British English

Personal Best

CB135570

Teacher's Book

A1
Beginner

Series Editor
Jim Scrivener

Author
Sheila Dignen

Richmond

THE COMPLETE PACKAGE

What is available for Personal Best

Teacher's Book + online access

- Teacher's Book with interleaved Student's Book
- Guidance notes, Answer Keys, Audio and Video scripts
- Access code for Richmond Learning Platform

Teacher's Resource Book

- Over 60 supplementary photocopiable resources
- Grammar, vocabulary and skills activities with Teacher's notes
- Copy-and-go grammar and vocabulary progress tests

Class Audio / Video pack

- Student's Book Audio CDs
- Student's Book Video DVD

Student's Book + online access

- 10 units of class material
- Review and Practice sections every 2 units
- Grammar Practice, Vocabulary Practice and Communication Practice sections
- Access code for Richmond Learning Platform

Workbook + audio

- Practice of the language and skills in the Student's Book
- For homework or self-study
- Review and Practice sections every unit
- Additional Writing Practice section
- Downloadable audio MP3s

Language App

- Fun games and activities for extra grammar and vocabulary practice
- Rewards and scores to show progress

Digital Book

- Complete digital version of the course
- Answer Keys, Class Audio and Video
- Use on any interactive whiteboard, or with a computer and projector.

Richmond Testing

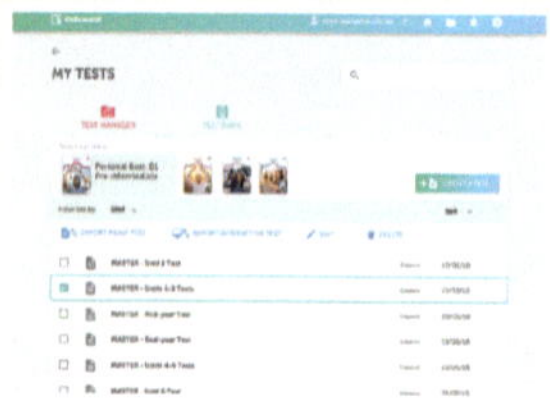

- Download unit, progress and mid-/ end-term tests
- Editable versions
- Richmond Test Manager for digital and customized tests

Richmond Learning Platform

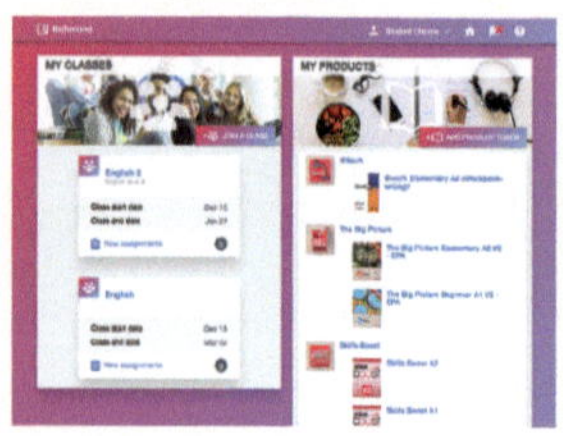

- Extended practice activities for grammar, vocabulary and skills
- Class Audio MP3 and Video MP4
- Assign, track and mark activities and tests

CONTENTS

CONTENTS

Language App, unit-by-unit grammar and vocabulary games

A personal welcome to Personal Best

by **Jim Scrivener**, Series Editor

Jim is an internationally respected writer, teacher trainer, materials designer, course leader and educational consultant. His work is mainly focused on practical classroom methodology and teaching techniques – on what works in the classroom. Over the years, he has taught and trained in many different teaching and learning environments around the world. Jim is an established and regular conference presenter. His books have twice won the Duke of Edinburgh English Speaking Union awards as well as the International House prize and the ARELS Frank Bell Prize.

I'd like to show you some of the features I really like about this book and point out some ways that you can get the most out of it. There are two key ideas that power the concept of *Personal Best*:

It's Personal The course focuses on students as individuals who learn at different speeds and have different strengths and weaknesses.

It helps learners achieve their Best To help students reach their full potential, we have focused on the vital role of **PRACTICE**. The course makes sure that students can actually *take away the language they can use*.

How is Personal Best different?

LANGUAGE

Grammar is taught in stand-alone lessons, separate from skills work. In many coursebooks, students have to understand difficult reading or listening passages before they can extract and study grammar points. In *Personal Best* language work is not tangled up within long reading or listening texts.

The pronunciation syllabus focuses on connected speech to help with recognising and producing language.

Lexis is prioritized. *Personal Best* includes two or more vocabulary sets per unit. **Vocabulary items are useful and relevant** for students and are used in discussions or tasks or for other work on a topic.

Above all, **PRACTICE** is given priority in the course.

SKILLS

There is a comprehensive skills syllabus. Students can see what is being focused on in the Listening Builder, Conversation Builder, Text Builder and Skill boxes.

Reading and listening skills pages are designed not as vehicles for grammar presentations, but develop learner skills and strategies.

Serious attention is paid to helping students speak and write better. Students are challenged to make use of selected functional language and to improve specific speaking or writing skills. There are clear task goals and cumulative aims for speaking and writing activities.

PRACTICE *at the heart of learning*

So, how do students learn a language? Just by turning the pages of a book and doing the exercises? As every experienced teacher knows, doing the work, page after page, doesn't necessarily mean that the students take away anything useful from a lesson. We need to make sure that there is deeper learning. The most important way that this can happen is through a quantity of focused, meaningful practice.

We believe that typically students struggle with new language because they simply don't get sufficient practice. They need lots of safe opportunities to try out using new language. *Personal Best* offers them a wealth of practice in a variety of exercises, tasks and games in the **Student's Book**, **Workbook**, the Personal Best **Language App**, the **Richmond Learning Platform** and the innovative '3xPractice' feature in the **Teacher's Book**.

Moving beyond the 'correct answer'

Teachers typically ask students to do each coursebook exercise on their own (or possibly in a pair) and then they check the answers together in the whole class (or students do this individually using a list of answers). The class then typically moves on to new work.

Just collecting a list of correct answers doesn't necessarily mean that students have really understood the language point. Students might get a correct answer by luck, by guessing, by listening to other students, by copying, by pretending that they agree with what you said, etc.

When students call out their answers, teachers usually hear the students who are stronger, faster or louder – and say 'good' to their answers. But it's important to remember that these students are, of course, the ones who have already got the correct answers. It's the other students we need to be interested in. And just because some students have a correct answer, it doesn't mean that they can actually *use* the items. A correct answer is the first step towards helping students to use the items, not the final goal.

It can be quite a big leap from doing an exercise (such as filling in answers on the page) to really feeling confident with the language items themselves. One simple and enjoyable way you could try is by revisiting an exercise more than once – to go back to it after the original task and checking it has been completed and re-explore it, like a gold miner, digging deeper to find more treasure.

By repeatedly reading, remembering, studying, saying and just 'playing with' the language, it is far more likely to lodge deeper in your students' minds and become part of their usable database of language.

What is '3xPractice'?

How can I help my students to really learn the items they study? How can that learning be deeper and more long-lasting? The **3xPractice** feature encourages students to play around with new language and experiment with forms and meanings so that they are 'nudged' towards greater internalisation, memorisation and personalisation.

In the *Personal Best* Teacher's Book, we will offer you lots of ideas for **3xPractice** so that, if you want to and have time, you could really exploit the exercises and get much more learning value out of them. You may not want to do this every time you do an exercise – but I encourage you to try it sometimes, to see how much more an exercise can reveal beyond just the 'correct answer'.

Enjoy using Personal Best

I really hope you enjoy using this course with your students – and don't forget to check out all those extra ideas we've put together in the Teacher's Book. You'll find warmers, extra activities, concept questions and plenty more.

Can a course book help students to reach their personal best? Not on its own, certainly – but perhaps, together with your skill and interest and personal touches, you may find a course here that not only helps your students to learn more and learn deeper than they thought possible but also helps you as a teacher to teach to your personal best.

Approach to Language teaching: A and C Lessons

Lessons A and C always focus on Language. They cover grammar, vocabulary and pronunciation and use accessible, graded texts or audio to contextualise the language point. There is an emphasis on practice via clearly staged activities with additional practice in the **Grammar Practice**, **Vocabulary Practice** and **Communication Practice** sections, the **Personal Best Language App**, the **Workbook** and the **Richmond Learning Platform**.

LANGUAGE Lesson A – Grammar, vocabulary and pronunciation

Each unit is constructed around a useful and stimulating topic.

Each lesson has clear aims for grammar and vocabulary.

Clear grammar boxes give a summary of the structures being taught.

Grammar practice sections provide more explanations, examples and opportunities for practice.

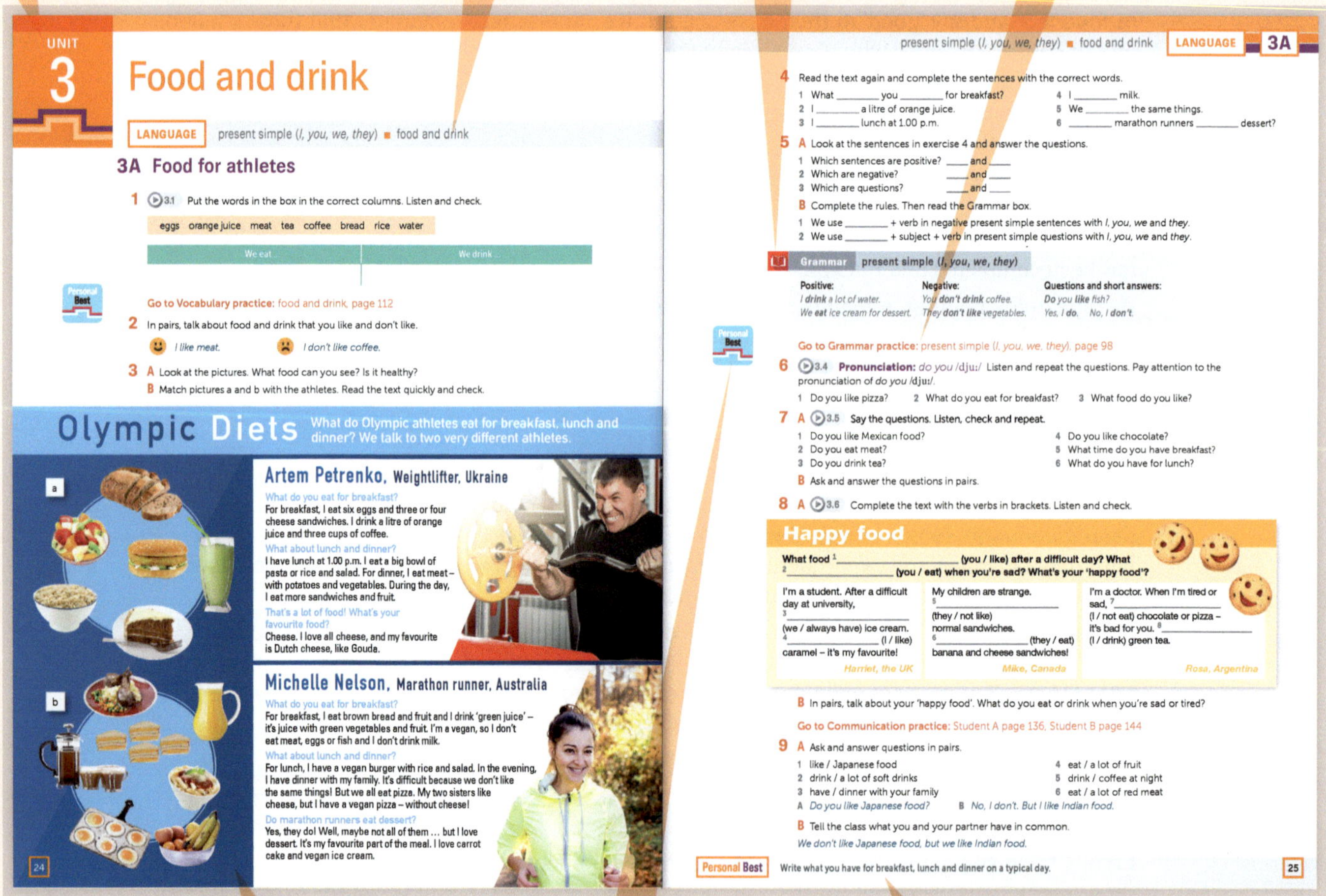

UNIT 3

Food and drink

LANGUAGE present simple (*I, you, we, they*) ■ food and drink

3A Food for athletes

1 3.1 Put the words in the box in the correct columns. Listen and check.

eggs orange juice meat tea coffee bread rice water

We eat ...	We drink ...

Go to Vocabulary practice: food and drink, page 112

2 In pairs, talk about food and drink that you like and don't like.

I like meat. *I don't like coffee.*

3 A Look at the pictures. What food can you see? Is it healthy?

B Match pictures a and b with the athletes. Read the text quickly and check.

Olympic Diets What do Olympic athletes eat for breakfast, lunch and dinner? We talk to two very different athletes.

a

b

Artem Petrenko, Weightlifter, Ukraine

What do you eat for breakfast?
For breakfast, I eat six eggs and three or four cheese sandwiches. I drink a litre of orange juice and three cups of coffee.
What about lunch and dinner?
I have lunch at 1.00 p.m. I eat a big bowl of pasta or rice and salad. For dinner, I eat meat – with potatoes and vegetables. During the day, I eat more sandwiches and fruit.
That's a lot of food! What's your favourite food?
Cheese. I love all cheese, and my favourite is Dutch cheese, like Gouda.

Michelle Nelson, Marathon runner, Australia

What do you eat for breakfast?
For breakfast, I eat brown bread and fruit and I drink 'green juice' – it's juice with green vegetables and fruit. I'm a vegan, so I don't eat meat, eggs or fish and I don't drink milk.
What about lunch and dinner?
For lunch, I have a vegan burger with rice and salad. In the evening, I have dinner with my family. It's difficult because we don't like the same things! But we all eat pizza. My two sisters like cheese, but I have a vegan pizza – without cheese!
Do marathon runners eat dessert?
Yes, they do! Well, maybe not all of them … but I love dessert. It's my favourite part of the meal. I love carrot cake and vegan ice cream.

24

present simple (*I, you, we, they*) ■ food and drink LANGUAGE 3A

4 Read the text again and complete the sentences with the correct words.

1 What ______ you ______ for breakfast?
2 I ______ a litre of orange juice.
3 I ______ lunch at 1.00 p.m.
4 I ______ milk.
5 We ______ the same things.
6 ______ marathon runners ______ dessert?

5 A Look at the sentences in exercise 4 and answer the questions.

1 Which sentences are positive? ___ and ___
2 Which are negative? ___ and ___
3 Which are questions? ___ and ___

B Complete the rules. Then read the Grammar box.

1 We use ______ + verb in negative present simple sentences with *I, you, we* and *they*.
2 We use ______ + subject + verb in present simple questions with *I, you, we* and *they*.

Grammar present simple (*I, you, we, they*)

Positive:	Negative:	Questions and short answers:
*I **drink** a lot of water.*	*You **don't drink** coffee.*	***Do** you **like** fish?*
*We **eat** ice cream for dessert.*	*They **don't like** vegetables.*	*Yes, I **do**. No, I **don't**.*

Go to Grammar practice: present simple (*I, you, we, they*), page 98

6 3.4 **Pronunciation:** *do you* /dju:/ Listen and repeat the questions. Pay attention to the pronunciation of *do you* /dju:/.

1 Do you like pizza? 2 What do you eat for breakfast? 3 What food do you like?

7 A 3.5 Say the questions. Listen, check and repeat.

1 Do you like Mexican food?
2 Do you eat meat?
3 Do you drink tea?
4 Do you like chocolate?
5 What time do you have breakfast?
6 What do you have for lunch?

B Ask and answer the questions in pairs.

8 A 3.6 Complete the text with the verbs in brackets. Listen and check.

Happy food

What food [1] ______ (you / like) after a difficult day? What [2] ______ (you / eat) when you're sad? What's your 'happy food'?

I'm a student. After a difficult day at university, [3] ______ (we / always have) ice cream. [4] ______ (I / like) caramel – it's my favourite! *Harriet, the UK*

My children are strange. [5] ______ (they / not like) normal sandwiches. [6] ______ (they / eat) banana and cheese sandwiches! *Mike, Canada*

I'm a doctor. When I'm tired or sad, [7] ______ (I / not eat) chocolate or pizza – it's bad for you. [8] ______ (I / drink) green tea. *Rosa, Argentina*

B In pairs, talk about your 'happy food'. What do you eat or drink when you're sad or tired?

Go to Communication practice: Student A page 136, Student B page 144

9 A Ask and answer questions in pairs.

1 like / Japanese food
2 drink / a lot of soft drinks
3 have / dinner with your family
4 eat / a lot of fruit
5 drink / coffee at night
6 eat / a lot of red meat

A *Do you like Japanese food?* B *No, I don't. But I like Indian food.*

B Tell the class what you and your partner have in common.

We don't like Japanese food, but we like Indian food.

Personal Best Write what you have for breakfast, lunch and dinner on a typical day.

25

The language presentation texts are short and carefully graded to allow students to focus on the teaching point.

Every grammar point is practised on the **Personal Best Language App**.

Stronger students, or those who finish quickly, can engage with the language further in a **Personal Best** activity. Alternatives for weaker students are provided in the **Teacher's Book**.

LANGUAGE Lesson C – Grammar, vocabulary and pronunciation

A selection of key lexical items connected to the lesson topic is presented.

Vocabulary practice sections present and practise additional topic vocabulary.

Each language lesson has one **Pronunciation** focus. The **Personal Best Language App** also contains a variety of pronunciation exercises.

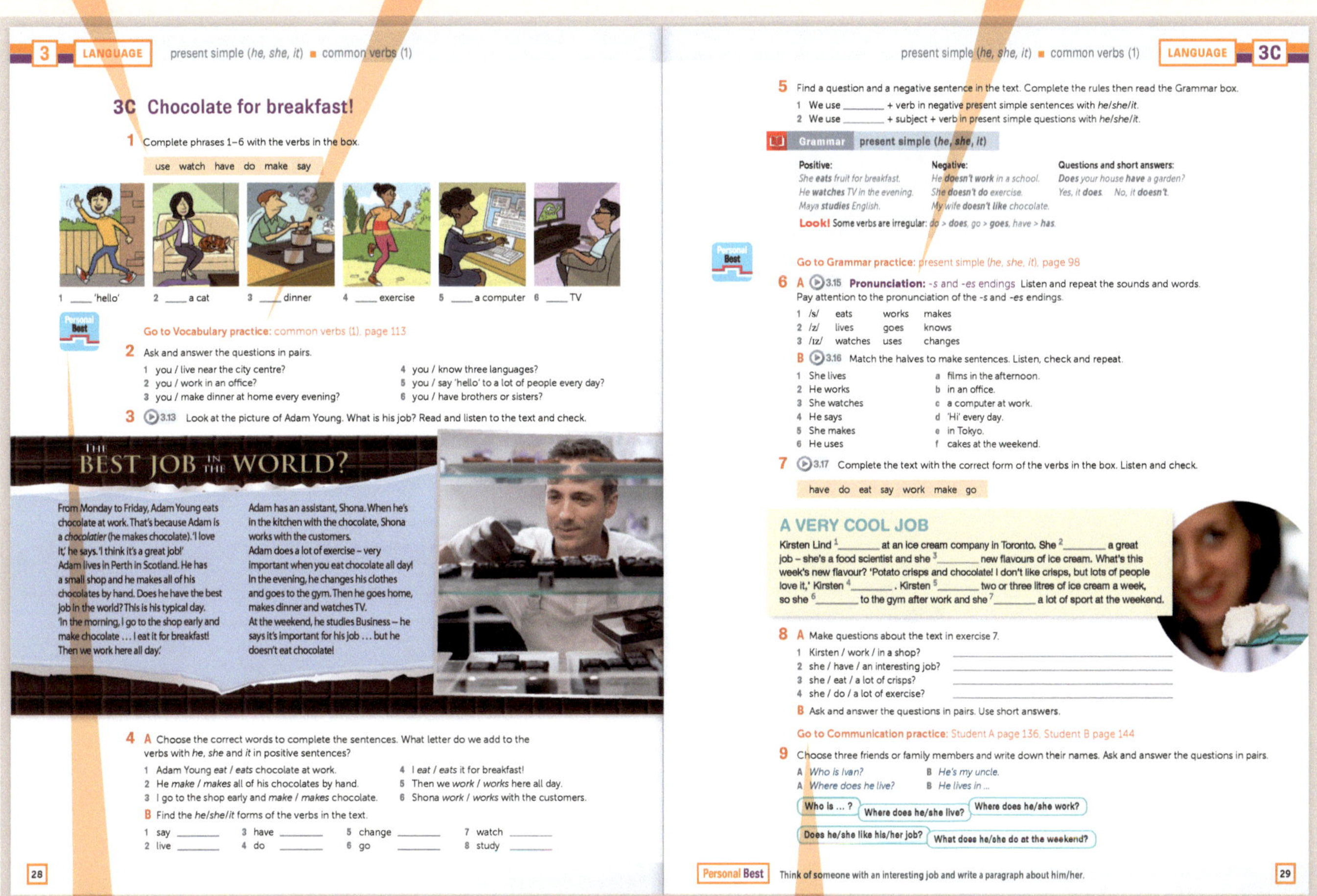

3 LANGUAGE present simple (*he, she, it*) ■ common verbs (1)

3C Chocolate for breakfast!

1 Complete phrases 1–6 with the verbs in the box.

use watch have do make say

1 ____ 'hello' 2 ____ a cat 3 ____ dinner 4 ____ exercise 5 ____ a computer 6 ____ TV

Personal Best

Go to Vocabulary practice: common verbs (1), page 113

2 Ask and answer the questions in pairs.

1 you / live near the city centre?
2 you / work in an office?
3 you / make dinner at home every evening?
4 you / know three languages?
5 you / say 'hello' to a lot of people every day?
6 you / have brothers or sisters?

3 3.13 Look at the picture of Adam Young. What is his job? Read and listen to the text and check.

THE BEST JOB IN THE WORLD?

From Monday to Friday, Adam Young eats chocolate at work. That's because Adam is a *chocolatier* (he makes chocolate). 'I love it,' he says. 'I think it's a great job!'
Adam lives in Perth in Scotland. He has a small shop and he makes all of his chocolates by hand. Does he have the best job in the world? This is his typical day.
'In the morning, I go to the shop early and make chocolate … I eat it for breakfast! Then we work here all day.'
Adam has an assistant, Shona. When he's in the kitchen with the chocolate, Shona works with the customers.
Adam does a lot of exercise – very important when you eat chocolate all day! In the evening, he changes his clothes and goes to the gym. Then he goes home, makes dinner and watches TV.
At the weekend, he studies Business – he says it's important for his job … but he doesn't eat chocolate!

4 A Choose the correct words to complete the sentences. What letter do we add to the verbs with *he, she* and *it* in positive sentences?

1 Adam Young *eat / eats* chocolate at work.
2 He *make / makes* all of his chocolates by hand.
3 I go to the shop early and *make / makes* chocolate.
4 I *eat / eats* it for breakfast!
5 Then we *work / works* here all day.
6 Shona *work / works* with the customers.

B Find the *he/she/it* forms of the verbs in the text.

1 say ______ 2 live ______ 3 have ______ 4 do ______ 5 change ______ 6 go ______ 7 watch ______ 8 study ______

28

present simple (*he, she, it*) ■ common verbs (1) LANGUAGE 3C

5 Find a question and a negative sentence in the text. Complete the rules then read the Grammar box.

1 We use ______ + verb in negative present simple sentences with *he/she/it*.
2 We use ______ + subject + verb in present simple questions with *he/she/it*.

Grammar present simple (*he, she, it*)

Positive:	Negative:	Questions and short answers:
*She **eats** fruit for breakfast.*	*He **doesn't work** in a school.*	***Does** your house **have** a garden?*
*He **watches** TV in the evening.*	*She **doesn't do** exercise.*	*Yes, it **does**. No, it **doesn't**.*
*Maya **studies** English.*	*My wife **doesn't like** chocolate.*	

Look! Some verbs are irregular: *do* > ***does***, *go* > ***goes***, *have* > ***has***.

Personal Best

Go to Grammar practice: present simple (*he, she, it*), page 98

6 A 3.15 **Pronunciation:** *-s* and *-es* endings Listen and repeat the sounds and words. Pay attention to the pronunciation of the *-s* and *-es* endings.

1 /s/ eats works makes
2 /z/ lives goes knows
3 /ɪz/ watches uses changes

B 3.16 Match the halves to make sentences. Listen, check and repeat.

1 She lives a films in the afternoon.
2 He works b in an office.
3 She watches c a computer at work.
4 He says d 'Hi' every day.
5 She makes e in Tokyo.
6 He uses f cakes at the weekend.

7 3.17 Complete the text with the correct form of the verbs in the box. Listen and check.

have do eat say work make go

A VERY COOL JOB

Kirsten Lind [1]______ at an ice cream company in Toronto. She [2]______ a great job – she's a food scientist and she [3]______ new flavours of ice cream. What's this week's new flavour? 'Potato crisps and chocolate! I don't like crisps, but lots of people love it,' Kirsten [4]______ . Kirsten [5]______ two or three litres of ice cream a week, so she [6]______ to the gym after work and she [7]______ a lot of sport at the weekend.

8 A Make questions about the text in exercise 7.

1 Kirsten / work / in a shop? ______
2 she / have / an interesting job? ______
3 she / eat / a lot of crisps? ______
4 she / do / a lot of exercise? ______

B Ask and answer the questions in pairs. Use short answers.

Go to Communication practice: Student A page 136, Student B page 144

9 Choose three friends or family members and write down their names. Ask and answer the questions in pairs.

A *Who is Ivan?* B *He's my uncle.*
A *Where does he live?* B *He lives in …*

Who is … ? / Where does he/she live? / Where does he/she work? / Does he/she like his/her job? / What does he/she do at the weekend?

Personal Best Think of someone with an interesting job and write a paragraph about him/her.

29

Every vocabulary set is practised on the **Personal Best Language App**.

Communication practice sections provide additional pairwork activities to practise the language.

Approach to Skills teaching: B Lessons

Each B and D lesson focuses on development of one of the four skills: reading, listening, writing or speaking.
Each B lesson focuses on one of the receptive skills, i.e. listening or reading. The listening lessons feature a video webshow called *Learning Curve*. The listening and reading lessons feature **Skill**, **Text builder** and **Listening builder** boxes.

SKILLS Lesson B – Listening

Each lesson has clear aims for the Listening Skill and Listening builder features.

Each listening lesson features a vocabulary set. Key lexical items are previewed on the page and exemplified in the video.

Each listening lesson is built around the Learning Curve webshow, which presents documentaries and vox pops on the unit topic. Students are exposed to a variety of accents and to features of natural spoken speech.

The vox pops also act as models for short speaking tasks where students talk about their own experiences.

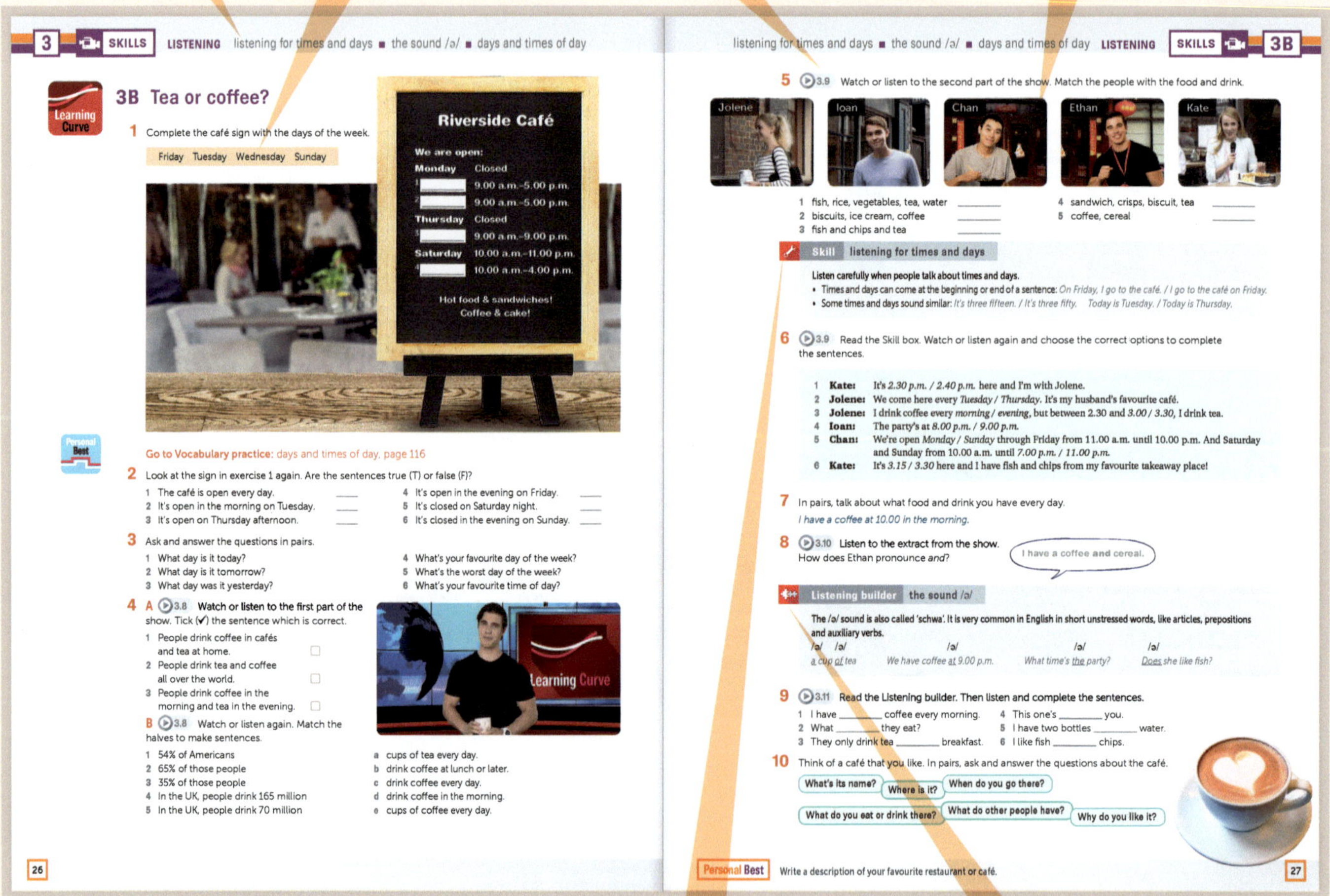

3 SKILLS LISTENING listening for times and days ■ the sound /ə/ ■ days and times of day

3B Tea or coffee?

1 Complete the café sign with the days of the week.

Friday Tuesday Wednesday Sunday

Go to Vocabulary practice: days and times of day, page 116

2 Look at the sign in exercise 1 again. Are the sentences true (T) or false (F)?

1 The café is open every day. ___
2 It's open in the morning on Tuesday. ___
3 It's open on Thursday afternoon. ___
4 It's open in the evening on Friday. ___
5 It's closed on Saturday night. ___
6 It's closed in the evening on Sunday. ___

3 Ask and answer the questions in pairs.

1 What day is it today?
2 What day is it tomorrow?
3 What day was it yesterday?
4 What's your favourite day of the week?
5 What's the worst day of the week?
6 What's your favourite time of day?

4 A 3.8 **Watch or listen to the first part of the show.** Tick (✓) the sentence which is correct.

1 People drink coffee in cafés and tea at home. ☐
2 People drink tea and coffee all over the world. ☐
3 People drink coffee in the morning and tea in the evening. ☐

B 3.8 Watch or listen again. Match the halves to make sentences.

1 54% of Americans
2 65% of those people
3 35% of those people
4 In the UK, people drink 165 million
5 In the UK, people drink 70 million

a cups of tea every day.
b drink coffee at lunch or later.
c drink coffee every day.
d drink coffee in the morning.
e cups of coffee every day.

26

listening for times and days ■ the sound /ə/ ■ days and times of day LISTENING SKILLS 3B

5 3.9 Watch or listen to the second part of the show. Match the people with the food and drink.

Jolene Ioan Chan Ethan Kate

1 fish, rice, vegetables, tea, water ______
2 biscuits, ice cream, coffee ______
3 fish and chips and tea ______
4 sandwich, crisps, biscuit, tea ______
5 coffee, cereal ______

Skill listening for times and days

Listen carefully when people talk about times and days.
- Times and days can come at the beginning or end of a sentence: *On Friday, I go to the café. / I go to the café on Friday.*
- Some times and days sound similar: *It's three fifteen. / It's three fifty. Today is Tuesday. / Today is Thursday.*

6 3.9 Read the Skill box. Watch or listen again and choose the correct options to complete the sentences.

1 **Kate:** It's *2.30 p.m. / 2.40 p.m.* here and I'm with Jolene.
2 **Jolene:** We come here every *Tuesday / Thursday*. It's my husband's favourite café.
3 **Jolene:** I drink coffee every *morning / evening*, but between 2.30 and *3.00 / 3.30*, I drink tea.
4 **Ioan:** The party's at *8.00 p.m. / 9.00 p.m.*
5 **Chan:** We're open *Monday / Sunday* through Friday from 11.00 a.m. until 10.00 p.m. And Saturday and Sunday from 10.00 a.m. until *7.00 p.m. / 11.00 p.m.*
6 **Kate:** It's *3.15 / 3.30* here and I have fish and chips from my favourite takeaway place!

7 In pairs, talk about what food and drink you have every day.

I have a coffee at 10.00 in the morning.

8 3.10 **Listen to the extract from the show.** How does Ethan pronounce *and*?

I have a coffee and cereal.

Listening builder the sound /ə/

The /ə/ sound is also called 'schwa'. It is very common in English in short unstressed words, like articles, prepositions and auxiliary verbs.

/ə/ /ə/ *a cup of tea* — /ə/ *We have coffee at 9.00 p.m.* — /ə/ *What time's the party?* — /ə/ *Does she like fish?*

9 3.11 **Read the Listening builder. Then listen and complete the sentences.**

1 I have ______ coffee every morning.
2 What ______ they eat?
3 They only drink tea ______ breakfast.
4 This one's ______ you.
5 I have two bottles ______ water.
6 I like fish ______ chips.

10 Think of a café that you like. In pairs, ask and answer the questions about the café.

What's its name? Where is it? When do you go there? What do you eat or drink there? What do other people have? Why do you like it?

Personal Best Write a description of your favourite restaurant or café.

27

Each listening lesson focuses on and practises a particular listening skill, such as listening for the main idea(s) or identifying the key points.

Each listening lesson focuses on and practises a particular aspect of connected speech, such as contractions, linking, sentence stress, etc.

SKILLS Lesson B – Reading

Each lesson has clear aims for the Reading Skill and Text builder features.

Reading Skill boxes focus on and practise a particular reading skill, such as approaching a text, skimming and scanning, etc.

Each reading lesson is built around a full-page text.

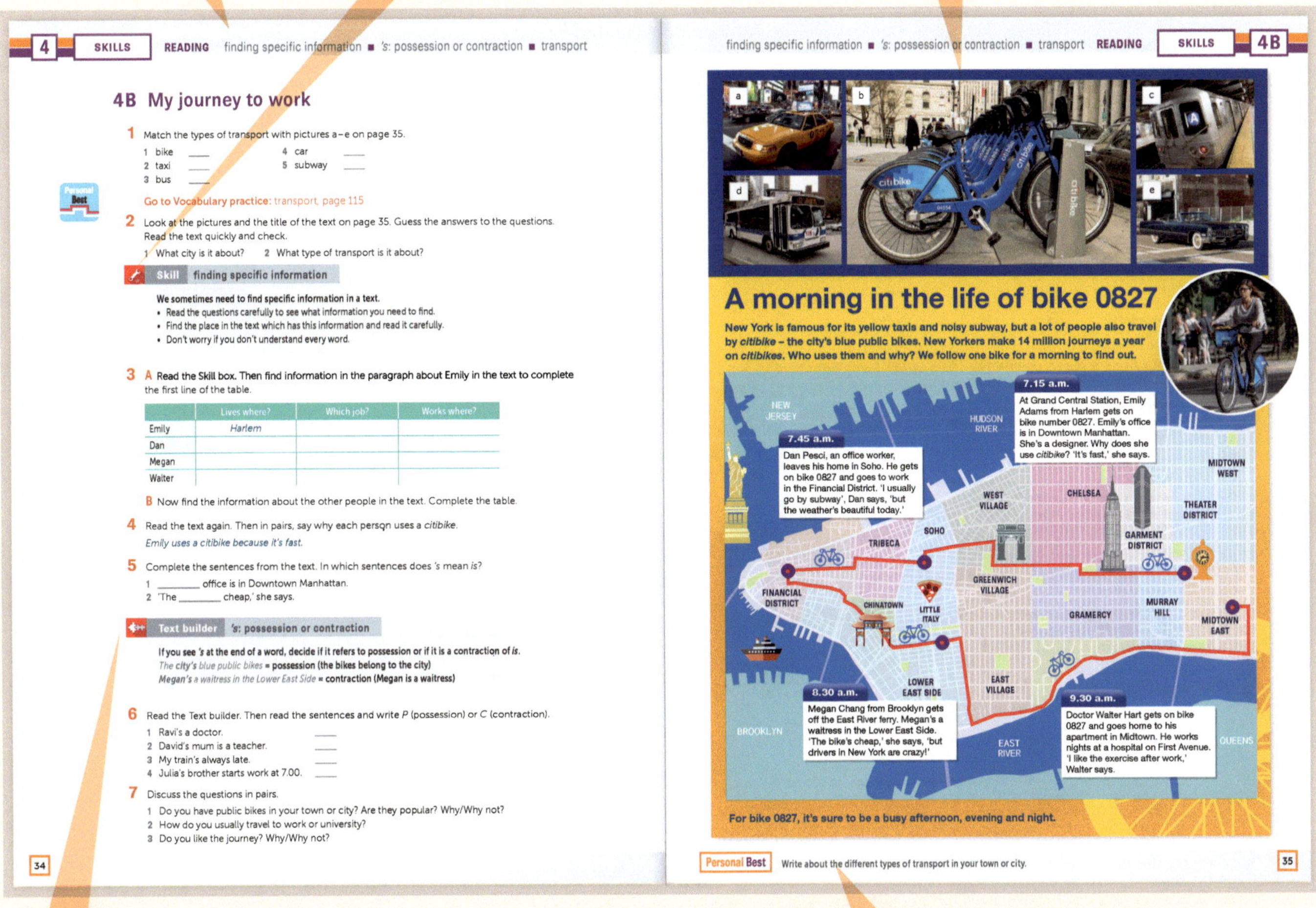

4 SKILLS READING finding specific information ■ 's: possession or contraction ■ transport

4B My journey to work

1 Match the types of transport with pictures a–e on page 35.

1 bike ___
2 taxi ___
3 bus ___
4 car ___
5 subway ___

Personal Best

Go to Vocabulary practice: transport, page 115

2 Look at the pictures and the title of the text on page 35. Guess the answers to the questions. Read the text quickly and check.

1 What city is it about? 2 What type of transport is it about?

Skill finding specific information

We sometimes need to find specific information in a text.

- Read the questions carefully to see what information you need to find.
- Find the place in the text which has this information and read it carefully.
- Don't worry if you don't understand every word.

3 A Read the Skill box. Then find information in the paragraph about Emily in the text to complete the first line of the table.

	Lives where?	Which job?	Works where?
Emily	*Harlem*		
Dan			
Megan			
Walter			

B Now find the information about the other people in the text. Complete the table.

4 Read the text again. Then in pairs, say why each person uses a *citibike*.

Emily uses a citibike because it's fast.

5 Complete the sentences from the text. In which sentences does *'s* mean *is*?

1 ________ office is in Downtown Manhattan.
2 'The ________ cheap,' she says.

Text builder 's: possession or contraction

If you see 's at the end of a word, decide if it refers to possession or if it is a contraction of *is*.
The city's blue public bikes = **possession (the bikes belong to the city)**
Megan's a waitress in the Lower East Side = **contraction (Megan is a waitress)**

6 Read the Text builder. Then read the sentences and write *P* (possession) or *C* (contraction).

1 Ravi's a doctor. ___
2 David's mum is a teacher. ___
3 My train's always late. ___
4 Julia's brother starts work at 7.00. ___

7 Discuss the questions in pairs.

1 Do you have public bikes in your town or city? Are they popular? Why/Why not?
2 How do you usually travel to work or university?
3 Do you like the journey? Why/Why not?

34

finding specific information ■ 's: possession or contraction ■ transport READING SKILLS 4B

A morning in the life of bike 0827

New York is famous for its yellow taxis and noisy subway, but a lot of people also travel by *citibike* – the city's blue public bikes. New Yorkers make 14 million journeys a year on *citibikes*. Who uses them and why? We follow one bike for a morning to find out.

7.15 a.m. At Grand Central Station, Emily Adams from Harlem gets on bike number 0827. Emily's office is in Downtown Manhattan. She's a designer. Why does she use *citibike*? 'It's fast,' she says.

7.45 a.m. Dan Pesci, an office worker, leaves his home in Soho. He gets on bike 0827 and goes to work in the Financial District. 'I usually go by subway', Dan says, 'but the weather's beautiful today.'

8.30 a.m. Megan Chang from Brooklyn gets off the East River ferry. Megan's a waitress in the Lower East Side. 'The bike's cheap,' she says, 'but drivers in New York are crazy!'

9.30 a.m. Doctor Walter Hart gets on bike 0827 and goes home to his apartment in Midtown. He works nights at a hospital on First Avenue. 'I like the exercise after work,' Walter says.

For bike 0827, it's sure to be a busy afternoon, evening and night.

Personal Best Write about the different types of transport in your town or city.

35

Text builder boxes focus on aspects of text cohesion, sequencing, referencing or language associated with a particular genre such as narratives or articles.

Stronger students, or those who finish quickly, can engage with the language further in a **Personal Best** activity. Alternatives for weaker students are provided in the **Teacher's Book**.

Approach to Skills teaching: D Lessons

Each B and D lesson focuses on development of one of the four skills: reading, listening, writing or speaking.
Each D lesson focuses on one of the productive skills, i.e. speaking or writing. The speaking lessons feature a video webshow called *Learning Curve*. The writing and speaking lessons feature **Skill**, **Text builder** and **Conversation builder** boxes
The D lessons bring together the language and skills practised in the unit in a supported *Personal Best* productive task.

SKILLS Lesson D – Speaking

Each lesson has clear aims for the Conversation builder and Speaking Skill features.

Like the listening skills lessons, each speaking skills lesson is built around the *Learning Curve* webshow. In speaking lessons, the hosts talk about their personal lives through video diaries, and we see them in different situations.

Each speaking lesson focuses on and practises a particular function, such as telling a personal story or speaking on the phone. The Conversation builder highlights the functional language from the video and gives students target expressions to take away.

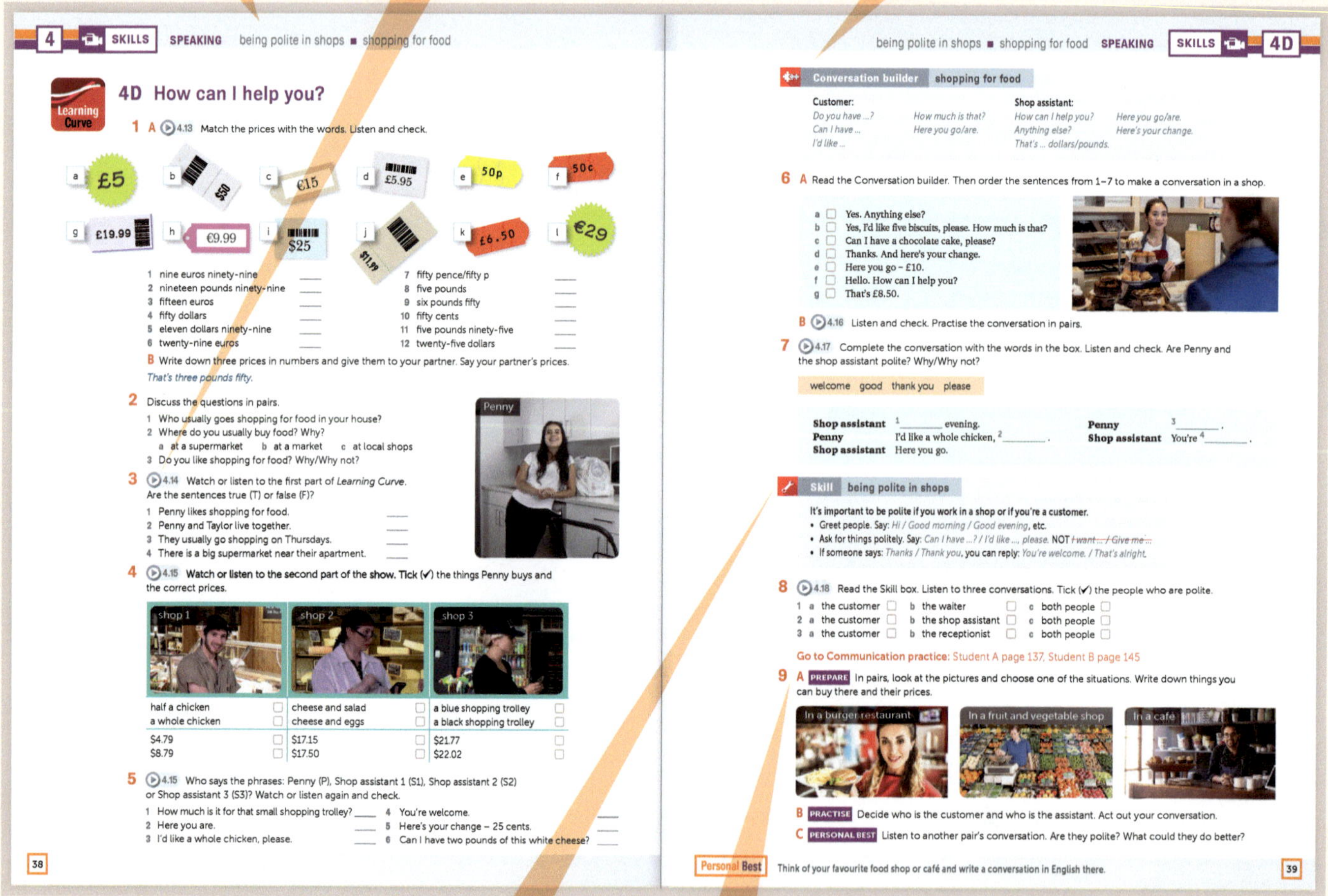

4 SKILLS SPEAKING being polite in shops ■ shopping for food

4D How can I help you?

1 A 4.13 Match the prices with the words. Listen and check.

a £5 b $50 c €15 d £5.95 e 50p f 50c
g £19.99 h €9.99 i $25 j $11.99 k £6.50 l €29

1 nine euros ninety-nine ___
2 nineteen pounds ninety-nine ___
3 fifteen euros ___
4 fifty dollars ___
5 eleven dollars ninety-nine ___
6 twenty-nine euros ___
7 fifty pence/fifty p ___
8 five pounds ___
9 six pounds fifty ___
10 fifty cents ___
11 five pounds ninety-five ___
12 twenty-five dollars ___

B Write down three prices in numbers and give them to your partner. Say your partner's prices.
That's three pounds fifty.

2 Discuss the questions in pairs.
1 Who usually goes shopping for food in your house?
2 Where do you usually buy food? Why?
a at a supermarket b at a market c at local shops
3 Do you like shopping for food? Why/Why not?

3 4.14 Watch or listen to the first part of *Learning Curve*. Are the sentences true (T) or false (F)?
1 Penny likes shopping for food. ___
2 Penny and Taylor live together. ___
3 They usually go shopping on Thursdays. ___
4 There is a big supermarket near their apartment. ___

Penny

4 4.15 Watch or listen to the second part of the show. Tick (✓) the things Penny buys and the correct prices.

shop 1	shop 2	shop 3
half a chicken ☐	cheese and salad ☐	a blue shopping trolley ☐
a whole chicken ☐	cheese and eggs ☐	a black shopping trolley ☐
$4.79 ☐	$17.15 ☐	$21.77 ☐
$8.79 ☐	$17.50 ☐	$22.02 ☐

5 4.15 Who says the phrases: Penny (P), Shop assistant 1 (S1), Shop assistant 2 (S2) or Shop assistant 3 (S3)? Watch or listen again and check.
1 How much is it for that small shopping trolley? ___
2 Here you are. ___
3 I'd like a whole chicken, please. ___
4 You're welcome. ___
5 Here's your change – 25 cents. ___
6 Can I have two pounds of this white cheese? ___

38

being polite in shops ■ shopping for food SPEAKING SKILLS 4D

Conversation builder shopping for food

Customer:
Do you have ...?
Can I have ...
I'd like ...
How much is that?
Here you go/are.

Shop assistant:
How can I help you?
Anything else?
That's ... dollars/pounds.
Here you go/are.
Here's your change.

6 A Read the Conversation builder. Then order the sentences from 1–7 to make a conversation in a shop.
a ☐ Yes. Anything else?
b ☐ Yes, I'd like five biscuits, please. How much is that?
c ☐ Can I have a chocolate cake, please?
d ☐ Thanks. And here's your change.
e ☐ Here you go – £10.
f ☐ Hello. How can I help you?
g ☐ That's £8.50.

B 4.16 Listen and check. Practise the conversation in pairs.

7 4.17 Complete the conversation with the words in the box. Listen and check. Are Penny and the shop assistant polite? Why/Why not?

welcome good thank you please

Shop assistant [1] ______ evening.
Penny I'd like a whole chicken, [2] ______ .
Shop assistant Here you go.
Penny [3] ______ .
Shop assistant You're [4] ______ .

Skill being polite in shops

It's important to be polite if you work in a shop or if you're a customer.
- Greet people. Say: *Hi / Good morning / Good evening*, etc.
- Ask for things politely. Say: *Can I have ...? / I'd like ..., please.* NOT ~~*I want ... / Give me ...*~~
- If someone says: *Thanks / Thank you*, you can reply: *You're welcome. / That's alright.*

8 4.18 Read the Skill box. Listen to three conversations. Tick (✓) the people who are polite.
1 a the customer ☐ b the waiter ☐ c both people ☐
2 a the customer ☐ b the shop assistant ☐ c both people ☐
3 a the customer ☐ b the receptionist ☐ c both people ☐

Go to Communication practice: Student A page 137, Student B page 145

9 A PREPARE In pairs, look at the pictures and choose one of the situations. Write down things you can buy there and their prices.

In a burger restaurant
In a fruit and vegetable shop
In a café

B PRACTISE Decide who is the customer and who is the assistant. Act out your conversation.
C PERSONAL BEST Listen to another pair's conversation. Are they polite? What could they do better?

Personal Best Think of your favourite food shop or café and write a conversation in English there.

39

Each speaking lesson focuses on and practises a particular speaking skill, such as showing interest or taking turns, which is exemplified in the video.

Each speaking lesson ends the unit with a step-by-step personalization activity where students follow three steps to consolidate the Conversation builder and Speaking Skill worked on in the lesson.

SKILLS Lesson D – Writing

Each lesson has clear aims for the Writing Skill and Text builder features.

A range of text types are modelled and exemplified, including blogs, emails and essays.

Each writing lesson focuses on and practises a particular writing skill, such as making notes or writing formally.

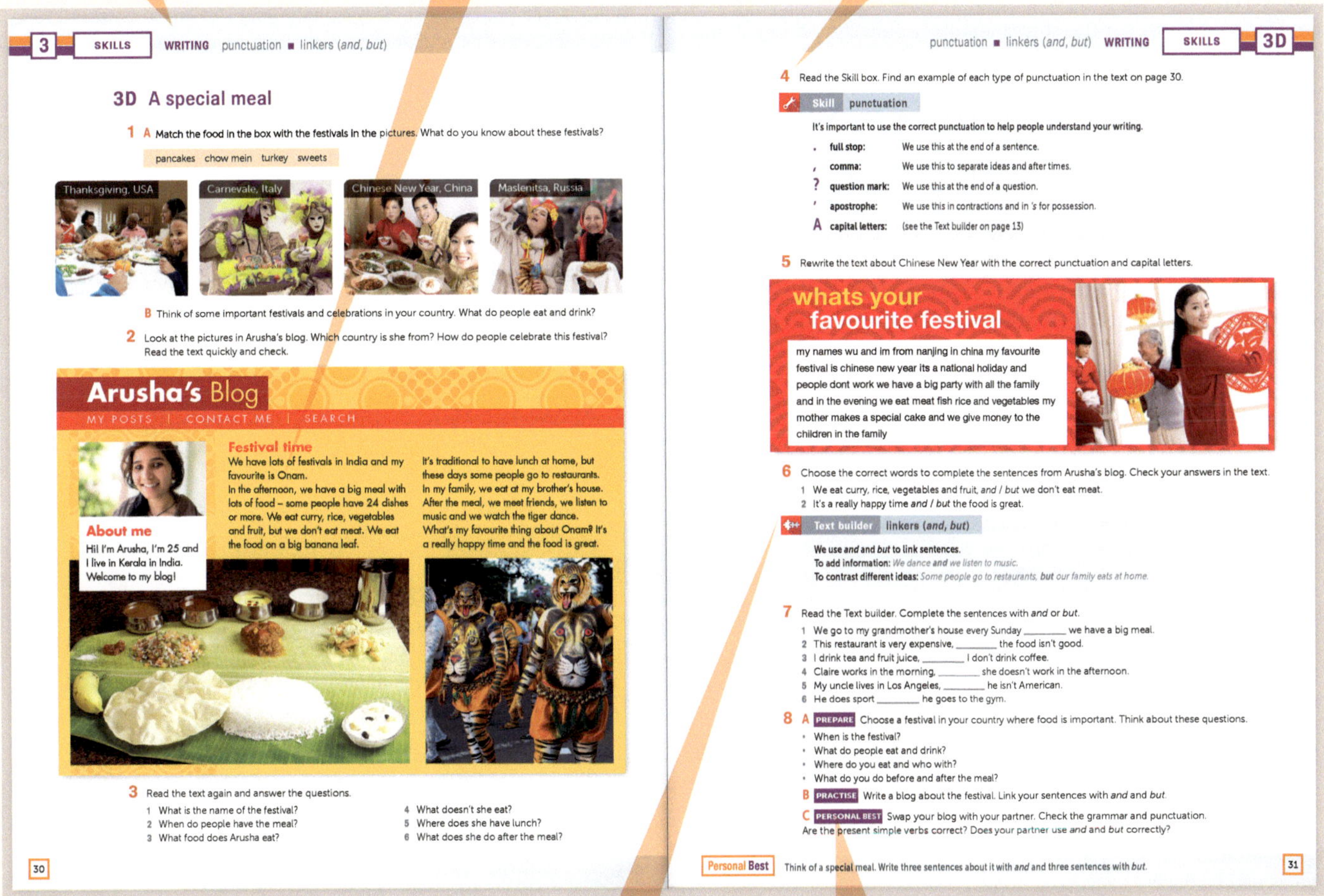

3 SKILLS WRITING punctuation ■ linkers (*and*, *but*)

3D A special meal

1 A Match the food in the box with the festivals in the pictures. What do you know about these festivals?

pancakes chow mein turkey sweets

Thanksgiving, USA | Carnevale, Italy | Chinese New Year, China | Maslenitsa, Russia

B Think of some important festivals and celebrations in your country. What do people eat and drink?

2 Look at the pictures in Arusha's blog. Which country is she from? How do people celebrate this festival? Read the text quickly and check.

Arusha's Blog

MY POSTS | CONTACT ME | SEARCH

About me
Hi! I'm Arusha, I'm 25 and I live in Kerala in India. Welcome to my blog!

Festival time
We have lots of festivals in India and my favourite is Onam.
In the afternoon, we have a big meal with lots of food – some people have 24 dishes or more. We eat curry, rice, vegetables and fruit, but we don't eat meat. We eat the food on a big banana leaf.
It's traditional to have lunch at home, but these days some people go to restaurants. In my family, we eat at my brother's house. After the meal, we meet friends, we listen to music and we watch the tiger dance.
What's my favourite thing about Onam? It's a really happy time and the food is great.

3 Read the text again and answer the questions.
1 What is the name of the festival?
2 When do people have the meal?
3 What food does Arusha eat?
4 What doesn't she eat?
5 Where does she have lunch?
6 What does she do after the meal?

30

punctuation ■ linkers (*and*, *but*) WRITING SKILLS 3D

4 Read the Skill box. Find an example of each type of punctuation in the text on page 30.

Skill punctuation

It's important to use the correct punctuation to help people understand your writing.

.	**full stop:**	We use this at the end of a sentence.
,	**comma:**	We use this to separate ideas and after times.
?	**question mark:**	We use this at the end of a question.
'	**apostrophe:**	We use this in contractions and in *'s* for possession.
A	**capital letters:**	(see the Text builder on page 13)

5 Rewrite the text about Chinese New Year with the correct punctuation and capital letters.

whats your favourite festival

my names wu and im from nanjing in china my favourite festival is chinese new year its a national holiday and people dont work we have a big party with all the family and in the evening we eat meat fish rice and vegetables my mother makes a special cake and we give money to the children in the family

6 Choose the correct words to complete the sentences from Arusha's blog. Check your answers in the text.
1 We eat curry, rice, vegetables and fruit, *and* / *but* we don't eat meat.
2 It's a really happy time *and* / *but* the food is great.

Text builder linkers (*and*, *but*)

We use *and* and *but* to link sentences.
To add information: *We dance **and** we listen to music.*
To contrast different ideas: *Some people go to restaurants, **but** our family eats at home.*

7 Read the Text builder. Complete the sentences with *and* or *but*.
1 We go to my grandmother's house every Sunday ________ we have a big meal.
2 This restaurant is very expensive, ________ the food isn't good.
3 I drink tea and fruit juice, ________ I don't drink coffee.
4 Claire works in the morning, ________ she doesn't work in the afternoon.
5 My uncle lives in Los Angeles, ________ he isn't American.
6 He does sport ________ he goes to the gym.

8 A PREPARE Choose a festival in your country where food is important. Think about these questions.
- When is the festival?
- What do people eat and drink?
- Where do you eat and who with?
- What do you do before and after the meal?

B PRACTISE Write a blog about the festival. Link your sentences with *and* and *but*.

C PERSONAL BEST Swap your blog with your partner. Check the grammar and punctuation. Are the present simple verbs correct? Does your partner use *and* and *but* correctly?

Personal Best Think of a special meal. Write three sentences about it with *and* and three sentences with *but*.

31

Each writing lesson focuses on and practises a particular function such as expressing reasons and results or use of pronouns. The Text builder highlights an aspect of written English to help students build their own texts.

Each writing lesson ends the unit with a step-by-step personalization activity where students follow the three steps to consolidate the Text builder and Writing Skill worked on in the lesson.

Welcome to *Learning Curve*: the webshow for Personal Best

What is Learning Curve?

Learning Curve is an exciting webshow about interesting things from around the world. Located and filmed in New York and London, the *Learning Curve* hosts present documentaries, interview people on the street, and also talk about their personal lives through video diaries.

Learning Curve exposes students to natural spoken language and develops a range of speaking and listening skills. There is a variety of interaction: monologues to camera, narratives in flashback, two-way dialogues, phone conversations, video conference calls, and group conversations.

How is the webshow integrated into the course?

All the video content is integrated seamlessly into the course with one video lesson per unit in the Listening (B) or the Speaking (D) lesson.

How and when do I watch Learning Curve?

There is a clear *Learning Curve* icon on the Student's Book page where video appears (or the corresponding audio should be played). This icon also appears in the Teacher's Book. Students can watch each show in its entirety (for enjoyment or familiarisation purposes), or it can be broken down into more manageable chunks, as recommended in each lesson. Each one is self-contained, so if one is missed for any reason, that won't affect the enjoyment of the next show.

Watching the video itself is our recommended option where technology allows, but if you are not able to play video in class, all of the video is supplied as audio only both as MP3 and on the Class Audio CDs. The scripts for the video are included in this Teacher's Book and can also be downloaded from the **Richmond Learning Platform**.

How does Learning Curve help to develop skills?

Too often students are frustrated that while they can understand their course book audio, they quickly feel lost when exposed to language outside the classroom. By using video to develop listening and speaking skills, students will build the skills and confidence to cope better with real life language environments; for example, recognizing that it isn't always necessary to understand every word when listening for specific information or gist; or that an awareness of 'filler expressions' can help students decode spoken language, as well as help them to sound more natural when they produce these themselves.

The videos help to bridge the gap between the classroom and the real world by exposing students to natural spoken English with well-staged and supported exercises.

Meet the hosts!

Ethan Moore

Ethan works in the New York City studio with Penny. He's from Connecticut. He enjoys travelling and is a very sociable person.

Kate McRea

Kate is from Los Angeles and works in the London studio with Simon. She loves being outdoors and is very sporty.

Penny Abernathy

Penny is British and works in the New York City studio with Ethan. She has a busy social life in New York, but sometimes she misses her family and friends. She shares a flat with her friend, Taylor.

Simon Collins

Simon, who's from the south of England, works in the London studio with Kate. He loves tennis, theatre and music. He isn't very keen on shopping – or trying new things! He and Penny were friends at school.

You will also meet ...

Jack Goode

Jack has his own restaurant, The Goode Food Restaurant, where he is the head chef, and he's also a food blogger and restaurant critic. Jack was at university with Simon and they have been best friends for years.

Taylor Weiss

Taylor is from the Midwest in the USA. She lives in New York City with Penny and works as a personal trainer. She loves yoga and hates being late!

Marc Kim

Marc's family are from South Korea. He lives in New York City, where he works as the IT specialist at *Learning Curve*. He is also a part-time student.

Approach to practice: In class

Student's Book: Practice section

There is an extensive **Practice** section at the back of the Student's Book for **Grammar**, **Vocabulary** and **Communication Practice**. Students are directed here from the relevant stages in the lesson. These sections should be done in class to get the maximum benefit from the course and can be used for revision later in the course.

The **Grammar Practice** section provides a clear overview of the grammar for the lesson.

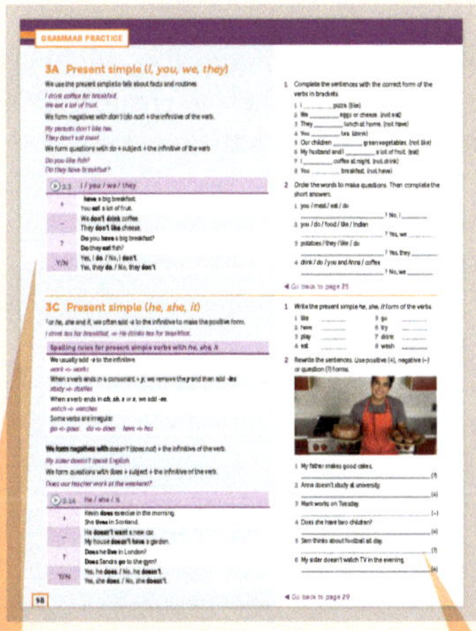

Explanations, usage notes and tables

Additional exercises practise both form and meaning of new grammar.

The **Vocabulary Practice** section includes full lexical sets (two or three per unit).

Picture-dictionary style vocabulary presentations

Additional exercises for extended practice

The **Communication Practice** section provides two or three speaking tasks per unit.

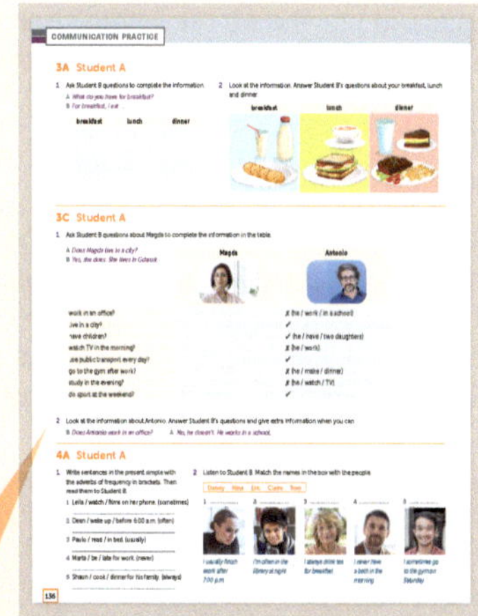

One pairwork task for every grammar point (two per unit) and one for every speaking lesson (every two units)

Review and Practice

There are six **Review and Practice** sections that revise grammar, vocabulary and functional language across units. They use a variety of exercises and end with a short, fun **Personal Best** section that allows for language recall in a more productive way.

Review and Practice sections appear every two units and give further opportunities to practise grammar and vocabulary.

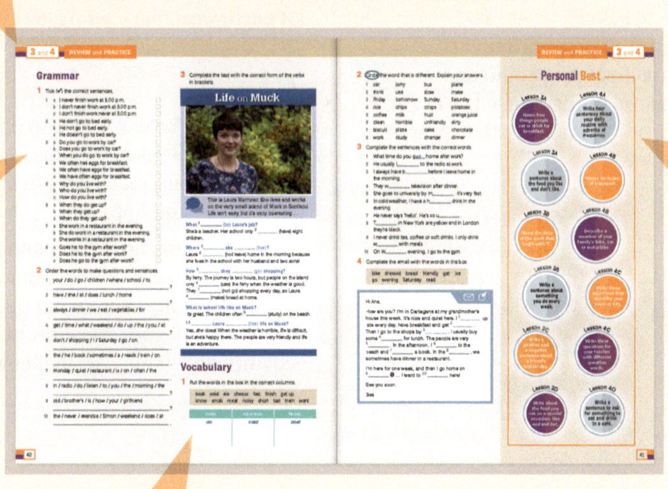

A variety of exercises revise the grammar from the previous two units. Grammar points are tested separately and in combination.

Personal Best questions and prompts give the opportunity to revise a number of language and skills points from the preceding two units, allowing for language recall and personalization.

A variety of exercises revise the vocabulary from the previous two units. Vocabulary from different units and lessons is reviewed together.

Approach to practice: Self study

Richmond Learning Platform

The **Richmond Learning Platform** complements the practice offered in the Workbook and on the **Personal Best Language App** with **extra practice activities**, a **forum**, **messaging** and **storage** areas, and a powerful and ground-breaking test management system.

Students

Students can practise all the language and skills from the Student's Book on the platform and receive instant feedback. They can try exercises up to three times to learn from their mistakes.

Teachers

Teachers can track students' progress and level of self-study activity and assign ready-made activities from the platform or their own tailored tasks. A set of sophisticated tools enable teachers to see at a glance how students are progressing and to analyse and compare the progress made by individual students and groups.

There is a full range of downloadable editable or print-and-go **resources**, including the worksheets and progress tests from the Teacher's Resource Book, audio scripts, wordlists and answer keys. Teachers have their own cloud storage area and can share activities from there with their students.

Testing

The **Richmond Test Bank** offers ready-made interactive, editable or PDF tests, and the **Test Manager** enables teachers to create their own interactive or print tests from a wide range of activities and tailor them to their students' needs.

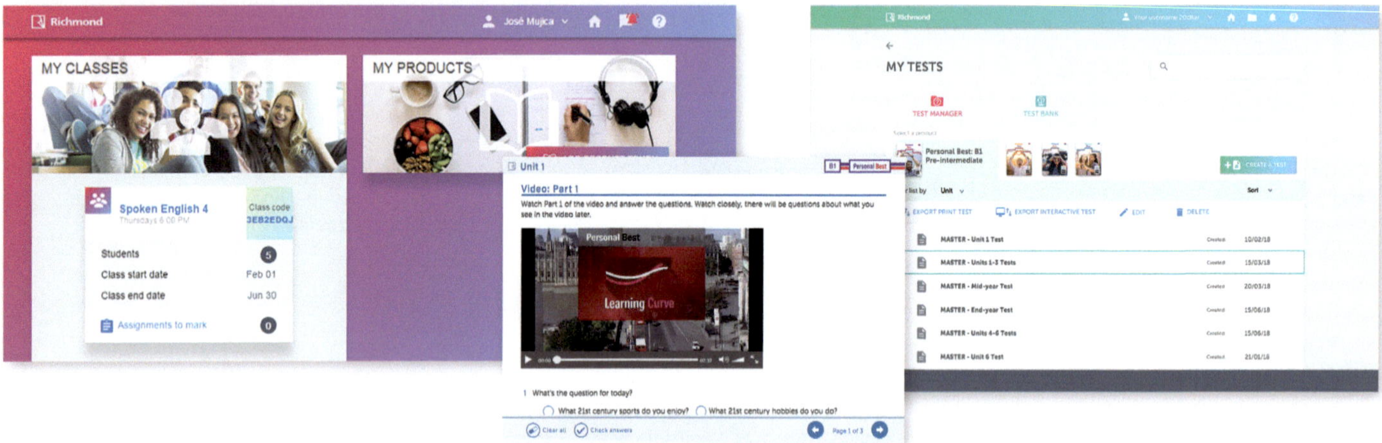

Personal Best Language Practice App

The **Personal Best Language App** offers free, self-study practice of the language content from the Student's Book. Grammar and vocabulary are the main focus, although pronunciation is also incorporated. The App includes accompanying audio and images from the Student's Book. Each level of the course has a corresponding App. This provides further optional self-study practice of the grammar and vocabulary of that level.

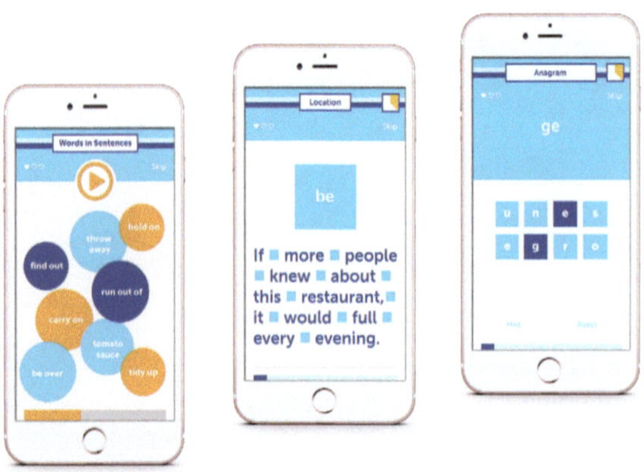

There are three different games for each grammar point and three for each vocabulary set from the Student's Book.

Making the most of the App

A clear App icon on the Student's Book and Teacher's Book page indicates wherever a grammar point or vocabulary set has practice material available on the App.

Students access the App on an individual basis and use it in their own time (e.g. as optional homework or as on-the-go mobile learning) to internalise what they have learnt in class. The App provides motivation for short bursts of practice through timed activities and game-like challenges with instant feedback.

Workbook

The **Workbook** provides a page of practice for each **Student's Book** lesson and an additional **Review and Practice** spread to revise the content from the whole unit.

The Workbook offers comprehensive self-study practice of the language and skills taught in the Student's Book. It provides practice not only of grammar, vocabulary and pronunciation but for all four skills – reading, listening, writing and speaking – for the corresponding Student's Book lessons. The audio is available as MP3 download on the **Richmond Learning Platform**.

Each grammar point is practised using a variety of controlled exercises.

Each pronunciation point has accompanying audio with a practice exercise. This is available as an MP3 download on the **Richmond Learning Platform**.

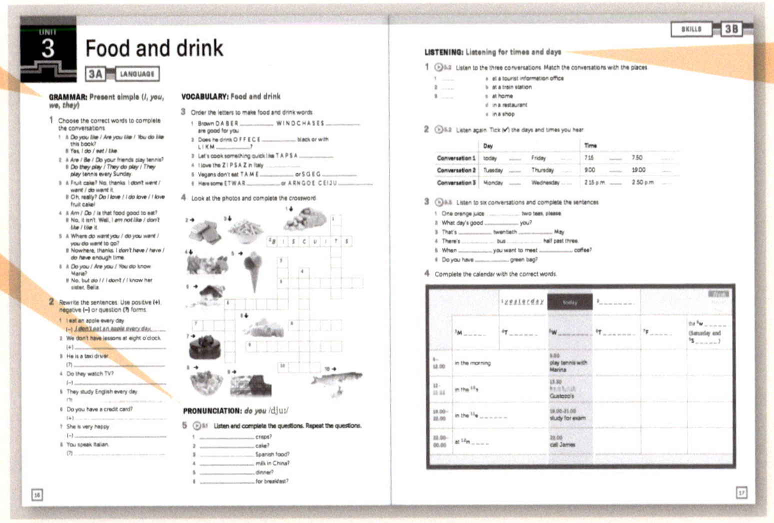

Each reading or listening skill is practised using texts or audio on a topic related to the **Student's Book** lesson.

Each vocabulary set is practised using a variety of exercises.

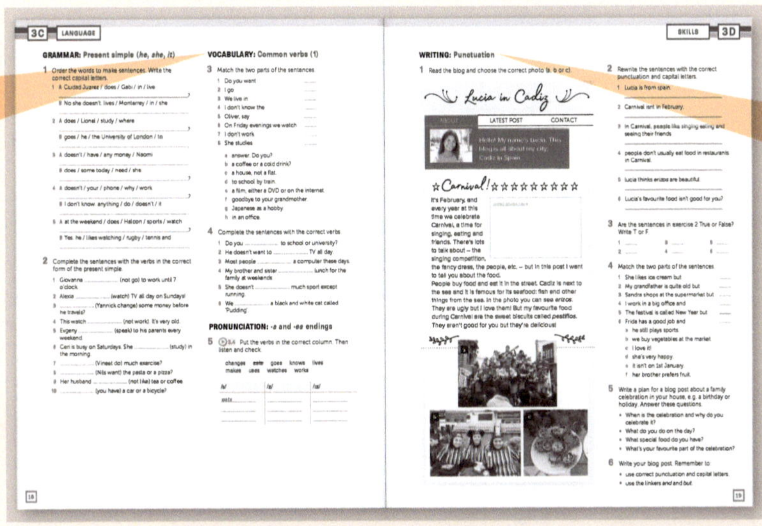

Each writing or speaking skill is practised using texts and exercises on a topic related to the **Student's Book** lesson.

At the back of the **Workbook**, there are five additional pages devoted to further writing skills practice, such as making notes or writing a narrative. These feature more model texts and exercises to practise the writing skill of the unit.

The **Review and Practice** section features podcasts and blogs from the *Learning Curve* team. This section revises the language taught in the unit and provides further listening and reading practice.

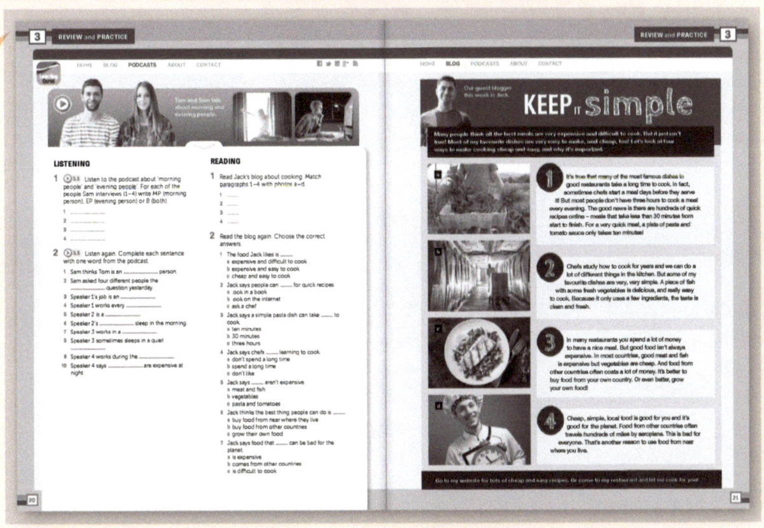

Teacher's Components

Teacher's Book

The **Teacher's Book** is a comprehensive, full-colour resource that incorporates the complete **Student's Book.** It provides all the necessary procedural guidance to teach the Student's Book lessons as well as extra ideas to extend and support students. There is a unique **3xPractice** feature for each lesson to help teachers and students go deeper into the activities and experiment with forms and meanings.

Each full-sized, colour **Student's Book** page is next to its accompanying teaching notes.

The **Overview** gives a short summary of the unit content and aims.

The **aims** of each lesson are clearly outlined.

There is an accessible easy-to-use **warmer** activity at the start of each lesson to interest and engage students in the topic.

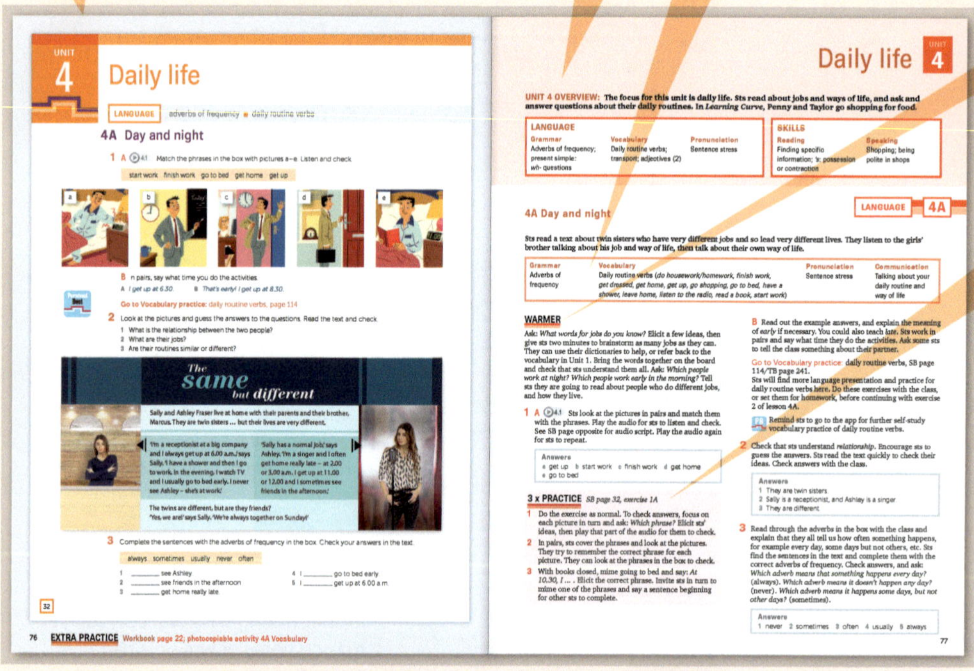

3xPractice boxes encourage students to engage more deeply with the language in three steps.

Extra Practice activities offer ideas for further extending and exploiting the topic and language or skill of the lesson.

Personal Best boxes provide activities for weaker students. They are easy for teachers to set up and for individual students to work through on their own.

Concept check questions ensure students have understood the grammar teaching point, or the text builder / listening builder/ conversation builder language presented in the lesson.

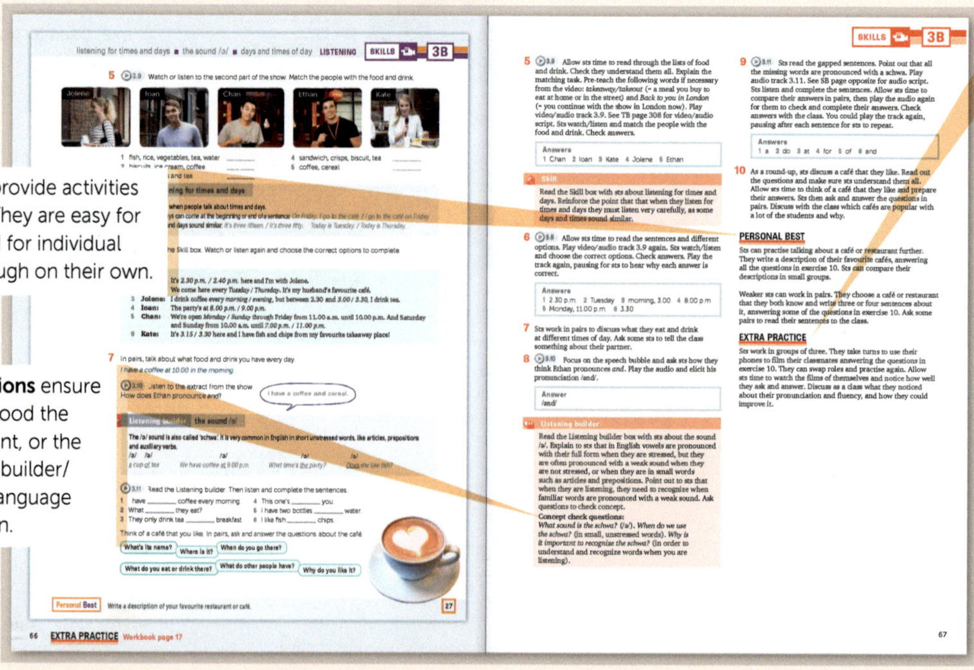

Teacher's Resource Book

The **Teacher's Resource Book** provides extensive photocopiable materials and unit tests. The photocopiable activities can be used as a change of focus or used as revision at a later stage. The unit tests help with recall and provide a sense of progress. There are photocopiable activities for grammar, vocabulary and skills.

Students work in pairs or groups to complete engaging tasks that practise the language or skills from the lesson.

The teacher's notes provide preparation and procedural notes as well as extra practice ideas.

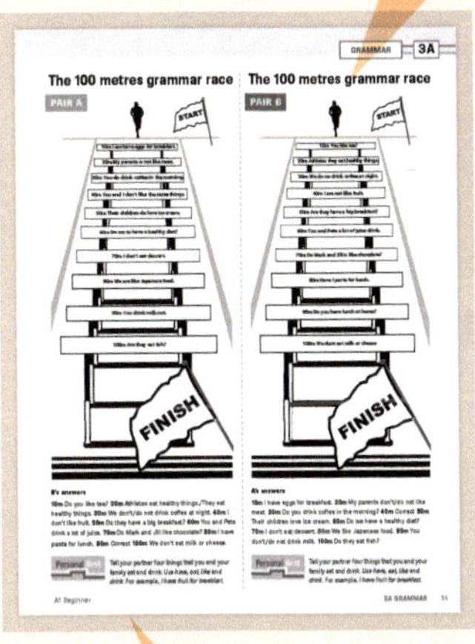

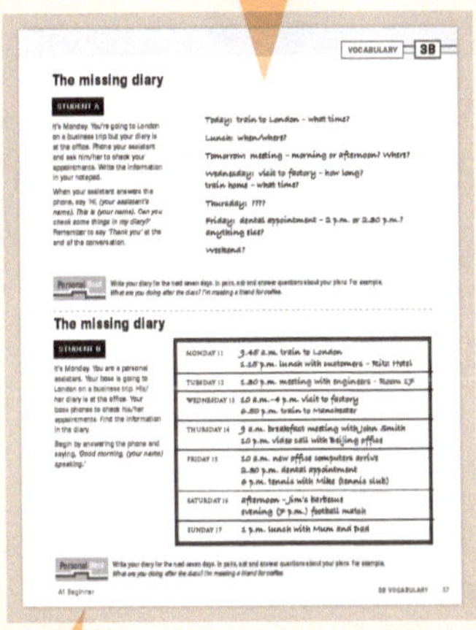

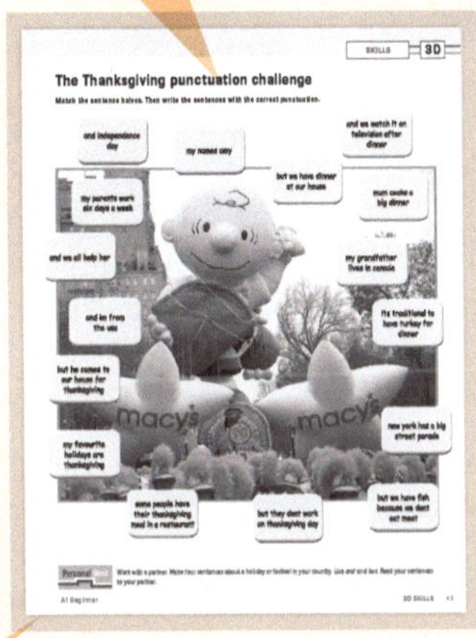

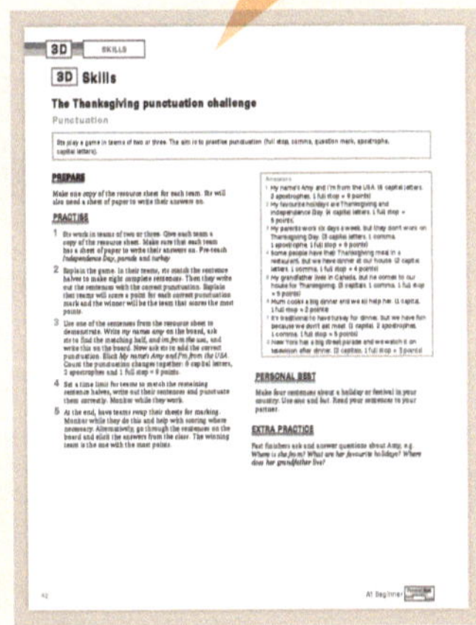

A follow-up **Personal Best** task at the end of each activity allows a more personal response.

The **Teacher's Resource Book** also provides photocopiable Unit Language Tests to check students' progress quickly in class or as homework.

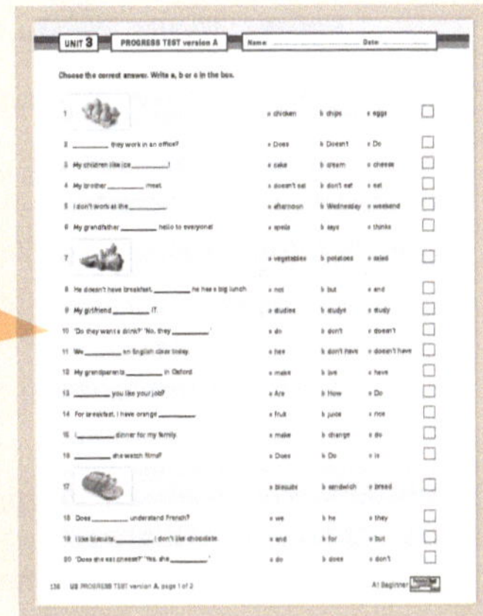

Audio / Video pack

The **Audio and Video pack** includes the Class Audio CDs and Class Video DVDs. All audio and video is also available to download from the Richmond Learning Platform.

Digital Book

This is a complete projectable digital resource for the teacher: it provides the Student's Book in digital format with embedded audio, video, scripts, notes and answers, for use with a smart board or projector.

UNIT 1

My life

LANGUAGE the verb *be* (*I, you*) ■ greetings ■ classroom language

Hello

1 1.1 Read and listen. Match conversations 1–3 with pictures a–c.

1 **Wendy** Good morning. Are you Emma, the new teacher?
Emma Yes, I am.
Wendy I'm Wendy. Nice to meet you. You're in Class 3.
Emma Thanks, Wendy. See you later.

2 **Emma** Hello, I'm Emma. What's your name?
Kiko Hi, my name's Kiko.
Emma Nice to meet you, Kiko.
Kiko Are you a student here?
Emma No, I'm not. I'm your teacher!

3 **Kiko** Emma, this is my friend, Misha.
Emma Hello. Mmm, you aren't in Class 3, Misha.
Misha No, I'm in Class 4 and I'm late! Goodbye!
Emma Bye, Misha!

2 Put the words from the conversations in the correct columns. Can you add any other words?

Bye Good morning
Hi See you later

Hello	Goodbye

3 **A** 1.2 Listen and repeat the highlighted phrases from the conversations in exercise 1. How do you say them in your language?

B Practise the conversations from exercise 1 in groups of four.

4 **A** Complete the sentences with the words in the box. Then check your answers in the conversations.

're 'm 'm not aren't Are

1 I ________ Wendy.
2 You ________ in Class 3.
3 ________ you a student here?
4 No, I ________ .
5 You ________ in Class 3, Misha.

B 1.3 Listen and repeat the contractions in **bold**. Then read the Grammar box.

1 I am = **I'm** 2 You are = **You're** 3 You are not = **You aren't**

Grammar the verb *be* (*I, you*)

Positive:
I'm *Wendy.*
You're *in Room 4.*

Negative:
You aren't *in Class 3.*
I'm not *a student.*

Questions and short answers:
Are you *a teacher?*
Yes, ***I am****.* *No,* ***I'm not****.*

Go to Grammar practice: the verb *be* (*I, you*), page 96

My life

UNIT 1

UNIT 1 OVERVIEW: This unit looks at personal information and introductions. Sts practise introducing themselves, exchanging personal information and completing a form. In *Learning Curve*, Simon and Kate talk to people about where they are from and what their jobs are.

LANGUAGE

Grammar	Vocabulary	Pronunciation
The verb *be*	Greetings; classroom language; countries and nationalities; jobs; numbers 0–100; adjectives (1)	The alphabet; word stress; numbers

SKILLS

Listening	Writing
Listening for information about people; contractions	Completing a form; capital letters

LANGUAGE **Hello**

Hello

Sts listen to conversations in which people meet and introduce themselves, and then practise introducing themselves. They listen to some classroom language, and learn the alphabet.

Grammar	Vocabulary	Pronunciation	Communication
The verb be (*I, you*)	Classroom language (*Can you repeat that, please?; Excuse me, what does … mean?; Go to page … ; How do you say …; in English?; How do you spell that?; Listen and repeat; Look at the picture; Sorry, I don't understand; Open/Close your books; Sorry I'm late; Work in pairs.*)	The alphabet	Introducing yourself

WARMER

Introduce yourself by saying, *Hello, my name's …* . Ask sts to turn to their partner to say *hello*, and say their name.

1 1.1 Use the pictures to teach the words *teacher*, *student* and *class*. Play the first conversation. See SB page opposite for audio script. Elicit which picture it matches. Sts listen and match the conversations with the pictures. Check answers.

Answers
1 c 2 a 3 b

2 Draw the two columns from the table on the board. Point to the box and say *Bye*, waving your hand. Elicit which column it should be added to. Sts then complete the task. Check answers.

Answers
Hello: Good morning, Hi Goodbye: Bye, See you later

3 A 1.2 Sts listen and repeat. See SB page opposite for audio script. Elicit how sts would say each phrase in their language.

B If necessary, play audio 1.1 again, pausing after each line for sts to repeat. Sts then practise the conversations in pairs.

4 A Sts complete the sentences with the correct words, then check in the conversations in exercise 1. Check answers.

Answers
1 'm 2 're 3 Are 4 'm not 5 aren't

B 1.3 Play the audio, pausing after each contraction for sts to repeat. See SB page opposite for audio script.

Grammar

Read the Grammar box with sts about the verb *be*. Explain that the verb *be* is irregular, so sts need to learn all the forms. Point out that we usually use contractions rather than full forms (*I'm, you're* etc.), but we always use full forms in short answers, e.g. *Yes, I am.* NOT ~~*Yes, I'm*~~. Point out the inverted word order in questions. Ask questions to check concept.

Concept check questions:
I'm Wendy – correct? (yes). *I'm a teacher – positive or negative?* (positive). *What's the negative form?* (I'm not a teacher). *You a student – correct?* (no – you're a student). *What's the negative form?* (You aren't a student). *Are you a student? – correct?* (yes). *What's the answer?* (Yes, I am/No, I'm not).

Go to Grammar practice: the verb *be (I, you)*, SB page 96/TB page 205
Sts will find more language reference, presentation and practice for the verb *be (I, you)* here. Do these exercises with the class, or set them for homework, before continuing with exercise 5A.

PB Remind sts to go to the app for further self-study grammar practice of the verb *be (I, you)*.

5 A 1.5 Complete the conversation. Listen and check.

Kiko Hello. What's [1]________ name?
Eleni [2]________ name's Eleni.
Kiko Nice to [3]________ you, Eleni. I [4]________ Kiko.
Eleni Nice to meet you, Kiko. [5]________ you a student here?
Kiko [6] Yes, I ________ .

B In pairs, practise the conversation using your names.

6 Introduce yourself and your partner to another pair.

A *Hello, I'm Caro. This is Pablo.*
B *Nice to meet you. My name's Malika and this is Petra.*

7 1.6 Read the phrases and write *Teacher* or *Student*. Listen and check.

1 ________
Open your books.

2 ________
Excuse me, what does 'late' mean?

3 ________
Sorry, I don't understand.

4 ________
Listen and repeat.

5 ________
How do you say 'buenos días' in English?

6 ________
Work in pairs.

Go to Vocabulary practice: classroom language, page 106

8 1.8 **Pronunciation:** the alphabet Listen and repeat the sounds, words and letters.

/eɪ/	/iː/	/e/	/aɪ/	/əʊ/	/uː/	/ɑː/
late	meet	yes	my	no	you	class
Aa Hh Jj Kk	Bb Cc Dd Ee Gg Pp Tt Vv	Ff Ll Mm Nn Ss Xx Zz	Ii Yy	Oo	Qq Uu Ww	Rr

9 1.9 Listen to the conversations. Write the names of the students.

Class 3
Student names:
1 ______________________
2 ______________________
3 ______________________

ABC School of English

Go to Communication practice: Student A page 134, Student B page 142

10 Introduce yourself to five students. Ask the questions and write the answers.

What's your name? How do you spell that?

Personal Best Write a conversation between a teacher and a new student.

5 A 1.5 Sts complete the conversation with the correct words. Play audio track 1.5 for sts to listen and check. See SB page opposite for audio script. Write the missing words on the board for sts to check spellings.

Answers
1 your 2 My 3 meet 4 'm 5 Are 6 am

B Model the activity by having the conversation with a confident student. Encourage them to use their own name. Sts then practise the conversation in pairs.

3 x PRACTICE *SB page 5, exercise 5B*

1 Do the exercise as normal. To check answers, read out each gapped sentence in turn, with three possible answers, e.g. *What's you name/What's your name/ What's my name?* Sts say the correct sentence. Sts then practise the conversation in pairs.

2 In pairs, sts cover the conversation. They try to remember each line of the conversation in turn, then reveal it to check.

3 Ask sts to close their books. Write prompts for the conversation on the board, e.g.
Hello / name ?
My ...
nice / meet / I ...
nice / meet / student?
✓
Sts use the prompts to practise the conversation again.

6 Invite four sts to come to the front of the class. Give them each a name: *Caro*, *Pablo*, *Malika* and *Petra*. Help each of the students in turn to model the example conversation, introducing themselves and using gestures to introduce each other. Ask them to repeat the conversation again, this time using their own names. Put sts into groups of four to practise introducing themselves using their own names. Change the groups around for sts to practise again if necessary.

7 1.6 Read out the first speech bubble and ask: *Who says this? A teacher or a student?* Elicit the answer. In pairs, sts read the remaining speech bubbles and decide who says each one. Play audio track 1.6. See SB page opposite for audio script. Sts listen and check. Check answers, and check that sts understand all the phrases.

Answers
1 T 2 S 3 S 4 T 5 S 6 T

Go to Vocabulary practice: classroom language, SB page 106/TB page 225.
Sts will find more language presentation and practice for classroom language here. Do these exercises with the class, or set them for homework, before continuing with exercise 8.

PB Remind sts to go to the app for further self-study vocabulary practice of classroom language.

8 1.8 Focus on the alphabet and explain that for this task the alphabet is not arranged in its usual order, but is arranged according to the way we pronounce each letter. Play the first group of letters and point out that they are all pronounced with the same vowel sound /eɪ/. Play audio track 1.8 once through for sts to listen and read. See SB page opposite for audio script. Play the audio again, pausing for sts to repeat the sounds and letters.

9 1.9 Play the first conversation and elicit the student's name. See TB page 306 for audio script. Elicit how to spell the name, and write it in on the board. Play the remaining conversations. Sts listen and write the names. Check answers.

Answers
1 Kenan Zorlu
2 Camila Bernardi
3 Hiro Matsumoto

Go to Communication practice
Divide the class into Student A and Student B. All 'Student A' sts should go to SB page 134. All 'Student B' sts should go to SB page 142. Go to TB page 281 for the teacher notes. Do the activity, then continue with exercise 10.

10 Demonstrate the conversation with a confident student, then ask two confident students to demonstrate it again. Allow sts to move around the classroom, introducing themselves to five of their classmates and writing their names.

PERSONAL BEST

Sts can practise introducing themselves further. They work in pairs and write a conversation between a teacher and a new student. They can use conversation 2 in exercise 1 on page 4 to help. Sts can then role-play their conversations in pairs.

With weaker sts, ask for two volunteers to come to the front of the class and be a teacher and a student. Assign their roles, then indicate the teacher and ask: *What does he/she say?* Elicit the first line of a conversation from the class, e.g. *Hello, I'm ...* . Write this on the board. Continue in this way, eliciting each line of a conversation and writing on the board. Sts can then practise the conversation, with the two volunteers modelling each line.

1A Where's she from?

a

b

1 A In pairs, match the flags with the countries.

A *What's a?* **B** *I think it's Mexico.*

c

d

e

f

g

h

1 Argentina ____
2 Brazil ____
3 China ____
4 Mexico ____
5 Spain ____
6 Turkey ____
7 the UK ____
8 the USA ____

B 1.10 Listen, check and repeat.

2 A 1.11 Listen to the conversation. Repeat it in pairs.

A Where are you from?
B I'm from Salta.

A Where's Salta?
B It's in Argentina.

B In pairs, practise the conversation using the cities and countries.

Toledo / Spain Izmir / Turkey Harbin / China York / the UK

3 Look at the picture. Match the countries from exercise 1 with the nationalities.

1 British *the UK*
2 Spanish ____
3 Mexican ____
4 American ____
5 Argentinian ____
6 Chinese ____
7 Turkish ____
8 Brazilian ____

Personal Best

Go to Vocabulary practice: countries and nationalities, page 107

4 1.13 Do the quiz in pairs. Listen and check.

THE COUNTRIES QUIZ

1 What nationality is Lewis Hamilton?
a He's British.
b He's American.

5 Which sentence is correct?
a Sydney is the capital of Australia.
b Sydney isn't the capital of Australia.

2 Where is Mount Fuji?
a It's in China.
b It's in Japan.

6 Is *ceviche* Mexican or Peruvian?
a It's Mexican.
b It's Peruvian.

3 Is this elephant from India or Africa?
a It's from India.
b It's from Africa.

7 Where is the Bosphorus?
a It's in Turkey.
b It's in Russia.

4 Is Elsa Pataky Russian?
a Yes, she is.
b No, she isn't.

8 What nationality is Paulo Coelho?
a He's Italian.
b He's Brazilian.

EXTRA PRACTICE Workbook page 4; photocopiable activity 1A Vocabulary

1A Where's she from?

Sts listen to conversations in which people talk about their country and nationality, and practise talking about their own country and nationality.

Grammar	Vocabulary	Pronunciation	Communication
Verb be (*he, she, it*)	Countries and nationalities (*China/Chinese, Spain/Spanish, the UK/British*, etc.); numbers 0-10	Word stress (*Japan, Japanese*, etc.)	Talking about countries and nationalities

WARMER

Say: *My name's ... I'm from ...* (say your country). Invite one or two students to say their names and where they are from. Write the names of the countries they mention on the board. You could ask sts to spell the name of their country for you, to revise the letters of the alphabet. Teach the words *country* and *nationality*.

1 A Read through the country names with the class and make sure sts understand them all. Point to the first flag and ask: *What's a?* Elicit some possible answers, encouraging sts to say: *I think it's ...* Sts work in pairs to match the flags with the countries.

B 1.10 Play audio track 1.10. See SB page opposite for audio script. Sts listen and check their answers. See which pair got the most answers right. Play the audio again for sts to repeat.

Answers
1 c 2 f 3 h 4 a 5 e 6 d 7 b 8 g

2 A 1.11 Teach the word *city*. Play audio track 1.11. See SB page opposite for audio script. Sts listen and read. Play the audio again, pausing after each line for sts to repeat.

B Demonstrate an example conversation, using the first city and country. Sts then practise the conversations in pairs. Ask some pairs to perform one of the conversations for the class.

3 Point to the picture and read out the speech bubble. Ask: *Where's she from?* (the UK) *What's her nationality?* (British). Sts match the countries from exercise 1 with the nationalities. Check answers, and model pronunciation of the nationalities.

Answers
2 Spain 3 Mexico 4 the USA 5 Argentina 6 China
7 Turkey 8 Brazil

3 x PRACTICE *SB page 6, exercise 3*

1 Do the exercise as normal. To check answers, call out each nationality in turn and get all sts to shout the correct country name at the same time. Say the correct country and nationality together, and get sts to repeat.

2 In pairs, sts cover exercise 3. They look at the country names in exercise 1 again and try to remember the nationalities. They can look at exercise 3 again to check.

3 Ask sts to close their books, then put them into teams. Call out the country names from exercise 1. Teams race to say the correct nationality.

Go to Vocabulary practice: countries and nationalities, SB page 107/TB page 227.
Sts will find more language presentation and practice for countries and nationalities here. Do these exercises with the class, or set them for homework, before continuing with exercise 4 of lesson 1A.

PB Remind sts to go to the app for further self-study vocabulary practice of countries and nationalities.

4 1.13 Read through the quiz questions with the class and make sure sts understand them all. Sts do the quiz in pairs. You could set a time limit for this, to make it competitive. Play audio track 1.13. See TB page 306 for audio script. Sts listen and check their answers. See which pair got the most correct answers.

Answers
1 a 2 b 3 a 4 b 5 b 6 b 7 a 8 b

5 A Match the pronouns *he*, *she* and *it* with the people and things.

1 he
2 she
3 it

a Elsa Pataky
b *ceviche*
c Lewis Hamilton

B Tick (✓) the form of the verb *be* that we use with *he*, *she* and *it*. Then read the Grammar box.

1 am ☐ 2 is ☐ 3 are ☐

Grammar **the verb *be* (*he*, *she*, *it*)**

Positive:
*He'**s** Japanese.*
*She'**s** from Mexico.*

Negative:
*Barcelona **isn't** the capital of Spain.*
*She **isn't** Australian.*

Questions and short answers:
***Is** it from India?*
*Yes, it **is**. No, it **isn't**.*

Personal Best

Go to Grammar practice: the verb *be* (*he*, *she*, *it*), page 96

6 A 1.15 **Pronunciation:** word stress Listen and repeat the words. Pay attention to the underlined stressed syllables.

Ja<u>pan</u> Japa<u>nese</u> <u>Me</u>xico <u>Me</u>xican <u>I</u>taly I<u>ta</u>lian <u>Tur</u>key <u>Tur</u>kish

B 1.16 Underline the stress in the countries and nationalities. Then listen, check and repeat.

1 I'm Brazilian. 2 She's from Germany. 3 It's Chinese. 4 Is he from Argentina?

7 In pairs, ask and answer the question *Where's ... from?* about the people and things.

A *Where's Zara from?*
B *Is it Italian?*
A *No, it isn't. It's Spanish.*

Zara

Ryan Gosling

Mercedes

Thalia

Neymar

Chow mein

8 A 1.17 Listen and repeat the numbers.

0	1	2	3	4	5	6	7	8	9	10
zero/oh	one	two	three	four	five	six	seven	eight	nine	ten

B 1.18 What are the international dialling codes for the countries? Listen and write the answers.

1 China + ________
2 Colombia + ________
3 India + ________
4 Mexico + ________
5 Spain + ________
6 Turkey + ________

Go to Communication practice: Student A page 134, Student B page 142

9 A In pairs, write six more quiz questions about countries and nationalities.

B Work with another pair. Ask and answer your quiz questions.

A *What is the capital of Wales? a) It's Glasgow. b) It's Cardiff.*
B *It isn't Glasgow – that's in Scotland. I think it's Cardiff.*
A *That's right! Your turn.*

Personal Best Write six sentences about people and things you like. Say where they are from.

EXTRA PRACTICE Workbook page 4; photocopiable activity 1A Grammar

5 A Sts look at the quiz in exercise 4 again and match the pronouns with the people and things. Check answers and check that sts understand the meaning of the pronouns.

> **Answers**
> 1 c 2 a 3 b

B Say: *He am British? He is British? He are British?* Elicit the correct answer.

> **Answer**
> 2

Grammar

Read the Grammar box with sts about the verb *be* (*he*, *she*, *it*). Remind sts that the verb *be* is irregular, so they need to learn all the forms. Point out that we usually use contracted forms rather than full forms (*he's*, *it's*, etc.), but we always use full forms in short answers, e.g. *Yes, he is*. NOT ~~*Yes, he's*~~. Point out the inverted word order in questions. Ask questions to check concept.

Concept check questions:
He Japanese – correct? (no – *he's* Japanese). *Positive or negative?* (positive). *She not Brazilian – correct?* (no – she *isn't* Brazilian). *Positive or negative?* (negative). *She's from Germany – can you make this into a question?* (Is she from Germany?). *What's the short answer to this question?* (Yes, she is/No, she isn't).

Go to Grammar practice: verb *be* (*he*, *she*, *it*), SB page 96/TB page 205
Sts will find more language reference, presentation and practice for the verb *be* (*he*, *she*, *it*) here. Do these exercises with the class, or set them for homework, before continuing with exercise 6A of lesson 1A.

PB Remind sts to go to the app for further self-study grammar practice of the verb *be* (*he*, *she*, *it*).

6 A 1.15 Demonstrate the meaning of *syllable* by saying some words for countries and counting the number of syllables by clapping. Play audio track 1.15 for sts to listen and repeat the words. See SB page opposite for audio script. Point out the underlined part of each word and explain the meaning of *stress* and *stressed* syllable. Point out that the same syllable is not always stressed in the country and nationality, e.g. Ja<u>pan</u>, Japa<u>nese</u>.

B 1.16 Sts work in pairs and underline the stressed syllables in the countries and nationalities. Play audio track 1.16. See SB page opposite for audio script. Sts listen and check their answers, then listen again and repeat.

> **Answers**
> 1 Bra<u>zil</u>ian 2 <u>Ger</u>many 3 Chi<u>nese</u> 4 Argen<u>ti</u>na

7 Read out the example conversation. Teach the phrase *I don't know*, which sts may need. Sts work in pairs to guess where the people and things are from. Check answers, and see which pair guessed the most answers correctly.

> **Answers**
> Ryan Gosling – Canada
> Mercedes – Germany
> Thalía – Mexico
> Neymar – Brazil
> Chow mein – China

8 A 1.17 Play audio track 1.17. See SB page opposite for audio script. Sts listen and repeat. Point out the tricky spelling of *eight*.

B 1.18 Read out the question and make sure sts understand it. Point out the plus sign and teach the word *plus*. Play the first number and ask sts to write it down. See TB page 306 for audio script. Check the answer. Play the rest of the audio track. Sts listen and write the numbers. Allow sts time to compare their answers in pairs, then play the audio again for them to listen and check. Check answers.

> **Answers**
> 1 8 6 2 5 7 3 9 1 4 5 2 5 3 4 6 9 0

Go to Communication practice
Divide the class into Student A and Student B. All 'Student A' sts should go to SB page 134. All 'Student B' sts should go to SB page 142. Go to TB page 281 for the teacher notes. Do the activity, then continue with exercise 9A of lesson 1A.

9 A Sts work in pairs and write six more quiz questions. Remind them to think about the word order and position of the verb *be* in their questions. You could elicit a few example questions for sts to use as models. Monitor and help while sts are working, and make sure their questions are correctly formed.

B Read out the example conversation and make sure sts understand everything. Put pairs together into groups of four to ask and answer their questions. Sts could repeat the activity by testing another pair of sts. Ask who managed to answer all their classmates' questions correctly.

1B Welcome to *Learning Curve*!

1 Match the jobs in the box with pictures a–f.

doctor engineer office worker police officer taxi driver waiter

Personal Best

Go to Vocabulary practice: jobs, page 108

2 A 1.20 Look at the picture. Listen and complete the conversation.

A What's my job?
B Are you an [1]________ ?
A No, I'm not. Try again!
B Are you a [2]________ ?
A Yes, I am.

B In pairs, play 'What's my job?'.

3 1.21 Watch or listen to the start of a webshow called *Learning Curve*. Match the cities with the people.

1 New York a Simon, Kate, Marina
2 London b Ethan, Penny, Mohammed, Marc

Skill listening for information about people

We often listen to information about people.

- Don't worry if you don't understand everything the speakers say.
- Read the questions and think about the information you need to listen for: name, job, nationality, etc.
- Listen for the verb *be*: *I'm ... / He's ... / She's ...* etc.

4 1.21 Read the Skill box. Watch or listen again and choose the correct information about the people.

Simon Collins
Nationality: British
Job: [1] *TV presenter / receptionist*

Ethan Moore
Nationality: [2] *American / British*
Job: TV presenter

Penny Abernathy
Nationality: English and [3] *Italian / Argentinian*
Job: TV presenter

Marina Ivanova
Nationality: Russian
Job: [4] *receptionist / teacher*

Mohammed Bensallem
Nationality: American
Job: [5] *TV presenter / office worker*

Marc Kim
Nationality: *American*
Job: [6] *doctor / IT specialist*

Kate McRea
Nationality: [7] *American / Argentinian*
Job: TV presenter

 EXTRA PRACTICE Workbook page 5; photocopiable activity 1B Vocabulary

1B Welcome to *Learning Curve*!

Sts learn vocabulary for jobs, then meet the *Learning Curve* team and watch or hear about people who live and work in different cities. They then talk about where they live and the jobs that they do.

Listening	Skill	Listening builder	Vocabulary
Sts watch a video or listen to a recording about where people live and the jobs they do.	Listening for information about people	Contractions	Jobs: (*an actor, a chef, a doctor, an engineer, an IT worker, an office worker, a police officer, a receptionist, a shop assistant, a singer, a student, a taxi driver, a teacher, a tour guide, a TV presenter, a waiter/a waitress*)

WARMER

Say: *I'm a teacher*. Write the word *teacher* on the board and say: *It's my job*. Write the word *job* on the board and repeat *I'm a teacher. It's my job*. Ask one or two students: *Where are you from? What's your job?*

1 Sts match the jobs with the pictures.

Answers
a taxi driver b waiter c office worker d police officer
e engineer f doctor

Go to Vocabulary practice: jobs, SB page 108/TB page 229
Sts will find more language presentation and practice for jobs here. Do these exercises with the class, or set them for homework, before continuing with exercise 2A of lesson 1B.

PB Remind sts to go to the app for further self-study vocabulary practice of jobs.

2 A 1.20 Mime driving, to show what the student in the picture is doing. Play audio track 1.20. See SB page opposite for audio script. Sts listen and complete the conversation. Check answers. Explain the meaning of *try again*.

Answers
1 engineer 2 taxi driver

B Put sts into pairs to take turns to mime and guess.

Each unit features an episode of *Learning Curve*, a webshow intended for international students to engage in English language and culture. It is presented by a range of hosts who present documentaries and vox pops (in B lessons which focus on listening skills) and also talk about their personal lives through video diaries (in D lessons which focus on speaking skills). You and your students can watch the videos in class, or download them from the Learning Platform to watch at home. You can watch the episode in its entirety (for enjoyment or familiarization purposes), or you can break it down into more manageable chunks, as recommended in each lesson. It is also available as an 'audio-only' option for teaching environments without access to video. Students hear speakers from the UK and the USA (exposing them to both British and American English accents) as well as from other countries. The video allows students to practise particular listening skills and gives them exposure to features of natural spoken speech. See TB page 14 for more information on *Learning Curve*.

3 1.21 All the B lessons in this level which focus on listening skills are accompanied by video. In this episode of *Learning Curve*, Simon and the team talk to people about jobs. Pre-teach the following words if necessary from the video: *programme* and *studio*. Play video or audio track 1.21. See TB page 306 for video/audio script. Sts listen and match the cities with the people. Check answers.

Answers
1 b 2 a

Skill

Read the Skill box with sts about listening for information about people. Pre-teach the following words if necessary from the video: *IT specialist*, *internet*, *technology*, *statistics* and *popular*. Play video or audio track 1.21 again.

4 Sts watch or listen and choose the correct information. Check answers.

Answers
1 TV presenter 2 American 3 Argentinian
4 receptionist 5 office worker 6 IT specialist
7 American

5 1.22 Watch or listen to the rest of the show. Who isn't in London now? Where is he/she?

6 1.22 Watch or listen again. Complete the information with countries and jobs.

1 Viktor: from: ________ job: ________ and ________
2 Sarah: from: ________ job: ________
3 Pedro: from: ________ job: ________

7 **A** In pairs, ask and answer the questions about the three people.

Where is ... from? | What's his/her job?

B In pairs, ask and answer the questions about you.

Where are you from? | What's your job?

8 1.23 Listen and read what Kate says. How does she say the contractions in **bold**? What do they mean?

Listening builder contractions

In English, we often use contractions, especially when we speak.
I'm *from the United States.* = ***I am*** *from the United States.*
She ***isn't*** *a student.* = *She* ***is not*** *a student.*
What's *your job?* = ***What is*** *your job?*

9 1.24 Read the Listening builder. Listen and write the contractions.

1 ________ Spanish.
2 ________ your name?
3 He ________ a doctor.
4 ________ from Japan.
5 ________ an engineer.
6 The ________ here.

10 1.25 In pairs, look at the pictures of Jia and Luis. Guess the information about the people. Listen to the conversations and check.

job? | nationality? | Where now?

11 Write the names of three friends or members of your family. In pairs, ask and answer questions about them.

A *Where's Saanvi from?* B *She's from Nagpur.*
A *What's her job?* B *She's an IT worker.*
A *Where is she now?* B *She's in Mumbai.*

Personal Best Choose five classmates and write their jobs, e.g. *Carla's a teacher.*

EXTRA PRACTICE Workbook page 5

5 1.22 Focus on the three pictures of people and model pronunciation of their names. Explain to sts that they are going to watch or listen to the second half of the show. Read out the questions, then play video/audio track 1.22. See TB page 306 for video/audio script. Sts watch/listen and answer the questions. Check answers.

Answers
Pedro. He's in Alaska.

6 1.22 Pre-teach the following words if necessary from the video: *familiar with, fan, busy, tourist, meeting, wonderful*. Ask questions to elicit the meanings, e.g. *Which word means someone who likes something a lot?* (fan). *Which word means someone who visits a city?* (tourist). Teach the meanings. Point to the gapped information and explain that the information belongs with each person in order: Viktor, Sarah and Pedro. Elicit that after *from* sts need to add a country. Play video/audio track 1.22 again. Sts watch/listen and complete the information with countries and jobs. Check answers. Play the track again, pausing for sts to hear why each answer is correct.

Answers
1 Poland 2 taxi driver 3 engineer 4 Canada
5 teacher 6 Chile 7 police officer

7 **A** Ask: *Where's Viktor from?* Elicit the answer (*He's from Poland*). Ask: *What's his job?* Elicit the answer. Sts work in pairs to ask and answer questions about the three people.

B Ask one or two sts: *Where are you from? What's your job?* Elicit answers, and teach any additional job names if necessary. Sts then work in pairs to ask and ask the questions. Ask some sts to tell the class about their partner's country and job.

8 1.23 Focus on the speech bubble, and point out the contractions. Explain that contractions are two words that are joined together. Play audio track 1.23. See SB page opposite for audio script. Discuss with the class how Kate says the contractions, and what they mean.

Answers
I'm = I am
What's = What is

Listening builder

Read the Listening builder box with sts about contractions. Read out the sentences with contractions and those with full forms, to model pronunciation of both. Explain that we often use full forms in writing, but we usually use contractions when we speak. Ask questions to check concept.

Concept check questions:
What do we call two words joined together? (a contraction). *Do we use contractions when we write, or when we speak?* (when we speak). *I am a doctor – can you say that with a contraction?* (I'm a doctor). *What is your job? – Can you say that with a contraction?* (What's your job). *He isn't a taxi driver – what does 'isn't' mean?* (is not).

9 1.24 Allow sts time to read the gapped sentences, then play audio track 1.24. See SB page opposite for audio script. Sts listen and write the contractions. Check answers, and elicit what each contraction means.

Answers
1 I'm 2 What's 3 isn't 4 It's 5 You're 6 teacher's

10 1.25 Focus on the photos and the questions. Read out the task and make sure sts understand that they have to guess the information. Ask: *Where's Jia from? What's her job? Where is she now?* Elicit a few guesses from individual sts. Put sts into pairs to guess the information, then play audio track 1.25. See TB page 307 for audio script. Sts listen and check their answers. Check answers with the class and play the track again for sts to hear the answers. Ask who guessed correctly.

Answers
1 job: office worker; nationality: Chinese; Where now? New York/the USA
2 job: student/waiter; nationality: Colombian; Where now? the UK

11 As a round-up, sts discuss information about their friends and family members. Ask sts individually to write the names of three friends or family members. Put them into pairs to ask and answer questions about the people. Ask some sts to tell the class something about one of their friends or family members.

PERSONAL BEST

Sts can practise talking about jobs further. They choose five classmates and write sentences about their jobs. Ask some sts to read their sentences to the class.

Weaker sts can write sentences to answer the questions in exercise 10 about themselves, e.g. *I'm a student. I'm from Argentina. I'm in London now*. Ask some sts to read their sentences to the class.

EXTRA PRACTICE

Sts work in groups of three. They take turns to use their phones to film their classmates answering the questions in exercise 11. They can swap roles and practise again. Allow sts time to watch the films of themselves and notice how well they ask and answer questions about personal information. Discuss as a class what they noticed about their speaking, and how they could improve it.

1C We are the champions

1 A Write the numbers in the box in the correct order.

sixteen thirteen fourteen seventeen twelve twenty ~~eleven~~ fifteen nineteen eighteen

eleven, ______

B Look at the pictures and read the numbers. Tick (✓) the numbers that are correct.

1 twenty-three ☐

2 fifty-four ☐

3 eighty-six ☐

4 sixty-eight ☐

5 one hundred ☐

6 thirty ☐

Go to Vocabulary practice: numbers 0–100, page 111

2 A In pairs, ask and answer the question *How old is …?* for the people in the picture.

A *How old is Kyle?* B *I think he's 40.*

B 1.27 Listen and write the ages.

Kyle ______ Martin ______ Lorna ______

3 A Look at the picture. What do you know about the rock band Queen? Do you know any songs or the names of the band members?

B Read the introduction to the interview. What is the name of the band?

Queen for a night

No, this isn't a photo of Freddie Mercury and the rock band Queen. It's Dave Bryant, a teacher, and his band 'Queen for a night'. They're on a UK tour and tonight they're in Manchester. I'm with Dave and Jim from the band.

So Jim, are you all teachers?

Jim No, we aren't. I'm an engineer and Ed and Mick are doctors.

And where are you from?

Dave I'm from London, Jim and Ed are from Oxford and Mick's from Bristol. We're old friends from university.

How's the tour?

Jim It's good, but it's hard. It's a big tour – fourteen cities – and we aren't so young now!

Really? How old are you?

Dave Mick and I are forty-seven. And you and Ed are fifty …

Jim I'm not fifty! Ed's fifty … I'm forty-nine.

Dave Oh yes. Sorry, Jim!

And what's your favourite Queen song?

Dave That's easy! It's *We Are the Champions*!

10

1C We are the champions

Sts read and listen to an interview with a member of a Queen tribute band. They then invent their own band and practise interviewing each other about their personal information.

Grammar	Vocabulary	Pronunciation	Communication
The verb *be* (*we, you, they*)	Numbers 0–100; adjectives (1) (*bad, beautiful, big, boring, cheap, difficult, easy, expensive, good, happy, interesting, old, sad, small, ugly, young*)	Numbers	Talking about numbers

WARMER

Revise numbers 0–10 by getting sts to count to ten as a class. Get them to count again, going around the class, with each student saying a number. Hold up different numbers of fingers and get sts to say the numbers. Gradually speed up, until sts are confident with all the numbers.

1 A Sts work in pairs to write the numbers in the correct order. They can use their dictionaries to help. You could do this as a race. Check answers and model pronunciation of the numbers.

Answers
eleven, twelve, thirteen, fourteen, fifteen, sixteen, seventeen, eighteen, nineteen

B Teach the numbers *twenty, thirty, forty, fifty, sixty, seventy, eighty, ninety* and *a hundred*. Sts work in pairs to look at the numbers and tick the ones that are correct. Check answers and elicit the correct numbers for the remaining pictures.

Answers
1, 4 and 5 are correct. 2 forty-five 3 eighty 6 fifty

3 x PRACTICE *SB page 10, exercise 1B*

1 Do the exercise as normal. To check answers, read out each number in turn. Ask sts to put up their left hand if they think it is correct, and their right hand if they think it is not correct. Confirm the answer and, where the number on the page was incorrect, elicit the correct number.

2 In pairs, sts cover the words in exercise 1B. They look at the pictures and try to remember the numbers. They can look at their answers again to check, or ask you if they are not sure.

3 Ask sts to close their books, and put them into teams. Write random numbers from 0–100 on the board, one at a time. Teams race to say each number correctly. They get a point for a correct answer, but lose a point if they say it incorrectly.

Go to Vocabulary practice: numbers 0–100, SB page 111/TB page 235
Sts will find more language presentation and practice for numbers from 0–100 here. Do these exercises with the class, or set them for homework, before continuing with exercise 2A of lesson 1C.

PB Remind sts to go to the app for further self-study vocabulary practice of numbers 0–100.

2 A 1.27 Draw sts' attention to the picture. Ask *How old is Kyle?*, elicit some guesses but don't confirm the answer. Sts work in pairs to ask and answer about all three people.

B Play audio track 1.27. See TB page 307 for audio script. Sts listen and complete the ages. Check answers. Play audio track 1.27 again, pausing after each line for sts to repeat.

Answers
Kyle 42, Martin 14, Lorna 65

3 A Point to the picture and read out the questions. Check that sts understand the meaning of *rock band*. Elicit what sts know about the band Queen. Elicit the name *Freddie Mercury*, and elicit the names of some of the band's well-known songs, e.g. 'We Will Rock You', 'Bohemian Rhapsody', 'We are the Champions', 'Don't Stop Me Now'.

B Teach the meaning of *tour, tonight* and *night*. Elicit or explain that Manchester and Bristol are cities in the UK. Sts read the introduction and answer the question. Check the answer.

Answer
Queen for a night.

4 1.28 Read and listen to the interview. Complete the information about the band.

	Dave	Jim	Ed	Mick
job				
city				
age				

5 **A** Read the sentences from the interview. Match the people in **bold** with the pronouns *we*, *you* and *they*.

1 **Mick and I** are forty-seven. ____ 2 **Jim and Ed** are from Oxford. ____ 3 And **you and Ed** are fifty. ____

B Tick (✓) the form of the verb *be* we use when we talk about more than one person. Then read the Grammar box.

a *am / am not* ☐ b *is / isn't* ☐ c *are / aren't* ☐

Grammar the verb *be* (*we, you, they*)

Positive:	Negative:	Questions and short answers:
*We**'re** old friends.*	*We **aren't** young.*	***Are** you all teachers?*
*They**'re** on a UK tour.*	*They **aren't** the rock band Queen.*	*Yes, we **are**.* *No, we **aren't**.*

Personal Best

Go to Grammar practice: the verb *be* (*we, you, they*), page 96

6 **A** 1.30 **Pronunciation:** numbers Listen and repeat the numbers. Pay attention to how the stress changes.

1 a thir<u>teen</u> b <u>thir</u>ty 2 a four<u>teen</u> b <u>for</u>ty 3 a fif<u>teen</u> b <u>fif</u>ty

B 1.31 Listen and tick (✓) the numbers you hear. Listen again and repeat.

1 a He isn't 16. ☐ b He isn't 60. ☐ 3 a We aren't 17. ☐ b We aren't 70. ☐
2 a She's 18. ☐ b She's 80. ☐ 4 a They're 19. ☐ b They're 90. ☐

Go to Communication practice: Student A page 134, Student B page 142

7 Match adjectives 1–4 from the text with their opposites in the box.

bad small old difficult

1 young ________ 2 good ________ 3 big ________ 4 easy ________

Personal Best

Go to Vocabulary practice: adjectives (1), page 109

8 Describe the pictures in pairs. Use positive and negative forms.

Picture a: They're big. They aren't small.

9 **A** In small groups, imagine you are in a band and complete the table.

The name of the band	Your names	Your ages	Nationalities

B Work with another group. Interview each other about your bands.

What's the name of your band? What are your names? How old are you? Where are you from?

Personal Best Write a short paragraph about a band you like.

EXTRA PRACTICE Workbook page 6; photocopiable activities 1C Grammar and 1C Vocabulary

4 1.28 Point out the interview text on page 10. Focus on the table and check that students understand *job*. Play audio track 1.28. See SB page 10 for audio script. Sts listen and complete the table. Check answers, and check that sts understand *engineer* and *doctor*.

Answers
Dave: teacher, London, forty-seven
Jim: engineer, Oxford, forty-nine
Ed: doctor, Oxford, fifty
Mick: doctor, Bristol, forty-seven

5 A Read out the first sentence and ask sts to find the same sentence in the interview on page 10. Ask them to match the bold words with the correct pronoun. Sts then match the remaining bold words with the pronouns. Check answers, and check that sts understand the pronouns.

Answers
1 we 2 they 3 you

B Say: *We am from Oxford / We is from Oxford / We are from Oxford – which is correct?* Elicit the correct answer.

Answer
c

Grammar

Read the Grammar box with sts about the verb *be (we, you, they)*. Remind sts that the verb *be* is irregular, and they need to learn all the parts. Ask questions to check concept.

Concept check questions:
We are forty-five – correct? (yes). *Positive or negative?* (positive). *Can you make it negative?* (We aren't forty-five). *They are from London – correct?* (yes). *Can you make it into a question?* (Are they from London?). *What's the answer to that question?* (Yes, they are/No, they aren't).

Go to Grammar practice: the verb *be (we, you, they)*, SB page 96/TB page 205.
Sts will find more language reference, presentation and practice for the verb *be* (*we, you, they*) here. Do these exercises with the class, or set them for homework, before continuing with exercise 6A of lesson 1C.

PB Remind sts to go to the app for further self-study grammar practice of the verb *be (we, you, they)*.

6 A 1.30 Play the audio once for sts to listen. See SB page opposite for audio script. Point out the underlined syllables, and point out how the stress is different in the different words. Play the audio again for sts to repeat.

B 1.31 Play the first sentence of the audio. See TB page 307 for audio script. Elicit which sentence sts hear. Play the rest of the audio. Sts listen and tick the sentences they hear. Play the audio again as you check the answers, so sts can hear the correct answers. Play the audio once more for sts to repeat.

Answers
1 a 2 b 3 b 4 a

Go to Communication practice
Divide the class into Student A and Student B. All 'Student A' sts should go to SB page 134. All 'Student B' sts should go to SB page 142. Go to TB page 281 for the teacher notes. Do the activity, then continue with exercise 7 of lesson 1C.

7 Focus on adjectives 1–4 and ask sts to find them in the interview on page 10. Sts then match them with the opposites in the box. They can use their dictionaries to help. Check answers, and check that sts understand all the adjectives.

Answers
1 old 2 bad 3 small 4 difficult

Go to Vocabulary practice: adjectives (1), SB page 109/ TB page 231.
Sts will find more language presentation and practice for adjectives (1) here. Do these exercises with the class, or set them for homework, before continuing with exercise 8 of lesson 1C.

PB Remind sts to go to the app for further self-study vocabulary practice of adjectives (1).

8 Focus on the first picture and read out the example sentences. In pairs, sts look at the remaining pictures and describe them using positive and negative sentences. Elicit possible answers.

Suggested answers
b They're bad. They aren't good. They're young. They aren't old.
c They're new. They aren't old.
d They're difficult. They aren't easy.

9 A Put sts into groups of four or five. Tell them they are going to make their own band. Focus on the table and make sure sts understand everything. Tell them they can invent information about themselves if they don't want to give real information.

B Read out the four questions and make sure sts understand them all. Put groups together to interview each other. Encourage them to all join in with asking and answering the questions, rather than just leaving it to one or two sts. Monitor and help while they are working. Ask: *Who has a good band? Why is it good?*

PERSONAL BEST

Sts can practise using the verb *be* further. They write a short paragraph about a band they like. Sts can compare their paragraphs in small groups and discuss which bands have a good name, and which bands they all like.

Weaker sts can work in pairs and write three sentences about a band they both like. Ask some sts to read their sentences to the class.

1D What's your email address?

1 Match the places in the box with pictures a–c.

hotel car rental office gym

a

b

c

2 **A** Look at the form. Match it with one of the pictures in exercise 1.

B 1.33 Listen to the conversation. Which piece of information in the form is **incorrect**?

Customer Information — CARS-4-U

Title	MR ☑ MRS ☐ MS ☐		
Surname	Martin	First name(s)	Louis
Nationality	French	Date of birth	17/06/1980
Address	35 Rue Pasteur, Paris		
Postcode	75099		
email address	louis.martin@mymail.com		
Phone number	33 1 80 26 58		

Skill completing a form

When you complete a form, read all the instructions and sections carefully.

- Use the correct *title*. *Mr* = a man, *Mrs* = a married woman, *Ms* = a woman (married or unmarried).
- Your *surname* is your family name.
- Write your *date of birth* in numbers: the day/the month/the year: *13/09/1995*.
- For email addresses: @ = 'at' and .com = 'dot com'.

3 Read the Skill box. Match sections 1–9 with information a–i.

1 postcode
2 date of birth
3 address
4 surname
5 first name
6 email address
7 title
8 phone number
9 nationality

a Smith
b M42 3GN
c Ms
d s.smith@cjbrooks.com
e 07700 900 357
f 23/11/1988
g British
h Sarah
i 36 Charles Street, Manchester

EXTRA PRACTICE Workbook page 7

1D What's your email address?

Sts study a car hire form that someone has completed. They study the use of capital letters, then practise completing a form with personal information.

Writing	Skill	Text builder
Completing a form	Completing a form	Capital letters

WARMER

Play a game to revise the alphabet. Starting at the front of the class, sts each say one letter of the alphabet in turn. If they make a mistake or cannot think of the next letter, they are out. Go round two or three times, speeding up each time, until sts are confident. Ask sts to write three new words from lesson 1C on a piece of paper, without their partner seeing. Sts then work in pairs and spell their words to each other. Their partner writes the words. See who manages to write all the words correctly.

1 Sts work in pairs and match the words with the pictures. They can use their dictionaries to help. Check answers, and check that sts understand all the words. Model and drill pronunciation of the words.

Answers
a hotel b gym c car rental office

2 A Sts look at the form and match it with one of the pictures. Check the answer, then read through the form with the class and check that sts understand all the information in it. Model pronunciation of the words for the types of information, e.g. *title, surname, address*.

Answer
c

B 1.33 Explain to sts that one piece of information in the form is not correct. Play audio track 1.33. See TB page 307 for audio script. Sts listen and find the incorrect piece of information. Check the answer. Play the audio again if necessary as you check, so that sts can hear the correct and incorrect information.

Answer
The postcode is 75009, not 75099.

Skill

Read the Skill box with sts about completing a form. Read out the email address on the form to demonstrate how to say email addresses.

3 Sts match the sections with the information. Check answers.

Answers
1 b 2 f 3 i 4 a 5 h 6 d 7 c 8 e 9 g

3 x PRACTICE *SB page 12, exercise 3*

1. Do the exercise as normal. To check answers, say each section in turn. Demonstrate to sts that they should put their hand completely up if they are confident about the answer, half-way up if they are half confident, and only a small way up if they are not very confident. Ask a confident student to give the answer.
2. In pairs, sts cover 1–9 in exercise 3, then look at just a–i and try to remember the word for each kind of information. They can uncover 1–9 again to check.
3. Ask sts to close their books. Say individual pieces of information in turn, e.g. *Spanish, 07904 100 200, Ana*. In pairs, sts race to say the word for that kind of information (nationality, phone number, first name).

4 In pairs, ask and answer questions about you, using the information in exercise 3.

A *What's your surname?* **B** *It's Taylor.*
A *How do you spell that?* **B** *It's T-A-Y-L-O-R.*

5 Look at answers a–i in exercise 3. Tick (✓) the information with capital letters.

1 first name ☐
2 surname ☐
3 email address ☐
4 nationality ☐
5 street names ☐
6 cities ☐

Text builder capital letters

In English, we use capital letters (*A*, *B*, *C*, *D*, etc.) for the following:
- the first word in a sentence: *What's your name?*
- the personal pronoun *I*: *Hello, I'm Robert.*
- the names of people and places: *Emma is from Oxford.*
- countries, nationalities and languages: *We're from China. We're Chinese.*
- postcodes: *SN2 5EF*

6 **A** Read the Text builder. Find one **incorrect** capital letter in each sentence.

1 My friend Lena is American. She's From Florida.
2 Hello, I'm Antonio. I'm a new Student.
3 Our Address is 173 London Avenue, Manchester, M73 6XL.
4 This is Mesut. He's from Turkey and he's Twenty-one.

B Rewrite the sentences with capital letters.

1 what's his job? is he a doctor? ____________
2 my address is 3 white street, glasgow gl33 4sc. ____________
3 they aren't from germany. they're from poland. ____________
4 i'm your new english teacher. my name's jack. ____________

7 **A** **PREPARE** Look at the form. Check that you understand all the information you need to write.

ATLAS HOTEL

Customer Information

Title Mr ☐ Mrs ☐ Ms ☐ Other ☐
Surname ____________
First name(s) ____________
Date of birth ____________
Nationality ____________
Address ____________
Postcode ____________
Email address ____________
Phone number ____________

B **PRACTISE** Complete your form. Remember to use capital letters correctly.

C **PERSONAL BEST** Swap your form with a partner. Is it clear and easy to read? Are the capital letters correct?

Personal Best Design a form for a gym. Complete it with information about a family member.

13

4 Read out the example questions and answers. Sts work in pairs to ask and answer questions. Monitor and help while sts are working. Ask some sts questions about their partner, e.g. *What's (Pedro's) surname?*

5 Sts look at the answers in exercise 3 and tick the information with capital letters. Check answers.

Answers
1, 2, 4, 5

Text builder

Read the Text builder box with sts about capital letters. Explain that we use capital letters in some kinds of information, e.g. your name, the names of cities, the names of streets, etc. Point out that only the first letter is a capital in each case, but point out that we use all capital letters for postcodes. Ask sts which uses are the same in their language, and which are different. Ask questions to check concept.

Concept check questions:
Do we use capital letters for names? (yes). *First names and surnames?* (yes). *All the letters in a name?* (no, only the first letter). *What other information do we use capital letters for?* (cities, street names, nationality, postcode). *Which kind of information do we use all capital letters for?* (postcode).

6 A Sts read the sentences and find one incorrect capital letter in each one. Check answers.

Answers
1 From 2 Student 3 Address 4 Twenty-one

B Point out to sts that the first letter in a sentence is always a capital letter, and we always write the pronoun *I* with a capital letter. Sts rewrite the sentences with capital letters. Check answers by asking individual sts to come and write the correct sentences on the board.

Answers
1 What's his job? Is he a doctor?
2 My address is 3 White Street, Glasgow GL33 4SC.
3 They aren't from Germany. They're from Poland.
4 I'm your new English teacher. My name is Jack.

7 Sts follow the steps to complete a form.

A PREPARE Sts look at the form and prepare their ideas. They can ask you if they are not sure about anything.

B PRACTISE Sts complete the form with information about themselves. Refer them back to the Skill box for tips on how to fill in a form, and refer them to the Text builder box to remind them about how to use capital letters.

C PERSONAL BEST Sts work in pairs. They swap their forms with a partner and give feedback on how clear and easy to read it is, and whether capital letters are used correctly. Point out to sts that they should always be positive and encouraging when they give feedback to a partner.

PERSONAL BEST

Sts can practise completing a form further. In pairs, they design a form for a gym. They then each complete it with information about a family member. Sts can swap forms and give feedback on how clear and easy to read it is, and the use of capital letters.

Weaker sts could copy the form from exercise 2 on page 12, then complete it with information about a family member. They can swap forms and give feedback on the use of capital letters.

EXTRA PRACTICE

As a class, brainstorm ideas for a form for joining a library. Draw the form on the board and ask sts to make two copies. On one copy, sts add information about a fictional person who wants to join the library. Tell students they could use the name and details of a celebrity, a character in a film, etc., or they could invent someone. Tell them not to show it to their partner. Sts then take turns to ask and answer questions, to complete their second form with their partner's information. Tell sts they should not show each other their forms, but must do it all by speaking and spelling words where necessary. When they have finished, sts can compare their forms, to see if they have written all their partner's information correctly. Discuss as a class which parts of the form were the most difficult.

UNIT 2

People and things

LANGUAGE singular and plural nouns ■ *this, that, these, those* ■ personal objects

2A The man with only 15 things

1 2.1 In pairs, match the words in the box with objects a–f. Listen and check.

a book a bag keys a watch an umbrella a camera

a 
b 
c 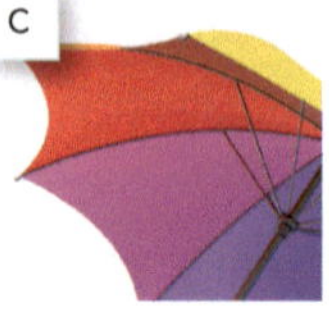
d 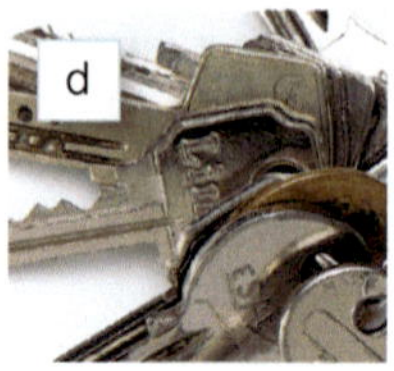
e 
f 

Personal Best

Go to Vocabulary practice: personal objects, page 110

2 Look at exercise 1 and answer the questions. Then read the Grammar box.

1 Which noun do we use with *an*? ________ 2 Which noun is plural? ________

Grammar singular and plural nouns

Singular nouns:	*a key*	*an umbrella*	*a watch*
Plural nouns:	*keys*	*umbrellas*	*watches*

Personal Best

Go to Grammar practice: singular and plural nouns, page 97

3 **A** Imagine you live with only 15 things. What are your 15 things?

B Read the text. Are your 15 things the same as Andrew's?

15 countries *with* 15 things

This is Andrew Hyde, and that's his book: *15 countries with 15 things*. Andrew is from Colorado in the USA and he's a writer and traveller. And it's true – he's a man with only 15 things!

THESE ARE HIS 15 THINGS:

1 ___ bag	6 ___ wallet	13 ___ shoes
2 ___ smartphone	7 ___ jacket	14 ___ towel
3 ___ camera	8 ___ trousers	15 ___ wash bag
4 ___ iPad	9 & 10 ___ shirts	
5 ___ sunglasses	11 & 12 ___ shorts	

Andrew is back in the USA now, but is he happy with just those 15 things? Yes, he says. Life is easy without a lot of things.

14

People and things

UNIT 2

UNIT 2 OVERVIEW: This unit focuses on people, their family and their possessions. Sts practise talking about their possessions and their own family. In *Learning Curve*, Kate and Simon talk about the time.

LANGUAGE		
Grammar	**Vocabulary**	**Pronunciation**
Singular and plural nouns; *this, that, these, those*; possessive adjectives	Personal objects; colours; family and friends	/ɪ/ and /iː/; *'s*

SKILLS	
Reading	**Speaking**
Preparing to read; adjectives and nouns	Telling the time; asking for information politely

LANGUAGE 2A

2A The man with only 15 things

Sts read a text about an American who travelled to 15 different countries with only 15 things in his bag. They read about what an office worker carries in her bag, and then talk about what they have in their own bag.

Grammar	Vocabulary	Pronunciation	Communication
Singular and plural nouns; *this, that, these, those*	Personal objects (*bag, book, camera, credit card, glasses, keys, mobile phone, pen, pencil, purse, sunglasses, tablet, umbrella, wallet, watch*)	/ɪ/ and /iː/	Talking about your personal possessions

WARMER

Point to some familiar objects from around the classroom, e.g. a pen, a book, and ask: *What's this?* Elicit any words the sts already know and write them on the board. Tell sts they are going to practise talking about the things they have.

1 2.1 Sts look at the pictures in pairs and match them with the words. Play the audio for sts to listen and check. See TB page 307 for audio script.

Answers
a a bag b a camera c an umbrella d keys e a book f a watch

Go to Vocabulary practice: personal objects, SB page 110/TB page 233.
Sts will find more language presentation and practice for vocabulary for personal objects here. Do these exercises with the class, or set them for homework, before continuing with exercise 2 of lesson 2A.

PB Remind sts to go to the app for further self-study vocabulary practice of vocabulary for personal objects.

2 Refer sts back to the words in exercise 1. Read out the first question and explain the meaning of *noun*. Sts work in pairs to answer the questions. Check answers as a class.

Answers
1 umbrella 2 keys

Grammar

Read the Grammar box with sts about singular and plural nouns. Explain that singular nouns refer to just one thing, and plural nouns refer to more than one. Explain that we use *a/an* with singular nouns, and that plural nouns usually end in *-s* or *-es*. Ask questions to check concept.

Concept check questions:
Book, bag, watch – what kind of words are they? (nouns). *A book – singular or plural?* (singular). *Three book – correct?* (no – *three books*). *A watch – singular or plural?* (singular). *What's the plural form?* (watches). *A umbrella – correct?* (no – an umbrella).

Go to Grammar practice: singular and plural nouns. SB page 97/TB page 207.
Sts will find more language reference, presentation and practice for singular and plural nouns here. Do these exercises with the class, or set them for homework, before continuing with exercise 3A of lesson 2A.

PB Remind sts to go to the app for further self-study grammar practice of singular and plural nouns.

3 A Give sts time to make a list individually of their 15 things. They can use a dictionary to find words they don't know, or they can ask you. Put sts into small groups to compare their ideas. Ask groups to tell the class which things are on all their lists.

B Check/explain the meaning of *with* and *without*. Sts then read the text and compare their lists with Andrew's. Ask the class which of their things are the same as Andrew's.

4 Look at the list of Andrew's things again. Write *a* or *an* for singular nouns, and – for plural nouns.

5 Complete the sentences from the text with the pronouns in the box. Which words do we use with singular nouns? Which ones with plural nouns? Then read the Grammar box.

that those this these

1 ________ is Andrew Hyde.
2 ________'s his book.
3 ________ are his 15 things.
4 Is he happy with just ________ 15 things?

Grammar *this, that, these, those*

Things that are near us:
***This** is my bag.*
***These** are my keys.*

Things that aren't near us:
***That**'s my car.*
***Those** are my friends.*

Personal Best

Go to Grammar practice: *this, that, these, those*, page 97

6 A 2.5 **Pronunciation:** /ɪ/ and /iː/ Listen and repeat the sounds and words.

/ɪ/	this	it	is	six
/iː/	these	he	three	keys

B 2.6 In pairs, say the sentences. Listen, check and repeat.

1 This is my city.
2 These are my keys.
3 Is that tree Japanese?
4 She's six and he's three.

Go to Communication practice: Students A and B page 135

7 Choose the correct words to complete the text.

What's in your bag?

Maria Clara, office worker, Rio de Janeiro

[1] *This / These* is my bag and [2] *this / these* are my things. This [3] *is / are* my book. It's in English! [4] *These / That* are my keys. [5] *This / These* key is for my house and [6] *that / those* key is for my car. [7] *This is / That's* my car over there – it's [8] *a / an* sports car! What's this? It's [9] *a / an* umbrella. It's very small! And the last thing? These are [10] *a / –* sunglasses!

8 A 2.7 Listen and match conversations 1–3 with pictures a–c.

a

b

c

B 2.7 Complete the phrases from the conversations with *this, that, these* and *those*. Listen again and check.

1	**Jack**	What's ________?	**Helen**	________ is my bag.
2	**Woman**	Jorge, who's ________ over there?	**Jorge**	________'s Sergio.
3	**Man**	Hi, Karen. What are ________?	**Karen**	________ are my cameras.

9 Put some things from your bag on the desk. In pairs, ask and answer questions about the things.

A *What's that?*
B *This is a book. It's in Spanish.*
A *And what are those?*
B *These are my keys.*

Personal Best Write about the things in your bag, as in exercise 7.

4 Read out the first item on Andrew's list again (bag) and ask: *a bag? an bag? bag?* Elicit the answer (a bag). Sts complete the task. Check answers.

Answers
1 a 2 a 3 a 4 an 5 – 6 a 7 a 8 – 9, 10 – 11, 12 – 13 – 14 a 15 a

5 Ask sts to find the first sentence in the text on page 14 and elicit the correct pronoun (*This*). Check that sts understand the sentence. Sts find the remaining sentences in the text and complete them with the correct pronouns. Check answers, and check that sts understand the sentences. Read out the two questions and elicit the answers.

Answers
1 This 2 That 3 These 4 those
We use *this* and *that* with singular nouns. We use *these* and *those* with plural nouns.

Grammar

Read the Grammar box with sts about *this, that, these, those*. Explain that we use *this* and *that* with singular nouns, and we use *these* and *those* with plural nouns. Use gestures to demonstrate the difference between *this is my book* (near you) and *that is my book* (not near you). Do the same to demonstrate *these are my books* and *those are my books*. Ask questions to check concept.

Concept check questions:
This is my book – is it near me? (yes). *What do I say if it isn't near me?* (That's my book). *This is my keys – correct?* (No – *these are* my keys). *What do I say if they aren't near me?* (Those are my keys).

Go to Grammar practice: *this, that, these, those*. SB page 97/TB page 207.
Sts will find more language reference, presentation and practice for *this, that, these, those* here. Do these exercises with the class, or set them for homework, before continuing with exercise 6A of lesson 2A.

PB Remind sts to go to the app for further self-study grammar practice of *this, that, these, those*.

6 A 2.5 Play audio track 2.5. See SB page opposite for audio script. Sts listen and notice the two vowel sounds. Play the audio again for sts to listen and repeat.

B 2.6 Model pronunciation of the first two sentences. Explain to sts that they should focus on the /ɪ/ and /iː/ sounds. Sts practise saying the sentences in pairs. Play audio track 2.6. Sts listen and check their answers, then listen again and repeat.

Go to Communication practice
Divide the class into Student A and Student B. All sts (A & B) should go to SB page 135. Go to TB page 283 for the teacher notes. Do the activity, then continue with exercise 7 of lesson 2A.

7 Sts read the text and choose the correct words to complete it. Check answers with the class.

Answers
1 This 2 these 3 is 4 These 5 This 6 that
7 That's 8 a 9 an 10 –

3 x PRACTICE *SB page 15, exercise 7*

1. Do the exercise as normal. To check answers, tell sts you are going to read out the whole text with some correct answers and some incorrect. Tell them they should make a particular sound (e.g. a beep) when you read an incorrect answer.
2. With books closed, read out the text again, omitting some words, e.g. *This ... my bag. ... are my things*. You could cough or beep to indicate a gap. Sts guess the missing words.
3. With books closed, write some key words from the text on the board, e.g. *my bag, my things, book, English*. In pairs, sts try to rewrite the text from memory. They can look at the text again to check. Ask who managed to remember it all.

8 A 2.7 Focus on the pictures, then play the first conversation. Elicit which picture it matches. Play the remaining conversations. Sts listen and match them with the pictures. See TB page 307 for audio script. Check answers.

Answers
1 b 2 c 3 a

B 2.7 Sts complete the sentences with the correct words. Play the audio for them to listen and check. Check answers.

Answers
1 that, This 2 that, That 3 those, These

9 Read out the example questions and answers. Demonstrate the task by taking some things out of your bag. Encourage sts to ask questions about the things, and answer them. Sts then work in pairs to ask and answer questions about their own things. Monitor and help with vocabulary if necessary while sts are working.

PERSONAL BEST

Sts can practise talking about their things further. They write a text about the things in their bag, using the text in exercise 7 as a model. Sts can compare their texts in pairs and check the use of *this, that, these, those*.

With weaker sts, write four sentence beginnings on the board: *This is ..., That's .., These are ..., Those are ...* . Sts complete them with their own ideas, then compare their sentences in pairs.

2B Lost!

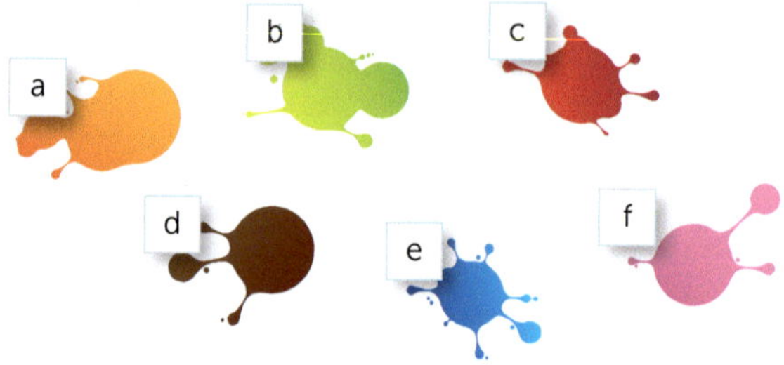

1 **A** Match the words in the box with the colours.

blue brown green orange pink red

Personal Best

Go to Vocabulary practice: colours, page 110

B In pairs, point to objects in the classroom. Ask and answer *What colour is that/are those...?*

A *What colour are those books?* **B** *They're orange.*

Skill preparing to read

Before you read a text, look at other information to help you prepare.
- Think about the style of the text. Is it from a magazine, a website, a letter?
- Look at the pictures. What people, places and things can you see?
- Read the title. What does it mean?

2 **A** Read the Skill box. What do you think the text on page 17 is about? Tick (✓) a, b or c.

a lost tourists in London ☐ **b** transport in London ☐ **c** lost objects in London ☐

B Read the text quickly and check your answer.

3 Read the text again. Are the sentences true (T) or false (F)?

1 The Lost Property Office is in London. ____
2 The objects are all from buses. ____
3 Tim Carlisle is a tour guide every day. ____
4 The laptop is new. ____
5 All the instruments are expensive. ____
6 The £15,000 is in the office now. ____

4 Complete the sentences with the words in the box. Check your answers in the text.

expensive violin guitars cheap

1 These ________ are ________ .
2 That's an ________ ________ .

Text builder adjectives and nouns

adjective + noun: *£15,000 in a **brown envelope**.*
noun + *be* + adjective: *This **laptop is new**.*

Look! Adjectives don't change with plural nouns: *It's an **expensive instrument**. They're **expensive instruments**.*

5 Read the Text builder. Order the words to make sentences.

1 good it's a camera ____________________
2 sunglasses they're expensive ____________________
3 green bag the is ____________________
4 are the brown wallets ____________________
5 fast a it's car ____________________

6 **A** 2.9 Read and listen to the conversation in a Lost Property Office.

B In pairs, change the highlighted words and have a new conversation.

A Hello, can I help you?
B Do you have my wallet? It's a small, black wallet. It's expensive.
A One moment. Is this your wallet?
B Yes, that's it!

 EXTRA PRACTICE Workbook page 11; photocopiable activity 2B Vocabulary

2B Lost!

Sts read about the large number of things that end up in the Lost Property Office for Transport for London, then practise asking for something they have lost.

Vocabulary	Reading	Skill	Text builder
Colours (*black, blue, brown, gold, green, grey, orange, pink, purple, red, silver, white, yellow*)	Sts read a text about the things in the Lost Property Office for Transport for London.	Preparing to read	Adjectives and nouns

WARMER

Mime using a camera and ask: *What's this?* Elicit the word. Invite sts in turn to mime using something. You could refer them back to page 14 or the Vocabulary practice on page 110 for ideas. Other sts guess the words. As they guess the words, write them on the board and check that sts understand them.

1 A Sts work in pairs and match the words with the colours. They can use a dictionary to help. Check answers.

Answers
a orange b green c red d brown e blue f pink

Go to Vocabulary practice: colours, SB page 110/TB page 233.
Sts will find more language presentation and practice for colours here. Do these exercises with the class, or set them for homework, before continuing with exercise 1B of lesson 2B.

PB Remind sts to go to the app for further self-study vocabulary practice of colours.

B Demonstrate the task by pointing to some objects in the classroom and asking questions, e.g. *What colour is that book? What colour are those pens?* Sts then work in pairs and practise asking and answering questions.

Skill

Read the Skill box with sts about preparing to read. Check they understand *information, prepare, style, magazine, website, letter, places* and *title*. Point out that thinking about a text before you read it can help you to understand it more easily. Read the three options with the class and make sure sts understand them all.

2 A Sts look at the pictures, read the title and think about the style of the text, then guess what it is about. Elicit some possible answers, and encourage sts to explain why they think this is the correct answer. Don't confirm the answer at this stage.

B Sts read the text quickly to check their answer. Point out to sts that they shouldn't worry at this stage if they don't understand everything in the text. Check the answer with the class.

Answer
c

3 Check that sts understand the meaning of *true* and *false*. Read through the six sentences with the class, and check that sts understand them all. Read out the first sentence again and ask: *Is this true or false?* Ask sts to read the first two paragraphs of the text to check. Elicit the answer. Sts read the text again and decide if the remaining sentences are true or false. Check answers, referring to the text for evidence.

Answers
1 T 2 F 3 F 4 T 5 F 6 F

4 Sts complete the sentences with the missing words, then check their answers in the text. Allow sts time to compare their answers in pairs, then check with the class.

Answers
1 guitars, cheap 2 expensive violin

Text builder

Read the Text builder box with sts about adjectives and nouns. Elicit that nouns are words such as *bag, book* and *umbrella* that refer to things, and adjectives are words such as *big, good* and *expensive* that describe things. Explain that adjectives usually come before a noun, e.g. *a big bag, a red bus*, NOT ~~*a bag big, a bus red*~~. Point out that adjectives can also come after the verb *be*, e.g. *This bag is big, That bus is red*. Point out that adjectives stay the same with singular and plural nouns, e.g. *a new camera, two new cameras*, NOT ~~*two news cameras*~~. Ask questions to check concept.

Concept check questions:
A black taxi – correct? (yes). *A bus red – correct?* (no – a red bus). *Do adjectives go before a noun or after a noun?* (before a noun). *One blue car, two blues cars – correct?* (no – two *blue cars*). *Are adjectives plural when the noun is plural?* (no – adjectives don't change). *This is a big camera – This camera …* (is big). *These are red buses – These buses …* (are red).

5 Sts order the words to make sentences. Check answers.

Answers
1 It's a good camera. 2 They're expensive sunglasses.
3 The bag is green. 4 The wallets are brown.
5 It's a fast car.

6 A 2.9 Refer sts to the conversation, then play audio track 2.9. See SB page opposite for audio script. Sts read and listen to the conversation.

B Demonstrate the task with a confident student. Sts then work in pairs to make a new conversation. They can swap roles and practise again. Ask some sts to perform their conversations for the class.

Lost in London

22,000 mobile phones, 12,000 credit cards, a green 'Incredible Hulk' toy, £15,000 in a brown envelope …

These are some of the things in the Transport for London Lost Property Office. Every year, 300,000 objects are lost on buses, trains and taxis in the city. I'm at the office in central London, and with me is Tim Carlisle. Tim is a worker here, but today he's my tour guide.

'Look at all these things – wallets, glasses, bags, shoes, mobile phones – they're all here,' Tim tells me. 'Look at this laptop – it's new.'

In a different part of the office are musical instruments. 'These guitars are cheap, but that's an expensive violin,' he says.

'What's over there?' I ask.

'Those are umbrellas. Big umbrellas, small umbrellas, blue umbrellas, pink umbrellas …'

'And what about the envelope with £15,000?' I ask. 'Is it still here?'

'No,' Tim says. 'An old man collected it last month. He's 80 years old and he doesn't like banks!'

And that's the end of my tour. It's time for me to go. Now, where's my phone?

Personal Best Write a conversation in a Lost Property Office.

PERSONAL BEST

Sts can practise talking about lost things further. In pairs, they write a conversation in a Lost Property Office. They can use the conversation in exercise 6 on page 16 as a model, but encourage them to change some of the wordings if they can, e.g. the assistant could ask another question about the object. You could teach a few more phrases to help sts, e.g. *OK, Thank you*.

Weaker sts could make a list of three things they have, using adjectives to describe them, e.g. *It's a new phone. It's small.* They can compare their lists in pairs.

EXTRA PRACTICE

With books closed, write the following matching task on the board:

1 a green	a envelope
2 a brown	b man
3 pink	c toy
4 an old	d umbrellas

Sts work in pairs and match the halves of the phrases from memory. They can check their answers in the text. Check answers, and check that sts understand all the phrases.

Answers
1 c **2** a **3** d **4** b

EXTRA PRACTICE

With books closed, write the following numbers on the board and teach sts how to say them.

1 15,000
2 80
3 12,000
4 22,000

In pairs, sts try to remember the meaning of the numbers in the text. They can look at the text again to check their answers.

Answers
1 £15,000 in a brown envelope
2 the old man is 80
3 12,000 credit cards
4 22,000 mobile phones

EXTRA PRACTICE

In pairs or small groups, sts imagine the Lost Property Office at their school and make a list of what is in it. Encourage them to use their imaginations! Monitor and help while they are working, helping with vocabulary if necessary. They can then prepare a conversation in which they show someone around the office, with one of them as a tour guide and the other person asking questions. Ask pairs or groups in turn to perform their conversations for the class.

2C My family

1 Match the people in the box with pictures a–d.

husband and wife   mother and son   father and daughter   brother and sister

a

b

c

d

2 Put the words from exercise 1 in the correct columns.

Male ♂	Female ♀
brother	*sister*

Personal Best

Go to Vocabulary practice: family and friends, page 111

3 **A** Discuss the questions in pairs.

1 Are you from a big family or a small family?
2 Do you live with your family?
3 Does anyone in your family live in a different city or country?

B Read the text quickly. What is Laura's family situation? Is she sad about it?

Long-distance families

Are you part of a 'long-distance' family? Are your brothers or sisters in a different city or country? Are you a long way from your parents or children? Tell us your stories.

Laura Wickham

Hi! My name's Laura. My husband Seamus and I are long-distance parents! We live in Cork in Ireland. Our daughter Amy is 30 years old and she's in Australia. Our son Conor is 26 years old and he's in the USA.

Amy and Conor are a long distance from us, but their lives are very interesting. Amy's an IT worker in Perth. Her husband Pete is from there. He's an engineer. Pete is Australian. Conor's a surfing teacher in Los Angeles. He loves California and its beautiful beaches, so it's his dream job! Conor's girlfriend Nicole is a Hollywood actor … well, that's her dream. At the moment, she's a waitress.

We're on Skype a lot with our children, but it's difficult with the time differences. Am I sad that they're so far away? Sometimes, but the important thing is that they're happy.

4 Read the text again. Match the information with the people.

1 This person is 30 years old.
2 This person is a waitress.
3 This person lives in Cork.
4 This person is a surfing teacher.
5 This person is Australian.

a Seamus
b Amy
c Pete
d Conor
e Nicole

 EXTRA PRACTICE Workbook page 12; photocopiable activity 2C Vocabulary

2C My family

Sts learn vocabulary for family members, and read about a long-distance family, with people in three different countries. They then practise talking about their own family.

Grammar	Vocabulary	Pronunciation	Communication
Possessive adjectives, *'s* for possession	Family and friends (*boyfriend, brother, children, daughter, father, girlfriend, grandfather, grandmother, husband, mother, parents, sister, son, wife*)	*'s*	Talking about family and friends

WARMER

With books closed, tell sts you are going to say a word to them and they should write down the first three words that come into their head. Tell them they can write the words in their own language if they don't know the words in English. Tell them not to think too much, but just write the first words they think of. Write the word *family* on the board and elicit or explain the meaning. Allow sts time to write their words, then find the English words in their dictionaries if necessary. Ask sts in turn what words they wrote. Write all the words on the board to give you a word picture of what family means to your sts. See which words were written the most often.

1 Read through the words in the box with the class and teach the meanings. Sts then look at the pictures and match them with the words. Check answers. Model and drill pronunciation of the words.

Answers
a brother and sister
b mother and son
c husband and wife
d father and daughter

3 x PRACTICE *SB page 18, exercise 1*

1 Do the exercise as normal. To check answers, point to each picture in turn and offer alternatives, e.g. *Mother and son? Brother and sister?* Students respond by saying yes or no. Model and drill pronunciation of the words, and point out the tricky spelling of *daughter*.

2 In pairs, sts cover the words, then look at the pictures again and try to remember the words for each picture. They can look at the words again to check.

3 With books closed, say some sentences to give clues for the words, e.g. *I'm your sister, you are my* ... (brother). Sts race to say the correct words. Invite sts to spell each word when they give the correct answer.

2 Check that sts understand the symbols and the words *male* and *female*. Sts write the words in the correct columns. Tell sts to copy the spellings carefully. Check answers.

Answers
male: brother, husband, son, father
female: sister, wife, mother, daughter

Go to Vocabulary practice: family and friends, SB page 111/TB page 235.
Sts will find more language presentation and practice for words for family and friends here. Do these exercises with the class, or set them for homework, before continuing with exercise 3A of lesson 2C.

PB Remind sts to go to the app for further self-study vocabulary practice of words for family and friends.

3 A Read out the three questions and make sure sts understand them all. Sts discuss the questions in pairs. Ask some sts to tell the class something about their partner.

B Use the map to elicit or teach *Ireland*, *Australia* and *the USA*. Read out the questions and check that sts understand them. Sts read the text quickly to answer the questions. Remind sts that when they read a text for the first time, they shouldn't worry if they don't understand everything. Check answers with the class.

Answers
Laura lives with her husband, but her son and daughter live in other countries. She is sometimes sad, but she thinks it's important that her children are happy.

4 Ask sts to read the information about the people. Check they understand everything. Model pronunciation of the names *Seamus* /ˈʃeɪməs/ and *Amy* /ˈeɪmiː/. Sts read the text again and match the information with the people. Check answers.

Answers
1 b 2 e 3 a 4 d 5 c

5 Complete the sentences from the text with the words in the box.

our my her its his their

1 ________ name's Laura.
2 ________ son Conor is 26 years old.
3 ________ lives are very interesting.
4 ________ husband Pete is from there.
5 He loves California and ________ beautiful beaches.
6 It's ________ dream job!

6 A Choose the correct option to complete the sentence from the text.

Conor's / Pete's / Seamus's girlfriend Nicole is a Hollywood actor.

B What ending do we add to names and nouns to show possession? Read the Grammar box.

Grammar possessive adjectives, 's for possession

Possessive adjectives:

I	my:	*I'm a teacher. **My** name's Karen.*
you	your:	*Are you OK? **Your** phone's broken.*
he	his:	*He's a tour guide. **His** job's interesting.*
she	her:	*She's Chinese, but **her** husband's British.*
it	its:	*Sydney's a great city. **Its** beaches are beautiful.*
we	our:	*We're in Class 3 and **our** teacher's very good!*
they	their:	*Jo and Ben aren't here. They're in **their** car.*

's for possession:

***Kim's** mother is from Germany.*
*Is this **Amy's** book?*
***My son's** new phone is expensive.*

Go to Grammar practice: possessive adjectives, 's for possession, page 97

7 A 2.12 **Pronunciation:** *'s* Listen and repeat. Pay attention to the *'s* sound.

son's daughter's Amy's Conor's my husband's my sister's

B 2.13 In pairs, say the sentences. Then listen, check and repeat.

1 My husband's name is Felipe.
2 Our son's girlfriend is French.
3 My wife's parents are from Canada.
4 Sara's brother's girlfriend is a doctor.

Go to Communication practice: Student A page 135, Student B page 143

8 2.14 Look at the people. In pairs, guess their relationship. Listen and check.

A *I think Jim is Tom Hanks's son.* **B** *Yes, or maybe he's his brother.*

9 Choose five people in your family and write down their names. In pairs, ask and answer questions about the people.

A *Who is Azra?* **B** *She's my brother's wife.*

Who is he/she? How old is he/she? What is his/her job?

Personal Best Write a description of your family.

19

5 Read out the first gapped sentence. Ask sts to find the sentence in the text, and elicit the correct word to complete it. Sts look at the text again and complete the sentences with the correct words. Check answers and check that sts understand all the sentences.

Answers
1 My 2 Our 3 Their 4 Her 5 its 6 his

6 A Sts find the sentence in the text and choose the correct option to complete it. Check the answer, and check that sts understand the sentence.

Answer
Conor's

B Read out the question and check sts understand the meaning of possession. Use the example in exercise 6A to elicit the answer.

Answer
's

Grammar

Read the Grammar box with sts about possessive adjectives and *'s* for possession. Explain that we use possessive adjectives with a noun, to say who something belongs to, e.g. *my name, his brother, her husband*. Point out that the form does not change for singular or plural nouns, e.g. *my book, my books; his teacher, his teachers*. Explain that we add *'s* to a name or a noun to show that something belongs to that person, e.g. *Amy's mother, Paul's sister, my brother's camera*. Point out that the form is the same when it is followed by a singular or plural noun, e.g. *Paul's brother, Paul's brothers*. Ask questions to check concept.

Concept check questions:
This is me bag – correct? (no – my bag). *My bag, my bags – correct?* (yes). *What's the possessive adjective for 'he'?* (his). *What's the possessive adjective for 'you'?* (your). *That's Amy umbrella – correct?* (no – *Amy's* umbrella). *My sister name is Maria – correct?* (no – my *sister's* name). *My sister's book, my sister's books – correct?* (yes).

Go to Grammar practice: possessive adjectives, *'s*, SB page 97/TB page 207.
Sts will find more language reference, presentation and practice for possessive adjectives and *'s* here. Do these exercises with the class, or set them for homework, before continuing with exercise 7A of lesson 2C.

PB Remind sts to go to the app for further self-study grammar practice of possessive adjectives and *'s*.

7 A 2.12 Allow sts time to read through the words, then play audio track 2.12 once for sts to listen and notice the *'s* sound. See SB page opposite for audio script. Play the audio again for sts to repeat.

B 2.13 Sts practise saying the sentences in pairs, paying attention to the *'s* sound. Play audio track 2.13 for sts to listen and check their pronunciation. See SB page opposite for audio script. Play the audio again for sts to repeat the sentences.

Go to Communication practice
Divide the class into Student A and Student B. All 'Student A' sts should go to SB page 135. All 'Student B' sts should go to SB page 143. Go to TB page 283 for the teacher notes. Do the activity, then continue with exercise 8 of lesson 2C.

8 2.14 Focus on the photos and ask sts which people on the top row they recognize. Elicit what they know about each celebrity. Explain that the people on the bottom row are all related to the celebrities. Read out the example answer and teach the meaning of *maybe*. Ask: *Who do you think Jim is?* Elicit one or two ideas. Sts then work in pairs to talk about the photos. Play audio track 2.14. See Answers for audio script. Sts listen to check their ideas. Check the answers with the class, and ask who guessed all the answers correctly.

Answers
Jim Hanks is Tom Hanks's brother.
Louise Adams is Victoria Beckham's sister.
Jaden Smith is Will Smith's son.
Gerard Piqué is Shakira's boyfriend.
Judy Murray is Andy Murray's mother.

9 Read out the task and the example questions, then demonstrate the task by writing the name of someone in your family on the board. Invite sts to ask you questions about the person. Sts then write down five names of people in their family, and work in pairs to ask and answer questions about them. Ask some sts to tell the class something they learned about their partner's family.

PERSONAL BEST

Sts can practise talking about their family further by writing a description of their family. They can compare their descriptions in pairs and ask more questions to find out more about the people.

Weaker sts can choose three people in their family and write a sentence about each one. Ask some sts to read some of their sentences to the class.

2D What time is it?

1 A 2.15 In pairs, match the times in the box with the clocks. Listen and check.

five o'clock | ten past eight | quarter past ten | half past six | quarter to twelve | five to four

1 ______ 2 ______ 3 ______ 4 ______ 5 ______ 6 ______

B 2.16 Complete the times. Listen, check and repeat.

1 It's eleven ______ .

2 It's ______ three.

3 It's ______ twelve.

4 It's ______ nine.

2 A 2.17 Watch or listen to the start of *Learning Curve*. Choose the correct options to complete the sentences.

1 Kate is ____ .
  a at home b on holiday c at work
2 ____ are on the phone.
  a Kate's parents b Kate's friends c Kate's brothers
3 They are in ____ .
  a Boston b Los Angeles c London
4 Kate has ____ and a sister.
  a no brothers b one brother c two brothers

B 2.17 Watch or listen again and answer the questions.

1 What time is it in London? ______
2 What time is it in Los Angeles? ______

Conversation builder — telling the time

Asking for the time:
What time is it?
What's the time?
What time's the film?
What time's the next bus?

Talking about times:
It's ten o'clock.
It's seven a.m./p.m.
The film is at twenty past eight.
The bus is in ten minutes.

3 A Read the Conversation builder. Match the questions with pictures a–d.

a
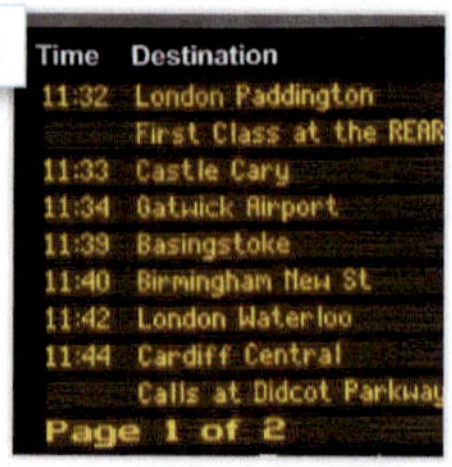

b
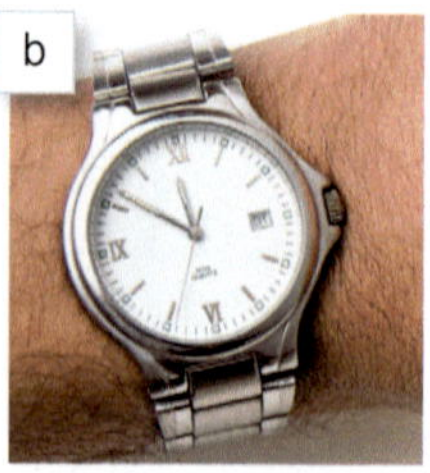

c
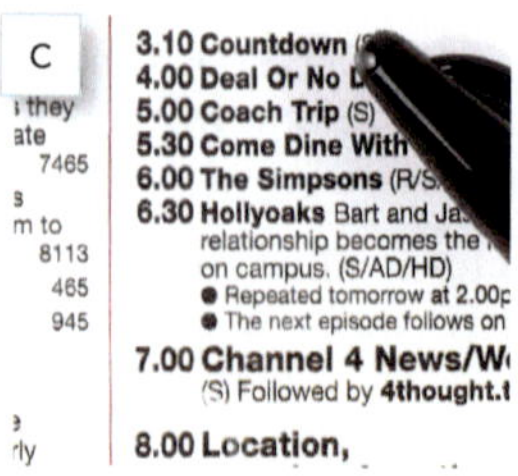

d

1 What's the time? ____
2 What time is *The Simpsons*? ____
3 What time is it in New York? ____
4 What time's the train to Birmingham? ____

B Ask and answer the questions in pairs.

EXTRA PRACTICE Workbook page 13

2D What time is it?

Sts hear people talking about the time. They then practise telling the time and asking for information politely.

Speaking	Skill	Conversation builder
Sts watch a video or listen to a recording of people talking about the time. They then practise talking about the times of different events.	Asking for information politely, e.g. *Excuse me, Please, Thank you.*	Telling the time

WARMER

Point to a clock if there is one in the classroom, and teach the word *clock*. Alternatively, draw one on the board. Then look at your wrist, as if you are looking at a watch, and teach the word *watch*. Take out your phone and show the time on your phone. Ask: *What time is it?* Write the question on the board. Model and drill pronunciation of the question. Say what time it is now, e.g. *It's ten o'clock.*

1 A 2.15 Put sts into pairs to look at the clocks and match the times with the clocks. Play audio track 2.15. See SB page opposite for audio script. Sts listen and check their answers. Play the audio again for sts to repeat.

Answers
1 half past six
2 quarter to twelve
3 five o'clock
4 ten past eight
5 five to four
6 quarter past ten

B 2.16 Sts work individually or in pairs to complete the times. Play audio track 2.16. See TB page 307 for audio script. Sts listen and check their answers. Play the audio again for them to repeat.

Answers
1 o'clock
2 quarter past
3 half past
4 twenty-five to

3 x PRACTICE *SB page 20, exercise 1B*

1 Do the exercise as normal. Before you play the recording, point to each clock in turn and ask: *What time is it?* Elicit the answers, then play the recording for sts to check.

2 Ask sts to cover the words. They look at the clocks again and try to remember how to say each time. They can look at the words and their answers again to check.

3 In pairs, sts draw three more clocks, showing different times, and decide how to say them. Monitor and help while they are working. They then swap clocks with another pair and practise saying the times they are given. Ask some sts to come to the board and draw one of their clocks, then say the time.

2 A 2.17 All the D lessons in this level which focus on speaking skills are accompanied by video. In this episode of *Learning Curve*, Kate introduces members of her family and talks about what time it is and her new job.

Allow sts time to read the gapped sentences and the options. Teach the words *awake*, *asleep* and *tired*. Remind sts of the meaning of *studio*. Play video/audio track 2.17. See TB page 307 for video/audio script. Sts watch or listen and choose the correct options. Check answers with the class.

Answers
1 a 2 a 3 b 4 c

B 2.17 Read out the two questions and elicit the answers if sts can remember them. Don't confirm their answers yet. Play the video/audio again. Sts watch or listen and answer the questions. Check answers with the class.

Answers
1 2.30 a.m. / half past two in the morning
2 6.30 p.m. / half past six in the evening

Conversation builder

Read the Conversation builder box with sts about telling the time. Make sure they understand that *What's the time?* and *What time is it?* are different forms of the same question, and both are correct. Point out the use of *a.m.* for mornings, and *p.m.* for afternoons and evenings. Point out the use of *at* to say when something happens, e.g. *Dinner is at eight o'clock*. Point out the use of *in* for future time, e.g. *The film is in five minutes*. Ask questions to check concept.

Concept check questions:
How can you ask about the time now? (What time is it? / What's the time?). *How can you ask about the time of a train?* (What time's the train?). *It's half past two – is it before two o'clock or after?* (after). *It's 6 p.m. – is it morning or afternoon?* (afternoon). *The train's in two o'clock – correct?* (no – the train's *at* two o'clock). *I have to wait ten minutes for a bus. What can I say?* (The bus is in ten minutes).

3 A Read out the first question and elicit which picture it matches. Sts read the remaining questions and match them with the pictures. Check answers.

Answers
1 b 2 c 3 d 4 a

B Sts ask and answer the questions in pairs. Ask some individual sts the questions to check their answers.

Answers
1 11.52 2 6.00 3 9.00 4 11.40

4 2.18 Watch or listen to the rest of the show. Match the times in the box with the people.

8.15 9.00 3.00 8.45 12.30

5 A 2.18 Match the questions with the people from exercise 4. Watch or listen again and check.

1 When's the match? ________
2 OK, what time is it? ________
3 Excuse me. What time's the James Bond film? ________
4 Excuse me. What time is it, please? ________
5 Where's the 67 bus? ________

B Which questions are polite? Why?

Skill asking for information politely

When you ask for information, it's important to be polite.

- Use *Excuse me* or *Sorry* to get the person's attention.
- At the end of the conversation, say *Thank you* or *Thanks*.
- If you want to be extra polite, say *Please* at the end of questions.

6 2.19 Read the Skill box. In pairs, guess the missing words from the conversations. Listen and check.

Woman 1 [1]________ . What time is it, [2]________ ?
Kate It's 8.15. Quarter past.
Woman 1 Oh! I'm late. [3]________ very much.

Woman 2 [4]________ , what time is the 67 bus?
Kate Next bus ... 8.45. It's in ten minutes.
Woman 2 Oh, 8.45, not 8.35. Ten minutes. OK. [5]________ .

7 In pairs, practise asking for information politely.

Questions	Answers
what / the teacher's name	It's Leanne.
what time / next bus to Cambridge	It's at 12.20 p.m.
where / the museum	It's that building.
what / name of this restaurant	It's The Golden Dragon.
what / the school's phone number	It's 354 269.

Go to Communication practice: Student A page 135, Student B page 143

8 A PREPARE In pairs, choose the cinema or the airport and invent the missing information.

★ SILVER CINEMA ★

FILM	TIME	SCREEN
Star Wars	________	________
Titanic	________	________
The Wizard of Oz	________	________

Airport departures 10:05

Flight	Time	Gate
Stockholm	________	________
Beijing	________	________
Lima	________	________

B PRACTISE In pairs, ask and answer questions about the films or the flights. Remember to be polite.

C PERSONAL BEST Invent information for the other situation and repeat the activity. Is your speaking better this time?

Personal Best Write a conversation with a tourist in your local train or bus station.

EXTRA PRACTICE Workbook page 13

4 2.18 Focus on the times in the box and elicit how to say them. Teach the different ways to say *8.15*, *8.45* and *12.30* (eight fifteen/quarter past eight, etc.). Focus on the five people and explain the task. Pre-teach the following words if necessary from the video: *match* (= a sports game) and *Follow me*, then play video/audio track 2.18. See TB page 307 for video/audio script. Sts watch or listen and match the times with the people. Check answers, then play the video/audio again for sts to hear the answers in context.

> **Answers**
> 1 12.30 2 8.15 3 8.45 4 3.00 5 9.00

5 A 2.18 Read out the first question and ask: *Who asks this question?* Elicit the answer. Sts then match the questions with the five people. Play video/audio track 2.18 again for sts to check their answers. Check answers with the class.

> **Answers**
> 1 Man 2 2 Simon 3 Man 1 4 Woman 1 5 Woman 2

B Discuss with the class which questions are polite and why. Elicit or explain that we use phrases such as *Excuse me* and *please* to make a question polite.

> **Answer**
> 3 and 4

Skill

Read the Skill box with sts about asking for information politely. Elicit or give a few examples of questions from exercise 5A with the phrases added, to make them polite, e.g. *Sorry. When's the match? Excuse me. Where's the 67 bus, please?*

6 2.19 Put sts into pairs to look at the conversation and guess the missing words. Elicit a few ideas, but don't confirm them. Play audio track 2.19. See SB page opposite for audio script. Sts listen and check their answers. Check answers with the class. Sts could then practise the conversations in pairs.

> **Answers**
> 1 Excuse me 2 please 3 Thank you 4 Sorry
> 5 Thanks

7 Read out the first prompt and elicit a polite question to ask for the information. Focus on the answers. Point out how to say *twelve twenty p.m.* and explain that in English phone numbers are usually said as individual numbers, so the phone number here would be *three five four, two six nine*. Sts practise asking for the information in pairs. Ask some pairs to perform one of their conversations for the class.

Go to Communication practice

Divide the class into Student A and Student B. All 'Student A' sts should go to SB page 135. All 'Student B' sts should go to SB page 143. Go to TB page 283 for the teacher notes. Do the activity then continue with exercise 8 of lesson 2D.

8 Sts follow the steps to have a conversation in which they ask about the time and other information.

A PREPARE Focus on the information and make sure sts understand *screen* and *gate*. Elicit that both of these require a number. Sts work in pairs to complete the information.

B PRACTISE Sts work in pairs to have a conversation in which they ask for information. They can swap roles and practise again. Remind them to use phrases to be polite.

C PERSONAL BEST Discuss with sts how easy or difficult they found the task. Sts then invent information for the other situation and repeat the activity. They can swap roles and practise again. Point out to sts that it might feel artificial to practise in this way, but the more times they practise conversations like this, the easier they will find them when they are in a real-life situation.

PERSONAL BEST

Sts can work in pairs and prepare a new conversation in a train or bus station in their town or city. They could then practise their conversation in their pairs. Ask some sts to perform their conversations for the class.

Weaker sts can work in new pairs and this time focus more on their listening skills. They choose one of the situations and have another conversation, but the person giving information invents it as they answer. The person listening must listen carefully and write it down. When they have finished, they can check with their partner to see if they have written the information correctly. They can swap roles and practise again.

EXTRA PRACTICE

Put sts into groups of three. Two sts repeat the conversation from exercise 8 in which they ask for information. The third student uses their phone to film the other two. Sts can swap roles and practise again. Watching themselves on film will help sts to evaluate how well they can ask for information politely.

Grammar

1 Choose the correct options to complete the sentences.

1 Hi Laura, I ________ Khalid's brother. Nice to meet you.
a 's
b 're
c 'm

2 How old ________ your grandfather?
a are
b is
c am

3 ________ these your glasses?
a Am
b Is
c Are

4 A Is your sister's boyfriend from Brazil?
B No, ________ .
a he isn't
b she isn't
c I'm not

5 A What's this?
B It's ________ old book.
a –
b a
c an

6 ________ my mother over there with the blue umbrella.
a These are
b This is
c That's

7 My wife's a chef and this is ________ new restaurant.
a she's
b her
c his

8 My ________ surname is Chen.
a grandfather's
b grandfather
c grandfathers

2 Rewrite the sentences with the new words.

1 He's an English teacher.
They *'re English teachers* .

2 These are my red pens.
This ________________________ .

3 We're happy with our new tablets.
I ________________________ .

4 Those expensive cars are Italian.
That ________________________ .

5 I'm a student in India.
She ________________________ .

6 My brother's an office worker and this is his bag.
My brothers ________________________ and
these ________________________ .

3 Choose the correct options to complete the text.

A HOLLYWOOD FAMILY

[1] *These / This* is Zooey Deschanel. She's [2] *a / an* actor and a singer. [3] *She / Her* sister Emily is an actor too. She's in the TV show *Bones*. What [4] *'s / 're* their mother's job? An actor. And [5] *their / our* father's job? [6] *Her / His* job is in films too! That's not all – Zooey's [7] *sister's / sisters* husband is … an actor. They [8] *'re / 's* from California in the USA and they're a Hollywood family. They [9] *are / aren't* the only family like this. From Marlon Brando's family to Will Smith's family, they [10] *'m / 're* easy to find in Hollywood.

Vocabulary

1 Put the words in the box in the correct columns.

~~difficult~~ engineer grandfather interesting IT worker mobile phone mother pencil receptionist small watch wife

Jobs	Adjectives	Family	Personal objects
	difficult		

Grammar

1 Sts read the sentences and questions and choose the correct options to complete them. Check answers.

Answers
1 c
2 b
3 c
4 a
5 c
6 c
7 b
8 a

2 Sts rewrite the sentences with the new words. Check answers.

Answers
2 is my red pen
3 'm happy with my new tablet
4 expensive car is Italian
5 's a student in India
6 are office workers, are their bags

3 Ask sts to read the text through quickly for general meaning, ignoring the options. Ask: *What's Zooey's job?* (she's an actor and a singer). Sts read the text again and choose the correct words to complete it. Check answers.

Answers
1 This
2 an
3 Her
4 's
5 their
6 His
7 sister's
8 're
9 aren't
10 're

3 x PRACTICE *SB page 22, exercise 3*

1 Do the exercise as normal. When you check the answers, read the text aloud, including some correct answers and some incorrect. Ask sts to call out when you read out an incorrect answer. Discuss as a class why it is incorrect, and why the correct answer is right.

2 Ask sts to close their books. They work in pairs and try to remember as much as they can about Zooey and her family. You could write some prompts on the board to help them, e.g. *sister, TV show Bones, mother, father, films*. They can check by looking in their books.

3 Sts work in pairs and prepare an interview with Zooey. As a class, brainstorm some questions they could ask, e.g. *Where are you from? What's your job? Who is Emily? What TV show is she in?* Sts can then role-play an interview with Zooey, using information from the text. They can swap roles and practise again.

Vocabulary

1 Sts put the words in the correct columns. As an extension, sts could add one or two more words to each column.

Answers

Jobs	Adjectives	Family	Personal objects
engineer	difficult	grandfather	mobile phone
IT worker	interesting	mother	pencil
receptionist	small	wife	watch

2 Circle the word that is different. Explain your answers.

1	black	new	orange	gold
2	chef	tour guide	TV presenter	grandmother
3	French	Polish	Russian	Canada
4	fifty	thirteen	fourteen	seventeen
5	son	glasses	purse	keys
6	Hi	Bye	Hello	Good morning
7	bad	boring	ugly	happy
8	father	daughter	boyfriend	husband

3 Choose the correct options to complete the sentences.

1 Jing Wei is ________ . She's from Shanghai.
a doctor b Chinese c brother

2 Excuse me, what does 'building' ________ ?
a say b understand c mean

3 My sister's daughter is six and her ________ is four.
a son b children c husband

4 That camera is very ________ .
a new b young c sad

5 Russia is a very ________ country.
a small b easy c big

6 I'm from ________ . I'm American.
a the UK b the USA c Argentina

7 **A** It's ten past nine.
B Sorry I'm ________ .
a student b teacher c late

8 Macu is a ________ . She's in her car all day.
a shop assistant b taxi driver c girlfriend

9 **A** What colour is a chef's hat?
B It's ________ .
a white b small c pink

10 The pages of this old ________ are yellow.
a tablet b wallet c book

4 Complete the conversation with the words in the box.

nineteen Germany Italian waitress
bag student girlfriend later

Max Who's that girl with Frank? Is she his sister?
Sue No. That's his new [1]________ .
Max Wow! Is she from here?
Sue No, she's from [2]________ .
Max She's beautiful. How old is she?
Sue She's [3]________ .
Max Is she a [4]________ at the university?
Sue No, she's a [5]________ at the [6]________ restaurant in Green Road.
Max Oh no, I'm late for class. See you [7]________ .
Sue Hey ... is that your [8]________ ?
Max Yes, it is. Thanks!
Sue Bye.

Personal Best

Lesson Hello Write a phrase to introduce a friend to someone.

Lesson 2A Name four objects in your bag.

Lesson 1A Name five nationalities, but not your own.

Lesson 2A Describe one of your personal objects.

Lesson 1B Describe someone, including their job and nationality.

Lesson 2B Write two of your favourite colours.

Lesson 1B Write three questions to ask a new student in your class.

Lesson 2B Describe something in the classroom.

Lesson 1C Write the ages of three people in your family.

Lesson 2C Write two sentences about people in your family.

Lesson 1D Write three words that always start with capital letters.

Lesson 2D Write what time it is now.

2 Sts circle the word that is different in each set. Check answers, and ask sts to explain in each case why the word is different. As an extension, sts could write two or three sentences using some of the words.

Answers
1 new (not a colour)
2 grandmother (not a job)
3 Canada (not a nationality)
4 fifty (not a teen number)
5 son (not a personal object)
6 Bye (not a greeting similar to *hello*)
7 happy (not a negative adjective)
8 daughter (not male)

3 Sts read the sentences and choose the correct options to complete them. Check answers.

Answers
1 b
2 c
3 a
4 a
5 c
6 b
7 c
8 b
9 a
10 c

3 x PRACTICE *SB page 23, exercise 3*

1 Do the exercise as normal. When you check the answers, read out each sentence in turn and ask sts to call out the correct answer all together when you reach the gap. Ask a student who called out the correct answer to repeat it and say why the others are not correct.

2 Ask sts to close their books. Write the correct answers on the board, e.g. *Chinese, mean, son*. In pairs, sts try to remember the sentence for each correct answer. They can look at their books to check.

3 Sts work in pairs. They choose five sentences from exercise 3 and rewrite them using one of the incorrect answers, e.g. *Jing Wei is a doctor. Excuse me, I don't understand*. Put pairs together into groups of four. They take turns to read their sentences to each other, saying which number sentence it is, and omitting the answer, e.g. *Jing Wei is a* ______. *Excuse me, I don't* ______. The other pair guesses the answer.

4 Sts read the conversation and complete it with the correct words. Check answers.

Answers
1 girlfriend
2 Germany
3 nineteen
4 student
5 waitress
6 Italian
7 later
8 bag

Personal Best

At the end of each *Review and practice* double-page spread, there is a *Personal Best* section. The aim here is to provide a quick challenge to change the pace and allow for language recall and personalization.

These questions and prompts give sts the opportunity to revise a number of language and skills points from the preceding two units in a more productive way. The points being revised are referenced according to which lesson they appear in (e.g. Lesson 2A). They cover grammar, vocabulary, text builder language from reading and writing lessons, and conversation builder language from speaking lessons. Sts work individually, in pairs or in groups, according to the class dynamic and the time available. Set a time limit if you would like to add a competitive element. Encourage sts to refer back to the relevant lessons if they are having difficulties. The aim is for them to respond to the prompts and engage with the target language in a personal way. Their answers will vary. Monitor and help as necessary and get feedback on sts' answers.

WORKBOOK REVIEW AND PRACTICE

Students will find two pages of Review and Practice at the end of each unit of their Workbooks.
Unit 1, pages 8 and 9
Unit 2, pages 14 and 15

UNIT 3

Food and drink

LANGUAGE present simple (*I, you, we, they*) ■ food and drink

3A Food for athletes

1 3.1 Put the words in the box in the correct columns. Listen and check.

eggs orange juice meat tea coffee bread rice water

We eat ...	We drink ...

Go to Vocabulary practice: food and drink, page 112

2 In pairs, talk about food and drink that you like and don't like.

I like meat. *I don't like coffee.*

3 **A** Look at the pictures. What food can you see? Is it healthy?

B Match pictures a and b with the athletes. Read the text quickly and check.

Olympic Diets

What do Olympic athletes eat for breakfast, lunch and dinner? We talk to two very different athletes.

a

b

Artem Petrenko, Weightlifter, Ukraine

What do you eat for breakfast?

For breakfast, I eat six eggs and three or four cheese sandwiches. I drink a litre of orange juice and three cups of coffee.

What about lunch and dinner?

I have lunch at 1.00 p.m. I eat a big bowl of pasta or rice and salad. For dinner, I eat meat – with potatoes and vegetables. During the day, I eat more sandwiches and fruit.

That's a lot of food! What's your favourite food?

Cheese. I love all cheese, and my favourite is Dutch cheese, like Gouda.

Michelle Nelson, Marathon runner, Australia

What do you eat for breakfast?

For breakfast, I eat brown bread and fruit and I drink 'green juice' – it's juice with green vegetables and fruit. I'm a vegan, so I don't eat meat, eggs or fish and I don't drink milk.

What about lunch and dinner?

For lunch, I have a vegan burger with rice and salad. In the evening, I have dinner with my family. It's difficult because we don't like the same things! But we all eat pizza. My two sisters like cheese, but I have a vegan pizza – without cheese!

Do marathon runners eat dessert?

Yes, they do! Well, maybe not all of them ... but I love dessert. It's my favourite part of the meal. I love carrot cake and vegan ice cream.

24

 EXTRA PRACTICE Workbook page 16; photocopiable activity 3A Vocabulary

Food and drink

UNIT 3

UNIT 3 OVERVIEW: The topic of this unit is food and drink. Sts talk about food and drink that they like. In *Learning Curve*, Kate and Ethan talk to people about when they eat and drink and what they have. Sts read about people they know and the jobs they do. Finally, they read a blog about a festival and write about their favourite festival and the food people eat to celebrate it.

LANGUAGE

Grammar	Vocabulary	Pronunciation
Present simple	Food and drink; times and days; common verbs	do you /djuː/; *-s* and *-es* endings

SKILLS

Listening	Writing
Listening for times and days; the sound /ə/	Punctuation; linkers (*and, but*)

LANGUAGE 3A

3A Food for athletes

Sts read about the foods that two athletes eat every day, and their favourite foods. They listen to people talking about food they eat when they are sad, and practise talking about the food they eat and enjoy.

Grammar	Vocabulary	Pronunciation	Communication
Present simple (*I, you, we, they*)	Food and drink (*biscuit, bread, cake, cheese, chicken, chips, chocolate, coffee, crisps, eggs, fish, fruit, ice cream, meat, milk, orange juice, pasta, pizza, potatoes, rice, salad, sandwich, tea, vegetables, water; have breakfast/lunch/dinner*)	*do you* /djuː/	Talking about food and drink

WARMER

Mime eating a meal and write the words *eat* and *food* on the board. Teach the meanings. Mime drinking a coffee and write the word *drink* on the board. Ask: *Do you know any words for food and drink in English?* Elicit words that sts know. Prompt them with ideas if necessary, focusing on international words such as *pizza, pasta, burger, coffee*. Tell sts that this unit is all about food and drink.

1 3.1 Read through the words in the box and elicit or teach the meanings. Sts put the words in the correct column. Play audio track 3.1. See Answers for audio script. Sts listen and check their answers. Play the audio again for sts to repeat.

Answers
We eat eggs. We eat meat. We eat bread. We eat rice.
We drink orange juice. We drink tea. We drink coffee. We drink water.

Go to Vocabulary practice: food and drink, SB page 112/ TB page 237.
Sts will find more language presentation and practice for food and drink vocabulary here. Do these exercises with the class, or set them for homework, before continuing with exercise 2 of lesson 3A.

PB Remind sts to go to the app for further self-study vocabulary practice of food and drink vocabulary.

2 Teach the meaning of *like* and *don't like* if necessary. Read out the examples, and give one or two more examples of food and drink you like and don't like. Sts discuss what they like and don't like in pairs. Ask some sts to make a sentence using *We like...* or *We don't like ...* about something they both like or don't like.

3 A Read out the questions and check that sts understand *healthy*. Model and drill pronunciation of the word. In pairs, sts try to identify the food in the pictures and say if it is healthy or not. Get feedback on their answers. Help sts to identify any items they are not sure about, e.g. the bowl of rice or the bowl of pasta.

Answers
a (brown) bread, fruit, juice, burger, rice, (carrot) cake
b meat with potatoes and vegetables, sandwiches, orange juice, coffee, pasta, eggs, fruit

B Focus on the two athletes, and read out their names and sports. Use the photos to teach the meaning of *weightlifter* and *marathon runner*. In pairs, sts match the collections of food (a and b) with the athletes. Discuss their ideas, but don't confirm the answers. Teach the meaning of *vegan*. Sts then read the text quickly to check their answers. Check answers with the class.

Answers
a Michelle b Artem

4 Read the text again and complete the sentences with the correct words.

1 What ________ you ________ for breakfast?
2 I ________ a litre of orange juice.
3 I ________ lunch at 1.00 p.m.
4 I ________ milk.
5 We ________ the same things.
6 ________ marathon runners ________ dessert?

5 A Look at the sentences in exercise 4 and answer the questions.

1 Which sentences are positive? ____ and ____
2 Which are negative? ____ and ____
3 Which are questions? ____ and ____

B Complete the rules. Then read the Grammar box.

1 We use ________ + verb in negative present simple sentences with *I*, *you*, *we* and *they*.
2 We use ________ + subject + verb in present simple questions with *I*, *you*, *we* and *they*.

Grammar present simple (*I, you, we, they*)

Positive:	Negative:	Questions and short answers:
I ***drink*** *a lot of water.*	*You* ***don't drink*** *coffee.*	***Do*** *you* ***like*** *fish?*
We ***eat*** *ice cream for dessert.*	*They* ***don't like*** *vegetables.*	*Yes, I* ***do****.* *No, I* ***don't****.*

Personal Best

Go to Grammar practice: present simple (*I, you, we, they*), page 98

6 3.4 **Pronunciation:** *do you* /djuː/ Listen and repeat the questions. Pay attention to the pronunciation of *do you* /djuː/.

1 Do you like pizza? 2 What do you eat for breakfast? 3 What food do you like?

7 A 3.5 Say the questions. Listen, check and repeat.

1 Do you like Mexican food?
2 Do you eat meat?
3 Do you drink tea?
4 Do you like chocolate?
5 What time do you have breakfast?
6 What do you have for lunch?

B Ask and answer the questions in pairs.

8 A 3.6 Complete the text with the verbs in brackets. Listen and check.

Happy food

What food [1] ________________ (you / like) after a difficult day? What [2] ________________ (you / eat) when you're sad? What's your 'happy food'?

I'm a student. After a difficult day at university, [3] ________________ (we / always have) ice cream. [4] ________________ (I / like) caramel – it's my favourite!

Harriet, the UK

My children are strange. [5] ________________ (they / not like) normal sandwiches. [6] ________________ (they / eat) banana and cheese sandwiches!

Mike, Canada

I'm a doctor. When I'm tired or sad, [7] ________________ (I / not eat) chocolate or pizza – it's bad for you. [8] ________________ (I / drink) green tea.

Rosa, Argentina

B In pairs, talk about your 'happy food'. What do you eat or drink when you're sad or tired?

Go to Communication practice: Student A page 136, Student B page 144

9 A Ask and answer questions in pairs.

1 like / Japanese food
2 drink / a lot of soft drinks
3 have / dinner with your family
4 eat / a lot of fruit
5 drink / coffee at night
6 eat / a lot of red meat

A *Do you like Japanese food?* **B** *No, I don't. But I like Indian food.*

B Tell the class what you and your partner have in common.

We don't like Japanese food, but we like Indian food.

Personal Best Write what you have for breakfast, lunch and dinner on a typical day.

4 Focus on the gapped sentences and teach the meaning of *breakfast, lunch* and *dessert*. Sts read the text again and complete the sentences with the correct words. Check answers.

Answers
1 do, eat 2 drink 3 have 4 don't drink 5 don't like
6 Do, eat

5 A Read out the questions in turn and elicit the answers.

Answers
1 2, 3 2 4, 5 3 1, 6

B Read out the gapped rules and elicit the missing words to form negatives and questions.

Answers
1 don't 2 do

Grammar

Read the Grammar box with sts about the present simple (*I, you, we, they*). Point out to sts that they already know the negative form of the verb *be* (*am not, isn't, aren't*), but the verb *be* is an exception, and most verbs use *don't* in negative sentences. Point out the inverted word order in questions: *Do you like…?* NOT ~~*You do like …?*~~ Ask questions to check concept.

Concept check questions:
I drink coffee – correct? (yes). *Can you change the sentence to 'we' and 'they'?* (we drink coffee, they drink coffee). *What verb form is this?* (present simple). *What word do we add to make the sentence negative?* (don't). *I eat meat – can you make it negative?* (I don't eat meat). *What word do we add to make a question?* (do). *You drink tea – can you make this a question?* (Do you drink tea?). *What's the answer?* (Yes, I do. No, I don't).

Go to Grammar practice: present simple (*I, you, we, they*), SB page 98/TB page 209
Sts will find more language reference, presentation and practice for the present simple (*I, you, we, they*) here. Do these exercises with the class, or set them for homework, before continuing with exercise 6 of lesson 3A.

PB Remind sts to go to the app for further self-study grammar practice of the present simple (*I, you, we, they*).

6 3.4 Explain that in speech, we often don't say the words *do you* in full, but shorten them. Play audio track 3.4 for sts to listen and notice the pronunciation of *do you*. See SB page opposite for audio script. Play the audio again for sts to listen and repeat the questions.

7 A 3.5 Sts work in pairs and practise saying the questions. Play audio track 3.5. See SB page opposite for audio script. Sts listen and check their answers, then listen again and repeat.

B Read through the questions again with the class and check that sts understand them all. Sts ask and answer the questions in pairs. Ask some sts to make sentences using *we*, to say something that is true for both of them.

8 A 3.6 Check that sts understand *caramel, banana* and *always*. Read out the first gapped sentence and elicit the correct verb form as an example. Sts complete the text with the correct verb forms. Play audio track 3.6 for sts to listen and check their answers. See SB page opposite for audio script.

Answers
1 do you like 2 do you eat 3 we always have 4 I like
5 They don't like 6 They eat 7 I don't eat 8 I drink

3 x PRACTICE *SB page 25, exercise 8A*

1 Do the exercise as normal. To check answers, play audio track 3.6, pausing before each gap. Elicit the answer from a student, then play the audio for sts to check.
2 With books closed, write the names of the three people in the text on the board. In pairs, sts try to remember what each person says and write sentences from the text from memory. They can look at the text again to check.
3 Sts choose one of the people in the text and try to memorize the sentences they say. They then cover the main text, leaving the questions uncovered. In pairs, they ask their partner the questions, and their partner answers from memory.

B Allow sts time to prepare their ideas individually. Sts then talk about their own 'happy food'. Ask some sts to tell the class about their happy food. Ask who has similar ideas.

Go to Communication practice
Divide the class into Student A and Student B. All 'Student A' sts should go to SB page 136. All 'Student B' sts should go to SB page 144. Go to TB page 285 for the teacher notes. Do the activity, then continue with exercise 9A of lesson 3A.

9 A Read out the example question and answer. Elicit one or two more of the questions, to check that sts can form them correctly. Check that sts understand *red meat*. Sts ask and answer the questions in pairs. Ask sts to note down things they have in common.

B Ask pairs in turn to tell the class what they have in common, using *we*.

PERSONAL BEST

Sts can practise talking about food and drink further. They write what they have for breakfast, lunch and dinner on a typical day. They can compare their ideas in pairs.

Weaker sts could list the foods and drinks they usually have for each meal, without writing sentences. They can compare their lists in pairs.

3B Tea or coffee?

1 Complete the café sign with the days of the week.

Friday   Tuesday   Wednesday   Sunday

Go to Vocabulary practice: days and times of day, page 116

2 Look at the sign in exercise 1 again. Are the sentences true (T) or false (F)?

1 The café is open every day. ____
2 It's open in the morning on Tuesday. ____
3 It's open on Thursday afternoon. ____
4 It's open in the evening on Friday. ____
5 It's closed on Saturday night. ____
6 It's closed in the evening on Sunday. ____

3 Ask and answer the questions in pairs.

1 What day is it today?
2 What day is it tomorrow?
3 What day was it yesterday?
4 What's your favourite day of the week?
5 What's the worst day of the week?
6 What's your favourite time of day?

4 **A** 3.8 Watch or listen to the first part of the show. Tick (✓) the sentence which is correct.

1 People drink coffee in cafés and tea at home. ☐
2 People drink tea and coffee all over the world. ☐
3 People drink coffee in the morning and tea in the evening. ☐

B 3.8 Watch or listen again. Match the halves to make sentences.

1 54% of Americans
2 65% of those people
3 35% of those people
4 In the UK, people drink 165 million
5 In the UK, people drink 70 million

a cups of tea every day.
b drink coffee at lunch or later.
c drink coffee every day.
d drink coffee in the morning.
e cups of coffee every day.

3B Tea or coffee?

Sts learn vocabulary for days and times of day, then hear about the different kinds of food and drink that people enjoy in cafés. They then talk about a café that they like.

Listening	Skill	Listening builder	Vocabulary
Sts watch a video or listen to a recording about what people eat and drink in cafés.	Listening for days and times of day	The sound /ə/	Days and times of day: (*Monday, Tuesday, Wednesday, Thursday, Friday, Saturday, Sunday; the weekend, today, tomorrow, yesterday, morning, afternoon, evening, night*)

WARMER

Ask: *What do you eat for breakfast? What do you drink?* Elicit a few ideas, then ask: *Do you have breakfast at home, or do you go to a café? Which cafés do you go to?* Elicit a range of answers from individual sts.

1 Say the days of the week in order, and get sts to repeat them. Sts then read the sign and complete it with the days of the week. Check answers, then read through the sign with the class and make sure sts understand *open*, *closed*, *hot food* and *cake*.

> **Answers**
> 1 Tuesday 2 Wednesday 3 Friday 4 Sunday

Go to Vocabulary practice: Days and times of day, SB page 116/TB page 245
Sts will find more language presentation and practice for days and times of day here. Do these exercises with the class, or set them for homework, before continuing with exercise 2 of lesson 3B.

PB Remind sts to go to the app for further self-study vocabulary practice of times and days.

2 Read out the first sentence and ask: *Is this true?* Elicit that it is false. Sts read the remaining sentences and decide if they are true or false. Check answers, referring back to the sign to explain why each sentence is true or false.

> **Answers**
> 1 F 2 T 3 F 4 T 5 F 6 T

3 Read through the questions with the class and make sure sts understand them all. Allow sts time to prepare their ideas individually, then put them into pairs to ask and answer the questions. Ask some sts to tell the class something about their partner, e.g. *(Ana's) favourite day of the week is Saturday*.

4 A 3.8 In this episode of *Learning Curve*, Kate talks to people about what they like to eat and drink. Allow sts time to read the three sentences. Check they understand all over the world. Ask: *Which sentence do you think is true?* Elicit a few ideas, but don't confirm them. Play video/audio track 3.8. See TB page 308 for video/audio script. Sts listen and tick the sentence that is correct. Check the answer.

> **Answer**
> 2

B 3.8 Read out the sentence beginnings and model pronunciation of the percentages and the numbers. Make sure sts understand the word *million*. Read out the sentence endings and make sure sts understand *later* and *cup of coffee*. Read out the first sentence beginning again and ask: *Which ending do you think is correct?* Elicit a few ideas, but don't confirm them. Play the video/audio track again. Sts listen and match the sentence halves. Check answers, playing the video or audio again for sts to hear the answers in context.

> **Answers**
> 1 c 2 d 3 b 4 a 5 e

5 3.9 Watch or listen to the second part of the show. Match the people with the food and drink.

1 fish, rice, vegetables, tea, water ________
2 biscuits, ice cream, coffee ________
3 fish and chips and tea ________
4 sandwich, crisps, biscuit, tea ________
5 coffee, cereal ________

Skill listening for times and days

Listen carefully when people talk about times and days.

- Times and days can come at the beginning or end of a sentence: *On Friday, I go to the café. / I go to the café on Friday.*
- Some times and days sound similar: *It's three fifteen. / It's three fifty.* *Today is Tuesday. / Today is Thursday.*

6 3.9 Read the Skill box. Watch or listen again and choose the correct options to complete the sentences.

1 **Kate:** It's *2.30 p.m. / 2.40 p.m.* here and I'm with Jolene.
2 **Jolene:** We come here every *Tuesday / Thursday*. It's my husband's favourite café.
3 **Jolene:** I drink coffee every *morning / evening*, but between 2.30 and *3.00 / 3.30*, I drink tea.
4 **Ioan:** The party's at *8.00 p.m. / 9.00 p.m.*
5 **Chan:** We're open *Monday / Sunday* through Friday from 11.00 a.m. until 10.00 p.m. And Saturday and Sunday from 10.00 a.m. until *7.00 p.m. / 11.00 p.m.*
6 **Kate:** It's *3.15 / 3.30* here and I have fish and chips from my favourite takeaway place!

7 In pairs, talk about what food and drink you have every day.
I have a coffee at 10.00 in the morning.

8 3.10 Listen to the extract from the show. How does Ethan pronounce *and*?

I have a coffee **and** cereal.

Listening builder the sound /ə/

The /ə/ sound is also called 'schwa'. It is very common in English in short unstressed words, like articles, prepositions and auxiliary verbs.

/ə/ /ə/ *a cup of tea* — /ə/ *We have coffee at 9.00 p.m.* — /ə/ *What time's the party?* — /ə/ *Does she like fish?*

9 3.11 Read the Listening builder. Then listen and complete the sentences.

1 I have ________ coffee every morning.
2 What ________ they eat?
3 They only drink tea ________ breakfast.
4 This one's ________ you.
5 I have two bottles ________ water.
6 I like fish ________ chips.

10 Think of a café that you like. In pairs, ask and answer the questions about the café.

What's its name? Where is it? When do you go there?
What do you eat or drink there? What do other people have? Why do you like it?

Personal Best Write a description of your favourite restaurant or café.

 EXTRA PRACTICE Workbook page 17

5 3.9 Allow sts time to read through the lists of food and drink. Check they understand them all. Explain the matching task. Pre-teach the following words if necessary from the video: *takeaway/takeout* (= a meal you buy to eat at home or in the street) and *Back to you in London* (= you continue with the show in London now). Play video/audio track 3.9. See TB page 308 for video/audio script. Sts watch/listen and match the people with the food and drink. Check answers.

Answers
1 Chan 2 Ioan 3 Kate 4 Jolene 5 Ethan

Skill

Read the Skill box with sts about listening for times and days. Reinforce the point that that when they listen for times and days they must listen very carefully, as some days and times sound similar.

6 3.9 Allow sts time to read the sentences and different options. Play video/audio track 3.9 again. Sts watch/listen and choose the correct options. Check answers. Play the track again, pausing for sts to hear why each answer is correct.

Answers
1 2.30 p.m. 2 Tuesday 3 morning, 3.00 4 8.00 p.m.
5 Monday, 11.00 p.m. 6 3.30

7 Sts work in pairs to discuss what they eat and drink at different times of day. Ask some sts to tell the class something about their partner.

8 3.10 Focus on the speech bubble and ask sts how they think Ethan pronounces *and*. Play the audio and elicit his pronunciation /ənd/.

Answer
/ənd/

Listening builder

Read the Listening builder box with sts about the sound /ə/. Explain to sts that in English vowels are pronounced with their full form when they are stressed, but they are often pronounced with a weak sound when they are not stressed, or when they are in small words such as articles and prepositions. Point out to sts that when they are listening, they need to recognize when familiar words are pronounced with a weak sound. Ask questions to check concept.

Concept check questions:
What sound is the schwa? (/ə/). *When do we use the schwa?* (in small, unstressed words). *Why is it important to recognize the schwa?* (in order to understand and recognize words when you are listening).

9 3.11 Sts read the gapped sentences. Point out that all the missing words are pronounced with a schwa. Play audio track 3.11. See SB page opposite for audio script. Sts listen and complete the sentences. Allow sts time to compare their answers in pairs, then play the audio again for them to check and complete their answers. Check answers with the class. You could play the track again, pausing after each sentence for sts to repeat.

Answers
1 a 2 do 3 at 4 for 5 of 6 and

10 As a round-up, sts discuss a café that they like. Read out the questions and make sure sts understand them all. Allow sts time to think of a café that they like and prepare their answers. Sts then ask and answer the questions in pairs. Discuss with the class which cafés are popular with a lot of the students and why.

PERSONAL BEST

Sts can practise talking about a café or restaurant further. They write a description of their favourite café or restaurant, answering all the questions in exercise 10. Sts can compare their descriptions in small groups.

Weaker sts can work in pairs. They choose a café or restaurant that they both know and write three or four sentences about it, answering some of the questions in exercise 10. Ask some pairs to read their sentences to the class.

EXTRA PRACTICE

Sts work in groups of three. They take turns to use their phones to film their classmates answering the questions in exercise 10. They can swap roles and practise again. Allow sts time to watch the films of themselves and notice how well they ask and answer. Discuss as a class what they noticed about their pronunciation and fluency, and how they could improve it.

3C Chocolate for breakfast!

1 Complete phrases 1–6 with the verbs in the box.

use watch have do make say

1 ____ 'hello'

2 ____ a cat

3 ____ dinner

4 ____ exercise

5 ____ a computer

6 ____ TV

Personal Best

Go to Vocabulary practice: common verbs (1), page 113

2 Ask and answer the questions in pairs.

1 you / live near the city centre?
2 you / work in an office?
3 you / make dinner at home every evening?
4 you / know three languages?
5 you / say 'hello' to a lot of people every day?
6 you / have brothers or sisters?

3 3.13 Look at the picture of Adam Young. What is his job? Read and listen to the text and check.

THE BEST JOB IN THE WORLD?

From Monday to Friday, Adam Young eats chocolate at work. That's because Adam is a *chocolatier* (he makes chocolate). 'I love it,' he says. 'I think it's a great job!'
Adam lives in Perth in Scotland. He has a small shop and he makes all of his chocolates by hand. Does he have the best job in the world? This is his typical day.
'In the morning, I go to the shop early and make chocolate … I eat it for breakfast! Then we work here all day.'
Adam has an assistant, Shona. When he's in the kitchen with the chocolate, Shona works with the customers.
Adam does a lot of exercise – very important when you eat chocolate all day! In the evening, he changes his clothes and goes to the gym. Then he goes home, makes dinner and watches TV.
At the weekend, he studies Business – he says it's important for his job … but he doesn't eat chocolate!

4 **A** Choose the correct words to complete the sentences. What letter do we add to the verbs with *he*, *she* and *it* in positive sentences?

1 Adam Young *eat* / *eats* chocolate at work.
2 He *make* / *makes* all of his chocolates by hand.
3 I go to the shop early and *make* / *makes* chocolate.
4 I *eat* / *eats* it for breakfast!
5 Then we *work* / *works* here all day.
6 Shona *work* / *works* with the customers.

B Find the *he*/*she*/*it* forms of the verbs in the text.

1 say ________
2 live ________
3 have ________
4 do ________
5 change ________
6 go ________
7 watch ________
8 study ________

EXTRA PRACTICE Workbook page 18; photocopiable activity 3C Vocabulary

3C Chocolate for breakfast!

Sts read about two people who work with food – a chocolatier who eats chocolate all day, and a food scientist who develops new ice cream flavours. They then talk about people they know, and the jobs they do.

Grammar	Vocabulary	Pronunciation	Communication
Present simple (*he, she, it*)	Common verbs (1) (*change, do, go, have, know, live, make, say, study, think, use, want, watch, work*)	-*s* and -*es* endings	Talking about jobs

WARMER

With books closed, put sts into pairs and give them two minutes to write as many words for food and drink as they can. Bring all the words together on the board and check that sts understand them all. See which pair wrote the most words correctly.

1 Read through the verbs in the box with the class and teach the meanings if necessary. In pairs, sts look at the pictures and complete the phrases. Check answers. Model and drill pronunciation of the phrases.

Answers
1 say 2 have 3 make 4 do 5 use 6 watch

3 x PRACTICE *SB page 28, exercise 1*

1 Do the exercise as normal. To check answers, read out each phrase in turn with three possible verbs, e.g. *use hello, have hello, say hello*. Sts say the correct phrase. Model and drill pronunciation of the phrases.

2 In pairs, sts cover the verbs, then look at the pictures and try to remember the phrases. They can look at the verbs again to check.

3 With books closed, write the nouns only from exercise 1 on the board. Divide the class into teams. Teams take turns to choose a noun and make a sentence using it with the correct verb, e.g. *I don't have a cat. I watch TV at the weekend*. If their sentence is correct, give them a point and cross the noun off the board. If the sentence is not correct, don't correct it, but move on to the next team. Continue until all the words are crossed off the board. See which team has the most points.

Go to Vocabulary practice: common verbs (1), SB page 113/TB page 239
Sts will find more language presentation and practice for common verbs (1) here. Do these exercises with the class, or set them for homework, before continuing with exercise 2 of lesson 3C.

PB Remind sts to go to the app for further self-study vocabulary practice of common verbs (1).

2 Check that sts understand all the question prompts. Elicit one or two questions as examples, then elicit example answers from one or two sts. Sts then ask and answer the questions in pairs.

3 3.13 Focus on the picture and read out the question. Encourage sts to guess what Adam's job is. Play audio track 3.13. See SB page opposite for audio script. Sts listen to check their answer. Check the answer with the class.

Answer
He's a chocolatier.

4 A Sts look at the text again and choose the correct verb forms to complete the sentences. Check answers, then elicit what letter we add to the verbs with *he, she* and *it*.

Answers
1 eats 2 makes 3 make 4 eat 5 work 6 works
We add -*s* to the verb.

B Sts find the *he/she/it* forms of the verbs in the text and write them. Check answers, and ask sts what they notice about the verb forms. Elicit that some verbs add -*es* rather than -*s*, -*y* changes to -*ies*, and some verbs are irregular, e.g. *has*.

Answers
1 says 2 lives 3 has 4 does 5 changes 6 goes
7 watches 8 studies

5 Find a question and a negative sentence in the text. Complete the rules then read the Grammar box.

1 We use ________ + verb in negative present simple sentences with *he*/*she*/*it*.
2 We use ________ + subject + verb in present simple questions with *he*/*she*/*it*.

Grammar **present simple (*he*, *she*, *it*)**

Positive:	Negative:	Questions and short answers:
*She **eats** fruit for breakfast.*	*He **doesn't work** in a school.*	***Does** your house **have** a garden?*
*He **watches** TV in the evening.*	*She **doesn't do** exercise.*	*Yes, it **does**.* *No, it **doesn't**.*
*Maya **studies** English.*	*My wife **doesn't like** chocolate.*	

Look! Some verbs are irregular: *do* > ***does***, *go* > ***goes***, *have* > ***has***.

Personal Best

Go to Grammar practice: present simple (*he*, *she*, *it*), page 98

6 **A** 3.15 **Pronunciation:** -*s* and -*es* endings Listen and repeat the sounds and words. Pay attention to the pronunciation of the -*s* and -*es* endings.

1 /s/ eats works makes
2 /z/ lives goes knows
3 /ɪz/ watches uses changes

B 3.16 Match the halves to make sentences. Listen, check and repeat.

1 She lives — a films in the afternoon.
2 He works — b in an office.
3 She watches — c a computer at work.
4 He says — d 'Hi' every day.
5 She makes — e in Tokyo.
6 He uses — f cakes at the weekend.

7 3.17 Complete the text with the correct form of the verbs in the box. Listen and check.

have do eat say work make go

A VERY COOL JOB

Kirsten Lind [1]________ at an ice cream company in Toronto. She [2]________ a great job – she's a food scientist and she [3]________ new flavours of ice cream. What's this week's new flavour? 'Potato crisps and chocolate! I don't like crisps, but lots of people love it,' Kirsten [4]________ . Kirsten [5]________ two or three litres of ice cream a week, so she [6]________ to the gym after work and she [7]________ a lot of sport at the weekend.

8 **A** Make questions about the text in exercise 7.

1 Kirsten / work / in a shop? ____________________
2 she / have / an interesting job? ____________________
3 she / eat / a lot of crisps? ____________________
4 she / do / a lot of exercise? ____________________

B Ask and answer the questions in pairs. Use short answers.

Go to Communication practice: Student A page 136, Student B page 144

9 Choose three friends or family members and write down their names. Ask and answer the questions in pairs.

A *Who is Ivan?* **B** *He's my uncle.*
A *Where does he live?* **B** *He lives in …*

Who is … ?
Where does he/she live?
Where does he/she work?
Does he/she like his/her job?
What does he/she do at the weekend?

Personal Best Think of someone with an interesting job and write a paragraph about him/her.

5 Elicit that we use *don't* to make negative sentences with *I, you* and *we*, and we use *do* to make questions. Ask sts to find a question and a negative sentence with *he/she/it* in the text. Elicit the answers and write them on the board. Read out the gapped rules and use the sentences on the board to elicit the missing words. Model and drill pronunciation of *does* and *doesn't*.

Answers
1 doesn't 2 does

Grammar

Read the Grammar box with sts about the present simple (*he, she, it*). Point out that most verbs add *-s* in positive sentences with *he/she/it*, but some add *-es*, and some verbs ending in *-y* change to *-ies*. Point out that some verbs are irregular, and sts need to learn them. Point out that in negative sentences and questions the *-s* isn't added to the main verb, e.g. *He doesn't eat fruit*. NOT ~~He doesn't eats fruit~~. Ask questions to check concept.

Concept check questions:
I like chocolate – correct? (yes). *He like chocolate – correct?* (no – *he likes* chocolate). *Do we always add -s after he/she/it?* (no – some verbs add *-es*, some verbs ending in *-y* change to *-ies*, and some verbs are irregular). *What's the form of 'have' with he/she/it?* (has). *I don't like cats – correct?* (yes). *She don't like cats – correct?* (no – *she doesn't like* cats). *She watches TV – can you make this a question?* (Does she watch TV?). *What's the short answer to this question?* (Yes, she does/ No, she doesn't).

Go to Grammar practice: the present simple (*he, she, it*), SB page 98/TB page 209.
Sts will find more language reference, presentation and practice for the present simple (*he, she, it*) here. Do these exercises with the class, or set them for homework, before continuing with exercise 6A of lesson 3C.

PB Remind sts to go to the app for further self-study grammar practice of the present simple (*he, she, it*).

6 A 3.15 Explain to sts that the *-s* and *-es* ending can be pronounced in three slightly different ways, depending on the verbs. Play the audio once for sts to listen and notice the pronunciation of the verb endings. See SB page opposite for audio script. Play the audio again for sts to repeat.

B 3.16 Sts match the sentence halves. Play audio track 3.16 once for sts to check their answers. Play the audio again for sts to repeat.

Answers
1 e 2 b 3 a 4 d 5 f 6 c

7 3.17 Read out the first gapped sentence of the text and elicit the correct verb form to complete it. Sts then complete the text with the correct verb forms. Play audio track 3.17. See SB page opposite for audio script. Sts listen to check their answers. Check with the class.

Answers
1 works 2 has 3 makes 4 says 5 eats 6 goes 7 does

8 A Read out the first question prompt and elicit the question. Sts then write the questions. Check answers.

Answers
1 Does Kirsten work in a shop?
2 Does she have an interesting job?
3 Does she eat a lot of crisps?
4 Does she do a lot of exercise?

B Allow sts time to read the questions again and prepare their answers. Encourage them to write short answers and add more information if possible. They then ask and answer the questions in pairs. Check answers with the class.

Answers
1 No, she doesn't. She works at an ice cream company.
2 Yes, she does.
3 No, she doesn't. She doesn't like crisps.
4 Yes, she does. She goes to the gym after work and she does sport at the weekend.

Go to Communication practice
Divide the class into Student A and Student B. All 'Student A' sts should go to SB page 136. All 'Student B' sts should go to SB page 144. Go to TB page 285 for the teacher notes. Do the activity, then continue with exercise 9 of lesson 3C.

9 Ask sts to write the names of three friends or family members, and write them down. Read out the example questions, and make sure sts understand them all. Sts work in pairs to ask and answer the questions about their friends and family members. Ask some sts to tell the class something about one of their partner's friends or family members.

PERSONAL BEST

Sts can practise using the present simple with *he/she/it* further. They write a short paragraph about someone with an interesting job. Sts can compare their paragraphs in small groups and discuss which job they think is interesting.

Refer weaker sts back to the texts on page 24. They can write three sentences about each of the athletes, e.g. *Artem eats six eggs for breakfast*. Ask some sts to read their sentences to the class.

3D A special meal

1 **A** Match the food in the box with the festivals in the pictures. What do you know about these festivals?

pancakes chow mein turkey sweets

Thanksgiving, USA

Carnevale, Italy

Chinese New Year, China

Maslenitsa, Russia

B Think of some important festivals and celebrations in your country. What do people eat and drink?

2 Look at the pictures in Arusha's blog. Which country is she from? How do people celebrate this festival? Read the text quickly and check.

Arusha's Blog

MY POSTS | CONTACT ME | SEARCH

About me

Hi! I'm Arusha, I'm 25 and I live in Kerala in India. Welcome to my blog!

Festival time

We have lots of festivals in India and my favourite is Onam.
In the afternoon, we have a big meal with lots of food – some people have 24 dishes or more. We eat curry, rice, vegetables and fruit, but we don't eat meat. We eat the food on a big banana leaf.

It's traditional to have lunch at home, but these days some people go to restaurants. In my family, we eat at my brother's house. After the meal, we meet friends, we listen to music and we watch the tiger dance.
What's my favourite thing about Onam? It's a really happy time and the food is great.

3 Read the text again and answer the questions.

1 What is the name of the festival?
2 When do people have the meal?
3 What food does Arusha eat?
4 What doesn't she eat?
5 Where does she have lunch?
6 What does she do after the meal?

3D A special meal

Sts read a blog about a festival in Kerala, India, and the food people eat to celebrate it. They study punctuation and the use of linkers, then write a blog about a festival in their country and the food people eat to celebrate it.

Writing	Skill	Text builder
A blog	Punctuation	Linkers (*and*, *but*)

WARMER

Ask individual sts questions about food, e.g. *Do you like ice cream? Do you eat a lot of crisps? Do you have a big breakfast?* Put sts into pairs to prepare three questions to ask their classmates about food. Put pairs together into groups of four to ask and answer their questions and find as many things as they can that they all agree on. Allow sts a few minutes to discuss, then ask groups in turn to tell the class what their group agrees on.

1 A Read through the words in the box with the class and explain the meanings if necessary. Sts look at the pictures in pairs and discuss what food they can see, and what they know about the festivals. Discuss the answers as a class.

Answer
Thanksgiving, USA: turkey (The festival of Thanksgiving takes place in November, to celebrate the first successful harvest by settlers to the USA. Families come together to have a big meal.)
Carnevale, Italy: sweets (Carnevale is a festival to celebrate the end of the Christian period of Lent. People dress up in costumes and celebrate.)
Chinese New Year, China: chow mein (Chinese New Year is a festival to celebrate the beginning of a new year. People celebrate with special food, and by giving money to children.)
Maslenitsa, Russia: pancakes (This week-long festival takes place just before the beginning of the Christian period of Lent, when rich food and celebrating are traditionally not allowed. People celebrate and eat pancakes.)

B Put sts into pairs to discuss festivals and celebrations in their country, and what people eat. Monitor and help with vocabulary as necessary. Get feedback on sts' discussions.

2 Focus on the pictures and encourage sts to speculate on what country Arusha is from, and how people celebrate this festival. Teach the meaning of *banana leaf*. Sts then read the text quickly to check their ideas. Check answers with the class and explain the meaning of *curry* if necessary.

Answers
She is from India. People have a big meal. After the meal, they meet friends, listen to music and watch the tiger dance.

3 Read out the questions and make sure sts understand them all. Sts read the text again and answer the questions. Check answers, referring back to the text to confirm the answers.

Answers
1 Onam
2 in the afternoon
3 curry, rice, vegetables and fruit
4 meat
5 at her brother's house
6 She meets friends, listens to music and watches the tiger dance.

3 x PRACTICE *SB page 30, exercise 3*

1 Do the exercise as normal. To check answers, tell sts you are going to read out the text and they should shout 'Stop!' when you reach the answer to a question. Read out the text and stop when sts tell you, to check each answer.

2 In pairs, sts cover the text and look at the questions again. They try to remember the answers, and try to remember as much detail as they can about the text. They can uncover the text again to check.

3 Tell sts to imagine they are Arusha and they are going to tell their partner about Onam. In pairs, sts take half the text each and read it again, to remember as many details as they can. Tell them they can write down a maximum of 10 words to help them remember. With books closed, sts take turns to use their notes and tell their partner about Onam.

4 Read the Skill box. Find an example of each type of punctuation in the text on page 30.

Skill **punctuation**

It's important to use the correct punctuation to help people understand your writing.

.	**full stop:**	We use this at the end of a sentence.
,	**comma:**	We use this to separate ideas and after times.
?	**question mark:**	We use this at the end of a question.
'	**apostrophe:**	We use this in contractions and in *'s* for possession.
A	**capital letters:**	(see the Text builder on page 13)

5 Rewrite the text about Chinese New Year with the correct punctuation and capital letters.

whats your favourite festival

my names wu and im from nanjing in china my favourite festival is chinese new year its a national holiday and people dont work we have a big party with all the family and in the evening we eat meat fish rice and vegetables my mother makes a special cake and we give money to the children in the family

6 Choose the correct words to complete the sentences from Arusha's blog. Check your answers in the text.

1 We eat curry, rice, vegetables and fruit, *and* / *but* we don't eat meat.
2 It's a really happy time *and* / *but* the food is great.

Text builder **linkers (*and*, *but*)**

We use *and* and *but* to link sentences.
To add information: *We dance* ***and*** *we listen to music.*
To contrast different ideas: *Some people go to restaurants,* ***but*** *our family eats at home.*

7 Read the Text builder. Complete the sentences with *and* or *but*.

1 We go to my grandmother's house every Sunday ________ we have a big meal.
2 This restaurant is very expensive, ________ the food isn't good.
3 I drink tea and fruit juice, ________ I don't drink coffee.
4 Claire works in the morning, ________ she doesn't work in the afternoon.
5 My uncle lives in Los Angeles, ________ he isn't American.
6 He does sport ________ he goes to the gym.

8 **A** **PREPARE** Choose a festival in your country where food is important. Think about these questions.

- When is the festival?
- What do people eat and drink?
- Where do you eat and who with?
- What do you do before and after the meal?

B **PRACTISE** Write a blog about the festival. Link your sentences with *and* and *but*.

C **PERSONAL BEST** Swap your blog with your partner. Check the grammar and punctuation. Are the present simple verbs correct? Does your partner use *and* and *but* correctly?

Personal Best Think of a special meal. Write three sentences about it with *and* and three sentences with *but*.

Skill

Read the Skill box with sts about punctuation, and refer sts back to the Text builder on page 13 to check the use of capital letters. Point out that we also use commas in lists, e.g. *I like bread, meat and cheese.*

4 Sts look at the text again to find an example of each type of punctuation. Discuss the answers, and discuss with sts any differences in punctuation between English and their language.

Example answers
full stop: We eat the food on a big banana leaf.
comma: I'm Arusha, I'm 25 ... (to separate ideas) In the afternoon, we ... (after times of day)
question mark: What's my favourite thing about Onam?
apostrophe: I'm Arusha... (contraction), my brother's house (possession)
capital letters: Arusha, Onam, I'm, We have lots of ...

5 Sts rewrite the text with the correct punctuation and capital letters. Allow sts time to compare their answers in pairs, then check with the class.

Answers
My name's Wu and I'm from Nanjing in China. My favourite festival is Chinese New Year. It's a national holiday and people don't work. We have a big party with all the family, and in the evening, we eat meat, fish, rice and vegetables. My mother makes a special cake and we give money to the children in the family.

6 Sts choose the correct words to complete the sentences, then check their answers in Arusha's blog. Check answers with the class.

Answers
1 but 2 and

Text builder

Read the Text builder box with sts about linkers. Explain that we use linkers to join ideas together in the same sentence. Explain that we use *and* to add more information that is similar, e.g. *I like fruit and vegetables. We have a big meal and my mother makes a cake.* Explain that we use *but* to add information that is different (a contrast), e.g. *I like fruit, but I don't like vegetables. We have a big meal, but my mother doesn't make a cake. Ask questions to check concept.*

Concept check questions:
Why do we use linkers? (to join ideas in the same sentence). *Do we use 'and' to add information, or to contrast different ideas?* (to add information). *When do we use 'but'?* (to contrast different ideas). *I like tea but coffee – correct?* (no – I like tea *and* coffee). *Why?* (because the ideas are similar). *I eat chicken and I don't eat red meat – correct?* (no – I eat chicken, *but* I don't eat red meat). *Why?* (because the ideas are different, so we want to contrast them).

7 Sts complete the sentences with the correct linkers. Check answers.

Answers
1 and 2 but 3 but 4 but 5 but 6 and

8 Sts follow the steps to write a blog.

A PREPARE Sts read the questions and prepare their ideas. Monitor while they are working, and help with vocabulary if necessary.

B PRACTISE Sts write their blog. Refer them back to the Skill box to remind them to use punctuation correctly, and refer them to the Text builder box to remind them about how to use *and* and *but*.

C PERSONAL BEST Sts work in pairs. They swap their blogs with a partner and give feedback on the grammar, punctuation, present simple verbs and the use of *and* and *but*. Remind sts that they should always be positive and encouraging when they give feedback to a partner, and should always find some aspects to praise.

PERSONAL BEST

Sts can practise writing about food and using linkers further. They think of a special meal and write six sentences about it, using *and* and *but*. Sts could read their sentences to each other, omitting *and* or *but*. Their partner listens and guesses the missing linkers.

Refer weaker sts back to the texts on page 28 and 29. In pairs, they find examples of *and* and *but*, and discuss why that linker is used in each example. Ask sts to read some of the examples to the class, and use them to reinforce the rules on the use of *and* and *but*.

EXTRA PRACTICE

Write on the board: It's a ______ happy time. Ask sts to find the sentence in Arusha's blog on page 30, and find the missing word. Elicit the word (*really*) and add it to the sentence. Point out that it makes the meaning of the adjective *happy* stronger. Give one or two more examples, e.g. *We have a really big meal. The food is really great*. As a class, brainstorm some adjectives to describe festivals and food, e.g. *important, big, healthy, bad for you, good for you*. In pairs, sts write two sentences using the adjectives, and adding *really* to make the meaning stronger. Ask pairs in turn to read their sentences to the class.

UNIT 4

Daily life

LANGUAGE adverbs of frequency ■ daily routine verbs

4A Day and night

1 A 4.1 Match the phrases in the box with pictures a–e. Listen and check.

start work   finish work   go to bed   get home   get up

a

b

c

d

e

B In pairs, say what time you do the activities.

A *I get up at 6.30.*   **B** *That's early! I get up at 8.30.*

Personal Best

Go to Vocabulary practice: daily routine verbs, page 114

2 Look at the pictures and guess the answers to the questions. Read the text and check.

1 What is the relationship between the two people?
2 What are their jobs?
3 Are their routines similar or different?

The same but different

Sally and Ashley Fraser live at home with their parents and their brother, Marcus. They are twin sisters … but their lives are very different.

'I'm a receptionist at a big company and I always get up at 6.00 a.m.,' says Sally. 'I have a shower and then I go to work. In the evening, I watch TV and I usually go to bed early. I never see Ashley – she's at work.'

'Sally has a normal job,' says Ashley. 'I'm a singer and I often get home really late – at 2.00 or 3.00 a.m. I get up at 11.00 or 12.00 and I sometimes see friends in the afternoon.'

The twins are different, but are they friends?
'Yes, we are!' says Sally. 'We're always together on Sunday!'

3 Complete the sentences with the adverbs of frequency in the box. Check your answers in the text.

always   sometimes   usually   never   often

1 I ________ see Ashley.
2 I ________ see friends in the afternoon.
3 I ________ get home really late.
4 I ________ go to bed early.
5 I ________ get up at 6.00 a.m.

 EXTRA PRACTICE Workbook page 22; photocopiable activity 4A Vocabulary

Daily life

UNIT 4

UNIT 4 OVERVIEW: The focus for this unit is daily life. Sts read about jobs and ways of life, and ask and answer questions about their daily routines. In *Learning Curve*, Penny and Taylor go shopping for food.

LANGUAGE		
Grammar	**Vocabulary**	**Pronunciation**
Adverbs of frequency; present simple: *wh-* questions	Daily routine verbs; transport; adjectives (2)	Sentence stress

SKILLS	
Reading	**Speaking**
Finding specific information; *'s*: possession or contraction	Shopping; being polite in shops

LANGUAGE 4A

4A Day and night

Sts read a text about twin sisters who have very different jobs and so lead very different lives. They listen to the girls' brother talking about his job and way of life, then talk about their own way of life.

Grammar	**Vocabulary**	**Pronunciation**	**Communication**
Adverbs of frequency	Daily routine verbs (*do housework/homework, finish work, get dressed, get home, get up, go shopping, go to bed, have a shower, leave home, listen to the radio, read a book, start work*)	Sentence stress	Talking about your daily routine and way of life

WARMER

Ask: *What words for jobs do you know?* Elicit a few ideas, then give sts two minutes to brainstorm as many jobs as they can. They can use their dictionaries to help, or refer back to the vocabulary in Unit 1. Bring the words together on the board and check that sts understand them all. Ask: *Which people work at night? Which people work early in the morning?* Tell sts they are going to read about people who do different jobs, and how they live.

1 A 4.1 Sts look at the pictures in pairs and match them with the phrases. Play the audio for sts to listen and check. See SB page opposite for audio script. Play the audio again for sts to repeat.

Answers
a get up b start work c finish work d get home
e go to bed

3 x PRACTICE *SB page 32, exercise 1A*

1 Do the exercise as normal. To check answers, focus on each picture in turn and ask: *Which phrase?* Elicit sts' ideas, then play that part of the audio for them to check.

2 In pairs, sts cover the phrases and look at the pictures. They try to remember the correct phrase for each picture. They can look at the phrases in the box to check.

3 With books closed, mime going to bed and say: *At 10.30, I ... .* Elicit the correct phrase. Invite sts in turn to mime one of the phrases and say a sentence beginning for other sts to complete.

B Read out the example answers, and explain the meaning of *early* if necessary. You could also teach *late*. Sts work in pairs and say what time they do the activities. Ask some sts to tell the class something about their partner.

Go to Vocabulary practice: daily routine verbs, SB page 114/TB page 241.
Sts will find more language presentation and practice for daily routine verbs here. Do these exercises with the class, or set them for homework, before continuing with exercise 2 of lesson 4A.

PB Remind sts to go to the app for further self-study vocabulary practice of daily routine verbs.

2 Check that sts understand *relationship*. Encourage sts to guess the answers. Sts read the text quickly to check their ideas. Check answers with the class.

Answers
1 They are twin sisters.
2 Sally is a receptionist, and Ashley is a singer.
3 They are different.

3 Read through the adverbs in the box with the class and explain that they all tell us how often something happens, for example every day, some days but not others, etc. Sts find the sentences in the text and complete them with the correct adverbs of frequency. Check answers, and ask: *Which adverb means that something happens every day?* (always). *Which adverb means it doesn't happen any day?* (never). *Which adverb means it happens some days, but not other days?* (sometimes).

Answers
1 never 2 sometimes 3 often 4 usually 5 always

4 **A** Put the adverbs of frequency in the box in the correct order.

sometimes usually never

100% — 0%

always ¹_______ often ²_______ ³_______

B Read the sentences in exercise 3 again. Do the adverbs of frequency come before or after the verbs? Read the Grammar box.

Grammar adverbs of frequency

100%		
	always:	*I **always** have breakfast at home.*
	usually:	*She **usually** has a shower in the morning.*
	often:	*I **often** get up late at the weekend.*
	sometimes:	*I **sometimes** get home at 1.00 a.m.*
0%	never:	*She **never** has dinner at home.*

Look! Adverbs of frequency come after the verb *be*: *We're **always** together on Sunday.*

Personal Best

Go to Grammar practice: adverbs of frequency, page 99

5 **A** 4.4 **Pronunciation:** sentence stress Listen to the sentences. Are the adverbs of frequency stressed or unstressed?

1 I usually get up at 7.00 a.m.
2 I always have a coffee for breakfast.
3 I never go to the gym.
4 I often make dinner in the evening.

B Listen again, check and repeat.

6 Change the adverbs of frequency in 5A so the sentences are true for you. In pairs, say the sentences with the correct stress.

A *I sometimes get up at 7.00 a.m.* **B** *Really? I never get up at 7.00 a.m.*

7 **A** Look at the table. Write five sentences about Sally and Ashley's brother, Marcus.

He always has breakfast in a café.

	Mon	Tue	Wed	Thu	Fri
1 have breakfast in a café	✓	✓	✓	✓	✓
2 watch TV in the morning	✓	✗	✓	✗	✓
3 work in the evening	✓	✗	✓	✓	✓
4 see friends after work	✗	✗	✗	✗	✓
5 go to bed before midnight	✗	✗	✗	✗	✗

B 4.5 Listen and check. What is Marcus's job?

Go to Communication practice: Student A page 136, Student B page 144

8 In pairs, compare yourself with members of your family. Use the activities in the boxes.

I always get up before 7.00 a.m., but my brother usually gets up late, at 9.30.

get up before 7.00 a.m. | eat fast food | watch TV in the morning | go to bed late

get home before 6.00 p.m. | have coffee for breakfast | have lunch at work | have a shower in the morning

Personal Best Describe your typical daily routine at the weekend.

EXTRA PRACTICE Workbook page 22; photocopiable activity 4A Grammar

4 A Focus on the table and point out the 100% and 0% extremes. Sts work in pairs to put the adverbs of frequency in the correct order. Check answers.

Answers
1 usually 2 sometimes 3 never

B Ask sts to look back at the sentences in exercise 3 to answer the question. Elicit the answer.

Answer
before

Grammar

Read the Grammar box with sts about adverbs of frequency. Elicit that adverbs of frequency tell us how often something happens. Point out that they come before the main verb, e.g. *I always get up early*. NOT ~~*I get up always early*~~. or ~~*I get up early always*~~. Ask questions to check concept.

Concept check questions:
What do adverbs of frequency tell us? (how often something happens). *Which adverb of frequency means every day, or every week?* (always). *Which adverb of frequency means 'on no days'?* (never). *If I usually do something, is that more than 50% of the time?* (yes). *If I sometimes do something, is that more than 50% of the time?* (no). *I see never my friends – correct?* (no – I *never see* my friends).

Go to Grammar practice: adverbs of frequency. SB page 99/TB page 211.
Sts will find more language reference, presentation and practice for adverbs of frequency here. Do these exercises with the class, or set them for homework, before continuing with exercise 5A of lesson 4A.

PB Remind sts to go to the app for further self-study grammar practice of adverbs of frequency.

5 A 4.4 Explain that 'sentence stress' refers to how strongly some words are said in a sentence. As an example, say: *I love my job!* (stressing *love*). Ask: *Which word is stressed?* (love). Say the sentence again and ask: *Is the word 'my' stressed?* (no). Play audio track 4.4. See SB page opposite for audio script. Sts listen to hear if the adverbs of frequency are stressed or unstressed.

B 4.4 Play the audio again for sts to check their answers. Check the answer with the class, then play the audio again for sts to repeat.

Answer
The adverbs of frequency are stressed.

6 Read out the task, then read out the example answers. Point out that we use *Really?* to express surprise. Model pronunciation of the word, with rising intonation. Sts work in pairs to say sentences about themselves and compare their ideas. Ask some sts to tell the class something about their partner.

7 A Focus on the table and make sure sts understand that *Mon, Tue, Wed* etc. are abbreviations for the days of the week. Read out the example answer and elicit another example from the class. Sts then write the sentences.

Answers
1 He always has breakfast in a café.
2 He often watches TV in the morning.
3 He usually works in the evening.
4 He sometimes sees friends after work.
5 He never goes to bed before midnight..

B 4.5 Play audio track 4.5. See TB page 308 for audio script. Sts listen and check their answers. Check answers with the class, then ask: *What is Marcus's job?*

Answer
Marcus is a chef.

Go to Communication practice
Divide the class into Student A and Student B. All 'Student A' sts should go to SB page 136. All 'Student B' sts should go to SB page 144. Go to TB page 285 for the teacher notes. Do the activity, then continue with exercise 8 of lesson 4A.

8 Read out the task, then read out the example answer. Go through the activities in the boxes and make sure sts understand them all. Give another example, comparing yourself with a member of your family, then allow sts time to prepare their ideas individually. Put sts into pairs to tell their partner their ideas, and compare their experiences. Ask some sts to tell the class something they learned about their partner.

PERSONAL BEST

Sts can practise talking about their daily routines. They work in pairs and describe their daily routine at the weekend. You could brainstorm some typical activities with the class and write them on the board to help sts, e.g. *stay in bed late, watch a film, do sport*, etc.

With weaker sts, write some sentence beginnings on the board: *At the weekend, I always …; I never …; I sometimes …; I often …* . Sts complete the sentences with their own ideas, then compare their sentences in pairs.

4B My journey to work

1 Match the types of transport with pictures a–e on page 35.

1 bike ____
2 taxi ____
3 bus ____
4 car ____
5 subway ____

Personal Best

Go to Vocabulary practice: transport, page 115

2 Look at the pictures and the title of the text on page 35. Guess the answers to the questions. Read the text quickly and check.

1 What city is it about? 2 What type of transport is it about?

Skill finding specific information

We sometimes need to find specific information in a text.
- Read the questions carefully to see what information you need to find.
- Find the place in the text which has this information and read it carefully.
- Don't worry if you don't understand every word.

3 **A** Read the Skill box. Then find information in the paragraph about Emily in the text to complete the first line of the table.

	Lives where?	Which job?	Works where?
Emily	*Harlem*		
Dan			
Megan			
Walter			

B Now find the information about the other people in the text. Complete the table.

4 Read the text again. Then in pairs, say why each person uses a *citibike*.

Emily uses a citibike because it's fast.

5 Complete the sentences from the text. In which sentences does *'s* mean *is*?

1 ________ office is in Downtown Manhattan.
2 'The ________ cheap,' she says.

Text builder 's: possession or contraction

If you see *'s* at the end of a word, decide if it refers to possession or if it is a contraction of *is*.
*The **city's** blue public bikes* = possession (the bikes belong to the city)
***Megan's** a waitress in the Lower East Side* = contraction (Megan is a waitress)

6 Read the Text builder. Then read the sentences and write *P* (possession) or *C* (contraction).

1 Ravi's a doctor. ____
2 David's mum is a teacher. ____
3 My train's always late. ____
4 Julia's brother starts work at 7.00. ____

7 Discuss the questions in pairs.

1 Do you have public bikes in your town or city? Are they popular? Why/Why not?
2 How do you usually travel to work or university?
3 Do you like the journey? Why/Why not?

 EXTRA PRACTICE Workbook page 23; photocopiable activity 4B Vocabulary

4B My journey to work

Sts read about *citibikes*, public bikes in New York City. They then talk about public transport in their town or city, and how they usually travel to work.

Vocabulary	Reading	Skill	Text builder
Transport (*by bike, by boat, by bus, by car, by ferry, by lorry, by motorbike, by plane, by train, by taxi, on foot, on the subway/underground/metro*)	Sts read a text about *citibikes* in New York.	Finding specific information	*'s*: possession or contraction

WARMER

Mime walking or driving and say: *This is how I usually go to work*. Invite individual sts to mime how they go to work or school. As they mime, write the words for the forms of transport on the board and teach the meanings. Teach the word *transport* and the phrase *journey to work*.

1 Sts work in pairs and match the types of transport with the pictures. They can use a dictionary to help. Check answers. Model and drill pronunciation of the words.

Answers
1 b 2 a 3 d 4 e 5 c

Go to Vocabulary practice: transport, SB page 115/TB page 243.
Sts will find more language presentation and practice for transport vocabulary here. Do these exercises with the class, or set them for homework, before continuing with exercise 2 of lesson 4B.

PB Remind sts to go to the app for further self-study vocabulary practice of transport vocabulary.

2 Sts look at the pictures and title and guess the answers to the questions. Elicit some possible answers, but don't confirm them. Sts then read the text quickly to check their answers. Check answers with the class.

Answers
1 New York 2 *citibikes*

Skill

Read the Skill box with sts about finding specific information in a text. Check they understand *specific*. Read out the task, and point out to sts that they need to first find the paragraph about Emily, then find the specific information to complete the first line of the table.

3 A Sts find the information and complete the table. Check answers, and check that sts understand *designer*.

Answers
designer, Downtown Manhattan

B Sts find the information about the other people to complete the table. You could set a time limit for this, to encourage sts to find the information quickly. Check answers.

Answers
Dan: Soho, office worker, the Financial District
Megan: Brooklyn, waitress, the Lower East Side
Walter: Midtown, doctor, First Avenue

4 Read out the task and check that sts understand *why* (= asking for a reason). Read out the example answer and make sure sts understand *because* (= giving a reason). Sts read the text again, then discuss in pairs why each person uses the bike. Check answers.

Answers
Dan uses a *citibike* because the weather is beautiful.
Megan uses a *citibike* because it's cheap.
Walter uses a *citibike* because he likes the exercise after work.

5 Sts find the sentences in the text and complete them with the missing words. Check answers, then ask: *In which sentence does 's mean is?* Elicit the answer.

Answers
1 Emily's 2 bike's
's means *is* in sentence 2.

Text builder

Read the Text builder box with sts about *'s* for possession and as a contraction. Explain that *'s* is spelled and pronounced the same way, but it has two very different uses. Elicit that it can show possession, e.g. *Dan's home is in Soho* and it can also be a contraction for *is*, e.g. *Dan's an office worker* (= Dan is). Point out that it is important to understand the meaning of *'s* in order to understand the meaning of the whole sentence. Ask questions to check concept.

Concept check questions:
What two uses does 's have? (possession and contraction). *What word is it a contraction for?* (is). *Walter's a doctor – possession or contraction?* (contraction). *What's the full form?* (Walter is a doctor). *Walter's home is in Midtown – possession or contraction?* (possession).

6 Sts read the sentences and decide if the *'s* is for possession or a contraction. Check answers.

Answers
1 C 2 P 3 C 4 P

7 Read out the question and check that sts understand *popular*. Sts discuss the questions in pairs. Get feedback on their discussions.

A morning in the life of bike 0827

New York is famous for its yellow taxis and noisy subway, but a lot of people also travel by *citibike* – the city's blue public bikes. New Yorkers make 14 million journeys a year on *citibikes*. Who uses them and why? We follow one bike for a morning to find out.

7.15 a.m.

At Grand Central Station, Emily Adams from Harlem gets on bike number 0827. Emily's office is in Downtown Manhattan. She's a designer. Why does she use *citibike*? 'It's fast,' she says.

7.45 a.m.

Dan Pesci, an office worker, leaves his home in Soho. He gets on bike 0827 and goes to work in the Financial District. 'I usually go by subway', Dan says, 'but the weather's beautiful today.'

8.30 a.m.

Megan Chang from Brooklyn gets off the East River ferry. Megan's a waitress in the Lower East Side. 'The bike's cheap,' she says, 'but drivers in New York are crazy!'

9.30 a.m.

Doctor Walter Hart gets on bike 0827 and goes home to his apartment in Midtown. He works nights at a hospital on First Avenue. 'I like the exercise after work,' Walter says.

For bike 0827, it's sure to be a busy afternoon, evening and night.

Personal Best Write about the different types of transport in your town or city.

PERSONAL BEST

Sts can practise talking about transport further. They write a description of the different types of transport in their town or city. Sts can compare their descriptions in small groups. Ask sts which towns and cities have good transport and why.

Weaker sts can write three sentences about when they use different types of transport, e.g. *I sometimes go to work by bus. I never travel by train*. Ask some sts to read their sentences to the class.

EXTRA PRACTICE

With books closed, write the following gapped sentences on the board.

1 At Grand Central Station, Emily ______ bike number 0827.

2 'I usually ______ by subway,' Dan says.

3 Megan ______ the East River ferry.

In pairs, sts try to guess the missing verbs. They can check their answers in the text. Check answers, and point out that we can use *get on* and *get off* with trains, buses, ferries, and bikes, e.g. *I get on the bus at 7.30. I get off the bus at 7.45.* Explain that we use get *in/into* and *get out of* for cars and taxis, e.g. *I get in my car at 7.45. I get out of my car at 8.15.* We can use *go by* with any type of transport, e.g. *I go by taxi/bus/bike*.

Ask sts to write three sentences about themselves using *get on, get off, get in, get out of* or *go by*. Ask some sts to read their sentences to the class.

Answers
1 gets on 2 go 3 gets off

EXTRA PRACTICE

Put sts into pairs or small groups, and ask them to write the next journey that bike 0827 makes. Ask them to think about who uses it, where they live, what job they do and why they use the bike that day. Encourage them to use their imagination. Monitor and help while sts are working. Ask pairs or groups in turn to read out their journeys. The class could vote for their favourite.

4C Where do you work?

1 Match the adjectives in the box with their opposites.

quiet clean hot fast unfriendly

1 dirty / ________ 2 cold / ________ 3 friendly / ________ 4 noisy / ________ 5 slow / ________

Personal Best

Go to Vocabulary practice: adjectives (2), page 116

2 A Write down two examples for each of these things.

a cold country | a large building in your country | a noisy job | a long river | a fast animal | a friendly café or shop in your town or city | a hot drink | a quiet place in your town or city

B Compare your answers in pairs. Do you have the same things?

3 Read the text quickly and answer the questions.

1 What is Tess's job? ________
2 Does she like her job? ________
3 What time does she start work? ________
4 Where does she live? ________

A Dirty Job?

Tess Mitchell is a refuse collector. It's dirty work and she gets up very early, but she loves her job.

What time do you start work?
I start work at 5.00 in the morning. I get up at 4.15 a.m. and have breakfast. Then I leave for work.

1________ do you work?
I work in south London. The refuse centre isn't far from my house.

2________ do you do on a typical day?
I drive the lorry to about 800 houses every day from Monday to Friday. That's a lot of rubbish!

3________ do you like the job?
Because the people are friendly and I work outside. Sometimes it's very cold early in the morning, but when the weather's nice, I love it.

4________ do you finish work?
I finish at 1.30 p.m. I'm a mum, so the hours are great. I get home at 2.00, have a shower, and then I go to my children's school to collect them.

5________ do you relax when you're not at work?
I play football with a women's football team and we train on Tuesday and Thursday evenings. At the weekend, I get up late!

36

 EXTRA PRACTICE Workbook page 24; photocopiable activity 4C Vocabulary

4C Where do you work?

Sts read an interview with a refuse collector about her job. They then practise asking and answering questions about their work and daily routines using *wh-* questions.

Grammar	Vocabulary	Pronunciation	Communication
Present simple: *wh-* questions	Adjectives (2) (*clean, cold, dirty, fast, friendly, horrible, hot, large, long, nice, noisy, quiet, short, slow, small, unfriendly*)	Sentence stress	Asking and answering questions about work and daily routines

WARMER

With books closed, write on the board: *chef, doctor, police officer, waiter, office worker*. Check that sts understand all the words. Point to the jobs and ask: *Which job is difficult? Which is easy? Why? Which job is boring? Which is interesting? Why?* Elicit answers from individual sts. Try to elicit ideas about the routines associated with each job, e.g. working at night, getting up early, working outside in bad weather, etc. Tell sts that in this lesson they are going to talk more about different jobs.

1 Read through the adjectives in the box with the class and teach the meanings. Check that sts understand the meaning of *opposite*. Sts then look at the pictures and match the adjectives with their opposites. Check answers. Model and drill pronunciation of all the adjectives.

Answers
1 clean 2 hot 3 unfriendly 4 quiet 5 fast

3 x PRACTICE *SB page 36, exercise 1*

1 Do the exercise as normal. To check answers, point to each picture in turn and say a sentence about it, e.g. *This job's dirty; Look, she's cold*. Then ask: *What's the opposite?* Elicit the answers, then model and drill pronunciation of the adjectives.

2 In pairs, sts cover the adjectives in the box, and the adjectives under each picture. They try to remember the pair of adjectives for each picture. They can look at the words and their answers again to check.

3 Say a sentence that is not true, using one of the adjectives, e.g. *A bike is fast – true?* Elicit a response, using the opposite adjective: *No, a bike is slow*. In pairs, sts write four untrue sentences using the adjectives. They then close their books. Put pairs together into groups of four. Pairs take turns to read their sentences to each other. Their classmates must respond using the opposite adjectives. Ask who responded to all the sentences correctly.

Go to Vocabulary practice: adjectives (2), SB page 116/ TB page 245.
Sts will find more language presentation and practice for adjectives (2) here. Do these exercises with the class, or set them for homework, before continuing with exercise 2A of lesson 4C.

PB Remind sts to go to the app for further self-study vocabulary practice of adjectives (2).

2 A Read through the ideas in the boxes with the class and make sure sts understand them all. Sts work individually to write down examples. Monitor and help while sts are working. They can use their dictionaries to look for the names of animals, or they can ask you.

B Sts compare their ideas in pairs and notice any that are the same. Ask some sts which of their answers were the same. See which answers were popular with the class.

3 Focus on the pictures and read out the questions. Put sts into pairs to guess the answers. Remind them not to read the text at this stage, but just to guess. Elicit some possible answers, but don't confirm them. Sts then read the text quickly to check their answers. Check answers with the class.

Answers
1 She's a refuse collector.
2 Yes, she does.
3 She starts work at 5.00 in the morning.
4 She lives in south London.

4 **A** Complete the questions in the text with the question words in the box. How do you say them in your language?

Why Where When What How

B Look at the questions in the text again. Order the words below from 1–4 to make a question. Then read the Grammar box.

☐ *do/does* ☐ main verb ☐ question word ☐ subject

Grammar **present simple: *wh-* questions**

Question word:	*do/does*:	Subject:	Main verb:
Where	*do*	*you*	*live?*
What	*does*	*your husband*	*do?*
How	*does*	*he*	*get to work?*
When	*do*	*your children*	*watch TV?*
What time	*do*	*they*	*get up?*
Why	*do*	*you*	*work at the weekend?*
Who	*do*	*you*	*work with?*

Personal Best

Go to Grammar practice: present simple: *wh-* questions, page 99

5 4.10 **Pronunciation:** question words Listen and repeat the question words. Do they begin with a /w/ sound or a /h/ sound?

1 where ____ 2 when ____ 3 who ____ 4 why ____ 5 how ____ 6 what ____

6 **A** 4.11 Order the words to make questions. Say the questions with the correct pronunciation of the question words. Listen, check and repeat.

1 you / have / how many / do / children ________________?
2 what / they / time / have breakfast / do ________________?
3 do / does / husband / your / what ________________?
4 he / when / does / work ________________?
5 at the weekend / you / what / do / do ________________?

B 4.12 Match questions 1–5 with answers a–e. Listen to the interview with Tess and check.

a In the afternoons and evenings.
b Two.
c He's a taxi driver.
d 7.30.
e We often go to the park.

Go to Communication practice: Student A page 137, Student B page 145

7 **A** Find out about your partner. Ask and answer the questions in the boxes in pairs.

What time / start work? | Who / live with? | How / get to English classes?

What / have for breakfast? | Where / usually go on holiday? | How / relax in the evening?

Why / study English? | When / do your English homework? | How many brothers and sisters / have?

B Swap partners. Ask and answer questions about your first partner.

A *What time does Sasha start work?* **B** *He usually starts work at 8.00 a.m.*

Personal Best Write ten questions for an interview with an actor/singer that you like.

37

4 A Put sts into pairs to complete the questions in the text with the correct question words. Check answers, and check that sts understand all the questions. Elicit how sts say the question words in their language.

> **Answers**
> 1 Where 2 What 3 Why 4 When 5 How

B Sts look at the word order in the questions in the text, then order the words to make a question. They could work in pairs for this. Check the answer.

> **Answers**
> 1 question word 2 do/does 3 subject 4 main verb

Grammar

Read the Grammar box with sts about the present simple: *wh-* questions. Explain that we use *wh-* questions to ask for more information. Elicit or explain that *where* asks about a place, *when* asks about a time, *who* asks about a person, *what* asks about a thing, *how* asks about a way of doing something, *why* asks about a reason, and *what time* asks about the time. Reinforce the point that in *wh-* questions, *do/does* comes before the subject, e.g. *Where do you live?* NOT ~~*Where you do live?*~~ or ~~*Where you live?*~~ Ask questions to check concept.

Concept check questions:

Why do we use wh- questions? (to ask for more information). *Which word asks about a place?* (where). *Which word asks about a person?* (who). *Which word asks about a reason?* (why). *What are the two ways to ask about a time?* (when, what time). *Where you work? – correct?* (no – Where do you work?). *When he have breakfast? – correct?* (no – When does he have breakfast?). *I want to know the time you start work – what's my question?* (What time/When do you start work?).

Go to Grammar practice: present simple: *wh-* questions, SB page 99/TB page 211.

Sts will find more language reference, presentation and practice for *wh-* questions in the present simple here. Do these exercises with the class, or set them for homework, before continuing with exercise 5 of lesson 4C.

PB Remind sts to go to the app for further self-study grammar practice of the present simple: *wh-* questions.

5 4.10 Allow sts time to read through the questions. Play the first question on audio track 4.10 and elicit which words are stressed (where, work). See SB page opposite for audio script. Play the rest of audio track 4.10 for sts to listen and underline the stressed words. Play the audio again as you check the answers, for sts to hear the stressed words. Play the audio once more for sts to repeat.

> **Answers**
> 1 where /w/ 2 when /w/ 3 who /h/ 4 why /w/
> 5 how /h/ 6 what /w/

6 A 4.11 Sts put the words in the correct order to make questions. Put sts into pairs to compare their answers and practise saying the questions with the correct stress. Play audio track 4.11. See Answers for audio script. Sts listen and check their answers. Play the audio again for sts to repeat the questions.

> **Answers**
> 1 How many children do you have?
> 2 What time do they have breakfast?
> 3 What does your husband do?
> 4 When does he work?
> 5 What do you do at the weekend?

B 4.12 Sts match the questions in exercise 6A with the answers. Play audio 4.12. See TB page 308 for audio script. Sts listen and check their answers. Check answers with the class.

> **Answers**
> 1 b 2 d 3 c 4 a 5 e

Go to Communication practice

Divide the class into Student A and Student B. All 'Student A' sts should go to SB page 137. All 'Student B' sts should go to SB page 145. Go to TB page 287 for the teacher notes. Do the activity, then continue with exercise 7A of lesson 4C.

7 A Read through the question prompts with the class and make sure sts understand them all. Elicit one or two full questions, and elicit a few example answers for these questions. Sts ask and answer the questions in pairs. Point out that they need to listen to their partner's answers carefully, because they are going to talk about them. They could make notes on their partner's answers if they wish.

B Put sts into different pairs, and read out the task and the example question and answer. Point out that sts need to change the question forms to match *he/she/it*, e.g. *Who does she live with?* and they need to remember the final *-s* or *-es* on the verbs in positive sentences, e.g. *She lives with her family*. Sts ask and answer questions about their first partner. Ask some sts to tell the class something they learned about one of their classmates.

PERSONAL BEST

Sts can practise asking questions further by writing ten questions for an interview with an actor or singer that they like. Encourage them to use each different *wh-* word at least once. They can compare their questions in pairs and speculate about what the answers might be.

With weaker sts, brainstorm some ideas for famous people they would like to interview. Sts then work in pairs and write four questions to ask them. Put pairs together into groups of four to compare their questions and speculate about what the answers might be.

4D How can I help you?

1 A 4.13 Match the prices with the words. Listen and check.

1 nine euros ninety-nine ____
2 nineteen pounds ninety-nine ____
3 fifteen euros ____
4 fifty dollars ____
5 eleven dollars ninety-nine ____
6 twenty-nine euros ____
7 fifty pence/fifty p ____
8 five pounds ____
9 six pounds fifty ____
10 fifty cents ____
11 five pounds ninety-five ____
12 twenty-five dollars ____

B Write down three prices in numbers and give them to your partner. Say your partner's prices.

That's three pounds fifty.

2 Discuss the questions in pairs.

1 Who usually goes shopping for food in your house?
2 Where do you usually buy food? Why?
a at a supermarket b at a market c at local shops
3 Do you like shopping for food? Why/Why not?

3 4.14 Watch or listen to the first part of *Learning Curve*. Are the sentences true (T) or false (F)?

1 Penny likes shopping for food. ____
2 Penny and Taylor live together. ____
3 They usually go shopping on Thursdays. ____
4 There is a big supermarket near their apartment. ____

4 4.15 Watch or listen to the second part of the show. Tick (✓) the things Penny buys and the correct prices.

shop 1		shop 2		shop 3	
half a chicken	☐	cheese and salad	☐	a blue shopping trolley	☐
a whole chicken	☐	cheese and eggs	☐	a black shopping trolley	☐
$4.79	☐	$17.15	☐	$21.77	☐
$8.79	☐	$17.50	☐	$22.02	☐

5 4.15 Who says the phrases: Penny (P), Shop assistant 1 (S1), Shop assistant 2 (S2) or Shop assistant 3 (S3)? Watch or listen again and check.

1 How much is it for that small shopping trolley? ____
2 Here you are. ____
3 I'd like a whole chicken, please. ____
4 You're welcome. ____
5 Here's your change – 25 cents. ____
6 Can I have two pounds of this white cheese? ____

Learning Curve

4D How can I help you?

Sts hear a conversation about shopping, and some conversations in a shop. They then practise having a conversation in a shop, using phrases to be polite.

Speaking	Skill	Conversation builder
Sts watch a video or listen to a recording of people shopping and talking about shopping. They then practise having a conversation in a shop.	Being polite in shops	Shopping for food

WARMER

Ask: *How often do you go shopping for food?* Elicit a range of answers, then ask: *What things do you buy every week?* Ask sts to list ten things they buy every week. They can refer back to page 24 if they need help with common food items. Put sts into pairs to compare their lists. Ask pairs in turn to tell the class which things are on both their lists.

1 A 4.13 Use the price tags to teach the word *price*. Point to the different currency signs and teach the words *dollar*, *pound* and *euro*. Point to the first price and say: *Can you find the words for this price in 1–12?* Elicit the correct words. Sts then match the remaining prices with the words. They could work in pairs for this. Play audio track 4.13. See SB page opposite for audio script. Sts listen and check their answers. Play the audio again, pausing for sts to repeat.

Answers
1 h 2 g 3 c 4 b 5 j 6 l 7 e 8 a 9 k 10 f
11 d 12 i

3 x PRACTICE *SB page 38, exercise 1A*

1. Do the exercise as normal. To check answers, read out each sign in turn, with a mistake, e.g. *a) five dollars, b) fifty cents*. Sts race to correct you. Then play the audio for sts to listen and check.
2. Ask sts to cover the words. In pairs, they look at the prices again and try to remember how to say each one. They can look at the words and their answers again to check.
3. Tell sts they are going to play *Bingo*. Ask them to choose six of the prices and write them on a piece of paper, then close their books. Read out the prices from exercise 1A in a random order, noting them down as you say them. If sts have that price written down, they can cross it off. The first student to cross all their prices off shouts 'Bingo!' Check their answers, and if they are correct, they are the winner.

B Sts write down three new prices, then swap with a partner. They practise saying the prices in pairs.

2 Read out the questions and make sure sts understand them all. Sts discuss the questions in pairs. Ask some sts to tell the class something about their partner.

3 4.14 In this episode of *Learning Curve*, Penny talks about shopping, then Penny and Taylor go shopping for food. Teach the words *flatmate, roommate, fridge* and *neighbourhood*. Allow sts time to read through the sentences. Make sure they understand everything. Play video/audio track 4.14. See TB page 308 for video/audio script. Sts watch/listen and decide if the sentences are true or false. Check answers, playing the video/audio again if necessary for sts to hear the answers. Pre-teach the following words if necessary from the video: *on foot, underground, subway, fridge, steps*. Ask questions to elicit the meanings, e.g. *Which word means a place you put food to keep it cold?* (fridge). *Which expression means you walk to a place?* (on foot). *Which two words mean a train that goes under the streets?* (underground/subway). Teach the meanings, then play the video/audio again for sts to hear the words in context.

Answers
1 F 2 T 3 T 4 F

4 4.15 Allow sts time to read through the food items and the prices. Make sure they understand all the food items, and make sure they understand *shopping trolley*. Elicit how to say the prices. Point out that $17.15 and $17.50 sound very similar, so they will have to listen carefully to hear the correct one. Pre-teach the following words if necessary from the video/audio: *groceries, change* (= money you get back when you pay for something), *stairs, empty, telly* and *tax*. Play video/audio track 4.15. See TB page 309 for video/audio script. Sts watch/listen and tick the things Taylor buys and the prices. Check answers, playing the video/audio again if necessary for sts to hear the answers.

Answers
Shop 1 a whole chicken $8.79
Shop 2 cheese and salad $17.15
Shop 3 a black shopping trolley $21.77

5 4.15 Read through the phrases with the class and explain the meanings if necessary. Sts decide from memory who said each phrase. Play video/audio track 4.15 again for sts to check their answers. Check answers with the class.

Answers
1 P 2 S2 3 P 4 S1 5 S3 6 P

Conversation builder | shopping for food

Customer:
Do you have ...?
Can I have ...
I'd like ...
How much is that?
Here you go/are.

Shop assistant:
How can I help you?
Anything else?
That's ... dollars/pounds.
Here you go/are.
Here's your change.

6 **A** Read the Conversation builder. Then order the sentences from 1–7 to make a conversation in a shop.

a ☐ Yes. Anything else?
b ☐ Yes, I'd like five biscuits, please. How much is that?
c ☐ Can I have a chocolate cake, please?
d ☐ Thanks. And here's your change.
e ☐ Here you go – £10.
f ☐ Hello. How can I help you?
g ☐ That's £8.50.

B 4.16 Listen and check. Practise the conversation in pairs.

7 4.17 Complete the conversation with the words in the box. Listen and check. Are Penny and the shop assistant polite? Why/Why not?

welcome good thank you please

Shop assistant 1________ evening.
Penny I'd like a whole chicken, 2________ .
Shop assistant Here you go.
Penny 3________ .
Shop assistant You're 4________ .

Skill | being polite in shops

It's important to be polite if you work in a shop or if you're a customer.
- Greet people. Say: *Hi / Good morning / Good evening*, etc.
- Ask for things politely. Say: *Can I have ...? / I'd like ..., please.* NOT ~~*I want ... / Give me ...*~~
- If someone says: *Thanks / Thank you*, you can reply: *You're welcome. / That's alright.*

8 4.18 Read the Skill box. Listen to three conversations. Tick (✓) the people who are polite.

1 a the customer ☐ b the waiter ☐ c both people ☐
2 a the customer ☐ b the shop assistant ☐ c both people ☐
3 a the customer ☐ b the receptionist ☐ c both people ☐

Go to Communication practice: Student A page 137, Student B page 145

9 **A** **PREPARE** In pairs, look at the pictures and choose one of the situations. Write down things you can buy there and their prices.

In a burger restaurant

In a fruit and vegetable shop

In a café

B **PRACTISE** Decide who is the customer and who is the assistant. Act out your conversation.

C **PERSONAL BEST** Listen to another pair's conversation. Are they polite? What could they do better?

Personal Best Think of your favourite food shop or café and write a conversation in English there.

Conversation builder

Read the Conversation builder box with sts about shopping for food. Explain that we use *Do you have ...?* *Can I have ...?* or *I'd like ...* to ask for something, and we use *How much is that?* to ask about the price. We use *Here you go* or *Here you are* when we give something to someone. Explain that shop assistants ask: *How can I help you?* to ask politely what you want, and they ask *Anything else?* to ask if you want another thing. Explain the meaning of *change*. Ask questions to check concept.

Concept check questions:
Which phrases can we use to ask for something in a shop? (Do you have ...? Can I have ...? I'd like ...). *How do we ask about the price?* (How much is that?). *What do we say when we give something to someone?* (Here you go, Here you are). *What does the shop assistant say to ask what you want?* (How can I help you?). *How do they ask if you want another thing?* (Anything else?). *If the price is £2, and I give the shop assistant £5, what do they say to me?* (Here's your change).

6 A Ask sts to read the sentences. Elicit which sentence comes first in the conversation (f). Sts order the sentences to make a conversation.

Answers
1 f 2 c 3 a 4 b 5 g 6 e 7 d

B 4.16 Play audio track 4.16 for sts to check their answers. Play the audio again, pausing after each line for sts to repeat. Sts can then practise the conversation in pairs. They can swap roles and practise again.

7 4.17 Read out the first gapped sentence and elicit the correct word to complete it. Sts complete the conversation with the correct words. Play audio track 4.17 for sts to check their answers. See SB page opposite for audio script. Check answers with the class, and make sure sts understand the conversation. Ask: *Are Penny and the shop assistant polite?* Elicit that they are polite, because they use words such as *please* and *thank you*.

Answers
1 Good 2 please 3 Thank you 4 welcome

Skill

Read the Skill box with sts about being polite in shops. Check they understand everything.

8 4.18 Explain the task, then play the first conversation in audio 4.18. See TB page 309 for audio script. Ask: *Who is polite? The customer? The waiter? Both people?* Elicit the answer, then play the other two conversations. Sts listen and decide who is polite. Check answers, playing the audio again if necessary to hear why each person is polite or not polite.

Answers
1 a 2 c 3 b

Go to Communication practice
Divide the class into Student A and Student B. All 'Student A' sts should go to SB page 137. All 'Student B' sts should go to SB page 145. Go to TB page 287 for the teacher notes. Do the activity, then continue with exercise 9 of lesson 4D.

9 Sts follow the steps to practise being polite in shops.

A PREPARE Sts work in pairs to choose one of the situations and write down things they can buy there. Alternatively, brainstorm ideas for each situation as a class, and write the things on the board.

B PRACTISE Sts work in their pairs and act out a conversation. Remind sts to use phrases from the Conversation builder box for shopping for food, and remind them to use phrases from the Skill box to be polite. Encourage them to use intonation and tone of voice to sound polite and friendly, too. They can swap roles and practise again.

C PERSONAL BEST Sts work in groups of four to listen to each other and give feedback on how polite they sounded and what they could do better. They could then work with a different partner and practise another of the situations.

PERSONAL BEST

Sts can practise shopping for food further. They think of their favourite food shop or café and write a conversation in English there. They could then work in pairs and practise their conversations.

Weaker sts can look back at the conversation in exercise 6A. In pairs, they can change the details of the conversation, then practise it in pairs again.

EXTRA PRACTICE

Put sts into groups of three. Two sts practise one of their conversations from exercise 9, or a new conversation with a different situation. The third student uses their phone to film the other two. Sts can swap roles and practise again. Watching themselves on film will help sts to evaluate how well they can shop for food, and how polite they sound.

Grammar

1 Tick (✓) the correct sentences.

1 a I never finish work at 5.00 p.m. ☐
b I don't never finish work at 5.00 p.m. ☐
c I don't finish work never at 5.00 p.m. ☐

2 a He don't go to bed early. ☐
b He not go to bed early. ☐
c He doesn't go to bed early. ☐

3 a Do you go to work by car? ☐
b Does you go to work by car? ☐
c When you do go to work by car? ☐

4 a We often has eggs for breakfast. ☐
b We often have eggs for breakfast. ☐
c We have often eggs for breakfast. ☐

5 a Why do you live with? ☐
b Who do you live with? ☐
c How do you live with? ☐

6 a When they do get up? ☐
b When they get up? ☐
c When do they get up? ☐

7 a She work in a restaurant in the evening. ☐
b She do work in a restaurant in the evening. ☐
c She works in a restaurant in the evening. ☐

8 a Goes he to the gym after work? ☐
b Does he to the gym after work? ☐
c Does he go to the gym after work? ☐

2 Order the words to make questions and sentences.

1 your / do / go / children / where / school / to
_______________________________________?

2 have / she / at / does / lunch / home
_______________________________________?

3 always / dinner / we / eat / vegetables / for
_______________________________________.

4 get / time / what / weekend / do / up / the / you / at
_______________________________________?

5 don't / shopping / I / Saturday / go / on
_______________________________________.

6 the / he / book / sometimes / a / reads / train / on
_______________________________________.

7 Monday / quiet / restaurant / is / on / often / the
_______________________________________.

8 in / radio / do / listen / to / you / the / morning / the
_______________________________________?

9 old / brother's / is / how / your / girlfriend
_______________________________________?

10 the / never / exercise / Simon / weekend / does / at
_______________________________________.

3 Complete the text with the correct form of the verbs in brackets.

Life on Muck

This is Laura Marriner. She lives and works on the very small island of Muck in Scotland. Life isn't easy, but it's very interesting …

What [1]________ (be) **Laura's job?**
She's a teacher. Her school only [2]________ (have) eight children.

Where [3]________ **she** ________ (live)**?**
Laura [4]________ (not leave) home in the morning because she lives in the school with her husband and two sons!

How [5]________ **they** ________ (go) **shopping?**
By ferry. The journey is two hours, but people on the island only [6]________ (use) the ferry when the weather is good. They [7]________ (not go) shopping every day, so Laura [8]________ (make) bread at home.

What is school life like on Muck?
It's great. The children often [9]________ (study) on the beach.

[10]________ **Laura** ________ (like) **life on Muck?**
Yes, she does! When the weather is horrible, life is difficult, but she's happy there. The people are very friendly and life is an adventure.

Vocabulary

1 Put the words in the box in the correct columns.

~~boat~~ ~~cold~~ ~~do~~ cheese fast finish get up know small meat noisy short taxi train want

Verbs	Adjectives	Nouns
do	*cold*	*boat*

Grammar

1 Sts read the sentences and tick the ones that are correct. Check answers and discuss with the class why the other sentences are incorrect.

Answers
1 a
2 c
3 a
4 b
5 b
6 c
7 c
8 c

2 Sts put the words in the correct order to make sentences and questions. Check answers.

Answers
1 Where do your children go to school?
2 Does she have lunch at home?
3 We always eat vegetables for dinner.
4 What time do you get up at the weekend?
5 I don't go shopping on Saturday.
6 He sometimes reads a book on the train.
7 The restaurant is often quiet on Monday.
8 Do you listen to the radio in the morning?
9 How old is your brother's girlfriend?
10 Simon never does exercise at the weekend.

3 x PRACTICE *SB page 40, Grammar exercise 2*

1 Do the exercise as normal. To check answers, read out the first word of each correct answer. Choose a student to say the next word, then go around the class, with each student saying the next word in the sentence. Other sts can correct them if they make a mistake.

2 Ask sts to close their books. Write prompts for each sentence and question on the board, e.g. *children/ school, lunch/home*. In pairs, sts try to remember the sentences and questions. They can look at their books and their answers again to check.

3 Sts work in pairs and prepare four questions to ask their classmates, using ideas in the sentences and questions, e.g. *Do you have lunch at home? Do you always eat vegetables for dinner?* Put pairs together into groups of four to ask and answer their questions. Ask some sts to tell the class something about their partner, e.g. *(Paul) always eats vegetables for dinner.*

3 Ask sts to read the text through quickly for general meaning. Ask: *Why is life difficult on Muck? Why is it interesting?* Elicit a range of answers. Sts read the text again and complete it with the correct words. Check answers.

Answers
1 is
2 has
3 does, live
4 doesn't leave
5 do, go
6 use
7 don't go
8 makes
9 study
10 Does, like

Vocabulary

1 Sts put the words in the correct columns. As an extension, sts could write two or three sentences using some of the words. For an extra challenge, they could try to use more than one word in each sentence, e.g. *This train is fast and noisy*.

Answers

Verbs	Adjectives	Nouns
finish	fast	cheese
get up	small	meat
know	noisy	taxi
want	short	train

2 Circle the word that is different. Explain your answers.

1	car	lorry	bus	plane
2	think	use	slow	make
3	Friday	tomorrow	Sunday	Saturday
4	rice	chips	crisps	potatoes
5	coffee	milk	fruit	orange juice
6	clean	horrible	unfriendly	dirty
7	biscuit	pizza	cake	chocolate
8	work	study	change	dinner

3 Complete the sentences with the correct words.

1 What time do you g*et* home after work?
2 He usually l________ to the radio at work.
3 I always have b________ before I leave home in the morning.
4 They w________ television after dinner.
5 She goes to university by m________ . It's very fast.
6 In cold weather, I have a h________ drink in the evening.
7 He never says 'hello'. He's so u________ .
8 T________ in New York are yellow and in London they're black.
9 I never drink tea, coffee or soft drinks. I only drink w________ with meals.
10 On W________ evening, I go to the gym.

4 Complete the email with the words in the box.

bike dressed bread friendly get live
go evening Saturday read

Hi Ana,

How are you? I'm in Cartagena at my grandmother's house this week. It's nice and quiet here. I [1]________ up late every day, have breakfast and get [2]________ . Then I go to the shops by [3]________ . I usually buy some [4]________ for lunch. The people are very [5]________ . In the afternoon, I [6]________ to the beach and [7]________ a book. In the [8]________ , we sometimes have dinner in a restaurant.

I'm here for one week, and then I go home on [9]________ ☹ … I want to [10]________ here!

See you soon.

Bea

Personal Best

Lesson 3A Name four things people eat or drink for breakfast.

Lesson 4A Write four sentences about your daily routine with adverbs of frequency.

Lesson 3A Write a sentence about the food you like and don't like.

Lesson 4B Name six types of transport.

Lesson 3B Name the days of the week that begin with 'T'.

Lesson 4B Describe a member of your family's bike, car or motorbike.

Lesson 3B Write a sentence about something you do every week.

Lesson 4C Write three adjectives that describe your town or city.

Lesson 3C Write a positive and a negative sentence about a friend's typical day.

Lesson 4C Write three questions for your teacher with different question words.

Lesson 3D Write about the food you eat on a special occasion. Use *and* and *but*.

Lesson 4D Write a sentence to ask for something to eat and drink in a café.

2 Sts circle the word that is different in each set. Check answers, and ask sts to explain in each case why the word is different. As an extension, sts could write two or three sentences using some of the words.

Answers
1 plane (doesn't travel on the road)
2 slow (not a verb)
3 tomorrow (not a day of the week)
4 rice (not made from potatoes)
5 fruit (not a drink)
6 clean (not a negative adjective)
7 pizza (not sweet)
8 dinner (not a verb)

3 Sts read the sentences and complete them with the correct words. Check answers.

Answers
2 listens
3 breakfast
4 watch
5 motorbike
6 hot
7 unfriendly
8 Taxis
9 water
10 Wednesday

3 x PRACTICE *SB page 41, exercise 3*

1 Do the exercise as normal. To check answers, ask sts to tick the three answers they are most sure of. For each sentence, ask a student who ticked that sentence to give the answer.
2 Ask sts to close their books. Call out prompts for each sentence in turn, e.g. *time/home/work*. Sts try to remember the sentences. You could do this as a game, awarding a point to the first student who gives each correct answer.
3 Put sts into small groups. They choose one of the sentences and take turns to say it, each changing one detail, e.g. *He usually listens to the radio at work./He always listens to the radio at work./He always listens to the radio at home./I always listen to the radio at home.* Ask groups in turn to read their final sentences to the class. See which group has managed to change their sentence the most.

4 Sts read the email and complete it with the correct words. Check answers.

Answers
1 get
2 dressed
3 bike
4 bread
5 friendly
6 go
7 read
8 evening
9 Saturday
10 live

Personal Best

At the end of each *Review and practice* double-page spread, there is a *Personal Best* section. The aim here is to provide a quick challenge to change the pace and allow for language recall and personalization.

These questions and prompts give sts the opportunity to revise a number of language and skills points from the preceding two units in a more productive way. The points being revised are referenced according to which lesson they appear in (e.g. Lesson 3A). They cover grammar, vocabulary, text builder language from reading and writing lessons, and conversation builder language from speaking lessons. Sts work individually, in pairs or in groups, according to the class dynamic and the time available. Set a time limit if you would like to add a competitive element. Encourage sts to refer back to the relevant lessons if they are having difficulties. The aim is for them to respond to the prompts and engage with the target language in a personal way. Their answers will vary. Monitor and help as necessary and get feedback on sts' answers.

WORKBOOK REVIEW AND PRACTICE

Students will find two pages of Review and Practice at the end of each unit of their Workbooks.
Unit 3, pages 20 and 21
Unit 4, pages 26 and 27

UNIT 5

All about me

LANGUAGE *can* and *can't* ■ common verbs (2)

5A When can you start?

1 Complete phrases 1–5 with the verbs in the box.

swim speak drive play call

1 ________ a car 2 ________ Chinese 3 ________ the piano 4 ________ a friend 5 ________ in the sea

Personal Best

Go to Vocabulary practice: common verbs (2), page 117

2 Read the job advert. What do you need for this job?

JOBS TO GO .COM

▶ FIND JOBS

▶ POST CV

▶ COMPANY PROFILES

SYDNEY CITY TOURS: TOUR GUIDE

Help tourists see the beautiful city of Sydney.

Do you know Sydney? Do you like working with people? Can you speak a foreign language? Do you want to work this summer?

If the answer is 'Yes', then contact us.

▶ CONTACT

3 5.2 Listen to a job interview. Tick (✓) the things Georgia can do. Does she get the job?

	Yes	No
1 Can you speak a foreign language?		
2 Can you drive?		
3 Can you work early in the morning?		
4 Can you swim well?		

4 **A** 5.2 Match the halves to make sentences. Listen again and check.

1 Some of the people can't
2 I can speak
3 Yes, I
4 No, I
5 When can you

a can.
b start?
c Chinese.
d can't – sorry.
e speak English.

B Choose the correct options to complete the rules. Then read the Grammar box.

1 We use *can* to talk about *abilities* / *daily routines*.
2 We use *can't* + verb in *questions* / *negatives*.
3 We use *can* + subject + verb in *questions* / *negatives*.

 EXTRA PRACTICE Workbook page 28; photocopiable activity 5A Vocabulary

All about me

UNIT 5

UNIT 5 OVERVIEW: This unit focuses on talking about yourself. Sts practise talking about their own abilities and write a personal profile. In *Learning Curve*, Kate and Simon interview people about the electronic devices they can't live without.

LANGUAGE

Grammar	Vocabulary	Pronunciation
can and *can't*; object pronouns	Common verbs (2); electronic devices; activities	*can* and *can't*; /h/

SKILLS

Listening	Writing
Listening for specific information; sentence stress	Describing yourself; *because*

LANGUAGE 5A

5A When can you start?

Sts read a job advert for a tour guide and listen to someone being interviewed about their abilities and suitability for the job. They read a second job advert for an *au pair*, and listen to two people who are interested in the job talking about their abilities. Sts then practise talking about their own abilities.

Grammar	Vocabulary	Pronunciation	Communication
can and *can't*	Common verbs (2) (*arrive, call, cook, dance, drive, give, help, look after, meet, play, sing, speak, swim, travel*)	*can* and *can't*	Talking about your abilities

WARMER

Tell sts you are going to tell them three things about you. Say three sentences about yourself, e.g. *I like rock music. I ride my bike to school every day. I never watch TV.* Ask sts individually to write three sentences with information about themselves. Put sts into small groups to compare their sentences. Ask some sts to tell the class something they learned about their classmates. Tell sts that in this unit they will practise talking more about themselves.

1 Put sts into pairs to look at the pictures and complete the phrases with the correct verbs. They can use their dictionaries to help. Model and drill pronunciation of the phrases.

> **Answers**
> 1 drive 2 speak 3 play 4 call 5 swim

Go to Vocabulary practice: common verbs (2), SB page 117/TB page 247.
Sts will find more language presentation and practice for common verbs (2) vocabulary here. Do these exercises with the class, or set them for homework, before continuing with exercise 2 of lesson 5A.

PB Remind sts to go to the app for further self-study vocabulary practice of common verbs (2).

2 Focus on the advert and check sts understand *tour guide* and *need*. Sts read the job advert and note down the things that you need for the job. Check answers.

> **Answer**
> You need to know Sydney, like working with people, speak a language and want to work this summer.

3 5.2 Read out the questions and check that sts understand *foreign language* and *early*. Play the first question and answer of audio track 5.2. See TB page 309 for audio script. Ask: *Can Georgia speak a foreign language?* Elicit the answer and point out that sts should tick the 'Yes' column. Play the rest of the audio. Sts listen and tick the things that Georgia can do. Check answers, playing the audio again if necessary. Ask: *Does she get the job?*

> **Answers**
> 1 Yes 2 Yes 3 No 4 Yes
> Yes, she gets the job.

4 A 5.2 Sts match the sentence halves. Allow them time to compare their answers in pairs, then play audio track 5.2 again for them to listen and check. Check answers.

> **Answers**
> 1 e 2 c 3 a 4 d 5 b

B Teach the meaning of *ability*. Read through the rules with the class and elicit the correct answers.

> **Answers**
> 1 abilities 2 negatives 3 questions

Grammar *can* and *can't*

Positive:
*I **can work** this summer.*
*Georgia **can swim** well.*

Negative:
*I **can't speak** Chinese.*
*They **can't cook**.*

Questions and short answers:
*__Can__ you **speak** a foreign language?*
*Yes, I **can**.* *No, I **can't**.*

Personal Best

Go to Grammar practice: *can* and *can't*, page 100

5 ▶5.4 **Pronunciation:** *can* and *can't* Listen and repeat. Pay attention to the difference between *can* /kæn/ or /kən/ and *can't* /kɑːnt/.

1 He can drive. 2 She can't swim. 3 Can you play the guitar? 4 Yes, I can.

6 **A** ▶5.5 Say the sentences with the correct pronunciation of *can* and *can't*. Listen, check and repeat.

1 I can swim two kilometres.
2 I can't sing well.
3 I can't speak German.
4 I can cook Italian food.
5 I can drive a car.
6 I can't play the piano.

B Say the sentences in pairs. Say if you think it's true or false for your partner.

A *I can swim two kilometres.* **B** *False. You can't swim two kilometres.*
A *You're right, I can't swim.*

7 **A** Read the job advert. What does an *au pair* do?

B ▶5.6 Emily and Ben are interested in the job. Listen and tick (✓) what they can and can't do.

AU PAIR

- **Can you look after children?**
- **Do you like sports and music?**
- **Do you want to work as an au pair this summer?**

We're a friendly American family with two children. We live in Madrid, Spain.

– Contact Lisa Jones for more information. –

Can he/she ...	 Emily	 Ben
cook?		
drive?		
speak Spanish?		
play tennis?		
swim?		
play the piano?		
play the guitar?		
sing?		

8 ▶5.7 In pairs, ask and answer the questions about Emily and Ben. Who is best for the job? Listen and check.

A *Can Emily cook?* **B** *Yes, she can.*

Go to Communication practice: Student A page 137, Student B page 145

9 **A** Ask your classmates questions 1–5. Find someone who says 'Yes, I can.' and write his/her name. Then ask for more information.

A *Can you speak a foreign language?* **B** *Yes, I can.*
A *Which language can you speak?* **B** *I can speak French.*

Questions	Name	More information
1 Can you speak a foreign language?		
2 Can you play an instrument?		
3 Can you dance?		
4 Can you cook?		
5 Can you play a sport?		

B In pairs, discuss what you found out about your classmates.

Sebastian can speak French.

Personal Best Write ten sentences about people in your class. Use *can* and *can't*.

EXTRA PRACTICE Workbook page 28; photocopiable activity 5A Grammar

Grammar

Read the Grammar box with sts about *can* and *can't*. Point out that *can* and *can't* are the same for all persons, e.g. *I can, we can, he can* NOT ~~*he cans*~~. Point out that *can* and *can't* are followed by the infinitive without *to*, e.g. *I can swim* NOT ~~*I can to swim*~~. Point out that in short answers, we just use *can/can't*, but not the main verb, e.g. *Can you swim? Yes, I can*. Ask questions to check concept.

Concept check questions:
What do we use 'can' and 'can't' to talk about? (abilities). *I can dance, but I can't swim – what ability do I have?* (dancing). *Do 'can' and 'can't' change in the he/she/it forms?* (no, they are the same in all forms). *You can sing – how do I make that into a question?* (Can you sing?). *What are the short answers?* (Yes, I can, No, I can't).

Go to Grammar practice: *can* and *can't*, SB page 100/TB page 213.
Sts will find more language reference, presentation and practice for *can* and *can't* here. Do these exercises with the class, or set them for homework, before continuing with exercise 5 of lesson 5A.

PB Remind sts to go to the app for further self-study grammar practice of *can* and *can't*.

5 5.4 Explain that although *can* and *can't* look similar, they are pronounced in different ways. Play audio track 5.4 for sts to listen and notice the pronunciation of *can* and *can't*. See SB page opposite for audio script. Play the audio again for sts to listen and repeat.

6 A 5.5 Sts work in pairs and practise saying the sentences. Play audio track 5.5. See SB page opposite for audio script. Sts listen and check their answers, then listen again and repeat.

B Ask a student to read out the first sentence. Ask another student: *Do you think that's true or false?* Invite the student to give their opinion and make a sentence with you. Ask the first student to confirm if it is true or false. In pairs, sts then say the sentences to each other and guess whether they are true or false. Get feedback on who guessed all their partner's sentences correctly.

7 A Pre-teach *to contact someone*. Sts read the job advert and answer the question. Check the answer.

Answer
An *au pair* looks after children for a family.

B 5.6 Read through the activities in the table with the class and make sure sts understand them all. Play audio track 5.6. See TB page 309 for audio script. Sts listen and tick what the people can do. Check answers.

Answers
Emily can: cook, drive, swim, play the piano
Ben can: cook, speak Spanish, play tennis, swim, play the guitar, sing

3 x PRACTICE *SB page 43, exercise 7B*

1 Do the exercise as normal. To check answers, say a sentence about each ability, with some true sentences and some false, e.g. *Emily and Ben can cook. Ben can drive but Emily can't.* Sts correct the false sentences.

2 Play audio track 5.6 again, pausing after each of the questions. Sts try to remember Emily or Ben's answer, referring to their answers in the table to help them. They then listen to check.

3 In pairs, sts each choose one of the people, Emily or Ben. Their partner asks the questions in the table, and they answer giving Emily or Ben's answers. Encourage them to add the extra information that Emily and Ben give, e.g. *I can sing, but I'm not very good.*

8 5.7 Explain to sts that they must now think about who is best for the job – Emily or Ben. Read out the example question and answer. Sts ask and answer questions and decide who is best for the job. Play audio track 5.7. See TB page 309 for audio script. Sts listen to check their answers. Ask who guessed correctly.

Answer
Ben

Go to Communication practice
Divide the class into Student A and Student B. All 'Student A' sts should go to SB page 137. All 'Student B' sts should go to SB page 145. Go to TB page 287 for the teacher notes. Do the activity, then continue with exercise 9A of lesson 5A.

9 A Focus on the table and allow sts time to read through the questions. Explain to sts that they are going to move around the classroom and ask their classmates questions about abilities, and they need to find a different person who answers 'Yes, I can' to each question. Explain that they also need to find out more information. Read out the example questions and answers, then read through the other questions with the class and elicit some possible follow-up questions to get more information. Sts move around the class to ask and answer questions and complete the table.

B Sts discuss in pairs what they learned about their classmates. Get feedback on their discussions.

PERSONAL BEST

Sts can practise talking about abilities further. They write ten sentences about people in their class using *can* and *can't*. They can compare their sentences in pairs.

Weaker sts could write four sentences about themselves, two using *can* and two using *can't*. Ask some sts to read their sentences to the class.

Learning Curve

5B I can't live without my phone

1 Match the words in the box with the electronic devices 1–6. Is your family like this?

headphones laptop smartphone MP3 player TV remote control

1 ________ 2 ________ 3 ________ 4 ________ 5 ________ 6 ________

Personal Best

Go to Vocabulary practice: electronic devices, page 118

2 Which electronic devices do you have? Discuss in pairs.

I have a laptop, but I don't have a tablet.

3 5.9 Watch or listen to the first part of *Learning Curve*. Tick (✓) the devices Kate mentions.

camera ☐ desktop computer ☐ TV ☐ smartphone ☐ laptop ☐ headphones ☐

Skill listening for specific information

We sometimes need to listen for specific information.

- Read the questions to find out what information you need.
- Think about the topic and what type of information it is, e.g. a person, a place, a number, etc.
- Listen carefully when the speakers talk about this topic.

4 5.9 Read the Skill box. Watch or listen again and choose the correct options to answer the questions.

1 Which sport does Kate do on Friday?
 a basketball b football c tennis
2 What language does she learn on her tablet and phone?
 a Spanish b French c Italian
3 What device can't she live without?
 a tablet b camera c phone
4 How many photos do people take every year?
 a one million b one billion c one trillion
5 How many televisions do people in the USA have?
 a 116 million b 123 million c 26 million

5B I can't live without my phone

Sts learn vocabulary for electronic devices, then watch or listen to an episode of *Learning Curve* in which people talk about the devices they can't live without. They then discuss which devices are important to them.

Listening	Skill	Listening builder	Vocabulary
Sts watch a video or listen to a recording of people talking about their electronic devices and why they couldn't live without them.	Listening for specific information	Sentence stress	Electronic devices (*desktop computer, DVD player, DVR (digital video recorder), earphones, headphones, laptop, MP3 player, radio, remote control, Sat Nav, smartphone, TV (television)*)

WARMER

Ask: *Who has a smartphone with them today? What can you use it for?* Elicit the different things you can use a smartphone for, e.g. making phone calls, texting, accessing social media, taking photos, using the internet. Make notes on the board. Ask: *Do you always have your smartphone with you? Do you ever leave it at home?* Elicit a range of answers, and see if anyone in the class does not have their phone with them at all times.

1 Read through the words in the box with the class and teach the meanings if necessary. Explain that these are all kinds of electronic devices. Sts match the words with the devices in the picture. Check answers, then ask: *Is your family like this?* Discuss as a class in what ways sts' families are like the family in the picture. Ask more questions to prompt discussion, e.g. *Do they spend a lot of time on electronic devices? When* do they put their devices down and talk to each other?

Answers
1 laptop 2 TV 3 remote control 4 MP3 player
5 headphones 6 smartphone

Go to Vocabulary practice: electronic devices, SB page 118/TB page 249.
Sts will find more language presentation and practice for electronic devices here. Do these exercises with the class, or set them for homework, before continuing with exercise 2 of lesson 5B.

PB Remind sts to go to the app for further self-study vocabulary practice of electronic devices.

2 Sts discuss in pairs which devices they have and don't have. Hold a brief class discussion, and see which devices are the most popular with the class.

3 5.9 In this episode of *Learning Curve*, Kate and Simon interview people about the electronic devices they can't live without. Read out the task, then play video/audio track 5.9. See TB page 310 for video/audio script. Sts watch/listen and tick the devices Kate mentions. Check answers.

Answers
camera, TV, smartphone, laptop

Skill

Read the Skill box with sts about listening for specific information. Explain that specific information might be the name of something, a time, a number, a person, etc.

4 5.9 Allow sts time to read through the questions and options. Check they understand the sports in question 1 and teach the meaning of *rock climbing* and *to work out* (= to do exercise in a gym). Check they know how to say the numbers in question 5 and understand the meanings. Read out question 5 and explain that the people who watch a TV programme are the *viewers*. Play video/audio track 5.9 again. Sts watch/listen and choose the correct options. Check answers, playing the video/audio again if necessary for sts to hear the correct answers.

Answers
1 a 2 b 3 c 4 c 5 a

5 5.10 Watch or listen to the rest of the show. Complete the sentences with the words in the box.

headphones DVR car laptop tablet music

1 Simon can't live without ________ or his ________ .

2 Parminder can't live without her ________ and ________ .

3 Vincent can't live without his ________ and his ________ .

6 5.10 Watch or listen again. Choose the correct options to complete the sentences.

1 Parminder uses her devices for *presentations / letters / games*.
2 She uses her devices *at the weekend / at night / every day*.
3 Vincent can play *the piano / the violin / the guitar*.
4 His car is from *1962 / 1967 / 1972*.
5 Simon travels *by underground / on foot / by car*.

7 5.11 Listen to Vincent's sentence. Is it easy to hear the underlined words? Why?

And when I get home, I watch TV at night.

Listening builder sentence stress

In English, we stress the important words in sentences. You can usually understand the general idea if you only hear these words.

I play basketball on Fridays with a women's team.
I work for a big company and we use all the top technology.

8 **A** 5.12 Read the Listening builder. Read and listen to sentences 1–4. Can you understand them?

1 ________ can't live without ________ phone. ________ ________ call people ________ take photos.
2 ________ brother's ________ doctor. ________ usually goes ________ ________ hospital ________ car.
3 Kevin wants ________ new laptop, ________ ________ very expensive.
4 ________ ________ morning, ________ always listen ________ ________ radio.

B 5.12 Listen again and complete the sentences with the unstressed words.

9 In pairs, talk about your electronic devices. Answer the questions.

1 What do you use your devices for?
2 Which device can't you live without? Why not?

A *I use my phone to listen to music and take photos. What about you?*
B *I don't use my phone to listen to music. I have an MP3 player.*

Personal Best Write about your favourite electronic device. Say when and where you use it.

EXTRA PRACTICE Workbook page 29

5 5.10 Allow sts time to read through the gapped sentences, and point out the words in the box. Remind sts that in this exercise they are listening for specific information, so they need to listen carefully. Play video/audio track 5.10. See TB page 310 for video/audio script. Sts watch/listen and complete the sentences with the correct words. Check answers.

Answers
1 music, headphones 2 laptop, tablet 3 DVR, car

6 5.10 Sts read the sentences. Check they understand all the words in the options, especially *presentations, by underground* and *on foot*. Elicit how to say the dates in question 4. Play video/audio track 5.10 again. Sts watch/listen and choose the correct options to complete the sentences. Check answers. Play the track again, pausing for sts to hear why each answer is correct.

Answers
1 presentations 2 every day 3 the guitar 4 1972
5 underground

7 5.11 Focus on the speech bubble, and point out the underlined words. Read out the question, then play audio track 5.11. See SB page opposite for audio script. Discuss the answer to the question as a class.

Answer
Yes, because they are stressed.

Listening builder

Read the Listening builder box with sts about sentence stress. Explain that stressed words are spoken more clearly than other words, and they are pronounced with strong vowels, not the schwa. Point out that the stressed words in a sentence are the important words, like the nouns, verbs and adjectives, so it is possible to understand the general idea of the sentence even if you don't hear all the smaller, unstressed words. Ask questions to check concept.

Concept check questions:
What does it mean if a word is stressed? (you say it clearly, and with strong vowels). *Which words are usually stressed in a sentence?* (important words like nouns, verbs and adjectives). *Which words are not stressed?* (small words like prepositions and articles). *Is it important to hear every word in a sentence?* (no, you can usually understand the general idea if you just hear the stressed words).

8 **A** 5.12 Sts read the gapped sentences. Elicit what some of the missing words might be. Play audio track 5.12. See SB page opposite for audio script. Sts listen, paying attention to the stressed words. Ask: *Can you understand the sentences?* Elicit that it is possible to understand them, even if you can't hear all the unstressed words clearly.

B 5.12 Play the audio again so students can complete the sentences with the unstressed words. Check answers.

Answers
1 I can't live without **my** phone. **I can** call people **and** take photos.
2 **My** brother's **a** doctor. **He** usually goes **to the** hospital **by** car.
3 Kevin wants **a** new laptop **but they're** very expensive.
4 **In the** morning, **I** always listen **to the** radio.

9 As a round-up, sts discuss the electronic devices that they use. They read the questions and prepare their answers, then discuss the questions in pairs. Encourage them to listen carefully to their partner's answers. Ask some sts to tell the class something about their partner.

PERSONAL BEST

Sts can practise talking about electronic devices further. They write about their favourite electronic device, saying when and where they use it. They can compare their paragraphs in small groups.

For weaker sts, write on the board: *I use my ... When? Where? What for?* Ask sts to choose an electronic device that they use, and write three sentences about it to answer the three questions on the board. Ask some sts to read their sentences to the class.

EXTRA PRACTICE

Sts work in groups of three. They take turns to use their phones to film their classmates asking and answering the questions in exercise 9. Allow sts time to watch the films of themselves. Watching themselves on film will help sts to evaluate how naturally and fluently they can speak.

5C I love it!

1 Match the words in the box with pictures a–f.

cycling walking cleaning swimming reading cooking

a 
b 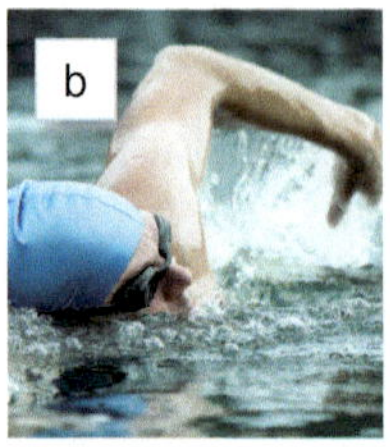
c 
d 
e 
f 

Personal Best

Go to Vocabulary practice: activities, page 119

2 A Write two activities in each column.

I love ...	I like ...	I don't like ...	I hate ...

B Tell your partner about what you love, like, don't like and hate.

A *I love cooking.* **B** *Really? I hate cooking. I love going out!*

3 A Look at the pictures on the webpage. What activities can you see?

B Read the text. Complete the sentences with *loves*, *likes*, *doesn't like* and *hates*.

1 Midori ________ listening to music. She ________ Adele.
2 Laura ________ shopping for food.
3 Diego ________ his grandad.
4 Josh ________ sleeping late because he ________ early mornings.
5 Ellie ________ watching movies with her friends and she ________ popcorn.

That's (i)nteresting

LIKES AND DISLIKES

I like listening to music. Adele is my favourite singer. I love her!

♥ 4 **Midori**

I like watching movies with my friends. We always have a big bowl of popcorn – I love it!

♥ 6 **Ellie**

My brother and I don't like shopping for food. Mum always takes us at the weekend!

♥ 7 **Laura**

I love my grandad. I can always talk to him and he helps me a lot.

♥ 12 **Diego**

I love sleeping late at weekends. Early mornings? I hate them!

♥ 3 **Josh**

5C I love it!

Sts read a web page where people have written about things they like and dislike. They then talk about things they like and dislike.

Grammar	Vocabulary	Pronunciation	Communication
Object pronouns (*me, you, him, her, it, us, them*)	Activities (*cleaning, cooking, cycling, dancing, going out, listening to music, meeting friends, reading, running, shopping, sleeping, swimming, walking, watching TV/films*)	/h/	Talking about activities you like and dislike

WARMER

With books closed, ask: *What do you usually do at the weekend?* Elicit a few ideas, e.g. *watch TV, meet friends*, then put sts into pairs and give them two minutes to write as many ideas as they can. Bring all the ideas together on the board and check that sts understand them all. See which activities are the most popular with the class.

1 Read through the activities in the box with the class and teach the meanings if necessary. In pairs, sts match the words with the pictures. Check answers. Model and drill pronunciation of the words.

Answers
1 walking 2 swimming 3 cooking 4 cleaning
5 cycling 6 reading

3 x PRACTICE *SB page 46, exercise 1*

1 Do the exercise as normal. To check answers, focus on each picture in turn and ask an individual student to say the correct word. Ask another student: *Do you agree?*

2 In pairs, sts cover the words, then look at the pictures and try to remember the words. They can look at the words and their answers again to check.

3 With books closed, mime one of the activities, e.g. mime *cycling*. Sts race to say the correct word. Invite sts in turn to mime the words for other sts to guess.

Go to Vocabulary practice: activities, SB page 119/TB page 251.
Sts will find more language presentation and practice for activities here. Do these exercises with the class, or set them for homework, before continuing with exercise 2A of lesson 5C.

PB Remind sts to go to the app for further self-study vocabulary practice of activities.

2 A Focus on the table and check that sts understand *love* and *hate*. Sts add two activities to each column.

B Read out the example answers, and remind sts that we use *Really?* to express surprise. Sts discuss their likes and dislikes in pairs. Ask some sts to tell the class which likes and dislikes they share, and which are different. You could teach the use of *both*, e.g. *We both love cycling*.

3 A Put sts into pairs to look at the pictures and identify the activities. Check answers, making sure sts use the *-ing* form for each activity,

Answers
listening to music, shopping, reading, sleeping, watching movies/films

B Focus on the first part of the text (Midori). Ask sts to read it, then focus on the first gapped sentence and elicit the complete sentence. Remind them if necessary about the *he/she/it* ending for present simple verbs (*likes*). Sts then read the rest of the text and complete the sentences with the correct words. Check answers.

Answers
1 likes, loves 2 doesn't like 3 loves 4 loves, hates
5 likes, loves

4 A Match the object pronouns in **bold** with the people and things. Read the text again and check.

1 I love **her**!
2 Mum always takes **us** at the weekend!
3 I can always talk to **him**.
4 He helps **me** a lot.
5 I hate **them**!
6 I love **it**!

a Diego
b early mornings
c Adele
d popcorn
e Laura and her brother
f Diego's grandad

B Choose the correct words to complete the sentences. Then read the Grammar box.

1 We use object pronouns instead of *people and things* / *times and places*.
2 We use object pronouns *before* / *after* verbs.

Grammar object pronouns

Subject pronouns:	Object pronouns:	
I	me	*I don't understand. Can you help **me**?*
you	you	*Are **you** Adam? This is for **you**.*
he	him	***He** isn't friendly. I don't like **him**.*
she	her	***She** works in your office. Do you know **her**?*
it	it	***It**'s perfect. I love **it**!*
we	us	***We**'re in the garden. Can you see **us**?*
they	them	***They**'re new here. I don't know **them**.*

Personal Best

Go to Grammar practice: object pronouns, page 100

5 A 5.15 **Pronunciation:** /h/ Listen and repeat. Pay attention to the sound /h/.

him her he help happy

B 5.16 Say the questions and sentences. Then listen, check and repeat.

1 Do you like him? 2 I can't see her. 3 He hates horses. 4 Hi, Harry. How are you?

6 5.17 Complete the conversation with object pronouns. Listen and check.

A Do you like Emma Stone?
B Yes, I do. I love [1]________ . She's great!
A What about Bruno Mars?
B Yes, I like [2]________ too.
A Do you like shopping for clothes?
B No, I hate [3]________ .
A Do you like Monday mornings?
B No, I hate [4]________ .
A What do you think of cats?
B I don't like [5]________ , but they like [6]________ !

Go to Communication practice: Student A page 138, Student B page 146

7 A Write three examples in each of the circles.

singers and bands
____
____
____

actors
____
____
____

food and drink
____
____
____

animals
____
____
____

activities
____
____
____

B In pairs, ask and answer questions about the people and things.

Do you like ...? What about ...? What do you think of ...?

8 Tell the class about you and your partner.

We both love cats. I like Ryan Gosling, but Carla doesn't like him.

Personal Best Write a conversation like the one in exercise 6 between you and someone in your family.

4 A Read out the first sentence and point out the bold pronoun. Ask: *Who does 'her' refer to?* Read out the possible answers a–f and elicit the correct answer (Adele). Ask sts to read the text about Midori again to check. Sts then complete the matching task and check their answers in the text. Check answers with the class.

Answers
1 c 2 e 3 f 4 a 5 b 6 d

B Read out the sentences and elicit the correct words to complete them, referring back to the sentences in 4A to help sts if necessary.

Answers
1 people and things 2 after

Grammar

Read the Grammar box with sts about object pronouns. Point out to sts that they already know the subject pronouns, which are used before a verb. Point out that *you* and *it* have the same subject and object pronouns, e.g. *You like cycling. I can see you. It is interesting. I like it.* But all the other object pronouns are different from the subject pronouns. Read out the examples, stressing the bold pronouns to reinforce the difference between subject and object pronouns. Ask questions to check concept.

Concept check questions:
What do pronouns refer to? (people and things). *When do we use subject pronouns?* (before a verb). *When do we use object pronouns?* (after a verb). ***We** like movies – subject or object pronoun?* (subject). *Jake likes **us** – subject or object pronoun?* (object). *Tom's over there – can you see he? – correct?* (no – can you see *him*?). *I have two brothers. I love they – correct?* (no – I love them). *She's nice – I like …* (her). *Which two object pronouns are the same as the subject pronouns?* (*you* and *it*).

Go to Grammar practice: object pronouns, SB page 100/ TB page 213.
Sts will find more language reference, presentation and practice for object pronouns here. Do these exercises with the class, or set them for homework, before continuing with exercise 5A of lesson 5C.

PB Remind sts to go to the app for further self-study grammar practice of object pronouns.

5 A 5.15 Model pronunciation of the /h/ sound in isolation and explain that many sts find this sound difficult to produce. Play audio track 5.15 once for sts to listen and notice the /h/ sound. See SB page opposite for audio script. Play the audio again for sts to listen and repeat.

B 5.16 Sts practise saying the sentences in pairs. Play audio track 5.16 once for sts to check their answers. See SB page opposite for audio script. Play the audio again for sts to repeat.

6 5.17 Read out the first gapped sentence of the conversation and elicit the correct object pronoun to complete it. Sts then complete the conversation with the correct object pronouns. Play audio track 5.17. See SB page opposite for audio script. Sts listen to check their answers. Check with the class.

Answers
1 her 2 him 3 it 4 them 5 them 6 me

Go to Communication practice
Divide the class into Student A and Student B. All 'Student A' sts should go to SB page 138. All 'Student B' sts should go to SB page 146. Go to TB page 289 for the teacher notes. Do the activity, then continue with exercise 7A of lesson 5C.

7 A Focus on the first category and elicit some examples of singers and bands that sts could add to it, e.g. *Rihanna*, *Adele*. Sts then complete the circles individually. If sts are struggling with some of the categories, e.g. *animals*, you could brainstorm some ideas with the class and write some words on the board for sts to choose from.

B Demonstrate the activity with a confident pair of sts. Ask one student to ask a question, and encourage the other student to answer. Sts then work in pairs to ask and answer questions.

8 Read out the example sentence and point out the use of *both*. Ask pairs in turn to tell the class something about themselves.

PERSONAL BEST

Sts can practise using object pronouns further. They write a conversation like the one in exercise 6 between them and someone in their family. Sts could practise their conversations in pairs.

Weaker sts could look at the conversation in exercise 6 again and make a few changes to make it true for them, e.g. by changing the names of the singers, or some of the activities, and changing the opinions. They can then practise the conversation in pairs.

5D My profile

1 A Look at the profile on the 'CityMeet' app. What do you think you can do with the app?

a find an apartment in a city **b** make new friends in a city **c** find a new job in a city

B Read the profile and check.

4G

Profile

CITY MEET

Tom Garcia
San Diego

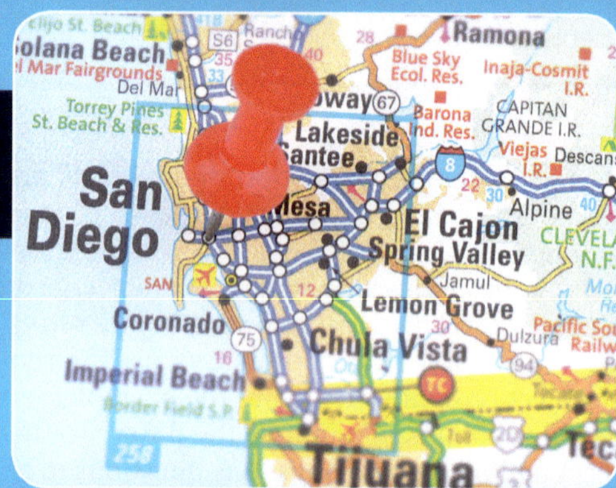

About me

Hi! I'm Tom Garcia. I'm twenty-nine. I work for a technology company. The company makes games and apps for mobile phones.

I'm from Oregon, but I live in San Diego, California. I'm new here. I share a small apartment near the beach with my best friend. I like San Diego because it's a beautiful city and the weather's great.

In my free time, I like running, playing the guitar and watching TV series. I also enjoy surfing because it's a great way to relax after work and I love the sea. I love making new friends and going out, so send me a message!

2 Read the profile again. Complete the sentences with the correct words.

1 Tom works for a ________ company.
2 He's from ________, but he lives in ________.
3 He lives near the ________ with his ________.
4 He thinks the weather in San Diego is ________.
5 He plays the ________ and watches ________ in his free time.
6 He loves making ________.

Skill describing yourself

When you write a text to describe yourself, use a different paragraph for each topic.

- personal information about you and your job: *Hi! My name's Fiona. I'm a teacher.*
- where you live: *I live in York. I share a flat with my best friend.*
- what you do in your free time: *In my free time, I like listening to music and cooking for friends.*
- information about your family: *I have a brother. His name's Paul and he's 18.*

3 Read the Skill box. Tick (✓) the topics which are in Tom's profile.

a his job ☐ **b** where he lives ☐ **c** his family ☐ **d** his free-time activities ☐

5D My profile

Sts read an online profile of a young American. They study tips for describing themselves and the use of *because*, then write their own online profile.

Writing	Skill	Text builder
An online profile	Describing yourself	*because*

WARMER

Ask: *What problems do people sometimes have when they move to a new city? What things can be difficult?* Elicit a range of ideas, e.g. finding somewhere to live, meeting people and making new friends, finding the best places to go shopping or go out, etc.

1 **A** Elicit the meaning of *profile* (= a description of a person). Explain that this profile is on an app. Sts look at the profile and guess what you can do with the app. Elicit a few ideas, but don't confirm them.

B Sts read the profile to check their ideas. Check the answer with the class and ask: *Do you think this is a good idea for an app? Why?*

Answer
b

2 Read out the first gapped sentence and elicit the correct word to complete it. Sts read the profile again and complete the sentences with the correct words. Check answers, and check that sts understand all the sentences.

Answers
1 technology
2 Oregon, San Diego
3 beach, best friend
4 great
5 guitar, TV series
6 new friends

Skill

Read the Skill box with sts about describing yourself. Check that sts understand *paragraph* and *topic*. Refer back to Tom's profile in exercise 1 to reinforce the point that you should use a different paragraph for each topic.

3 Sts then look at Tom's profile again and tick the topics he mentions. Check answers.

Answers
a, b, d

4 Complete Kimberley's profile with sentences a–c.

a I also love travelling because it's a great way to meet new people.
b I study French and Spanish. I can also speak Portuguese.
c We love San Diego because it's a fun and exciting city.

ABOUT ME

Hello! I'm Kimberley Watson and I'm a student at the University of San Diego. [1]____
I live in a house with four friends. We're all students. [2]____
In my free time, I like watching French films, running and going out with my friends. [3]____

5 Imagine Tom and Kimberley meet on CityMeet. Do they become friends? Choose an option and complete the sentence.

Tom and Kimberley *become / don't become* friends because ______________________________.

Text builder *because*

We use *because* to give a reason. It answers the question *Why?*
*I like San Diego **because** it's a beautiful city.*
Why do you like travelling? ***Because** it's a great way to meet new people.*

6 **A** Read the Text builder and find sentences with *because* in Tom and Kimberley's profiles. How do you say *because* in your language?

B Match 1–5 with a–e. Make sentences with *because*.

1 I live in a small flat
2 I go to work by bus
3 I like swimming
4 I don't often go to the gym
5 I like living in a village

a I'm usually tired after work.
b it's good exercise.
c it's quiet and the people are friendly.
d houses in my city are expensive.
e I can't drive.

7 Complete the sentences with your own ideas.

1 I love my city/town because ______________________________.
2 I'm often tired in the evening because ______________________________.
3 I like cooking because ______________________________.
4 I don't often go out because ______________________________.
5 I usually get up early because ______________________________.

8 **A** **PREPARE** Plan an online profile for you. Decide what information to include. Make notes about:

- your personal information
- your work or study
- where you live and who you live with
- your free-time activities and why you like them

B **PRACTISE** Write your profile. Use one paragraph for each topic. Remember to use *because* to give reasons.

C **PERSONAL BEST** Read your partner's profile. Does each paragraph contain one topic? Choose a paragraph that you like and tell your partner why you like it.

Personal Best Write a profile of a friend or someone in your family.

4 Read through sentences a–c with the class and make sure sts understand everything. Remind them if necessary of the use of *can* for abilities in sentence b. Sts read Kimberley's profile and decide on the best place for each sentence. To help them, encourage sts to think about the topic of each paragraph in the profile, and which sentence goes with each topic. Check answers.

> **Answers**
> 1 b 2 c 3 a

5 Sts read the two profiles again and decide if the people become friends and why or why not. Explain that there is no right answer for this task, but sts should use their own judgement. Discuss their ideas as a class.

Text builder

Read the Text builder box with sts about *because*. Explain that we use *because* to give a reason, to answer the question *why?*. Point out that we can use *because* as a linker to join two sentences together, e.g. *I love travelling because it's interesting*. We can also use it to give a reason as an answer to a direct question, e.g. *Why do you like travelling? Because it's interesting*. Ask questions to check concept.

Concept check questions:
Why do we use 'because' (to give a reason, and answer the question *why?*). *Can we use 'because' as a linker, to join sentences together?* (yes). *I like football. It's fun. – Can you join these sentences with 'because'?* (yes – I like football *because* it's fun). *When can you use 'because' at the beginning of a sentence?* (when it's the answer to a question with *why?*). *Why do you like this city? – can you think of an answer with 'because'* (e.g. ... *because* it's a big city and it's exciting).

6 A Sts find sentences with *because* in Tom and Kimberley's profiles. Check answers, then ask sts how they say *because* in their own language.

> **Answers**
> **Tom**
> I like San Diego because it's a beautiful city and the weather's great.
> I also enjoy surfing because it's a great way to relax after work and I love the sea.
> **Kimberley**
> We love San Diego because it's a fun and exciting city.
> I also love travelling because it's a great way to meet new people.

B Check that sts understand *flat*, *gym*, *village*, *houses* and *exercise*. Read out the first sentence beginning and add *because*. Elicit a possible ending (d). Sts match the remaining sentence halves and write sentences with *because*. Check answers.

> **Answers**
> 1 d 2 e 3 b 4 a 5 c

3 x PRACTICE *SB page 49, exercise 6B*

1 Do the exercise as normal. To check answers, ask sts in turn to read out the sentence beginnings. Ask other sts to complete each sentence with the correct reason.

2 In pairs, sts cover a–e and try to remember the reason for each sentence beginning. They can uncover a–e and look at their answers to check.

3 In pairs, sts write a different reason for each sentence beginning, e.g. *I live in a small flat because I don't like big houses*. Put pairs together into groups of four. They take turns to read out their reasons in a random order. The other pair guesses which sentence beginning each one goes with.

7 Sts complete the sentences with their own ideas. They can change the sentence beginnings to make them true for them if they like, e.g. *I don't like my town/city because ... .* Ask some sts to read some of their sentences to the class.

8 Sts follow the steps to write an online profile.

A PREPARE Sts read the notes and prepare their ideas. Monitor while they are working, and help if necessary.

B PRACTISE Sts write their profile. Refer them back to the Skill box to remind them how to organize their profile into different paragraphs, and refer them to the Text builder box to remind them how to use *because*.

C PERSONAL BEST Sts work in pairs. They swap their profile with a partner to check that each paragraph contains just one topic and give feedback on a paragraph they like.

PERSONAL BEST

Sts can practise describing people further. They write a profile about a friend or someone in their family. Point out that they need to use *he/she* forms of the verbs. Sts can share their profiles in pairs and give feedback on a paragraph they like.

Weaker sts can swap their profiles from exercise 8 with a partner. They rewrite their partner's profile using *he/she* forms. They can check their new profiles together for accuracy.

EXTRA PRACTICE

Write the following gapped sentences on the board:

1 I work ______ a technology company.
2 I share a small apartment ______ the beach ______ my best friend.
3 It's a great way to relax ______ work.
4 I'm a student ______ the University ______ San Diego.
5 I live ______ a house ______ four friends.

Explain to sts that the missing words are all prepositions (small words that tell us about place, time or relationships between people). Write these prepositions on the board: *after, at, for, in, near, of, with*. In pairs, sts complete the sentences from memory, then read the profiles of Tom and Kimberley again to check. Check answers.

> **Answers**
> 1 for 2 near, with 3 after 4 at, of 5 in, with

UNIT
6
Places

LANGUAGE *there is/are* ■ places in a town

6A City or village?

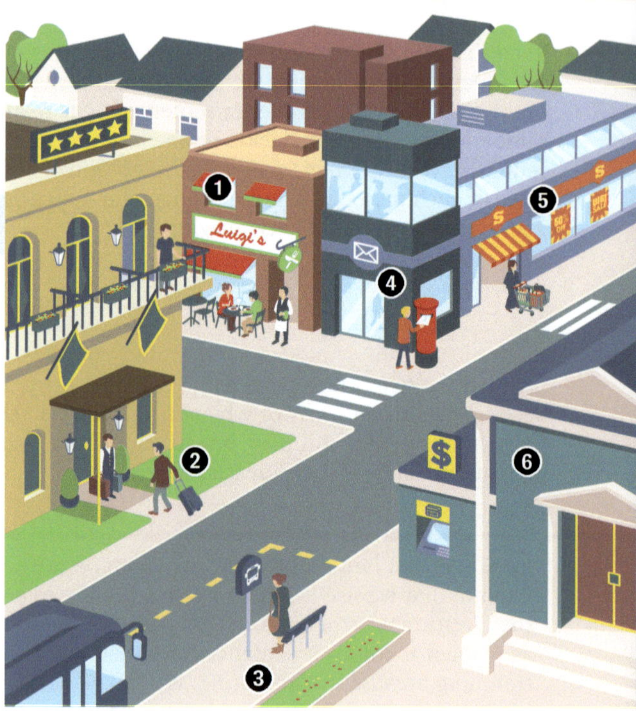

1 Match the words in the box with places 1–6.

bank bus stop restaurant hotel supermarket post office

1 ________ 3 ________ 5 ________
2 ________ 4 ________ 6 ________

Personal Best

Go to Vocabulary practice: places in a town, page 120

2 **A** Look at the pictures of Whycocomagh in Canada. Is it a city, town or village?

B Read the text and tick (✓) the things Whycocomagh has.

1 shopping centre ☐ 3 cinema ☐ 5 school ☐
2 supermarket ☐ 4 nightclub ☐ 6 restaurants ☐

An unusual job offer

Whycocomagh is a small village on the beautiful island of Cape Breton in Canada, but the local supermarket has a problem. It needs three new shop assistants and people don't want to come to live in Whycocomagh because it's very quiet and far from any big cities.

So the owners of the Farmer's Daughter store put an unusual job advert on Facebook. It says, *'We can't give you big money, but we can give you an awesome life'* … and they offer over 8 km^2 of free land!

Thousands of people from around the world are interested and want to work in the village, so now the supermarket has some new shop assistants. But what's the village really like? We talk to Kelly Jenkins, a teacher at the village school.

Tell us about Whycocomagh, Kelly.
It's small, but it's beautiful. There's a school, a post office and the local supermarket, of course! There are also some hotels and restaurants for tourists.

Is there a shopping centre or a cinema?
No, there isn't! There aren't any big shops and there isn't a cinema or a nightclub. But there are some wonderful people here. Everyone is very friendly.

Are there any problems?
Yes, there are … but life's boring without any problems!

3 Complete the sentences with the words in the box. Check your answers in the text.

isn't 's aren't are (x2) is

1 There ________ a school.
2 ________ there a shopping centre?
3 There ________ any big shops.
4 There ________ a cinema.
5 There ________ some wonderful people.
6 ________ there any problems?

Places

UNIT 6

UNIT 6 OVERVIEW: The topic for this unit is places. Sts read about life in cities and villages, then talk about the place where they live. They read about a student who lives on a boat before describing a room in their own home. In *Learning Curve*, sts watch or listen to Simon giving directions.

LANGUAGE		
Grammar	**Vocabulary**	**Pronunciation**
there is/are; prepositions of place	Places in a town; parts of the body; rooms and furniture	Linking consonants and vowels; sentence stress

SKILLS	
Reading	**Speaking**
Reading in detail; giving opinions	Checking information; asking for and giving directions

LANGUAGE 6A

6A City or village?

Sts read a text about a small village in rural Canada and the city of Lavasa in India. They listen to a conversation in which someone talks about the place where they live, then ask and answer questions about the place where they live.

Grammar	**Vocabulary**	**Pronunciation**	**Communication**
there is/are	Places in a town (*bank, bus stop, café, cinema, hospital, hotel, museum, nightclub, park, police station, post office, restaurant, school, shopping centre, supermarket, train station*)	Linking consonants and vowels	Talking about the place where you live

WARMER

Ask: *What can you see in a city?* Elicit a few ideas, e.g. shops, schools, then put sts into pairs and give them two minutes to make a list of all the things you can see in cities. They can use their dictionaries to help. Bring the words together on the board and check that sts understand them all. Ask: *Which things are there in your town or city? Which things can you see in a village?* Elicit answers, and elicit some differences between cities and villages. Tell sts they are going to read about the different places where people live.

1 Read through the words in the box with the class and teach the meanings if necessary. Sts look at the pictures in pairs and match them with the words. Check answers, then model and drill pronunciation of the words.

Answers
1 restaurant 2 hotel 3 bus stop 4 post office
5 supermarket 6 bank

3 x PRACTICE *SB page 50, exercise 1*

1 Do the exercise as normal. To check answers, focus on each place in turn and ask: *Is this a (cinema/bank)?* Elicit sts' ideas, then confirm the answers.

2 In pairs, sts cover the words and look at the pictures They try to remember the correct word for each place. They can look at the words in the box and their answers to check.

3 Refer sts to the Vocabulary practice section on page 120 and work through the exercises. Give a one-word clue for one of the places, e.g. *eat* (restaurant), *money* (bank). Sts race to say the correct place.

Go to Vocabulary practice: places in a town, SB page 120/TB page 253.
Sts will find more language presentation and practice for places in a town here. Do these exercises with the class, or set them for homework, before continuing with exercise 2A of lesson 6A.

PB Remind sts to go to the app for further self-study vocabulary practice of places in a town.

2 A Refer sts to the pictures and read out the question. Model pronunciation of the place name /waɪˈkɒgəmə/, and check that sts understand the difference between *city*, *town* and *village*. Encourage sts to guess the answers.

Answer
It's a village.

B Sts read the text quickly and tick the things that Whycocomagh has. Check answers.

Answer
2, 5, 6

3 Sts complete the sentences with the correct words, then check their answers in the text.

Answers
1 's 2 Is 3 aren't 4 isn't 5 are 6 Are

4 Look at the sentences in exercise 3 again and choose the correct options to complete the rules. Then read the Grammar box.

1 We use *there's* and *there isn't* with *singular / plural* nouns.
2 We use *there are* and *there aren't* with *singular / plural* nouns.
3 We use *some / any* with plural nouns in positive sentences.
4 We use *some / any* with plural nouns in negative sentences and questions.

Grammar *there is/are*

Positive:	Negative:	Questions:	Short answers:	
There's *a cinema.*	***There isn't*** *a museum.*	***Is there*** *a park?*	*Yes,* ***there is.***	*No,* ***there isn't.***
There are *some shops.*	***There aren't*** *any cafés.*	***Are there*** *any hotels?*	*Yes,* ***there are.***	*No,* ***there aren't.***

Personal Best

Go to Grammar practice: *there is/are*, page 101

5 In pairs, say if you want to live in Whycocomagh. Explain your answers.

I don't want to live in Wycocomagh because there ...

6 6.3 Complete the text with the correct form of *there is/are*. Listen and check.

This is the beautiful city of Lavasa in India. [1]________ some nice flats near the river. [2]________ a post office, a police station and [3]________ some great restaurants and cafés. [4]________ a train station, but if you need to travel by train, you can take a taxi to Pune, which is 60 km away. However, [5]________ something strange about Lavasa ... nobody lives here! [6]________ any people in the flats. At the weekends, [7]________ some tourists in the restaurants and hotels, but they're on holiday.

7 A 6.4 **Pronunciation:** linking consonants and vowels Listen and repeat the sentences from exercise 6. Pay attention to how the sounds link together.

1 There's‿a post‿office.
2 There‿isn't‿a train station.
3 There‿aren't‿any people.
4 There‿are some tourists.

B 6.5 Say the sentences linking the sounds together. Listen, check and repeat.

1 There's‿a hospital.
2 Is there‿a bank?
3 There‿are some‿offices.
4 There‿aren't‿any museums.
5 There‿isn't‿a park.
6 Are there‿any schools?

Go to Communication practice: Student A page 138, Student B page 146

8 A 6.6 Listen to the conversation. Where does Erica live? Is she happy there?

B 6.6 Are the sentences about the area where Erica lives true (T) or false (F)? Listen again and check.

1 There's a big park. ____
2 There's a supermarket. ____
3 There aren't any shops. ____
4 There's a café in her street. ____
5 There isn't a bus stop near her house. ____
6 There are some good restaurants. ____

9 Ask and answer the questions in pairs.

Where do you live? | Is it a city, a town or a village? | What's your area like? | Is there a ...? | Are there any ...?

Personal Best Write about a city, town or village you know well.

4 Read through the sentences in exercise 3 again. Focus on the sentences in exercise 4 and check that sts understand *singular*, *plural*, *positive* and *negative*. Sts work in pairs to read the rules and choose the correct options to complete them. Check answers.

Answers
1 singular 2 plural 3 some 4 any

Grammar

Read the Grammar box with sts about *there is/are*. Elicit that we use *there is/are* to talk about things that are in a place. Point out that with singular nouns we use *a* in both positive and negative sentences, e.g. *There is a school / There isn't a school*. Point out that with plural nouns, we use *some* in positive sentences and *any* in negative sentences, e.g. *There are some hotels. There aren't any hotels*. NOT ~~*There aren't some hotels*~~. Point out that in short answers, we have to use the full form of the verb, e.g. *Is there a school? Yes, there is*. NOT ~~*Yes, there's*~~. Ask questions to check concept.

Concept check questions:
When do you we use 'there is' and 'there are'? (to say what things are in a place). *Which forms do we use with singular nouns?* (there is/there isn't). *Which forms do we use with plural nouns?* (there are/there aren't). *There's a supermarket – correct?* (yes). *Can you make the sentence negative?* (There isn't a supermarket). *There are some cafés – correct?* (yes). *Can you make the sentence negative?* (There aren't any cafés).

Go to Grammar practice: *there is/are*. SB page 101/ TB page 215. Sts will find more language reference, presentation and practice for *there is/are* here. Do these exercises with the class, or set them for homework, before continuing with exercise 5 of lesson 6A.

PB Remind sts to go to the app for further self-study grammar practice of *there is/are*.

5 Read out the sentence and elicit a way of completing it, e.g. ... *there aren't any nightclubs*. Say: *I want to live in Wycogomagh because ...* . Elicit some possible answers, e.g. ... *because it's quiet*. Allow sts time to prepare their ideas individually, then put them into pairs to discuss their ideas. Elicit some possible answers from the class.

6 6.3 Focus on the picture and ask: *Where do you think it is?* Elicit a few ideas. Check that sts understand *flats*. Sts then read the text and complete it with the correct forms of *there is/are*. Play audio track 6.3. See SB page opposite for audio script. Sts listen to check their answers.

Answers
1 There are 2 There's 3 there are 4 There isn't
5 there is 6 There aren't 7 there are

7 A 6.4 Explain that when we speak, we often link words together, rather than saying them separately. Elicit the difference between consonants and vowels, and explain that we link consonants and vowels together. As an example, write on the board: *They put an‿advert on Facebook*. Say the sentence, emphasizing how the *n* of *an* links with *advert*. Play audio track 6.4. See SB page opposite for audio script. Sts listen and notice how the sounds link together.

B 6.5 Sts work in pairs and practise saying the sentences, linking the sounds together. Play the audio for sts to check their answers. Check the answers with the class, then play the audio again for sts to repeat.

Go to Communication practice
Divide the class into Student A and Student B. All 'Student A' sts should go to SB page 138. All 'Student B' sts should go to SB page 146. Go to TB page 289 for the teacher notes. Do the activity, then continue with exercise 8 of lesson 6A.

8 A 6.6 Read out the questions and teach the meaning of *area*, then play audio track 6.6. See TB page 310 for audio script. Sts listen and note down the answers to the questions. Check answers with the class, and ask: *Where is Dublin?* (in Ireland). *Is it a city?* (yes). Explain if necessary that Dublin is the capital city of Eire, the Republic of Ireland.

Answers
She lives in Dublin. Yes, she is happy there.

B 6.6 Read out the first sentence and ask: *Is this true or false?* (true). Sts read the remaining sentences and decide if they are true or false. Play audio track 6.6 again. Sts listen and check their answers. Check answers with the class.

Answers
1 T 2 F 3 F 4 T 5 F 6 F

9 Read out the questions, and elicit a few answers to the question: *What's your area like?* (e.g. *it's quiet, nice, horrible*). Elicit a few ways to complete the questions that are not completed, e.g. *Is there a park?, Are there any restaurants?* Ask a confident student about the area where they live, and elicit a few answers. Put sts into pairs to ask and answer questions. Ask some sts to tell the class something they learned about the area where their partner lives.

PERSONAL BEST

Sts can practise describing places further. They write a description of a city, town or village they know well. You could brainstorm a description of a place all the sts know and write it on the board as an example first.

With weaker sts, write some sentence beginnings on the board: *(Rome) is ... ; There's a ... ; There are some ... ; There aren't any ...* . Sts complete the sentences with their own ideas, then compare their sentences in pairs.

6B City art

1 A Look at the pictures of public art on page 53. Do you like them? Why/Why not?

B Read the text quickly. In which cities can you see the three pieces of art?

Skill reading in detail

We sometimes have to read part of a text in detail to understand it well.

- Read the question and find the paragraph of the text that has the information you need.
- Read the paragraph very carefully to answer the question.
- We sometimes use different words and phrases to give the same information.

2 Read the Skill box. Chose the correct options to complete the sentences. Underline the phrase in the text that helped you answer the questions.

1 Carla and Mason have ____ .
 a jobs at the same hotel **b** lots of cameras **c** different opinions about *Eye*
2 Bruno Catalano ____ .
 a makes sculptures **b** only has one arm **c** is from Spain
3 Elodie and Christine ____ .
 a are friends of the artist **b** live in Marseille **c** are on holiday
4 Günther ____ the lifesaver sculpture.
 a likes **b** doesn't like **c** doesn't give an opinion about
5 Helga works ____ .
 a in a school **b** in a restaurant **c** as a taxi driver

3 Match the words in the box with parts of the body 1–7 in the pictures on page 53.

head foot eye body leg hand arm

1 ________ 2 ________ 3 ________ 4 ________ 5 ________ 6 ________ 7 ________

Personal Best

Go to Vocabulary practice: parts of the body, page 121

4 Match the people with the opinions.

1 Carla	**a** 'I don't think it means anything.'
2 Mason	**b** 'I like it.'
3 Elodie and Christine	**c** 'I think this is really ugly.'
4 Günther	**d** 'In my opinion, that's what it means.'
5 Helga	**e** 'It's beautiful.'

Text builder giving opinions

Phrases: *In my opinion, … In my view, …*
Verbs: *I think/don't think … I like/don't like …*
Adjectives: *It's beautiful/ugly/interesting/boring/strange*, etc.

Look! We say: *I don't think it's ugly.*
NOT ~~*I think it isn't ugly.*~~

5 Read the Text builder. In pairs, describe the sculptures in the pictures and give your opinions.

a

b

c

6B City art

Sts read about some examples of city art in the USA, France and Germany. They then give their opinions of some other examples of city art.

Vocabulary	Reading	Skill	Text builder
Parts of the body (*arm, body, ear, eye, face, foot/ feet, hair, hand, head, knee, leg, mouth, nose, tooth/teeth*)	Sts read a text about city art in cities in the USA, France and Germany.	Reading in detail	Giving opinions

WARMER

Write the word *art* on the board and elicit or teach the meaning. Teach the words *painting* and *sculpture* too. Ask: *Where can you see art?* Elicit that you can see it in museums, and also outside, in towns and cities. Teach the expression *public art* and ask: *Is there any public art in your town or city? Do you like seeing art outside? Why/Why not?*

1 A Sts work in pairs and discuss whether they like the public art in the pictures. Discuss each sculpture with the class and encourage sts to join in and give their opinions, giving reasons for their answers.

B Check that sts understand the three subheadings in the text: *eye*, *travellers*, *lifesaver fountain*. Sts read the text quickly and answer the question. Check the answer with the class.

Answer
Eye – Dallas, USA; Travellers – Marseille, France; Lifesaver fountain – Duisburg, Germany

Skill

Read the Skill box with sts about reading in detail. Check they understand *detail*. Read out the first gapped sentence in exercise 2 and the three options. Elicit which paragraph of the text has the information they need (paragraph 1).

2 Ask sts to read each paragraph carefully to find the correct answer. Read out each option in turn and ask: *Is this correct? Why/Why not?* Elicit the detailed information in the text which gives the correct answer. Reinforce the point that the text uses different words and phrases to give the same information as the correct answer. Sts then complete the task. Check answers with the class, eliciting the correct information for each answer.

Answers
1 c 2 a 3 c 4 b 5 a

3 Read through the words in the box with the class and teach as necessary. Sts work in pairs to match the words with the parts of the body in the pictures on page 53. Check answers and point out the irregular plural form for *foot* (*feet*).

Answers
1 eye 2 head 3 arm 4 hand 5 body 6 leg
7 foot

Go to Vocabulary practice: parts of the body, SB page 121/TB page 255.
Sts will find more language presentation and practice for parts of the body here. Do these exercises with the class, or set them for homework, before continuing with exercise 4 of lesson 6B.

PB Remind sts to go to the app for further self-study vocabulary practice of parts of the body.

4 Read out the opinions and check that sts understand them all. Sts then read the text again and match the people with the opinions. Check answers.

Answers
1 d 2 a 3 e 4 c 5 b

Text builder

Read the Text builder box with sts about giving opinions. Explain that phrases such as *in my opinion* and *in my view* are slightly more formal than the other ways of giving opinions. Point out that some adjectives just describe something, e.g. *red*, *big*, *small*, but others give an opinion about it, e.g. *nice*, *boring*. Point out that with negative opinions, we usually use *I don't think*, e.g. *I don't think it's interesting*, NOT ~~*I think it isn't interesting*~~. Ask questions to check concept.

Concept check questions:
What two phrases can you use to give opinions? (in my opinion, in my view). *Which of these adjectives give opinions – big, beautiful, old, quiet, boring?* (beautiful, boring). *I like this sculpture – correct?* (yes). *Can you make the opinion negative?* (I don't like this sculpture). *I think it's beautiful – correct?* (yes). *Can you make the sentence negative?* (I don't think it's beautiful).

5 Focus on the pictures and check that students know the word *horse*. Allow sts time to prepare their opinions individually, then put them into pairs to compare their opinions. Discuss sts' opinions with the class and discuss which sculpture is the most popular and why.

I love it … but what is it?

There's art everywhere in our towns, cities and parks. Sometimes it's good, sometimes it's bad, but it's always interesting.

Eye

In the garden of a five-star hotel in Dallas, USA, there's a 10-metre-high eye, called *Eye*. 'It's really interesting,' says Carla, a receptionist at the hotel. 'There are cameras everywhere today, watching us. In my opinion, that's what it means.' Mason, a waiter from another hotel, doesn't agree. 'I don't think it means anything,' he says. 'It's just an eye!'

Travellers

In Marseille, France, there's an amazing sculpture by the French artist Bruno Catalano. It's a man on a journey. He only has one arm and he doesn't have a body. 'It's beautiful', say Elodie and her friend Christine, tourists from Paris. 'Perhaps it means that when we leave a place, we leave a part of us behind.'

Lifesaver fountain

This fountain in Duisburg in Germany is big and colourful. It has a person's legs, but a bird's head and feet. But what is it? And what do local people think? 'I usually like modern art,' says Günther, a taxi driver. 'But I think this is really ugly.' Helga, a teacher, disagrees. 'I like it,' she says. 'I often have lunch in a restaurant on this street. When I see the fountain, I feel happy.'

Personal Best Write about a piece of art you like and give your opinion of it.

 Workbook page 35

PERSONAL BEST

Sts can practise talking about art and giving their opinion further. They write a description of a piece of art that they like, and give their opinion of it. They can compare their descriptions in small groups and choose one to present to the class.

Weaker sts can work in pairs. They write a description of one of the sculptures in exercise 5 and give their opinion of it. Ask some pairs to read their descriptions to the class.

EXTRA PRACTICE

With books closed, write the following gapped sentences on the board.

1 It's ______ the garden ______ a five-star hotel.
2 She's a receptionist ______ the hotel.
3 ______ Marseille, there's a sculpture ______ a French artist.
4 It's a fountain ______ Duisburg ______ Germany.
5 I often have lunch ______ a restaurant ______ this street.

In pairs, sts try to guess the missing prepositions. They can check their answers in the text. Check answers, and point out that we can use *in* with cities and places such as restaurants, but we use *at* when we say where someone works (*The sculpture is in the hotel, I work at the hotel*). Point out the use of *on* with *street* (*on a street in Duisburg*).

Ask sts to write three sentences about themselves or a place they know, using *in*, *on* or *at*. Ask some sts to read their sentences to the class.

Answers
1 in, of **2** at **3** In, by **4** in, in **5** in, on

EXTRA PRACTICE

Put sts into pairs and ask them to imagine they are standing in front of one of the sculptures on page 53. Ask them to prepare a conversation, in which they describe the sculpture and give their opinion of it. Ask them not to mention the name of the sculpture. Monitor and help while sts are working, then ask pairs in turn to perform their conversation for the class. Other sts can listen, guess which sculpture they are describing, and say whether they agree with the opinions.

6C An unusual home

1 Match the furniture in the box with pictures a–f.

fridge table bed sofa wardrobe chair

a

b

c

d

e

f

Personal Best

Go to Vocabulary practice: rooms and furniture, page 122

2 In pairs, describe a room in your house. Can your partner guess the room?

A *There's a table and four chairs in this room.* **B** *Is it your kitchen?*
A *No, it's my living room!*

3 Look at the picture. Guess where Kirsten lives. Read the text and check.

Life on the water

For university students, a room in a flat or a house can be very expensive, but not for 20-year-old Kirsten Müller. Kirsten is a student at a business school in Berlin … and she lives on a boat! It's small, but it's home.

Kirsten is on the sofa in the living room. There's a small table in front of her. 'I study here every night,' she says. 'And I eat here too.' The kitchen has an electric cooker, and next to it, there's a small fridge. Kirsten cooks all her meals on the boat. 'It's perfect for me, but I can't invite lots of friends for dinner!'

The bedroom has a bed … and nothing else! All of Kirsten's clothes are in boxes under the bed because there isn't a wardrobe. Between the bedroom and the kitchen, there's a modern bathroom with a shower and a toilet.

Kirsten loves her home. It's cheap and the people on the other boats are friendly, but are there any problems? 'I don't like getting up in winter,' she says. 'It's very cold!'

4 Read the text again. Match the rooms in the box with the parts of the boat.

living room bathroom bedroom kitchen

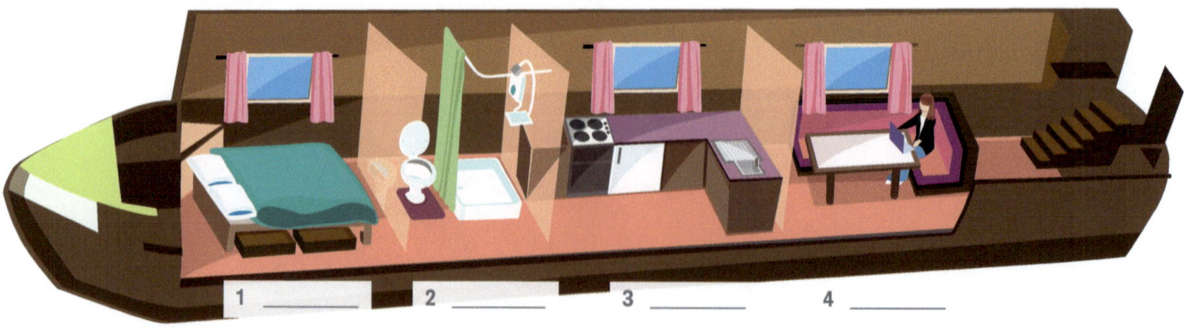

54

6C An unusual home

Sts read a text about a student who lives on a boat. They learn vocabulary for rooms and furniture, and practise saying where things are. They listen to a description of a room, then describe a room in their own home.

Grammar	Vocabulary	Pronunciation	Communication
Prepositions of place	Rooms and furniture (*bathroom, bedroom, kitchen, living room, study; bath, bed, chair, cooker, desk, fridge, lamp, shelves, shower, sofa, table, toilet, wardrobe, window*)	Sentence stress	Describing a room in your home

WARMER

Ask: *Where do you live? Is your home big or small? How many rooms are there?* Elicit a few answers from individual sts, then put sts into pairs to tell each other about their home. Read out the title of the lesson, *An unusual home*, and check that sts understand *unusual*. Tell sts that in this lesson they are going to read about an unusual home and practise describing their own home.

1 Sts work in pairs to look at the pictures and match them with the words in the box. Check answers. Model and drill pronunciation of the words.

Answers
a bed b chair c sofa d fridge e table f wardrobe

Go to Vocabulary practice: rooms and furniture, SB page 122/TB page 257.
Sts will find more language presentation and practice for rooms and furniture here. Do these exercises with the class, or set them for homework, before continuing with exercise 2 of lesson 6C.

PB Remind sts to go to the app for further self-study vocabulary practice of rooms and furniture.

2 Read out the model conversation. If necessary, remind sts of the use of *there is/are* to say what is in a place. Allow sts time to prepare their descriptions individually, then put them into pairs to describe the room and guess their partner's room. Ask who guessed correctly.

3 Focus on the picture and ask sts to guess where Kirsten lives. Elicit a few possible answers. Sts then read the text quickly to check their ideas. Check the answer with the class.

Answer
She lives on a boat.

4 Read through the rooms in the box with the class and check that sts understand them all. Read out the task and make sure sts understand what they have to do. Sts read the text again and match the rooms with the parts of the boat. Check answers.

Answers
1 bedroom 2 bathroom 3 kitchen 4 living room

3 x PRACTICE *SB page 54, exercise 4*

1 Do the exercise as normal. To check answers, point to each part of the boat in turn and ask: *Is this the (living room)?* Elicit the answers, then model and drill pronunciation of the words.

2 In pairs, sts cover the words in the box. They look at the picture of the boat again and try to name each room from memory. They can look at the words and their answers again to check.

3 In pairs, sts cover the text in exercise 3, They look at the picture of boat again and try to remember as many details as they can about each room, e.g. *There's a sofa in the living room, and there's a small table.* Ask them to write a sentence about each detail that they remember. Ask pairs in turn to read some of their sentences to the class. Ask other sts if they agree, but don't confirm the answers. Sts can check their ideas again in the text and give themselves a point for each correct sentence. See which pair got the most points.

5 Look at the diagram in exercise 4 again. Complete the sentences with the prepositions of place in the box. Check your answers in the text. Then read the Grammar box.

under	between	in	on	next to	in front of

1 Kirsten is ________ the sofa.
2 There's a small table ________ her.
3 The kitchen has an electric cooker, and ________ it, there's a small fridge.
4 All of Kirsten's clothes are ________ boxes ________ the bed.
5 ________ the bedroom and the kitchen, there's a modern bathroom.

Grammar **prepositions of place**

*There's a table **next to** the sofa.*
*My mobile phone is **in** my bag.*
*Your shoes are **under** the bed.*
*My keys are **on** the table.*
*My bedroom is **above** our living room.*
*Luca sits **between** Carlos and Emma.*
*Your car is **in front of** our house.*
*The cat is **behind** the sofa.*

Personal Best

Go to Grammar practice: prepositions of place, page 101

6 6.10 **Pronunciation:** sentence stress Listen and repeat the sentences. Pay attention to the underlined stressed words.

1 The camera is under my bed.
2 Your head is in front of the TV.
3 His shoes are next to the sofa.
4 The bathroom is behind the door.

7 **A** Complete the sentences with the correct prepositions of place.

1 The window is ________ the table.

2 Your keys are ________ the book.

3 The books are ________ the shelves.

4 There's a bed ________ the window and the chair.

B 6.11 In pairs, say the sentences with the correct stress. Listen, check and repeat.

8 **A** 6.12 Look at the picture and listen to the description. Find five differences between the description and the picture.

B 6.12 Compare your answers in pairs. Listen again and check.
There isn't a clock on the table. There's a lamp on the table.

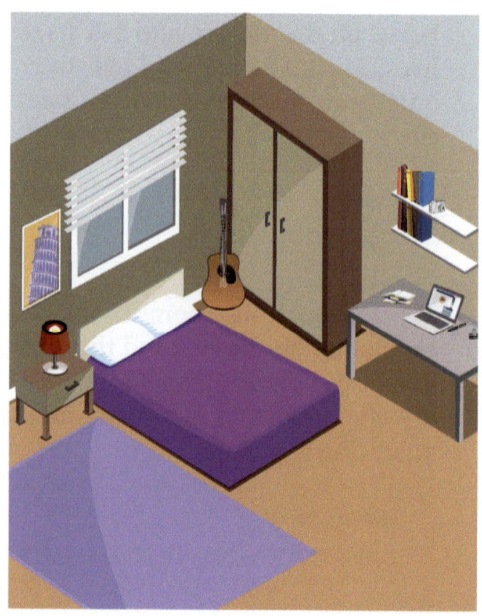

Go to Communication practice: Student A page 138, Student B page 146

9 **A** Think of a room in your house. Make notes about what furniture is in it and where it is.

B In pairs, describe your room. Your partner draws it. Then check your pictures.

10 Ask and answer the questions in pairs.
1 Do you live in a house or a flat?
2 Which is your favourite room? Why?
3 Imagine your ideal bedroom/living room/kitchen. What's in it?

Personal Best Write about your 'dream' home.

5 In pairs, sts look at the picture of the boat again and complete the sentences with the correct prepositions. They can check their answers in the text in exercise 3. Check answers with the class and check that sts understand all the prepositions.

Answers
1 on 2 in front of 3 next to 4 in, under 5 Between

Grammar

Read the Grammar box with sts about prepositions of place. Elicit that we use prepositions of place to say exactly where things are. Explain that prepositions are always followed by a noun or pronoun, e.g. *She's in the living room*, NOT ~~*She's in*~~. Point out that some prepositions are made up of more than one word, e.g. *in front of*, but they function in the same way as single words. Point out that *between* is always followed by *and*, e.g. *between the table and the sofa*. Ask questions to check concept.

Concept check questions:
On the table or in the table? (on). *In the living room or on the living room?* (in). *The fridge is next the cooker – correct?* (no – *next to* the cooker). *Above the window – what's the opposite?* (under the window). *In front of the TV – what's the opposite?* (behind the TV). *There's the kitchen, then the living room, then the bedroom – where is the living room?* (between the kitchen and the bedroom).

Go to Grammar practice: prepositions of place, SB page 101/TB page 215. Sts will find more language reference, presentation and practice for prepositions of place here. Do these exercises with the class, or set them for homework, before continuing with exercise 6 of lesson 6C.

PB Remind sts to go to the app for further self-study grammar practice of prepositions of place.

6 6.10 Allow sts time to read through the sentences. Play the first sentence on audio track 6.10 and point out that the underlined words are stressed. See SB page opposite for audio script. Play the rest of audio track 6.10 for sts to listen and notice the stressed words. Play the audio again for sts to repeat.

7 **A** Sts look at the pictures and complete the sentences with the correct prepositions of place. Check answers.

Answers
1 above 2 under 3 on 4 between

B 6.11 In pairs, sts practise saying the sentences with the correct stress. Play audio track 6.11. See Answers for audio script. Sts listen and check their answers. Play the audio again for them to repeat.

Answers
1 The window is above the table.
2 Your keys are under the book.
3 The books are on the shelves.
4 There's a bed between the window and the chair.

8 **A** 6.12 Focus on the picture and elicit some sentences describing where things are in it. Explain to sts that they will hear a description of the room, but there will be five differences between the description and the picture. Play audio track 6.12. See TB page 310 for audio script. Sts listen and note down the differences.

B 6.12 Sts compare their answers in pairs. Play the audio again for sts to check their answers. Check answers with the class, and see who noticed all the differences correctly.

Answers
There's a lamp on the table.
There is only one window, not two.
There isn't a chair in front of the desk.
The wardrobe is next to the desk.
The guitar is between the bed and the wardrobe.

Go to Communication practice
Divide the class into Student A and Student B. All 'Student A' sts should go to SB page 138. All 'Student B' sts should go to SB page 146. Go to TB page 289 for the teacher notes. Do the activity, then continue with exercise 9A of lesson 6C.

9 **A** Read through the task with the class and give some examples by writing notes about a room in your house on the board. Sts make their notes.

B In pairs, sts take turn to describe their room to their partner. Their partner must draw it, according to the description. Tell sts not to look at what their partner is drawing. When they have both finished, they can show each other their pictures and decide how accurate the pictures are. Get feedback on how accurately they managed to draw the rooms.

10 Read out the questions and make sure sts understand *favourite* and *ideal*. Allow sts time to prepare their answers individually. They then ask and answer the questions in pairs. Ask some sts to tell the class about their partner's ideal room.

PERSONAL BEST

Sts can practise describing rooms further by writing a description of their dream home. Encourage them to use their imagination! They can compare their descriptions in pairs and discuss which home they would like to live in.

With weaker sts, brainstorm some ideas for a dream home with the class, and make notes on the board, e.g. swimming pool in the garden, big room for parties. Sts then work in pairs and use the notes and their own ideas to write a description of the home. Ask some pairs to read their description to the class.

Learning Curve

6D Is there a post office near here?

1 In pairs, discuss what you usually do when you're lost.

a Ask someone in the street for directions.
b Go into a shop and ask for directions.
c Look at a map.
d Use a Sat Nav app on your phone.
e Walk around and hope you find the place.

2 6.13 Watch or listen to the first part of *Learning Curve*. Choose the correct words to complete the sentences.

1 Simon has *cereal and tea* / *eggs, toast and coffee* / *eggs, toast and tea* for breakfast.
2 He never goes to work *by car* / *by bike* / *on the underground*.
3 Kate always says *'the underground'* / *'the subway'* / *'the tube'*.
4 The man wants to find *a car park* / *a post office* / *the underground station*.

3 6.13 Complete the conversation with phrases a–e. Watch or listen again and check.

Man Excuse me. [1] ________
Simon Yes, there is. [2] ________
Go straight on. [3] ________
Man [4] ________
Simon [5] ________

a It's on the left, near the car park.
b Thank you very much.
c No problem.
d It's down the street.
e Is there a post office around here?

Conversation builder asking for and giving directions

Asking for directions:
Excuse me.
Is there a post office near here?
Is there a post office around here?
Where's the post office?

Giving directions:
Go straight on.
Go down this street.
Turn right/left at ...
It's on the right/left/corner.
It's near/next to/in front of ...

4 **A** Read the Conversation builder. In pairs, look at the maps and ask for and give directions to the places in orange.

A *Excuse me, where's the bank?* **B** *Go straight on ...*

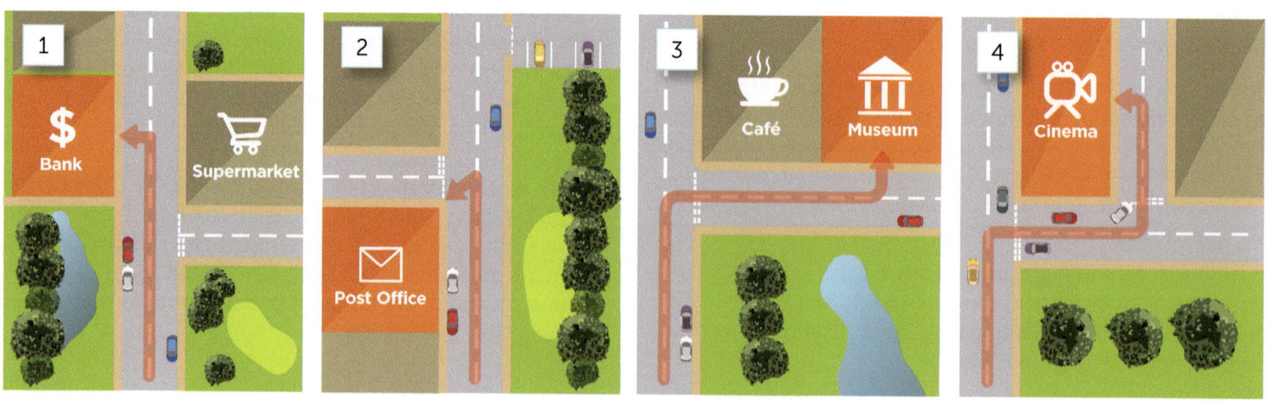

B 6.14 Listen and check. Are your conversations similar?

 EXTRA PRACTICE Workbook page 37

Learning Curve

6D Is there a post office near here?

Sts hear people asking for directions. They then practise asking for and giving directions, using phrases to check information.

Speaking	Skill	Conversation builder
Sts watch a video or listen to a recording of people asking for directions. They then practise asking for and giving directions.	Checking information	Asking for and giving directions

WARMER

Ask: *Do you sometimes visit other towns or cities? What cities do you like visiting? What are your favourite cities? Why?* Elicit a few answers. Ask: *What places do you go to when you visit a new city?* Elicit a range of answers, e.g. museums, restaurants, etc.

1 Focus on the picture and elicit that the person is looking at a map. Teach the words *lost* and *map* if necessary, and also teach the word *directions*. Sts work in pairs and discuss the questions. Ask some sts to tell the class what they and their partner do.

2 6.13 In this episode of *Learning Curve*, Simon gives people directions. Allow sts time to read the sentences and options. Pre-teach the following word if necessary from the video: *the tube* (= a British word for *the underground*). Play video/audio track 6.13. See TB page 310 for video/audio script. Sts listen and choose the correct words. Check answers.

Answers
1 eggs, toast and tea
2 by car
3 the subway
4 a post office

3 6.13 Allow sts time to read through the gapped conversation and the phrases. Read out the first gapped sentence and elicit the correct phrase. Sts then complete the conversation. Play video/audio track 6.13 again. Sts watch/listen and check their answers. Check answers, and make sure sts understand the completed conversation.

Answer
1 e 2 d 3 a 4 b 5 c

3 x PRACTICE *SB page 56, exercise 3*

1 Do the exercise as normal. To check answers, ask students in turn to read out one completed line of the conversation. Ask other students: *Is that right?*

2 Ask sts to cover phrases a–e. In pairs, they look at the conversation again and try to remember it, using just the gapped sentences. They can look at the phrases and their answers again to check.

3 Ask sts to close their books. Write a few prompts for the conversation on the board, e.g. *Post office? down / street / left / car park / thank you / problem*. Sts work in pairs and practise the conversation using the prompts. Play the video/audio track again for them to check.

Conversation builder

Read the Conversation builder box with sts about asking for and giving directions. Make sure they understand all the directions. Use gestures for *turn left/right* and *go straight on*. Point out that it is also important to use phrases to sound polite when asking for directions, e.g. *Excuse me. Thank you*. Ask questions to check concept.

Concept check questions:
I'm in a new city and I want to find a supermarket – what can I say? (Is there a supermarket near/around here?). *I want to find the station – what can I say?* (Excuse me, where's the station?). *Go down this street / Go straight on – same meaning?* (yes). *It's on the right – does that mean I go to the right?* (no, it means I will see it on my right side). *If I need to go to the right, what does the person say?* (turn right).

4 A Focus on the maps and make sure sts understand everything on them. Read out the example, and focus on the first arrow, leading to the bank. Elicit the rest of the directions to the bank. Sts then work in pairs and practise giving directions to the places. Monitor and help while they are working.

B 6.14 Play audio track 6.14. See TB page 310 for audio script. Sts listen and compare their conversations. Ask: *Are your conversations similar?* Sts could practise again if necessary.

5 6.15 Watch or listen to the second part of the show. Choose the correct options to answer the questions.

1 Where do the women want to go?
a To the cinema.
b To the shopping centre.
c To the supermarket.

2 What's the problem at the studio?
a There isn't any water.
b There isn't any tea.
c There isn't any electricity.

6 6.15 Watch or listen again. Complete the conversations with the phrases in the box.

a problem | show me | near here | did you say | repeat that | you mean

1 **Woman 1** Is there a shopping centre [1] ________ ?
Simon Yes, it's near the supermarket. Go down this street, turn right on Bethnal Green Road. Don't stop at Ebor Street. Go straight on.
Woman 2 Sorry, [2] ________ near the supermarket?

2 **Woman 1** Can you [3] ________ on the map?
Simon We're here. And there's the cinema. And there's the supermarket. The shopping centre is next to the supermarket. See?
Woman 2 Could you [4] ________ , please? More slowly.

3 **Kate** There's [5] ________ , so there's no water in the kitchen or the bathroom. But there's water under the receptionist's desk! Poor Marina.
Simon Sorry, did you say there's a problem on the street?
[6] ________ , a problem with the water?

Skill checking information

If you don't understand what someone says, you can:
- ask him/her to repeat: *Could you repeat that, please?* *Could you say that again?*
- ask him/her to speak more slowly: *Could you speak more slowly, please?*
- ask a question to check the information: *Did you say near the supermarket?* *You mean, a problem with the water?*

7 A 6.16 Read the Skill box. Listen and match phrases a–d with conversations 1–4. Where are the people in the situations?

a Sorry, did you say ...? ____
b Sorry, could you say that again, please? ____
c Sorry, could you repeat that, please? ____
d Sorry, could you speak more slowly, please? ____

B 6.16 Listen again and complete the information that the people repeat.

1 Turn right at the ________ . Then turn ________ at the ________ .
2 ________ . ________ @mail.com
3 70832 ________
4 £ ________

Go to Communication practice: Student A page 139, Student B page 147

8 A PREPARE In pairs, think of four places in your town. Think about how to get to the places from where you are now.

a train station or bus stop | a restaurant or café | a museum or tourist attraction | a shopping centre or supermarket

B PRACTISE Ask for and give directions. Check the information if you don't understand anything.

C PERSONAL BEST Swap partners and ask for and give directions to a new place. Are you more confident asking for directions in English?

Personal Best Write an email to a friend with directions to your house from the bus or train station.

57

5 6.15 Allow sts time to read the questions and possible answers. Pre-teach the following phrases if necessary from the video: *the internet is down* and *at your service* (= I am here to help you). Play video/audio track 6.15. See TB page 311 for video/audio script. Sts watch/listen and check their answers.

Answers
1 b 2 a

6 6.15 Allow sts time to read through the gapped conversations and words in the box. Play video/audio track 6.15 again. Sts watch/listen and complete the conversations. Allow sts time to compare their answers in pairs, then play the video/audio again for sts to check and complete their answers. Check answers with the class, and check that sts understand everything in the conversations.

Answers

1 near here	4 repeat that
2 did you say	5 a problem
3 show me	6 You mean

Skill

Read the Skill box with sts about checking information. Check they understand everything. Point out that intonation and tone of voice can help you to sound polite when you are checking information.

7 A 6.16 Allow sts time to read through the phrases. Play audio track 6.16. See TB page 311 for audio script. Sts listen and match each phrase with a conversation. Check answers.

Answers
a 4 b 3 c 2 d 1

B 6.16 Sts read the gapped sentences. Play audio track 6.16 again, pausing if necessary for sts to complete the information. Check answers.

Answers

1 post office, left, bank	3 569411
2 david, jackson454	4 3.50

Go to Communication practice
Divide the class into Student A and Student B. All 'Student A' sts should go to SB page 139. All 'Student B' sts should go to SB page 147. Go to TB page 291 for the teacher notes. Do the activity, then continue with exercise 8 of lesson 6D.

8 Sts follow the steps to ask for and give directions.

A PREPARE Allow sts time to read through the situations and prepare their ideas in pairs. You could brainstorm a few ideas with the class first.

B PRACTISE Sts work in pairs and take turns to ask for directions. Remind sts to use phrases from the Conversation builder box to ask for and give directions, and encourage them to use phrases from the Skill box to check information.

C PERSONAL BEST Sts swap partners and practise again. Encourage them this time to spend less time preparing and try to speak more fluently. Get feedback from sts on whether their speaking was better this time. Remind them that being good about speaking is all about practice, and it is often worth practising the same conversation two or three times until it starts to feel completely natural.

PERSONAL BEST

Sts can practise giving directions further. They write an email to a friend, giving directions to their house from the bus or train station. They can swap emails with a partner and give feedback on how clear the directions are.

Refer weaker sts back to the maps in exercise 4. They can work in pairs and write directions to one of the places on the maps.

EXTRA PRACTICE

Put sts into groups of three. Two sts practise a new conversation, or one of their conversations from exercise 8. They could stand up and act out the scene as they speak. The third student uses their phone to film the other two. Sts can swap roles and practise again. Watching themselves on film will help sts to evaluate how well they can ask for and give directions.

Grammar

1 Choose the correct options to complete the sentences.

1 On Saturday, I meet my friends ________ the shopping centre.
 a on b under c in
2 ________ any shelves in the living room.
 a There aren't
 b There are
 c There isn't
3 He can't ________ cakes. They're always horrible!
 a make b to make c makes
4 My friends live in the city. I meet ________ at the weekend.
 a they b them c us
5 There are ________ in the kitchen.
 a any biscuits
 b some biscuit
 c some biscuits
6 Your sunglasses are ________ to my laptop.
 a on b in front c next
7 A Is there a hospital in your town?
 B Yes, ________ .
 a there's
 b there is
 c there are
8 ________ drive a lorry?
 a Do you can
 b Can you
 c You can

2 Complete the conversations with the words in the box.

aren't any can can't her
isn't it next to on them

1 A ________ you swim?
 B Yes, I can, but there ________ a swimming pool in this town.
2 A Are there ________ restaurants near here?
 B Yes, there's an Italian restaurant ________ the supermarket on School Road.
3 A Where are my headphones? I want to use ________ .
 B They're ________ the desk.
4 A Who can speak Spanish? I ________ read this menu.
 B Give ________ to me. I know some Spanish.
5 A Selina's class is at 8.00 p.m., but there ________ any buses in the evening.
 B It's OK. I can drive ________ to the class.

3 Choose the correct options to complete the text.

A treehouse with a difference

If you want an unusual house, Jono Williams can [1] *make / makes* one for you. He's an engineer and he loves treehouses, but his new Skysphere is different – it's very small and it isn't [2] *in / under* a tree!

What's in the Skysphere?

[3] *There's / There are* a large bed, a TV and [4] *any / some* shelves. There's even a fridge for drinks [5] *between / in* the sofa! The windows are very large and Jono [6] *can / can't* see 360° around the house. There's Wi-Fi and he can [7] *use / using* his smartphone to play music and change the lights.

What does Jono do there?

Jono meets his friends at the Skysphere. They love [8] *them / it* too. They like listening to music and at night they can watch the stars.

Are there [9] *some / any* problems with Jono's house?

Only one … there [10] *isn't / aren't* a bathroom or a toilet.

Vocabulary

1 Put the words in the box in the correct columns.

museum lamp table DVD player remote control
head teeth park chair Sat Nav laptop desk
police station post office face foot

Places in a town	Electronic devices	Parts of the body	Furniture

Grammar

1 Sts read the sentences and choose the correct options to complete them. Check answers.

Answers
1 c
2 a
3 a
4 b
5 c
6 c
7 b
8 b

2 Sts read the conversations and complete them with the correct words. Check answers.

Answers
1 Can, isn't
2 any, next to
3 them, on
4 can't, it
5 aren't, her

3 Ask sts to read the text through quickly for general meaning. Ask: *What do Jono and his friends do in this house?* (they listen to music and watch the stars). Sts read the text again and choose the correct words to complete it. Check answers.

Answers
1 make
2 in
3 There's
4 some
5 in
6 can
7 use
8 it
9 any
10 isn't

3 x PRACTICE *SB page 58, Grammar exercise 3*

1 Do the exercise as normal. To check the answers, put sts into small groups and ask them to compare their answers and note down ones where they have different answers. Ask groups in turn which answers they disagree on, and discuss as a class which answers are correct for these and why. Then check the rest of the answers.

2 Ask sts to close their books. They work in pairs and try to remember as much as they can about the Skysphere. You could write some prompts on the board to help them, e.g. *small, bed, shelves, fridge, windows*. They can check by looking in their books.

3 In pairs, students design their own Skysphere and write some sentences to describe it, say what there is in it, and say what you can do there. Encourage sts to use their imagination! Pairs can present their own Skysphere to the class.

Vocabulary

1 Sts put the words in the correct columns. As an extension, sts could add one or two more words to each column.

Answers

Places in a town	Electronic devices	Parts of the body	Furniture
museum	lamp	head	DVD player
park	table	teeth	remote control
police station	chair	face	Sat Nav
post office	desk	foot	laptop

2 Circle the word that is different. Explain your answers.

1	toilet	bath	table	shower
2	ear	mouth	nose	hand
3	school	supermarket	restaurant	café
4	bank	kitchen	bedroom	living room
5	chair	arm	fridge	wardrobe
6	walking	reading	swimming	cycling
7	sing	speak	travel	call
8	DVD player	shelves	computer	Sat Nav

3 Choose the correct options to complete the sentences.

1 My city has two ________ .
a wardrobes b hospitals c bathrooms
2 What time does the bus ________ in the city centre?
a arrive b travel c go out
3 Her ________ is long and brown.
a eye b hair c mouth
4 There's a large ________ in the living room.
a bath b leg c sofa
5 She always uses ________ to listen to music on the bus.
a earphones b TV c shelves
6 A Where's the ________ ? B It's in the car.
a museum b toilet c Sat Nav
7 Is there any cheese in the ________ ?
a shower b fridge c DVR
8 At the weekend, I like ________ at the cinema.
a dancing b sleeping c watching films

4 Complete the conversations with the words in the boxes.

bedroom cooker windows desk nightclub cooking

Ama Hi, Ed! How are you? Do you like your new flat?
Ed No, not really. It's above a noisy [1]________ .
Ama Oh no! Is it big?
Ed No, it's very small. In the [2]________ , there's only a bed and a [3]________ , and there aren't any [4]________ in the bathroom.
Ama How's the kitchen? I know you like [5]________ .
Ed It's dirty and the [6]________ is very old ... but it's a good flat.
Ama What's good about it?
Ed It's cheap!

call station office speak drive stop

Sam Excuse me. Do you [7]________ English?
Fran Yes, I do.
Sam Where's the bus [8]________ ?
Fran It's in front of the post [9]________ , but there aren't any buses today.
Sam OK. Is there a train [10]________ near here?
Fran Yes, but it's a long walk. I can [11]________ you there if you want.
Sam No thanks, I can [12]________ a taxi.

Personal Best

Lesson 5A Write one positive and one negative sentence about your abilities.

Lesson 6A Name five places in your town.

Lesson 5B Name four electronic devices that you use.

Lesson 6A Write three questions to find out what there is in a friend's town.

Lesson 5C Name two activities that you like doing and two activities that you don't like doing.

Lesson 6B Write your opinion of a famous building.

Lesson 5C Write four sentences with different object pronouns.

Lesson 6B Name five parts of the body that you have two of.

Lesson 5D Write four sentences to describe yourself.

Lesson 6C Name four things in your house and describe where they are.

Lesson 5D Say why you like/don't like your town/city using *because*.

Lesson 6D Write directions from the classroom to a shop, café, school or bus stop.

2 Sts circle the word that is different in each set. Check answers, and ask sts to explain in each case why the word is different. As an extension, sts could write two or three sentences using some of the words.

Answers
1 table (not in bathroom)
2 hand (not part of head)
3 school (don't buy food there)
4 bank (not a room)
5 arm (not furniture)
6 reading (not an activity where you move)
7 travel (doesn't use voice)
8 shelves (not an electronic device)

3 Sts read the sentences and choose the correct words to complete them. Check answers.

Answers
1 b
2 a
3 b
4 c
5 a
6 c
7 b
8 c

3 x PRACTICE *SB page 59, exercise 3*

1 Do the exercise as normal. When you check the answers, read out each sentence in turn, inserting a correct or incorrect answer. Ask *Is this correct or incorrect? Why?*

2 Ask sts to close their books. Write the correct answers on the board, e.g. *hospitals, arrive.* Sts work in pairs and try to remember the sentences. They can look at their books to check.

3 Sts work in their pairs and choose four incorrect answers to write sentences with. Ask pairs in turn to read their sentences to the class, omitting the target word. Other sts listen and try to guess the missing words.

4 Sts read the conversations and complete them with the correct words. Check answers. As an extension, sts could choose one of the conversations, then change some of the details and practise it.

Answers
1 nightclub
2 bedroom
3 desk
4 windows
5 cooking
6 cooker
7 speak
8 stop
9 office
10 station
11 drive
12 call

Personal Best

At the end of each *Review and practice* double-page spread, there is a *Personal Best* section. The aim here is to provide a quick challenge to change the pace and allow for language recall and personalization.

These questions and prompts give sts the opportunity to revise a number of language and skills points from the preceding two units in a more productive way. The points being revised are referenced according to which lesson they appear in (e.g. Lesson 5A). They cover grammar, vocabulary, text builder language from reading and writing lessons, and conversation builder language from speaking lessons. Sts work individually, in pairs or in groups, according to the class dynamic and the time available. Set a time limit if you would like to add a competitive element. Encourage sts to refer back to the relevant lessons if they are having difficulties. The aim is for them to respond to the prompts and engage with the target language in a personal way. Their answers will vary. Monitor and help as necessary and get feedback on sts' answers.

WORKBOOK REVIEW AND PRACTICE

Students will find two pages of Review and Practice at the end of each unit of their Workbooks.
Unit 5, pages 32 and 33
Unit 6, pages 38 and 39

UNIT 7

All in the past

LANGUAGE past simple: *be* ■ celebrities

7A When they were young

1 Match the jobs in the box with pictures a–f.

musician politician film director writer footballer fashion model

a

b

c

d

e

f

Personal Best

Go to Vocabulary practice: celebrities, page 123

2 In pairs, describe celebrities. Can your partner guess who it is?

A *She's a tennis player. She's American. She's very good!* **B** *Is it Serena Williams?*

3 **A** Read the introduction of the text. Match the blue sign with one of the people a–e.

B Read the rest of the text. Match the other people with descriptions 1–4 and write their names on the blue signs. Check their names on page 139.

London's *famous houses*

London was home to lots of famous people from all over the world. Who were they and where were their houses? It's easy – just look for the blue signs on the buildings!

a

b

c

d

e

1869–1948
Lived here as a law student

1 He was a famous Indian politician, but he was also a student in London for three years. He was a vegetarian and in the 19th century it wasn't easy to find good vegetarian food in the city.

1945–1981
Singer and musician
Lived here
1972

2 In 1972, London was home to this Jamaican singer and his band. The musicians weren't famous then, but a year later their song *Stir It Up* was a big hit.

1890–1976
Writer
Lived here
1934–1941

3 This British writer wasn't from London, but she was here for seven years. Her crime stories were very popular around the world, and you probably know her famous detective – Hercule Poirot.

1853–1890
Artist
Lived here
1873–1874

4 This was the Dutch artist's home when he was 19 years old. He was in love with the owner's daughter, Eugenie. But was she interested in him? No, she wasn't!

All in the past

UNIT 7

UNIT 7 OVERVIEW: This unit focuses on the past. Sts read about what some well-known people did when they were young, and ask and answer questions about things they did themselves when they were young. In *Learning Curve*, Simon and Penny talk to people about Shakespeare and the theatre. Sts talk about things they did in the past and write an email about an interesting weekend away they had.

LANGUAGE

Grammar	Vocabulary	Pronunciation
Past simple: *be*; past simple: regular verbs	Celebrities; months and ordinals, time expressions	*was/were*; *-ed* endings

SKILLS

Listening	Writing
Listening for dates; linking consonants and vowels	Writing informal emails; sequencers

LANGUAGE 7A

7A When they were young

Sts read a text about houses in London that have blue plaques to show that famous people once lived there. They read about what some well-known celebrities did when they were young, and ask and answer questions about things they did themselves when they were young.

Grammar	Vocabulary	Pronunciation	Communication
Past simple: *be*	Celebrities (*artist, athlete, dancer, DJ, fashion model, film director, footballer, journalist, king, musician, photographer, politician, queen, racing driver, tennis player, writer*)	*was/were*	Talking about things from your past

WARMER

Teach the word *celebrity* and ask: *Who are your favourite celebrities?* Choose one or two celebrities and ask the class: *What do you know about this person?* Write one or two sentences on the board, e.g. *She's a singer*. Then ask: *What do you know about his/her life when he/she was young?* Elicit some ideas and write one or two sentences on the board using *was/were*. Point to the sentences on the board and teach the words *present* and *past*. Tell sts that in this unit they are going to practise talking about the past.

1 Sts work in pairs and match the jobs with the pictures. They can use their dictionaries to help. Model and drill pronunciation of the words.

Answers
a film director b musician c footballer d politician
e fashion model f writer

Go to Vocabulary practice: celebrities, SB page 123/TB page 259.
Sts will find more language presentation and practice for words for celebrities here. Do these exercises with the class, or set them for homework, before continuing with exercise 2 of lesson 7A.

PB Remind sts to go to the app for further self-study vocabulary practice of words for celebrities.

2 Read out the example answer. Give another description of a celebrity that sts will know, e.g. *He's a footballer. He's Portuguese. He's very good.* (Cristiano Ronaldo). Allow sts time to prepare one or two descriptions individually. They then describe their celebrities in pairs and try to guess who they are. Ask who guessed correctly.

3 A Explain to sts that in the UK, houses that famous people once lived in have blue plaques (signs) added to the outside, to tell people who lived in the house and when. Sts read the introduction and look at the sign, then match it with one of the famous people. Elicit the answer and elicit what sts know about Alfred Hitchcock (see answers below).

Answer
b (Alfred Hitchcock was an English and American film director known especially for his thrillers, including *Rear Window*, *Vertigo* and *Psycho*).

B Put sts into pairs to read the rest of the text and write the correct names on the plaques. If you think your sts may not recognize the people, you could focus on the pictures first and elicit the names of the people (see answers below). Check answers.

Answers
1 e (Mahatma Gandhi) 3 d (Agatha Christie)
2 c (Bob Marley) 4 a (Vincent van Gogh)

4 A Complete the sentences with the words in the box. Check your answers in the text.

was (x2) were (x2) wasn't weren't

1 Where ________ their houses?
2 He ________ a famous Indian politician.
3 It ________ easy to find good vegetarian food.
4 The musicians ________ famous then.
5 Her crime stories ________ very popular.
6 ________ she interested in him?

B Complete the rules. Then read the Grammar box.

1 The past simple forms of *is/isn't* = ________ / ________ .
2 The past simple forms of *are/aren't* = ________ / ________ .

Grammar **past simple: *be***

Positive:	Negative:	Questions:	Short answers:	
*He **was** a musician.*	*I **wasn't** an actor.*	***Was** she a writer?*	*Yes, she **was**.*	*No, she **wasn't**.*
*They **were** singers.*	*You **weren't** famous.*	***Were** you happy?*	*Yes, we **were**.*	*No, we **weren't**.*

Personal Best

Go to Grammar practice: past simple: *be*, page 102

5 A 7.3 **Pronunciation:** *was/were* Listen and repeat the question and answer. How are *was* and *were* pronounced?

A *Where were you yesterday?* **B** *I was at work.*

B In pairs, ask and answer the question *Where were you ...?* with the times in the boxes. Pay attention to the pronunciation of *was* and *were*.

A *Where were you at 7.30 this morning?* **B** *I was on the bus. I always go to work early. What about you?*
A *I was in bed!*

at 7.30 this morning | yesterday morning | yesterday at 2.00 p.m. | yesterday evening

Go to Communication practice: Student A page 139, Student B page 147

6 7.4 Complete the sentences with the correct form of *was* or *were*. Listen and check.

When they were young

- Singer Justin Timberlake and actor Ryan Gosling [1]________ presenters on a children's TV show when they [2]________ young.

- In 1990, J.K. Rowling [3]________ an English teacher in Portugal, but she [4]________ happy there. Seven years later, she [5]________ famous all over the world as the writer of the *Harry Potter* books.

- Actors and film directors Matt Damon and Ben Affleck [6]________ at school together, but they [7]________ in the same class.

- Athlete Usain Bolt [8]________ interested in cricket and football at school. His teachers [9]________ surprised because he [10]________ a very, very fast runner!

7 In pairs, ask and answer questions about when you were young. Use the ideas below.

A *What was the name of your first teacher?* **B** *Mrs Fuentes. She was really nice. What about you?*

1 What / the name of your first teacher?
2 / you a good student?
3 / you in a big class?
4 Who / your best friend?
5 What celebrities / popular when you / a child?
6 What films / popular?
7 What / your favourite TV programmes?
8 What / your favourite food?

Personal Best Think of someone famous that you like. Write a paragraph about their life when they were young.

4 A Read out the first gapped sentence and elicit the correct word (*were*). If sts struggle, ask them to find the sentence in the text on page 60. Sts then complete the remaining sentences and check their answers in the text. Check answers, and check that sts understand all the sentences.

Answers
1 were 2 was 3 wasn't 4 weren't 5 were 6 Was

B Read through the rules with the class and elicit the correct answers.

Answers
1 was/wasn't 2 were/weren't

Grammar

Read the Grammar box with sts about the past simple: *be*. Point out that we use the present simple to talk about things that are true now, and we use the past simple for things that were true in the past. Point out that in the present simple of *be* there are three forms (*am/am not, is/isn't, are/aren't*), but in the past simple there are only two forms (*was/wasn't, were/weren't*). Point out the word order in questions: *Was she famous?* NOT ~~*She was famous?*~~. Ask questions to check concept.

Concept check questions:
He is a film director – now or in the past? (now). *Can you change it so it is about the past?* (He was a film director). *They was musicians – correct?* (no – they *were* musicians). *Can you make the sentence negative?* (They weren't musicians). *She was a writer – can you make this into a question?* (Was she a writer?). *What are the two answers?* (Yes, she was/No, she wasn't).

Go to Grammar practice: past simple: *be*, SB page 102/ TB page 217.
Sts will find more language reference, presentation and practice for the past simple: *be* here. Do these exercises with the class, or set them for homework, before continuing with exercise 5A of lesson 7A.

PB Remind sts to go to the app for further self-study grammar practice of the past simple: *be*.

5 A 7.3 Play audio track 7.3 once for sts to listen to the question and answer. See SB page opposite for audio script. Play the audio again for sts to listen and repeat, then elicit that *was* and *were* are pronounced with the weak vowel /ə/ because they are unstressed. Point out that in British English, we don't usually pronounce the /r/ sound in *were* unless it is followed by a vowel, e.g. *They were asleep*.

Answers
was /wəz/
were /wə/

B Ask two confident sts to read out the example question and answer. Sts work in pairs and practise asking and answering the questions. Ask individual sts where their partner was at different times, e.g. *Where was (Ana) yesterday evening?* Elicit answers using *he/she* forms.

Go to Communication practice
Divide the class into Student A and Student B. All 'Student A' sts should go to SB page 139. All 'Student B' sts should go to SB page 147. Go to TB page 291 for the teacher notes. Do the activity, then continue with exercise 6 of lesson 7A.

6 7.4 Explain to sts that they are going to read about some celebrities when they were young. Read out the first gapped sentence and elicit the correct verb form (*were*). Sts read the text and complete it with the correct verb forms. Play audio track 7.4. See SB page opposite for audio script. Sts listen and check their answers. Check answers with the class.

Answers
1 were 2 were 3 was 4 wasn't 5 was 6 were
7 weren't 8 was 9 weren't 10 was

3 x PRACTICE *SB page 61, exercise 6*

1. Do the exercise as normal. To check answers, play the audio and pause before each missing verb form. Elicit some possible answers, encouraging sts to give reasons for their answers, e.g. it's plural because it's about more than one person. Play the audio to check, and pause again if sts got the answer wrong, to explain the correct answer.
2. Ask sts to cover the text. Read out the text again, with some correct verb forms and some incorrect. Ask sts to put up their hands or call out when they hear an incorrect verb form. Elicit the correct forms.
3. In pairs, sts cover the text and try to remember as many details as they can and write sentences, e.g. *J.K. Rowling was an English teacher*. Ask pairs in turn to read some of their sentences to the class. Sts can check their answers in the text.

7 In pairs, ask sts to write the questions first. Check these, then check that sts understand all the questions. Allow sts time to prepare their answers to the questions individually. They then work in pairs to ask and answer the questions. Ask some sts to tell the class something they learned about their partner.

Answers
2 Were you a good student?
3 Were you in a big class?
4 Who was your best friend?
5 What celebrities were popular when you were a child?
6 What films were popular?
7 What were your favourite TV programmes?
8 What was your favourite food?

PERSONAL BEST

Sts can practise talking about the past further. They think of someone famous and write a paragraph about them when they were young. They can compare their texts in pairs.

Weaker sts could write four sentences about themselves when they were young, using *was* and *wasn't*. Ask some sts to read their sentences to the class.

7B I was there in July

1 Order the months from 1–12.

☐ April ☐ August ☐ December ☐ February
☐ *1* January ☐ July ☐ June ☐ March
☐ May ☐ November ☐ October ☐ September

2 Look at the calendar. Match days a–f with dates 1–6.

1 the thirty-first of May ____ 4 the twelfth of May ____
2 the twentieth of May ____ 5 the first of May ____
3 the twenty-eighth of May ____ 6 the third of May ____

Go to Vocabulary practice: months and ordinals, page 124

May

1 a	2	3 b	4	5	6	7
8	9	10	11	12 c	13	14
15	16	17	18	19	20 d	21
22	23	24	25	26	27	28 e
29	30	31 f				

3 Ask and answer the questions in pairs.

1 What's the date today? 3 What's your favourite month?
2 When's your birthday? 4 When was the last public holiday?

4 **A** Look at the picture. What do you know about Shakespeare?

B Complete the text with the words in the box.

April *Hamlet* plays writer

William Shakespeare was a famous British [1]________ . He was born on 26 [2]________ 1564 and he died in April 1616. His [3]________ are popular all over the world. They include *Romeo and Juliet*, [4]________ and *Othello*.

5 7.7 Watch or listen to the first part of *Learning Curve*. Are the sentences true (T) or false (F)?

1 Shakespeare's plays are only about British people. ____
2 The Globe Theatre was Shakespeare's first theatre. ____
3 'Shakespeare in the Park' in New York is very expensive. ____
4 You can read Shakespeare's plays in 80 different languages. ____

Skill listening for dates

It's sometimes important to listen for specific years and months.

- Listen carefully because some months sound similar: *September, November* and *December.*
- Years are usually divided into two numbers: *1990 = nineteen ninety, 2008 = twenty oh eight.* For years after 2000, we sometimes use the whole number: *2009 = two thousand and nine.*
- We use ordinals to talk about centuries (100 years): *1900–1999 = the twentieth century.*

6 7.7 Read the Skill box. Watch or listen again. Complete the texts with the correct information.

The Globe Theatre was Shakespeare's first theatre. It was here in London during the [1]________ and [2]________ centuries, from [3]________ to about [4]________. This theatre looks just like the old Globe.

Every year, from [5]________ to [6]________ , there's a Shakespeare festival in Central Park in New York City. It's called 'Shakespeare in the Park'. 1,800 people can see a Shakespeare play at the Delacorte Theater for free!

62

7B I was there in July

Sts learn some vocabulary for months and ordinals and watch or listen to an episode of *Learning Curve* about the life and works of William Shakespeare. They talk about their own trips to the theatre, cinema or concerts.

Listening	Skill	Listening builder	Vocabulary
Sts watch a video or listen to a recording about William Shakespeare.	Listening for dates	Linking consonants and vowels	Months and ordinals (*January–December; first–thirty-first*)

WARMER

Play a game to revise counting from 1 to 50. Ask sts to stand up. Sts go around the class, counting from 1–50. If a student makes a mistake or cannot say the next number quickly enough, they sit down. Repeat the activity, speeding up, counting backwards, or counting in twos to make it more challenging.

1 Sts order the months from 1–12. You could do this as a race, to make it more challenging. Check answers, then model pronunciation of the months and get sts to repeat.

Answers

1 January	5 May	9 September
2 February	6 June	10 October
3 March	7 July	11 November
4 April	8 August	12 December

2 Focus on the calendar, and point out the days a–f. Sts work in pairs to match the days with the dates. Check answers, then model and drill pronunciation of the dates. Point out that we use ordinal numbers in dates, e.g. *the third of May*, NOT ~~*the three of May*~~.

Answers
1 f 2 d 3 e 4 c 5 a 6 b

Go to Vocabulary practice: months and ordinals, SB page 124/TB page 261.
Sts will find more language presentation and practice for months and ordinals here. Do these exercises with the class, or set them for homework, before continuing with exercise 3 of lesson 7B.

PB Remind sts to go to the app for further self-study vocabulary practice of months and ordinals.

3 Read out the questions and make sure sts understand them all. Sts ask and answer the questions in pairs. Ask some sts to tell the class their answers.

4 **A** Focus on the picture and elicit what sts know about Shakespeare.

B Check that sts understand *plays* and *writer*. Sts read the text and complete it with the correct words. Check answers. Ask sts if they know the stories of *Romeo and Juliet, Hamlet* or *Othello*.

Answers
1 writer 2 April 3 plays 4 *Hamlet*

5 7.7 In this episode of *Learning Curve*, Simon and Penny talk to people about theatre, plays and Shakespeare. Sts read the sentences. Check they understand *theatre* and *expensive*. Pre-teach the following words if necessary from the video: *playwright, entertainment, festival, to perform* and *in translation* (= translated into a different language). Read out the task, then play video/audio track 7.7. See TB page 311 for video/audio script. Sts watch/listen and decide if the sentences are true or false. Check answers, playing the video/audio again for sts to hear the correct answers.

Answers
1 F 2 T 2 F 2 T

Skill

Read the Skill box with sts about listening for dates. Say the dates in the Skill box, then write a few more years on the board and elicit how to say them, e.g. *2012, 1992, 2004, 1763.*

6 7.7 Allow sts time to read the gapped text. Play video/audio track 7.7 again. Sts listen and complete the text with the correct dates. Check answers by writing the dates on the board.

Answers
1 16th 2 17th 3 1599 4 1642 5 May 6 August

7 7.8 Watch or listen to the rest of the show. Match the people with sentences 1–4.

1 This person likes plays about love. ________
2 This person works at a theatre. ________
3 This person doesn't like Shakespeare. ________
4 This person likes plays about history. ________

8 7.8 Watch or listen again. Answer the questions with months or years.

1 When does Marty come to New York? ________ and ________
2 When were Elizabeth and Henry in Cambridge? ________
3 When was *A Midsummer Night's Dream* in Beijing? ________
4 When was *Henry IV* at the Hong Kong Arts Festival? ________

9 Ask and answer the questions in pairs.

Do you ever go to the theatre?
Which Shakespeare plays do you know?
Which types of plays do you like?
Do you like Shakespeare? Why/Why not?

10 7.9 Listen to Penny's sentence and look at the linked words. Pay attention to how the sounds join together.

Listening builder linking consonants and vowels

When a word ends in a consonant sound, and the next word starts with a vowel sound, we usually link the sounds together.
Hamlet‿is‿about‿a prince‿in Denmark.
I'm‿Elizabeth‿and this‿is my husband, Henry.
Sometimes the plays‿are‿in‿English‿and Chinese.

11 7.10 Read the Listening builder. Then listen and complete the sentences.

1 Hi, my name's Lucas ________ ________ ________ ________ .
2 In ________ ________ ________ ________ New York City for the first time.
3 The play ________ ________ ________ ________ king.
4 She was born on the ________ ________ ________ , 1999.
5 I like *Hamlet*, but I ________ ________ ________ the story.

12 Look at the pictures. Discuss the questions in pairs.

1 When was the last time you were at a theatre/a cinema/a concert?
2 Which play/film/band was it?
3 Was it good? Why/Why not?

Personal Best Write a description of your favourite play or film. Where does it happen? What's it about?

 EXTRA PRACTICE Workbook page 41

7 7.8 Pre-teach the following words if necessary from the video: *queue*, *balcony* (in a theatre), *king*, *feather*, *videochat*. Focus on the pictures and allow sts time to read the sentences. Play video/audio track 7.8. See TB page 311 for video/audio script. Sts watch/listen and match the people with the sentences. Check answers.

Answers
1 Elizabeth 2 Zhang 3 Marty 4 Henry

8 7.8 Sts read the questions. Play video/audio track 7.8 again. Sts watch/listen and answer the questions with a month or year. Check answers. Play the track again, pausing for sts to hear the answers.

Answers
1 March, October 2 July 3 2014 4 July

9 Allow sts time to prepare their ideas individually. They then ask and answer the questions in pairs. Ask some sts to tell the class something about their partner.

10 7.9 Focus on the speech bubble and point out the linked words. Read out the instruction, then play audio track 7.9. See SB page opposite for audio script. Sts listen and notice how the sounds join together.

Listening builder

Read the Listening builder box with sts about linking consonants and vowels. Make sure that sts understand the difference between consonants and vowels. Model some of the vowel sounds in English, (e.g. /e, ɪ, iː, ʊ, æ, ɒ/) then say a selection of consonant sounds (e.g. *s*, *t*, *d*, *n*) to illustrate the difference. Explain that when one word ends in a consonant sound, and the next word starts with a vowel, we link the sounds together, so the two words sound like one word. Ask questions to check concept.

Concept check questions:
What are vowel sounds? (e.g. /e, ɪ, iː, ʊ, æ, ɒ/). *What are consonant sounds?* (e.g. *b*, *t*, *n*, *s*). *When do we link consonants and vowels together?* (when one word ends in a consonant and the next word ends in a vowel). *He's – in – the – kitchen Which words do we link?* (He's‿in). *I like apples – which words do we link?* (like‿apples).

11 7.10 Allow sts time to read the gapped sentences. Play audio track 7.10. See TB page 312 for audio script. Sts listen and complete the sentences. Play the audio again if necessary for sts to check and complete their answers. Check answers with the class.

Answers
1 and I'm an actor
2 October I was in
3 was about an old
4 fourth of April
5 don't understand all

12 As a round-up, sts discuss their own experiences of the theatre, cinema and concerts. Read out the questions, and allow sts time to prepare their ideas individually. Put sts into pairs to discuss the question. Get feedback on their discussions.

PERSONAL BEST

Sts can practise talking about the theatre or cinema further. They write a description of their favourite play or film. Sts could read their descriptions to each other, without saying the name of the play or film, for their classmates to guess.

With weaker sts, write some more questions on the board, e.g. *Who are the characters in the play/film? What happens at the beginning? What happens at the end?* Sts can work in pairs. They think of a play or film that they both like and write three or four sentences about it, answering the questions on the board. Ask some pairs to read their sentences to the class.

EXTRA PRACTICE

Sts work in groups of three. They take turns to use their phones to film their classmates discussing the questions in exercise 12. Allow sts time to watch the films of themselves. Watching themselves on film will help sts to evaluate how naturally and fluently they can speak.

7C Famous decades

1 Match the decades in the box with a–f.

the nineties | the twenty-tens | the seventies | the noughties | the sixties | the eighties

2 Discuss the questions in pairs.

I was born in the eighties. What about you?

1 In which decade were you born?
2 Which decade has the best music and fashion, in your opinion?
3 Which was your favourite decade? Why?

3 7.11 In pairs, complete the quiz with the years in the box. Listen and check.

1969 | 1973 | 1985 | 1991 | 2004 | 2012

The Decades Quiz

On 4 February [1]________, Mark Zuckerberg started Facebook from his bedroom at university. He wanted 500 people to join. Now, more than 1.5 billion people use it!

In [4]________, Korean singer Psy danced *Gangnam Style* all over the world. The song was number 1 in 37 countries. Did you watch the video?

On 20 July [2]________, Neil Armstrong and Buzz Aldrin walked on the moon. 600 million people watched on TV or listened on the radio.

On 30 November [5]________, the USA and Norway played in the first Women's Football World Cup final in China. The result was a 2–1 win for the USA.

In April [3]________, Coca-Cola® tried a new recipe for their drink. People didn't like the flavour, and three months later, the original Coca-Cola was back in the shops.

On 3 April [6]________, Martin Cooper from Motorola called Joel Engel on the world's first mobile phone. Joel quickly stopped the call because he wasn't happy. He worked for rival company AT&T!

4 Read the quiz again. Write the past simple form of verbs 1–8.

1 start ________	3 watch ________	5 dance ________	7 call ________
2 walk ________	4 try ________	6 play ________	8 stop ________

5 **A** Look at the verbs in exercise 4 again and complete the rules.

1 We usually add the letters ____ to verbs to make the past simple form.
2 If the verb ends in *-e*, we add the letter ____ to make the past simple form.
3 If the verb ends in consonant + *y*, we remove the *y* and add the letters ____ to make the past simple form.
4 If the verb ends in consonant + vowel + consonant, we double the last consonant and add ____.

B Complete the sentences from the text to make the negative and question forms of the past simple. Does the main verb change form? Read the Grammar box.

1 People ________ like the flavour.   2 ________ you watch the video?

7C Famous decades

Sts do a quiz about past decades. They then read a text about the best decade for films, and ask and answer questions about things they did in the past.

Grammar	Vocabulary	Pronunciation	Communication
Past simple: regular verbs	Time expressions (*at the weekend, in 1999, last week/month/ year, ten years ago, yesterday*)	*-ed* endings	Talking about things you did in the past

WARMER

Write a few dates from the past on the board, e.g. *2015, 2009, 1998*. Elicit how to say the dates, and revise how to say dates in English if necessary. Then ask individual sts questions about the dates, using *was/were*, e.g. *Where were you in (2015)? Were you a student in (2009)? Were you at school in (2002)?* Use the opportunity to revise the use of *was/were* if necessary. Tell sts they are going to talk more about the past in this lesson.

1 Elicit or explain the meaning of *decade*. In pairs, sts match the decades with the numbers. Check answers, and model and drill pronunciation of the decades. Explain that the word *noughties* comes from the word *nought*, meaning zero.

Answers
a the sixties b the seventies c the eighties
d the nineties e the noughties f the twenty-tens

2 Allow sts time to prepare their answers individually. They then discuss the questions in pairs. Ask some sts to tell the class something they agree on.

3 7.11 Pre-teach *to join, recipe, flavour, result, mobile phone* and *rival*. In pairs, sts complete the quiz with the correct years. Play audio track 7.11. See SB page opposite for audio script. Sts listen and check their answers. See which pair got the most answers right.

Answers
1 2004 2 1969 3 1985 4 2012 5 1991 6 1973

4 Remind sts that we use the past simple to talk about the past. Focus on the first verb (*start*) and ask sts to find the past simple form in paragraph 1. Elicit the answer. Sts then find and write the remaining past simple forms. Check answers.

Answers
1 started 2 walked 3 watched 4 tried 5 danced
6 played 7 called 8 stopped

5 A Read out the first rule and elicit the answer. Sts work in pairs to complete the rules. Check answers.

Answers
1 ed 2 d 3 ied 4 ed

B Sts find the sentences in the text and complete them with the correct verb forms. Check answers, then ask the question to the class and elicit the answer.

Answers
1 didn't 2 Did
No, the main verb doesn't change form, but stays in the base form.

Grammar past simple: regular verbs

Positive:	Negative:	Questions and short answers:
*600 million people **watched** on TV.*	*They **didn't call** on a smartphone.*	***Did** you **try** the new drink?*
*Coca-Cola **tried** a new recipe.*	*Brazil **didn't play** in the final.*	*Yes, I **did**. No, I **didn't**.*

Personal Best

Go to Grammar practice: past simple: regular verbs, page 102

6 7.13 Complete the text with the past simple form of the verbs in brackets. Listen and check.

Were the nineties the best decade for films?

My brother [1] ________ (study) films at university and he thinks the nineties were the best decade for cinema. So last week, I [2] ________ (decide) to watch the film *Titanic* for the first time. It was in the cinema 20 years ago, but I was only two then.
I [3] ________ (love) it … but it's a sad story. It's about a real disaster that [4] ________ (happen) in 1912 in the Atlantic Ocean. Thousands of people [5] ________ (die) because the ship [6] ________ (not carry) enough lifeboats.
After that, I [7] ________ (want) to see more films from the nineties. So at the weekend, I [8] ________ (watch) *Jurassic Park*, *Forrest Gump* and *Pulp Fiction*. On Monday, it was *Toy Story*, and last night, I [9] ________ (start) watching *The Matrix* … but I [10] ________ (not finish) it because at 1.00 a.m. I [11] ________ (need) to go to bed. My brother was right – films from the nineties are amazing!

7 Complete the time expressions with the words in the box. Check your answers in the text in exercise 6.

in   ago   last (x2)   on   at (x2)

1 20 years ________
2 ________ week
3 ________ 1912
4 ________ the weekend
5 ________ night
6 ________ Monday
7 ________ 1.00 a.m.

Personal Best

Go to Vocabulary practice: time expressions, page 124

8 **A** 7.15 **Pronunciation:** *-ed endings* Listen and repeat the sentences from the text. Pay attention to the *-ed* endings in **bold**: /d/, /t/ and /ɪd/.

1 /d/ lov**ed** I lov**ed** it.
2 /t/ watch**ed** I watch**ed** *Jurassic Park*.
3 /ɪd/ need**ed** I need**ed** to go to bed.

B 7.16 Write the verbs in the box in the correct columns. Listen, check and repeat.

danced   wanted   played   tried   walked   visited

/d/	/t/	/ɪd/

Go to Communication practice: Student A page 139, Student B page 147

9 **A** In pairs, ask and answer the questions with the past simple form of the verbs. Write your partner's answers in the table.

A *When did you last watch a film on DVD?*
B *I watched a film on DVD about a year ago.*

When did you last …	Answers
1 watch / a film on DVD?	
2 study / for an exam?	
3 cook / chicken?	
4 play / a musical instrument?	
5 call / a friend on the phone?	

When was the last time you …	Answers
6 use / a computer?	
7 dance / with friends?	
8 relax / at home?	
9 talk / to a neighbour?	
10 listen / to the radio?	

B Tell the class about your partner.

Marco watched a film on DVD about a year ago.

Personal Best Choose six different time expressions and write a true past simple sentence for each one.

Grammar

Read the Grammar box with sts about the past simple: regular verbs. Point out that most verbs add *-ed* in the past simple form, but there are a few spelling rules sts need to learn. Point out that in the past simple, there is only one form for all persons (*I called*, *you called*, *they called*, etc). Point out that we use the base form of the verb, NOT the past simple form, in negative sentences and questions, e.g. *I didn't watch it.* NOT ~~*I didn't watched it*~~. *Did you watch it?* NOT ~~*Did you watched it?*~~. Point out the word order in the question form, e.g. *Did you play football?* NOT ~~*You did play football?*~~ Ask questions to check concept.

Concept check questions:

I watch a film last night – correct? (no – I *watched*). *What do we add to most verbs in the past simple?* (-ed). *What if the verb ends in -e?* (we add 'd'). *What is the past simple form of 'try'?* (tried). *What is the past simple form of 'stop?* (stopped). *I walked to school – can you make this negative?* (I *didn't walk* to school). *Can you make it into a question?* (*Did you walk* to school?).

Go to Grammar practice: past simple: regular verbs, SB page 102/TB page 217. Sts will find more language reference, presentation and practice for the past simple: regular verbs here. Do these exercises with the class, or set them for homework, before continuing with exercise 6 of lesson 7C.

PB Remind sts to go to the app for further self-study grammar practice of the past simple: regular verbs.

6 7.13 Read out the title of the text and elicit what films sts know from the 1990s. Read out the first gapped sentence and elicit the correct verb form. Sts then read the text and complete it with the correct verb forms. Play audio track 7.13. See SB page opposite for audio script. Sts listen and check their answers.

Answers
1 studied 2 decided 3 loved 4 happened 5 died
6 didn't carry 7 wanted 8 watched 9 started
10 didn't finish 11 needed

3 x PRACTICE *SB page 65, exercise 6*

1 Do the exercise as normal. To check answers, play the audio and pause before each missing verb form. Elicit the answer, then play the audio to check. Write the correct spellings on the board.

2 Ask sts to close their books. Read out the text again, making a beeping sound or coughing to indicate each gap. Sts try to remember the missing past simple verbs.

3 With books closed, write the base form of the verbs from the text on the board, e.g. *study*, *decide*, etc. In pairs, sts try to remember how each verb was used and write sentences. Sts can check their answers in the text.

7 Sts find the time expressions with the correct words, then check their answers in the text. Check answers, and check that sts understand all the time expressions. Point out the position of *ago*: *20 years ago*, NOT ~~*ago 20 years*~~.

Answers
1 ago 2 last 3 in 4 at 5 last 6 on 7 at

Go to Vocabulary practice: time expressions, SB page 124/TB page 261
Sts will find more language presentation and practice for time expressions here. Do these exercises with the class, or set them for homework, before continuing with exercise 8A of lesson 7C.

PB Remind sts to go to the app for further self-study vocabulary practice of time expressions.

8 A 7.15 Model pronunciation of the three sounds, /d/, /t/ and /ɪd/, in isolation. Play audio track 7.15 once for sts to listen and notice the pronunciations. See SB page opposite for audio script. Play the audio again for sts to listen and repeat.

B 7.16 Play audio track 7.16 once for sts to listen to the verbs. See SB page opposite for audio script. Play the audio again for sts to write the verbs in the box. Check answers, then play the audio once more for sts to check and repeat.

Answers
/d/ played, tried
/t/ danced, walked
/ɪd/ wanted, visited

Go to Communication practice
Divide the class into Student A and Student B. All 'Student A' sts should go to SB page 139. All 'Student B' sts should go to SB page 147. Go to TB page 291 for the teacher notes. Do the activity, then continue with exercise 9A of lesson 7C.

9 A Read out the example question and elicit one or two more questions as further examples. Sts prepare the questions in pairs. Check the form of the questions, and check that sts understand all the questions. In pairs, sts ask and answer the questions, and write their partner's answers. Point out that they should use full sentences in their answers, so they repeat the verb.

B Ask sts in turn to tell the class something about their partner.

PERSONAL BEST

Sts can practise talking about the past further. They write true sentences using six of the time expressions. They can compare their sentences in pairs.

For weaker sts, write four sentence beginnings on the board using different time expressions, e.g. *Last night, I ... ; At the weekend, I ...* . Sts complete the sentences with their own ideas. Ask some sts to read their sentences to the class.

7D A weekend away

1 In pairs, order the pictures from 1–6 to make a story about Elena and her father's trip to Oxford.

2 Read Elena's email and check the order of the pictures in exercise 1.

To: Becky Stewart

Subject: My weekend

Hi Becky,

How are things? I hope you're well.

Did I tell you about last weekend? I visited my sister Hannah. She lives in Oxford now. I wanted to go on my own … but Dad decided to come with me!

We travelled by train on Saturday. We arrived in Oxford and Hannah was at the train station. In the afternoon, we explored the city. First, we walked round the university. It was beautiful, but Dad stopped to take hundreds of photos! Then we visited an art gallery. Dad studied every painting and looked at every sculpture – we were there for hours! After that, Hannah and I wanted to go shopping, but Dad wanted to visit a museum. It was so boring!

It was a disaster! This weekend, I want to stay at home, or go away without Dad!

See you soon.

Elena

3 **A** Read the email again. Are the sentences true (T) or false (F)?

1 Elena and her dad travelled to Oxford. ____
2 They stayed in Oxford for a week. ____
3 Elena's dad didn't like the university. ____
4 They explored the university on foot. ____
5 They didn't stay in the art gallery for a long time. ____
6 Hannah and Elena didn't want to visit the museum. ____

B Look at the email again and answer the questions. Then read the Skill box.

1 How does Elena start her email?
2 How does she ask how her friend is?
3 How does she introduce her news?
4 How does she finish her email?

Skill **writing informal emails**

We write informal emails to friends and people we know well.

- Start the email in a friendly way: *Hi …, Hello …*
- Ask about the person: *How are you? How are things? I hope you're well.*
- Say why you are writing: *Did I tell you about …? I wanted to tell/ask you …*
- Finish the email in a friendly way: *See you soon, Bye for now, Take care.*

 EXTRA PRACTICE Workbook page 43

7D A weekend away

Sts read an informal email about a weekend away. They study tips for writing informal emails and the use of sequencers, then write their own informal emails about a weekend away.

Writing	Skill	Text builder
An informal email	Writing informal emails	Sequencers

WARMER

Ask: *Do you sometimes go away for a weekend? Who do you usually go with? Where do you go? What do you enjoy doing on a weekend away?* Elicit a range of answers from individual sts, e.g. visiting friends or relatives, visiting a new city, etc. Ask: *Where are your favourite places for a weekend away?* Elicit a few ideas.

1 Focus on the pictures and explain that they tell a story about a weekend away. Ask: *Which picture do you think comes first?* Elicit some possible answers. In pairs, sts order the pictures to make a story. Elicit a few possible answers, but don't confirm them.

2 Sts read the email to check their ideas. Check the answer with the class and ask: *Do you think this weekend away was fun? Why?*

Answers
1 a 2 f 3 e 4 c 5 d 6 b

3 **A** Read out the first sentence and ask: *Is this true?* (yes) Sts read the email again and decide if the remaining sentences are true or false. Check answers.

Answers
1 T 2 F 3 F 4 T 5 F 6 T

B Sts look at the email again and answer the questions. Check answers. Point out that the answers are all examples of informal language that we use in emails to friends and family members.

Answers
1 Hi Becky
2 How are things?
3 Did I tell you about last weekend?
4 See you soon.

Skill

Read the Skill box with sts about writing informal emails. Check that sts understand all the phrases.

4 Complete the email with the words in the box.

hope how hello tell now

To: George Hawkins
Subject: Fantastic weekend

[1]________ George,
[2]________ are you? I [3]________ you and the family are well.
I wanted to [4]________ you about last weekend. My daughter Elena and I travelled to Oxford. My other daughter, Hannah, moved there a few months ago, so we stayed with her.
On Saturday, we walked into town. First, we explored the university. It was very interesting. Elena loved all the old buildings! Then we visited an art gallery. We were there for hours – the girls didn't want to leave! After that, we looked around the museum. I was quite tired, but the girls really enjoyed it. It was a great weekend. I think Elena wants to do it again soon.
Bye for [5]________ .
Frank

5 Discuss the questions in pairs.

1 Who is Frank?
2 What differences are there between Frank and Elena's emails?
3 Do you enjoy visiting art galleries and museums? Why/Why not?

6 Order sentences a–c from 1–3. Check your answers in the email in exercise 4.

a ☐ After that, we looked around the museum.
b ☐ First, we explored the university.
c ☐ Then we visited an art gallery.

Text builder sequencers

We can show the order of events with *First*, *Then* and *After that*:
First, we walked into town. Then we visited the university. After that, we explored the centre.

Look! We usually use a comma after ***First*** and ***After that***.

7 Read the Text builder. Then write sentences in the past simple with sequencers.

First, we listened to some music. Then we cooked dinner ...

1 We / listen to / some music. We / cook / dinner. We / watch / a film.
2 She / visit / her sister. She / call / her mum. She / talk to / her dad.
3 I / walk to / my friend's house. We / study / English together. We / play / football.

8 **A** **PREPARE** Think of a weekend when you were somewhere interesting. Make notes about what happened. Think about:

- where you travelled to
- how you travelled
- who was with you
- where you stayed
- the places that you visited
- if you enjoyed it

Use these regular verbs to help you:

visit travel play walk watch listen to wait love cook explore stay talk enjoy need want try

B **PRACTISE** Write an email to a friend about your weekend. Use the Skill box and Text builder to help you.

C **PERSONAL BEST** Swap your email with your partner. Does your partner use the past simple correctly? Can you correct any mistakes?

Personal Best Write about a day when you visited a lot of places, like Elena's day in Oxford.

4 Sts complete the email with the correct words. Check answers. Ask sts to read Frank's email quickly, for general meaning. Ask: *Where did Frank go?* (to Oxford). *What places did he visit?* (the university, an art gallery and a museum).

Answers
1 Hello 2 How 3 hope 4 tell 5 now

5 Read through the questions with the class and make sure sts understand everything. Sts discuss the questions in pairs. Check answers.

Answers
1 Frank is Elena's and Hannah's dad
2 (possible answer) Frank enjoyed the university, the art gallery and the museum. Elena enjoyed the university, but she didn't enjoy the art gallery or the museum. She wanted to go shopping with Hannah.
3 Sts' own answers.

6 Explain to sts that they need to look at the events in the three sentences, and order them in the order that Frank and Elena did them. Sts order the sentences, then check their answers in the email in exercise 4. Check answers.

Answers
a 3 b 1 c 2

Text builder

Read the Text builder box with sts about sequencers. Explain that we use sequencers to show the order of events in a story. Point out the use of commas after *First* and *After that*, but not after *Then*. Ask questions to check concept.

Concept check questions:
Why do we use sequencers? (to shows the order of events in a story). *What do we use for the first event?* (First). *What do we use for the second event?* (Then). *What do we use for the third event?* (After that). *Which two sequencers have a comma after them?* (*First* and *After that*).

7 Sts write sentences using the sequencers. Check answers.

Answers
1 First, we listened to some music. Then we cooked dinner. After that, we watched a film.
2 First, she visited her sister. Then she called her mum. After that, she talked to her dad.
3 First, I walked to my friend's house. Then we studied English together. After that, we played football.

3 x PRACTICE *SB page 67, exercise 7*

1 Do the exercise as normal. To check answers, ask groups of three sts in turn to read out each sentence.

2 With books closed, write only the verb prompts for each sentence on the board, e.g. *listen, cook, watch*. In pairs, sts try to remember the sentences and write them. They can open their books to check.

3 Write the following verbs on the board: *watch, listen, talk, try, play, travel, visit, cook*. In pairs, sts write two sentences using sequencers. Encourage them to make their sentences original, e.g. *First, we visited a gallery. Then we watched a game of football. After that, we cooked some pasta*. Ask pairs to read their sentences to the class.

8 Sts follow the steps to write an informal email.

A PREPARE Sts read the notes and prepare their ideas. Monitor while they are working, and help with vocabulary if necessary. Encourage them to use some negative verbs, as well as positive ones.

B PRACTISE Sts write their email. Refer them back to the Skill box to remind them of the conventions of writing an email, and refer them to the Text builder box to remind them about how to use sequencers.

C PERSONAL BEST Sts work in pairs. They swap their emails with a partner to check that their partner has used past simple verbs correctly, and correct any mistakes.

PERSONAL BEST

Sts can practise writing about a day out. They write a description of a day when they visited a lot of places. Sts can share their descriptions in small groups and decide whose day was fun.

Refer weaker sts to the picture in exercise 8, and elicit that it shows London. In pairs, sts write sentences about the visit to London in the picture, using the verbs in 8A. Ask some pairs to read their sentences to the class.

EXTRA PRACTICE

Write the following gapped sentences on the board:
1 It ______ very interesting.
2 We ______ there for hours.
3 I ______ quite tired.
4 It ______ a great weekend.

Explain to sts that the missing words are all past simple forms of *be*. In pairs, sts complete the sentences from memory, then read Frank's email again to check. Check answers, and point out that sentences like these, which give more information can make an email or story more interesting.

Answers
1 was 2 were 3 was 4 was

UNIT 8

Travel

LANGUAGE past simple: irregular verbs ■ travel verbs

8A Incredible journeys

1 Complete the sentences with the verbs in the box.

get lost book fly miss ride take

1 Some of my friends ________ motorbikes to work.

3 I sometimes ________ the bus because I get up late.

5 I never ________ because I don't like it!

2 I always ________ train tickets early to get a good price.

4 If I go out at night, I usually ________ a taxi home.

6 I often ________ in a new town.

Personal Best

Go to Vocabulary practice: travel verbs, page 125

2 In pairs, say the sentences in exercise 1. Decide if they are true or false for your partner.

A *Some of my friends ride motorbikes to work.* **B** *False.*
A *You're right. All my friends drive to work.*

3 Look at the title and the picture. In pairs, guess what the story is about. Read the text and check.

Around the world *for love*

In January 2001, Ian Johnstone from Yorkshire in the UK went to work in Australia for a year, but his girlfriend Amy stayed at home. It was difficult to be so far away from her and after six months, Ian planned to visit her. He wanted to ask her to marry him, but he didn't tell her about his plans … it was a surprise visit!

Ian booked a flight and in July he flew from Sydney to London, with a stop in Singapore. But he didn't know about Amy's plans. She also wanted to surprise Ian with a visit, and at that exact moment, she was also on a plane … to Australia!

When Ian arrived in London, he bought some flowers and took the train to Yorkshire. Amy wasn't at home, so Ian waited for her. At the same time, Amy arrived at Ian's flat in Sydney. When his flatmate told her that Ian was 17,000 km away in England, Amy thought that it was a joke!

It wasn't possible for Ian or Amy to change their tickets, so they didn't see each other. But the story had a happy ending. Ian called Amy and asked her to marry him. And what did she say? She said 'yes', of course!

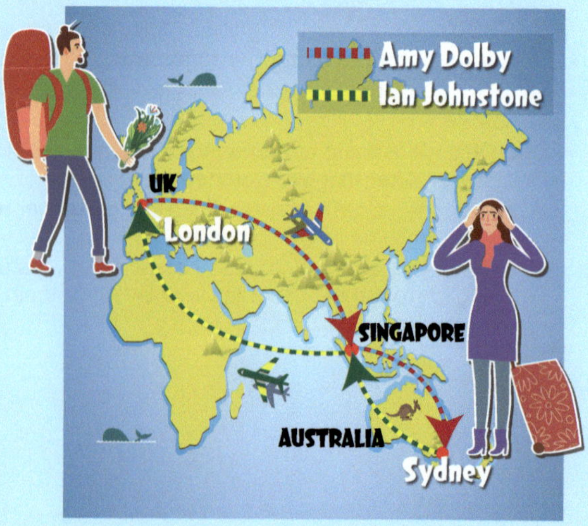

68

UNIT 8 Travel

UNIT 8 OVERVIEW: This unit focuses on the topic of travel. Sts read about a couple who flew halfway around the world to surprise each other. They listen to someone talking about their holiday, then talk about their own holiday or travel experiences. They practise talking about the weather and discuss how their own towns or cities have changed over time. In *Learning Curve*, Marc makes a phone call to a travel agent.

LANGUAGE

Grammar	Vocabulary	Pronunciation
Past simple: irregular verbs; *there was/were*	Travel verbs; weather and seasons; nature	Irregular past simple verbs; sentence stress

SKILLS

Reading	Speaking
Understanding the main idea; modifiers	Starting and ending a phone call at work; buying a ticket

LANGUAGE 8A

8A Incredible journeys

Sts read a text about a couple who travelled halfway around the world to surprise each other. They then read about a man who spent eleven years walking around the world. They study someone's travel plans, then listen to the person talking about what actually happened. They talk about their own experiences of holidays and travel.

Grammar	Vocabulary	Pronunciation	Communication
Past simple: irregular verbs	Travel verbs (*book, fly, get in, get lost, get off, get on, get out of, miss, ride, sail, take, walk*)	Irregular past simple verbs	Talking about holidays or journeys in the past

WARMER

Ask: *Where do you usually go on holiday?* Elicit a few ideas, then ask: *What do you enjoy about travelling? What do you dislike?* Elicit a few ideas, then put sts into pairs to discuss the good and bad things about travelling and make two lists. Ask pairs in turn to share their lists with the class, and write useful travel vocabulary on the board, e.g. *train, late, flight, wait, airport, delayed*, etc. See who in the class loves travelling, and who is less keen.

1 Focus on each picture in turn and read out the gapped sentence. Use the pictures to teach the meanings of words in the sentences, e.g. *motorbike, bus, late*. In pairs, sts complete the sentences with the correct verbs. They can use their dictionaries to help, or can try to guess the correct verbs. Check answers, and make sure sts understand all the completed sentences. Model and drill pronunciation of the verbs.

Answers
1 ride 2 book 3 miss 4 take 5 fly 6 get lost

3 x PRACTICE *SB page 68, exercise 1*

1 Do the exercise as normal. To check answers, focus on each gapped sentence in turn and read out three possible sentences, e.g. *Some of my friends book motorbikes/ride motorbikes/miss motorbikes to work.* Elicit the correct verbs and confirm the meaning.

2 In pairs, sts cover the sentences, and look at the pictures and wordpool box. They try to remember the correct sentence for each picture. They can look at the sentences and their answers to check.

3 With books closed, write the verbs from exercise 1 on the board and put sts into teams. Teams take turns to choose a verb and make their own sentence using it. If their sentence is correct, give them a point and cross the verb off the board. If their sentence is wrong, don't correct it, but move on to the next team. Continue until all the verbs are crossed off.

Go to Vocabulary practice: travel verbs, SB page 125/TB page 263.
Sts will find more language presentation and practice for travel verbs here. Do these exercises with the class, or set them for homework, before continuing with exercise 2 of lesson 8A.

PB Remind sts to go to the app for further self-study vocabulary practice of travel verbs.

2 Model the task with a confident student. Encourage the student to say if it is true or false for them. Sts then work in pairs to complete the task. Get feedback on who guessed correctly.

3 In pairs, sts look at the title and picture, and guess what the story is about. Point out to sts that guessing what a text is about before they read can help them to understand the text better. Sts read the text to check their ideas.

Answer
The text is about two people who flew to visit each other at the same time.

4 Are the sentences true (T) or false (F)? Read the text again and check.

1 Ian went to Australia with Amy. ____
2 He wanted to see his girlfriend. ____
3 Amy lived in London. ____
4 She travelled to Australia to see Ian. ____
5 They changed their tickets. ____
6 Amy didn't want to marry Ian. ____

5 **A** Look at the past simple verbs in **bold** in the sentence from the text. Which verb is regular and which is irregular?

Ian **booked** a flight and in July he **flew** from Sydney to London.

B Find the past simple form of the irregular verbs in the text. Then read the Grammar box.

1 go ________ 2 fly _flew_ 3 buy ________ 4 take ________ 5 think ________ 6 say ________

Grammar **past simple: irregular verbs**

Positive:	Negative:	Questions:	Short answers:
*Ian **went** to work in Australia.*	*Ian **didn't go** to work in Singapore.*	***Did** Ian **go** home?*	*Yes, he **did**.*
*He **flew** to London.*	*He **didn't fly** to Sydney.*	***Did** he **fly** alone?*	*No, he **didn't**.*
*He **bought** some flowers.*	*He **didn't buy** chocolate.*	***Did** he **buy** a ring?*	

Personal Best

Go to Grammar practice: past simple: irregular verbs, page 103

6 Complete the text with the past simple form of the verbs in brackets.

Around the world – on foot!

This is Jean Béliveau, a Canadian who walked around the world, through 64 countries in 11 years!

When [1]________ **he** ________ **(leave)?**
Jean [2]________ (leave) his home on 18 August 2000, and he [3]________ (not get) home until 2011. His wife, Luce, [4]________ (not go) with him, but she [5]________ (fly) to meet him eleven times.

Where [6]________ **he** ________ **(sleep)?**
He [7]________ (sleep) in people's homes, parks, schools, hospitals – and even in a police station! People also [8]________ (buy) him food and drink.

Why [9]________ **he** ________ **(do) it?**
He [10]________ (do) it because he wanted people to know about children's lives in other countries.

7 **A** 8.3 **Pronunciation:** irregular past simple verbs Listen and repeat the past simple verbs. Pay attention to the vowel sounds /ɒ/, /ɔː/ and /əʊ/.

1 /ɒ/ got lost 2 /ɔː/ bought thought 3 /əʊ/ rode drove

B 8.4 Underline the words in the sentences with the same vowel sounds. Listen, check and repeat.

1 I got on the bus.
2 We all bought a ticket.
3 I rode home on my bike.
4 He lost his new watch.
5 I thought it was a horse.
6 She drove to my home.

Go to Communication practice: Student A page 140, Student B page 148

8 **A** 8.5 Read Leanne's plans for a holiday to Croatia last summer. Then listen and correct the information with what really happened.

B In pairs, make sentences about Leanne's trip.

She didn't fly from Manchester. She flew from London.

My trip to Croatia

24 July: fly from Manchester to Dubrovnik
30 July: take bus to Split
5 August: sail to Šolta
10 August: take train to Zagreb and fly home
***Activities**: eat local food, swim in the sea, take photos … fall in love?*

9 Think about a holiday or journey. In pairs, ask and answer the questions in the boxes.

Where did you go? When did you go? How did you travel? Who did you go with? What did you do? Did you have a good time?

Personal Best Write about your partner's holiday or journey from exercise 9.

69

4 Read out the first sentence and ask: *Is it true or false?* (false). Elicit the part of the text which gives the information. Sts complete the task. Check answers.

> **Answers**
> 1 F 2 T 3 F 4 T 5 F 6 F

5 A Read out the sentence and elicit which verb is regular and which is irregular. Elicit that *flew* is the past simple of *fly*.

> **Answer**
> *booked* is regular, *flew* is irregular

B Ask sts to read the first sentence of the text again. Ask: *What is the verb in the sentence?* (went). *Which verb do you think it is the past simple of?* (go). Sts complete the task. Check answers.

> **Answers**
> 1 went 2 flew 3 bought 4 took 5 thought 6 said

Grammar

Read the Grammar box with sts about the past simple: irregular verbs. Point out to sts that they need to learn which verbs are irregular, and what the irregular forms are. Explain that in negative sentences and questions, irregular verbs behave in the same way as regular verbs, using the base form of the verb rather than the past simple form, e.g. *I didn't think about this*. NOT ~~*I didn't thought about this*~~. Ask questions to check concept.

Concept check questions:
Do irregular verbs add -ed in the past simple? (no). *Do all irregular verbs change in the same way in the past simple?* (no). *What's the past simple of 'go'?* (went). *What's the past simple of 'fly'?* (flew). *How do we form negatives in the past simple with irregular verbs?* (with *didn't* and the base form of the verb). *She didn't flew to New York – correct?* (no – She *didn't fly* to New York). *Can you make that into a question?* (Did she fly to New York?).

Go to Grammar practice: past simple: irregular verbs, SB page 103/TB page 219. Sts will find more language reference, presentation and practice for the past simple: irregular verbs here. Do these exercises with the class, or set them for homework, before continuing with exercise 6 of lesson 8A.

PB Remind sts to go to the app for further self-study grammar practice of the past simple: irregular verbs.

6 Read out the title of the text and check that sts understand *on foot*. Point out that all the verbs in brackets have got irregular past simple forms. Sts read the text and complete it with the correct verb forms. Check answers.

> **Answers**
> 1 did, leave
> 2 left
> 3 didn't get
> 4 didn't go
> 5 flew
> 6 did, sleep
> 7 slept
> 8 bought
> 9 did, do
> 10 did

7 A 8.3 Play audio track 8.3. See SB page opposite for audio script. Sts listen and notice the pronunciation. Point out that in English the pronunciation of words is not always clear from the spelling. Play the audio again for sts to repeat.

B 8.4 Read out the first sentence and elicit that *got* and *on* have the same vowel sound. In pairs, sts complete the task. Play audio track 8.4 for sts to check their answers. See SB page opposite for audio script. Check the answers, then play the audio again for sts to repeat.

> **Answers**
> 1 got, on
> 2 all, bought
> 3 rode, home
> 4 lost, watch
> 5 thought, horse
> 6 drove, home

Go to Communication practice
Divide the class into Student A and Student B. All 'Student A' sts should go to SB page 140. All 'Student B' sts should go to SB page 148. Go to TB page 293 for the teacher notes. Do the activity, then continue with exercise 8A of lesson 8A.

8 A 8.5 Read through the plans with the class. Ask: *Do you think this trip sounds fun?* Explain that Leanne's holiday didn't go according to the plan, so some things were different. Play audio track 8.5. See TB page 312 for audio script. Sts listen and correct the information. Check answers.

> **Answers**
> 25 July: flew from London to Dubrovnik
> 30 July: took taxi to Split
> 6 August: sail to Solta
> Didn't take photos
> Fell in love with Croatia

B Sts write negative and positive sentences to correct the information in the plans. Check answers.

> **Answers**
> She didn't fly on 24 July. She flew on 25 July.
> She didn't take the bus to Split. She took a taxi.
> She didn't sail to Šolta on 5 August. She sailed to Šolta on 6 August.

9 Read out the questions and ask: *Which verbs are irregular in the past simple?* You may have to remind them of the past simple form of *have* (had). Allow sts time to prepare their answers individually. Sts then ask and answer the questions in pairs. Ask some sts to tell the class about their partner's holiday or journey.

PERSONAL BEST

Sts can practise using the past simple and writing about holidays or journeys further. They write a description of their partner's holiday or journey from exercise 8. They can swap descriptions with their partner and correct any details that are wrong.

Weaker sts can work in pairs and change some of the details in Leanne's plans, e.g. *My trip to Italy*. They then write some sentences about her trip, using the past simple. Ask some sts to read their sentences to the class.

8B Crazy weather!

1 Match the weather phrases in the box with pictures a–d on page 71.

It's cold. It's sunny. It's raining. It's windy.

Personal Best

Go to Vocabulary practice: weather and seasons, page 126

2 In pairs, talk about the seasons in your country. Use *love/like/don't like/hate*.

I don't like autumn because it rains and it's cold and windy.

Skill understanding the main idea

When you see a text for the first time, try to understand the main idea quickly.

- Look at the title and pictures.
- Read the first line of each paragraph.
- Use this information to understand what the text is about.

3 **A** Read the Skill box. Then read the title and the highlighted sentences on page 71. Tick (✓) the main idea.

a Robbie had lots of problems with transport in Germany. ☐
b Robbie went on holiday and the weather changed a lot. ☐
c Robbie was in Berlin in the summer, but it snowed all week. ☐
d Robbie didn't like the weather in Germany, so he went to Ireland. ☐

B Read the whole text and check.

4 Are the sentences true (T) or false (F)? Read the text again and check.

1 Robbie went to Berlin with his girlfriend. ____
2 They had ice cream in Viktoria Park. ____
3 They waited on a train for three hours. ____
4 It rained at the Television Tower. ____
5 They didn't go to the concert because it snowed. ____
6 They arrived at the airport late and missed the flight. ____

5 Match the halves to make sentences from the text. Do the modifiers in **bold** come before or after the adjectives?

1 When we got off the plane, it was **very**
2 When we got to the park, it was **quite**
3 And in the afternoon, it was **really**
4 The views were**n't very**

a cold.
b good.
c windy.
d hot and sunny.

Text builder modifiers

We use modifiers before an adjective to make the meaning stronger or less strong:

really/very	*It was **really** sunny. The film was **very** exciting.*
quite	*The museum was **quite** interesting.*
not very	*The food wasn't **very** good.*

6 Read the Text builder. Then write sentences with the words and a modifier.

The weather today is very hot.

1 the weather today / hot
2 the *Star Wars* films / exciting
3 I think English / difficult
4 public transport in my country / expensive
5 my street / noisy
6 people in my city / friendly

7 In pairs, talk about your last trip or holiday. What was the weather like?

Last year, I visited Morocco. It was very hot and sunny in the day, and really cold at night.

 EXTRA PRACTICE Workbook page 47; photocopiable activity activities 8B Vocabulary and 8B Skills

8B Crazy weather!

Sts read about a trip to Berlin, in Germany, when the weather was very changeable. They then talk about the weather during their last trip or holiday.

Vocabulary	Reading	Skill	Text builder
Weather and seasons (*cloudy, cold, dry, foggy, hot, rain, snow, sunny, warm, wet, windy; spring, summer, autumn, winter*)	Sts read a text about a week of changeable weather during a visit to Berlin, in Germany.	Understanding the main idea	Modifiers

WARMER

Ask: *When do you usually go on holiday? In January? September?* Elicit a range of answers, and revise the months. Ask: *Why do you go in (August)?* Elicit answers, and elicit the idea that it is nice to go on holiday when the weather is good. Ask: *Is the weather always good in (August)?* Elicit the idea that the weather can change, and is not always good. Tell sts they are going to read about a trip to Germany, and practise talking about the weather.

1 Read through the weather phrases in the box with the class and teach the meanings if necessary. Sts match the weather phrases with the pictures. Check answers.

> **Answers**
> **a** It's sunny. **b** It's windy. **c** It's raining. **d** It's cold.

Go to Vocabulary practice: weather and seasons, SB page 126/TB page 265.
Sts will find more language presentation and practice for weather and seasons here. Do these exercises with the class, or set them for homework, before continuing with exercise 2 of lesson 8B.

PB Remind sts to go to the app for further self-study vocabulary practice of weather and seasons.

2 Read out the example sentence and give one or two more examples about your country, e.g. *I like summer because it's hot and sunny*. Sts talk about the seasons in pairs. Elicit some ideas from the class.

Skill

Read the Skill box with sts about understanding the main idea. Check they understand *main idea*. Point out to sts that they don't need to understand every word in a text in order to understand the main idea.

3 **A** Sts read the title and the highlighted sentences, then choose the main idea. Elicit some possible answers, but don't confirm them at this stage.

B Sts read the whole text to check their ideas. Check the answer with the class.

> **Answer**
> b

4 Sts read the text again and decide if the sentences are true or false. Check answers, eliciting the correct information from the text.

> **Answers**
> **1** T **2** F **3** T **4** T **5** F **6** F

5 Read out the first sentence beginning and elicit the correct ending. Sts complete the matching task. Check answers, then read out each completed sentence with and without the bold word. Elicit that the bold words change the meaning of the adjectives slightly.

> **Answers**
> **1** d **2** a **3** c **4** b

Text builder

Read the Text builder box with sts about modifiers. Explain that modifiers make the meaning of an adjective either stronger or less strong. Point out the graphic in the box, and explain that *really* and *very* make the meaning stronger, *quite* makes the meaning a little bit less strong, and *not very* makes the meaning much less strong. Ask questions to check concept.

Concept check questions:
What do modifiers do to adjectives? (make the meaning stronger or less strong). *I'm happy – I'm very happy: which is stronger?* (I'm very happy). *It's really cold – it's quite cold: which is stronger?* (it's really cold). *It was very warm – can you make this a bit less strong?* (it was *quite* warm). *Can you make it much less strong?* (it *wasn't very* warm).

6 Read out the example sentence and explain to sts that they can choose which modifier to use in each sentence. Encourage them to use a range of different modifiers. To check answers, ask pairs of sts to read out their sentences. Ask the class: *Which sentence has a stronger meaning?*

7 Read out the task and the example sentences. Allow sts to prepare their ideas individually. They then talk about their last trip or holiday in pairs. Ask some sts to tell the class about their partner's trip.

Travel news

Four Seasons In One Week

Robbie Irwin

Monday 12 March

My girlfriend and I arrived in Berlin today on holiday. We thought Germany was cold in March, so we only brought winter clothes, but we had a surprise. When we got off the plane, it was very hot and sunny! So this afternoon, we went to the shops and bought shorts and T-shirts and walked around the city centre. I even had an ice cream!

Wednesday 14 March

Today we decided to visit Viktoria Park, but the weather changed. It was warm when we left the hotel, so we wore our new shorts and T-shirts. But when we got to the park, it was quite cold. And in the afternoon, it was really windy. We decided to visit Museum Island, so we took a train back into the city … but a tree fell on the tracks, and we didn't move for three hours! After that, we went back to the hotel, changed our clothes and had dinner in a restaurant.

Thursday 15 March

The weather here is crazy – this morning it was sunny again! We decided to visit the famous Television Tower. It's over 350m tall and I wanted to take some photos of the city. But when we got to the top of the tower, it was cloudy and it started to rain – the views weren't very good. We bought some umbrellas and went to see a concert. When we came out – guess what? It was warm and sunny again!

Saturday 17 March

I can't believe it – it's 11.00 p.m. and we're still in Berlin Airport! It's really cold and it snowed all day. We took a taxi to the airport and when we arrived, we saw that there were no flights. The next flight is tomorrow morning at 7.00 a.m.

Sunday 18 March

Finally, we're back home in Ireland. We had bad luck with the weather, but we had a great trip and we loved Berlin.

a

b

c

d

Personal Best Write a paragraph about the weather in your town or city in different seasons.

PERSONAL BEST

Sts can practise talking about the weather further. They write a paragraph about the weather in their town or city in different seasons. They can compare their paragraphs in small groups and decide which places have nice weather.

Weaker sts can write one sentence about each season in their country. You could write the sentence beginnings on the board for them, e.g. *In the spring, it's ...* . Ask some sts to read their sentences to the class.

EXTRA PRACTICE

Divide the class into groups of four. Allocate one paragraph of the text on page 71 to each student (student 4 can have paragraphs 4 and 5). Sts read their paragraph again and note down all the regular and irregular past simple forms, and the base form of each verb. Point out that if a verb is used in a negative sentence in the text, they will have to look in their dictionary to find out if it is regular or irregular. In their groups, sts then share their lists with each other. Bring their ideas together on the board in two lists of *regular verbs* and *irregular verbs*. Remind sts that they need to learn which verbs are irregular, and what the irregular forms are.

Answers
regular verbs: arrive, walk, decide, change, move, want, start, snow, love
irregular verbs: think – thought, be – was/were, bring – brought, have – had, get – got, go – went, buy – bought, wear – wore, take – took, fall – fell, come – came, see – saw

EXTRA PRACTICE

Ask sts to imagine this was their holiday in Berlin, and they are showing a friend their holiday photos. Ask them to choose one of the photos and prepare to tell their partner about it. They can read the relevant paragraph of the text again and make some notes to help them. Tell them they could also change some of the details, as long as their description fits the picture. You could set a word limit of 10 or 12 words for sts' notes, to prevent them from writing too much. In pairs, sts then cover the text and tell their partner about their photo. Their partner listens and guesses the photo. If sts have their own holiday photos on their phones, they could then choose one of their own photos and tell a partner about their own holiday experiences, saying where they went, what they did and what the weather was like.

8C Then and now

1 Match the words in the box with the parts of the picture 1–6.

sky	field	forest	mountain	river	tree

1 ______ 4 ______
2 ______ 5 ______
3 ______ 6 ______

Personal Best

Go to Vocabulary practice: nature, page 127

2 Discuss the questions in pairs.

1 Which country is the picture in exercise 1?
2 What nature can you see out of the window?
3 Do you prefer beaches, mountains or forests? Why?

3 Read the introduction to a radio show. Answer the questions.

1 How many people live in Shenzhen? ______
2 Where does Liu Jiang live now? ______
3 What's her job? ______
4 When was she last in Shenzhen? ______

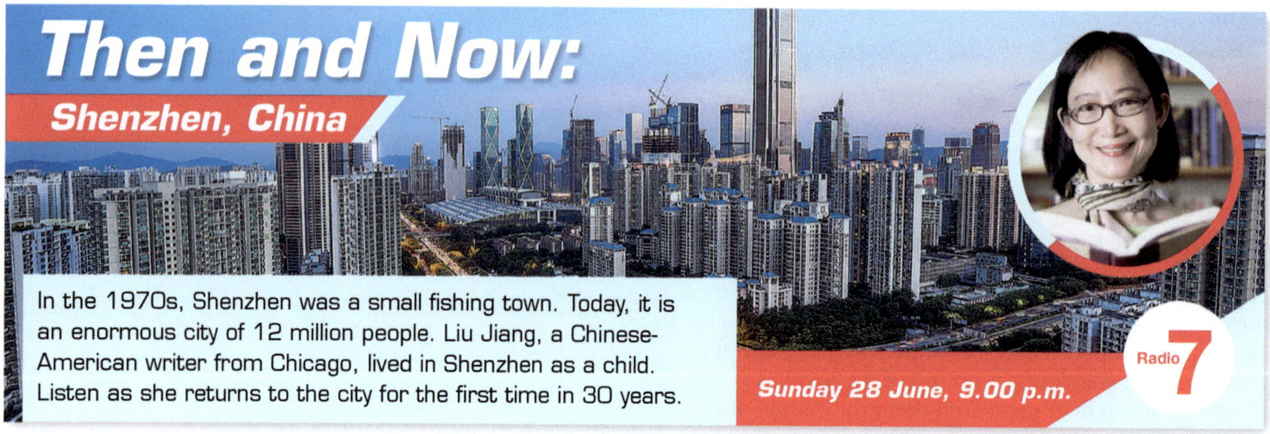

In the 1970s, Shenzhen was a small fishing town. Today, it is an enormous city of 12 million people. Liu Jiang, a Chinese-American writer from Chicago, lived in Shenzhen as a child. Listen as she returns to the city for the first time in 30 years.

4 8.8 Listen to the radio show. Tick (✓) the things that Shenzhen had 30 years ago and has today.

	Fields	Forest	Tall buildings	River	Train station	Airport	University
Shenzhen 30 years ago							
Shenzhen today							

5 **A** 8.8 Match the halves to make sentences and questions. Listen again and check.

1 **There were** fields
2 **There was** a forest
3 **There weren't** any cars
4 **Was there** public transport
5 **Were there** any trains
6 **There wasn't** a university

a or buses?
b here before.
c – everyone had bicycles.
d to travel around the country?
e where we played.
f around the town.

B Look at the words in **bold** in sentences 1–6 again. Choose the correct options to complete the rules. Then read the Grammar box.

1 We use *there was* and *there were* to talk about *the present* / *the past*.
2 We use *there was* and *there wasn't* with *singular* / *plural* nouns.
3 We use *there were* and *there weren't* with *singular* / *plural* nouns.

 EXTRA PRACTICE Workbook page 48; photocopiable activity 8C Vocabulary

8C Then and now

Sts read a text about the city of Shenzhen in China in the past and present, and listen to someone talking about returning to the city and seeing the changes. They then read about the ancient city of Pompeii, and talk about their own town or city in the past and present.

Grammar	Vocabulary	Pronunciation	Communication
there was/were	Nature (*beach, cloud, field, flower, forest, grass, mountain, river, sea, sky, sun, tree*)	Sentence stress	Talking about your town or city in the past and present

WARMER

Ask: *What's your town or city like? Is it big? Is it busy? How many people are there?* Elicit a few answers from individual sts, then ask: *What about in the past? What about 30 years ago? Was it smaller then? Was it quiet?* Elicit a few answers, and elicit that towns and cities change over time. Tell sts that in this lesson they are going to read and talk about cities in the past and the present.

1 Read through the words in the box with the class and teach the meanings if necessary. Sts then match the words with the parts of the picture. Check answers. Model and drill pronunciation of the words.

Answers
1 tree 2 mountain 3 forest 4 field 5 sky 6 river

3 x PRACTICE *SB page 72, exercise 1*

1 Do the exercise as normal. To check answers, read out each word in turn. Ask: *Which number is the (sky)?* Get sts to show each other in pairs. Ask one pair: *Do you agree about the answer?* If they agree, ask them to tell the class. Confirm the answer.

2 In pairs, sts cover the words in the box. They look at the picture again and try to name the different parts from memory. They can look at the words and their answers again to check.

3 Teach the phrases: *on the left, on the right, in the foreground, in the background*. Say a false sentence about the picture, e.g. *There's a big tree in the background*. Ask: *True or false?* In pairs, sts write three more true or false sentences about the picture. With books closed, pairs work together in groups of four to read their sentences to each other and guess from memory whether their classmates' sentences are true or false. They can look at the picture again to check. Ask who got all the answers right.

Go to Vocabulary practice: nature, SB page 127/TB page 267.
Sts will find more language presentation and practice for nature words here. Do these exercises with the class, or set them for homework, before continuing with exercise 2 of lesson 8C.

PB Remind sts to go to the app for further self-study vocabulary practice of nature words.

2 Sts discuss the questions in pairs. Discuss the answers briefly as a class.

Answer
1 China

3 Teach the meaning of *fishing town* and *enormous*. Sts read the introduction to the show and answer the questions. Check answers.

Answers
1 12 million 2 Chicago 3 writer 4 30 years ago

4 8.8 Allow sts time to read through the table. Elicit or explain that sts must tick the things that the city had 30 years ago, and the things that it has today. Play audio track 8.8. See TB page 312 for audio script. Sts listen and complete the table. Allow sts time to compare their answers in pairs. If necessary, play the audio again for them to check and complete their answers. Check answers with the class.

Answers

	Shenzhen 30 years ago	Shenzhen today
Fields	✓	
Forest	✓	
Tall buildings		✓
River	✓	✓
Train station	✓	✓
Airport		✓
University		✓

5 A 8.8 Read out the first sentence beginning and elicit the correct ending (f). Sts match the remaining sentence halves. Play audio track 8.8 again for sts to listen and check their answers. Check answers with the class and check that sts understand all the sentences and questions.

Answers
1 f 2 e 3 c 4 d 5 a 6 b

B In pairs, sts look at the words in bold in the sentences and choose the correct words to complete the rules. Check answers.

Answers
1 the past 2 singular 3 plural

Grammar *there was/were*

Positive:	Negative:	Questions	Short answers:	
There was *a train station.*	***There wasn't*** *an airport.*	***Was there*** *a university?*	*Yes,* ***there was****.*	*No,* ***there wasn't****.*
There were *lots of trees.*	***There weren't*** *any cars.*	***Were there*** *any shops?*	*Yes,* ***there were****.*	*No,* ***there weren't****.*

Personal Best

Go to Grammar practice: *there was/were*, page 103

6 Complete the text with the correct forms of *there was/were*.

This is Pompeii in Italy. In AD 79, a volcano destroyed the city. But what was life like for the 20,000 people that lived there before?
[1]________ about 200 cafés in the town. They sold eggs, cheese, bread and fruit. [2]________ also a market.
Children did lessons outside or at home, so [3]________ any school buildings. [4]________ some doctors, but [5]________ a hospital.
[6]________ a big amphitheatre, where [7]________ plays and concerts. And of course, [8]________ gladiators!

7 **A** 8.10 **Pronunciation:** sentence stress Listen and repeat the questions and short answers. Pay attention to the underlined stressed words.

1 Was there a train station? Yes, there was.
2 Was there an airport? No, there wasn't.
3 Were there any trees? Yes, there were.
4 Were there any cars? No, there weren't.

B 8.11 In pairs, ask and answer questions 1–4 about Pompeii. Remember to stress the correct words. Listen, check and repeat.

1 Were there any cafés?
2 Was there a market?
3 Were there any school buildings?
4 Was there a hospital?

Go to Communication practice: Student A page 140, Student B page 148

8 In pairs, look at the pictures and talk about Oxford Street in London in the past. Use the words in the box and your own ideas.

buses road shops horses and carriages tall buildings bus stops street lights taxis

There weren't any buses in the 19th century.

Oxford Street, 19th century Oxford Street, now

9 How is your town or city different from the past? In pairs, talk about the differences.

There was a cinema on Panama Street, but now there's a supermarket.

Personal Best Write about where you lived when you were a child.

Grammar

Read the Grammar box with sts about *there was/were*. Point out to sts that they are familiar with the use of *there is/are* in the present, and we use *there was/were* in a similar way to talk about things that existed in the past. Elicit that we use *there was/wasn't* with singular nouns, and *there were/weren't* with plural nouns. Remind sts that that we use *some* with plural nouns in positive sentences, and *any* in negative sentences, e.g. *There were some buses. There weren't any buses*. Ask questions to check concept.

Concept check questions:

There was a cinema in the city – does this describe the past or the present? (the past). *Can you make the sentence negative?* (there wasn't a cinema). *There was some trees – correct?* (no – there *were* some trees). *Can you make the sentence negative?* (there weren't any trees).

Go to Grammar practice: *there was/were*, SB page 103/ TB page 219. Sts will find more language reference, presentation and practice for *there was/were* here. Do these exercises with the class, or set them for homework, before continuing with exercise 6 of lesson 8C.

PB Remind sts to go to the app for further self-study grammar practice of *there was/were*.

6 Focus on the picture and explain that it shows the ancient city of Pompeii, in Italy. Elicit what sts know about the city. Teach the words *amphitheatre* and *gladiator*. Sts then read the text and complete it with the correct forms. Check answers.

Answers

1 There were	5 there wasn't
2 There was	6 There was
3 there weren't	7 there were
4 There were	8 there were

7 A 8.10 Point out the underlined words in the questions and short answers and explain that these are the stressed words. Play audio track 8.10. See SB page opposite for audio script. Sts listen and pay attention to the stressed words. Point out the different pronunciation of *was* and *were* when they are stressed and unstressed. Play the audio again for sts to repeat.

B 8.11 In pairs, sts practise saying the questions. Play audio track 8.11. See SB page opposite for audio script. Sts listen and check their pronunciation. You could play the audio again for them to listen and repeat. Sts then ask and answer the questions in pairs. Ask some pairs to ask and answer the questions for the class. Check that they are pronouncing the stressed and unstressed forms of *was* and *were* correctly.

Answers

1 Yes, there were.	3 No, there weren't.
2 Yes, there was.	4 No, there wasn't.

Go to Communication practice

Divide the class into Student A and Student B. All 'Student A' sts should go to SB page 140. All 'Student B' sts should go to SB page 148. Go to TB page 293 for the teacher notes. Do the activity, then continue with exercise 8 of lesson 8C.

8 Read through the task with the class, then read through the words in the box and make sure sts understand them all. Read out the example answer and explain *19th century*. Elicit one or two more examples. Sts then word in pairs to discuss the differences. Elicit answers from a range of students.

Possible answers

There was a road. There is a road now.
There were some shops. There are some shops now.
There were some horses and carriages. There aren't any horses and carriages now.
There weren't any tall buildings. There aren't any tall buildings now.
There weren't any bus stops. There are some bus stops now.
There weren't any street lights. There are some street lights now.
There weren't any taxis. There are some taxis now.

9 Read out the task and the example answer. Allow sts time to prepare their answers individually. They then talk about their town or city in pairs. Ask some sts to tell the class about their partner's town or city.

PERSONAL BEST

Sts can practise using *there was/were* further by writing a description of the place where they lived as a child. Encourage to include a range of sentences using *there was/wasn't* and *there were/weren't*. They can compare their descriptions in pairs and discuss which place sounds nice to grow up in.

Weaker sts can work in pairs. They cover exercise 8 and, from memory, write some sentences about Oxford Street in the 19th century and now. They can look at the pictures again to check. Ask some pairs to read their sentences to the class.

Learning Curve

8D A trip to Canada

1 Ask and answer the questions in pairs.

1 Why do you usually travel?
  a for work or study b to visit friends or family c to go on holiday d other
2 How do you prefer to travel? Why?
  a to take the train b to fly c to drive d other
3 How do you usually book your tickets when you travel?
  a online b on the phone c at a travel agent's d other

2 A 8.12 Watch or listen to the first part of *Learning Curve*. Answer the questions.

1 Why does Marc want to travel?
2 How does he prefer to travel?
3 How does he book the tickets?

B 8.12 Are the sentences true (T) or false (F)? Watch or listen again and check.

1 Marc works with technology. ____
2 He never buys tickets online. ____
3 He loves flying. ____
4 Clarisse is Marc's friend. ____
5 It's hot and sunny in California. ____
6 The journey to Montreal is 11 hours. ____

3 8.13 Complete the questions with the words in the box. Listen and check.

arrive how leave when return

1 **Clarisse** ________ do you want to leave?
Marc March 11.
2 **Clarisse** When would you like to ________ ?
Marc March 21.
3 **Marc** What time does the train ________ ?
Clarisse The train leaves from New York at 8.15 a.m.
4 **Marc** And when does it ________ in Montreal?
Clarisse 7.11 p.m.
5 **Marc** So, ________ much is it?
Clarisse It's $138 for a return ticket.

Conversation builder buying a ticket

Customer:
I'd like a single/return ticket to ...
What time does the train/bus/flight leave?
What time/When does it arrive?
How much is it?

Assistant:
What kind of ticket would you like?
Would you like a single or return ticket?
When do you want to return/leave?
It's ... for a single/return ticket.

4 Read the Conversation builder. Then in pairs, make conversations to buy the tickets.

A *I'd like a single ticket to Newcastle, please.*
B *When would you like to leave?*

Ticket type: SINGLE
Adults: ONE
From: LONDON KING'S CROSS
To: NEWCASTLE
Date: 14 JULY
Time: 12.05
Arrival: 14.55
Price: £65.00

OUTBOUND
Flight: RAX3498
Departing from: Frankfurt
21 September 10.00
Arriving at: Marrakesh
21 September 14.45

RETURN
Flight: RAX9912
Departing from: Marrakesh
5 October 12.35
Arriving at: Frankfurt
5 October 17.10
Price: €345.00

EXTRA PRACTICE Workbook page 49

8D A trip to Canada

Sts hear a conversation in which someone books a travel ticket. They then practise making a phone call to buy a ticket.

Speaking	Skill	Conversation builder
Sts watch a video or listen to a recording of someone booking a travel ticket. They then practise making a phone call to buy a ticket.	Starting and ending a phone call at work	Buying a ticket

WARMER

Ask: *Do you enjoy travelling to new places? What do you like about travelling? What don't you like?* Elicit a range of ideas. Teach the word *trip*. Ask: *Where was your last trip to? Did you enjoy it? Why? When is your next trip? Where is it to?* Elicit a range of answers.

1 Check that sts understand all the questions and possible answers. Sts ask and answer the questions in pairs. Ask some sts which of their answers were the same, and which were different.

2 A 8.12 In this episode of *Learning Curve*, Marc makes a phone call to buy some travel tickets. Ask sts what they know about Marc. Allow sts time to read the questions. Pre-teach the following words if necessary from the video: *round trip* (= travel to a place and back), *air conditioning*, *by mail* and *vacation*. Play video/audio track 8.12. See TB page 312 for video/audio script. Sts watch/listen and answer the questions. Check answers.

Answers
1 He wants to have a vacation.
2 He prefers to travel by train.
3 On the phone.

B 8.12 Allow sts time to read the sentences. Check they understand everything. Play video/audio track 8.12 again. Sts watch/listen and decide if the sentences are true or false. Check answers.

Answers
1 T 2 F 3 F 4 F 5 T 6 T

3 8.13 Read out the first gapped question and elicit the correct word to complete it. Sts complete the remaining questions with the correct words. Play audio track 8.13. See SB page opposite for audio script. Sts listen and check their answers. Check answers with the class and make sure sts understand all the questions.

Answers
1 When 2 return 3 leave 4 arrive 5 how

3 x PRACTICE *SB page 74, exercise 3*

1 Do the exercise as normal. To check the answers, focus on each question in turn. Ask a student what they think the completed question should be. Ask if anyone has a different answer. Discuss any different answers, then play the audio for that question and answer to confirm.

2 Sts work in pairs. One student closes their book. The other student reads out the answer to each question in turn, e.g. *March 11*. Their partner tries to remember the question. They can look at the conversations together again to check.

3 Sts work in pairs. One student takes on the role of Clarisse and the other student takes the role of Marc. They study their questions and answers and try to remember them. Tell them they can write down two words as prompts for each of their lines. With books closed, they then try to recreate the questions and answers, using their prompts. Play audio track 8.13 again for sts to see how much they remembered.

Conversation builder

Read the Conversation builder box with sts about buying a ticket. Explain the meaning of *single* and *return*. Point out the use of *I'd like* as a polite way of asking for something. Ask questions to check concept.

Concept check questions:
What's the name for a ticket to a place and back again? (a return ticket). *What about a ticket just to a place, but not back?* (a single ticket). *What time does the train leave? – Am I asking about the start or end of a trip?* (the start). *How can you ask about the end?* (What time does the train arrive?). *How can you ask about the price of a ticket?* (How much is it?).

4 Allow sts time to read the information on the tickets. Demonstrate the activity by taking the role of the customer. Say: *I'd like a single ticket to Newcastle, please*. Elicit the questions the assistant would ask, and reply using the information on the ticket. Sts then make conversations in pairs. Monitor and help while sts are working. Ask some sts to perform one of their conversations for the class.

5 **A** 8.14 Watch or listen to the second part of the show. Do you think Marc enjoyed his trip? Why/Why not?

B 8.14 Choose the correct options to complete the sentences. Watch or listen again to check.

1 Marc asks Clarisse about _____ .
  a places to eat b places to stay c public transport
2 The Wi-Fi in Montreal isn't good when _____ .
  a it snows b it rains c it's windy
3 On his trip, Marc helped people with their _____ .
  a coffee and sandwiches b French c Wi-Fi

6 8.15 Listen to the phrases from the conversations. Are they for starting or ending a phone call?

1 Hello, *Bon Voyage Travel.* This is Clarisse.
2 Thanks. Goodbye.
3 Hello, my name is Marc Kim. I'm Penny's friend.
4 Thanks for calling.

Skill starting and ending a phone call at work

When you speak on the telephone, remember to give important information and be polite.

- When you answer the phone, say *Hello* and identify yourself or your company: *Hello, Learning Curve. Hello, this is Clarisse / Clarisse speaking.*
- When you call someone, say who you are: *Hello, this is ... , My name's ...*
- When the conversation finishes, thank the person who called and say goodbye: *Thanks for calling. Thanks for your call.*

7 8.16 Complete the conversations with the missing words. Listen and check.

Brad Hello, *Easy Travel.* Brad [1]_________ .
Jenny Hi, [2]_________ is Jenny Foster. I'd like a single ticket to Seoul from Sydney, please.
...
Brad OK, Jenny. You leave on 15 June at 08.15 and you arrive in Seoul at 17.05.
Jenny Thanks very much.
Brad You're welcome. Thanks for your [3]_________ .
Jenny [4]_________ .

Go to Communication practice: Student A page 140, Student B page 148

8 **A** PREPARE Choose a type of transport and write down the information.

train

bus

plane

ferry

- where you want to go
- what type of ticket you want
- when you want to leave
- if/when you want to return

B PRACTISE Sit back-to-back with a partner. Act out a telephone call to buy a ticket. Then swap roles.

C PERSONAL BEST Listen to another pair. Write down three things that they do well.

Personal Best Write a conversation between a customer and a travel agent about a new trip.

5 A 8.14 Read out the question. Pre-teach the following words if necessary from the video: *Wi-Fi*, *snow* and *snowstorm*. Teach the meaning of *a discount*, *nearby*, *the Wi-Fi is down* and *to fix* (= to repair). Play video/audio track 8.14. See TB page 312 for video/audio script. Sts watch/listen and answer the question. Discuss the answer as a class, encouraging sts to give reasons for their answers.

B 8.14 Sts read the questions and choose the correct answers from memory. Play video/audio track 8.14 again. Sts listen and check their answers. Check answers with the class.

Answers
1 b 2 a 3 c

6 8.15 Focus attention on the speech bubbles. Play audio track 8.15. See SB page opposite for audio script. Sts listen and decide if each phrase is for starting or ending a phone call at work. Check answers. Sts could then work in pairs and practise saying the phrases, using their own names.

Answers
1 starting 2 ending 3 starting 4 ending

Skill

Read through the Skill box with the class about starting and ending a phone call at work. Point out the use of *This is ...* to introduce yourself. Point out that giving the right information and sounding friendly and polite are both important parts of communication at work.

7 8.16 Sts read the conversation and complete it with the missing words, referring back to the Skill box to help them. Play audio track 8.16. See SB page opposite for audio script. Sts listen and check their answers. Sts could then practise the conversation in pairs.

Answers
1 speaking 2 this 3 call 4 Goodbye

Go to Communication practice

Divide the class into Student A and Student B. All 'Student A' sts should go to SB page 140. All 'Student B' sts should go to SB page 148. Go to TB page 293 for the teacher notes. Do the activity, then continue with exercise 8 of lesson 8D.

8 Sts follow the steps to practise using the phone to buy a ticket.

A PREPARE Sts work individually and decide on the details of their trip.

B PRACTISE Sts work in pairs. If possible, get them to sit back-to-back, to give them the feeling they are on the phone. They act out a phone call to buy a ticket, then swap roles and practise again. Remind them to use phrases from the Conversation builder box for buying their ticket, and encourage them to use phrases from the Skill box to start and end their call.

C PERSONAL BEST Pairs work together in groups of four. They listen to each other's conversations and give feedback on three things their classmates do well. They then practise in new pairs. Get feedback on how well they think they did this time.

PERSONAL BEST

Sts can practise buying tickets further. They work in pairs and write a conversation about a new trip. They can practise their new conversation in their pairs.

Refer weaker sts back to the tickets in exercise 4 on page 74. They can choose one of the tickets and change some of the details on it, then write a conversation using that information. They can then practise their conversations in pairs.

EXTRA PRACTICE

Put sts into groups of three. Two sts can practise one of their conversations from exercise 8. The third student uses their phone to film the other two. Sts can swap roles and practise again. Watching themselves on film will help sts to evaluate how well they can make a phone call to buy tickets.

Grammar

1 Choose the correct options to complete the questions and sentences.

1 Where ________ last night?
a you were
b were you
c you was

2 Our taxi driver ________ very friendly.
a wasn't
b not was
c weren't

3 She ________ work at 7.00 p.m. last night.
a did finish
b finishes
c finished

4 ________ football at the weekend?
a Did you play
b You did play
c You played

5 They ________ to Oslo for a meeting.
a did fly
b flied
c flew

6 We had a map, so we ________ lost .
a didn't get
b didn't got
c not got

7 ________ a restaurant in your hotel?
a There was
b Was there
c Were there

8 ________ two police officers in the street last night.
a There was
b They were
c There were

2 Rewrite the questions and sentences in the past simple.

1 Does she play tennis with Laura?
________________________ last weekend?

2 There are two eggs in the fridge.
________________________ last night.

3 I don't have time for breakfast.
________________________ this morning.

4 I ride my bike to work.
________________________ yesterday.

5 Do you go to the gym?
________________________ last Saturday?

6 He gets on the 8.00 a.m. train.
________________________ yesterday.

3 Complete the text with the past simple form of the verbs in brackets.

In many countries people give food to birds in parks or in their gardens. But Gabi Mann from Seattle in the USA has a very special relationship with the birds in her neighbourhood – they bring *her* presents!

The story [1]________ (start) when Gabi [2]________ (be) four years old. She [3]________ (have) some food in the car and when she [4]________ (get out), the food fell on the ground. There [5]________ (be) a crow near the car and it [6]________ (fly) down to eat the food.

After that, Gabi [7]________ (not eat) all of her lunch at school. Instead she kept some and [8]________ (give) it to the birds on the way home. In 2013, she [9]________ (help) more birds and put food and water in the garden every morning. One day the crows started bringing things like buttons, rocks, small pieces of metal or plastic and even jewellery for Gabi. [10]________ they ________ (want) to say 'thank you' to her? Gabi thinks so. She collects these 'presents' and she now has more than 100. Her favourite is a metal heart. 'It shows me how much they love me,' she says.

Vocabulary

1 Put the words in the box in the correct columns.

summer April cold field fifth autumn first flower grass hot March May mountain winter ninth October second spring warm wet

Months	Ordinal numbers	Weather	Nature	Seasons

Grammar

1 Sts read the questions and sentences and choose the correct options to complete them. Check answers.

Answers
1 b
2 a
3 c
4 a
5 c
6 a
7 b
8 c

2 Students rewrite the questions and sentences in the past simple. Check answers.

Answers
1 Did she play tennis with Laura
2 There were two eggs in the fridge
3 I didn't have time for breakfast
4 I rode my bike to work
5 Did you go to the gym
6 He got on the 8.00 a.m. train

3 Use the picture to teach the word *crow*. Ask sts to read the text through quickly for general meaning. Ask: *Why does Gabi think the birds bring her presents?* (to say thank you for the food). Sts read the text again and complete it with the correct past simple verb forms. Check answers.

Answers
1 started
2 was
3 had
4 got out
5 was
6 flew
7 didn't eat
8 gave
9 helped
10 Did, want

3 x PRACTICE *SB page 76, Grammar exercise 3*

1 Do the exercise as normal. When you check the answers, focus on each verb and ask: *regular or irregular? singular or plural?* (for the forms of *be*). Elicit the answers to the questions, then elicit the correct verb forms.

2 Ask sts to close their books. Sts work in pairs and try to remember as much as they can about Gabi's story. They can check by looking in their books.

3 Put sts into groups of four and tell them they are going to retell the story from memory. In their groups, sts choose one paragraph each and try to memorize it. Tell them they can write down a maximum of six words to help them. Sts then close their books and try to tell the story in their groups, with each one telling their part of the story. Monitor and help while they are working. Ask some groups to tell the story for the class.

Vocabulary

1 Sts put the words in the correct columns. As an extension, sts could add one or two more words to each column.

Answers

Months	Ordinal numbers	Weather	Nature	Seasons
April	fifth	cold	field	summer
March	first	hot	flower	autumn
May	ninth	warm	grass	winter
October	second	wet	mountain	spring

2 Circle the word that is different. Explain your answers.

1	artist	musician	winter	dancer
2	week	rain	month	year
3	beach	dry	sea	river
4	spring	summer	autumn	windy
5	snow	ride	sail	fly
6	foggy	sunny	sky	cloudy
7	forest	sixth	third	fourth
8	king	queen	tree	politician

3 Choose the correct options to complete the sentences.

1 The summer in India is very ________ and wet.
a hot b sun c cold
2 My sister ________ the train at King's Cross Station.
a gets on b gets in c gets out
3 Don't ________ your bus! It leaves in five minutes.
a take b miss c get lost
4 There are lots of big trees in this ________ .
a flower b foggy c forest
5 Did you ________ your ticket to New York yesterday?
a fly b book c sail
6 He ________ of the car at the police station.
a got out b got off c got on
7 The ________ played the piano very well.
a musician b athlete c dancer
8 It was a beautiful day, so we ________ to the park.
a walked b watched c worked
9 With my smartphone, I never ________ in a new city.
a miss b get out c get lost
10 You can't swim in the ________ . It's very dangerous.
a river b field c sky

4 Complete the sentences with the words in the box.

ago 6.00 at (x2) summer in (x2)
Friday last on yesterday May

1 I went to Greece ________ year on holiday.
2 Did you meet your friends on ________ ?
3 He started work ________ 7.00 this morning.
4 We usually go shopping ________ Saturday.
5 We can take the train at ________ .
6 His birthday is ________ June.
7 He started a new job two weeks ________ .
8 The first of ________ is a public holiday.
9 I played tennis with my brother ________ .
10 What did you do ________ the weekend?
11 She lived in Bogotá ________ 2016.
12 We didn't go on holiday in the ________ .

Personal Best

Lesson 7A Name five celebrities with different jobs.

Lesson 8A List five irregular verbs and their past simple forms.

Lesson 7A Write where you were on two different days last week.

Lesson 8B Describe the weather in your favourite season.

Lesson 7B Write the birthdays of four friends or family members.

Lesson 8B Write three sentences with *quite*, *very* and *really* and an adjective.

Lesson 7C Write three sentences beginning *Last year …*, *Two years ago …* and *Yesterday …* .

Lesson 8C Name five things from nature you can see out of the window.

Lesson 7C List five regular verbs and their past simple forms.

Lesson 8C Write two sentences about your home as a child. Use *There was …* and *There were …* .

Lesson 7D Describe what you did yesterday with *First*, *Then* and *After that*.

Lesson 8D Write three sentences for buying a train ticket.

2 Sts circle the word that is different in each set. Check answers, and ask sts to explain in each case why the word is different. As an extension, sts could write two or three sentences using some of the words.

Answers
1 winter (not a profession/job)
2 rain (not a period of time)
3 dry (not a place in nature)
4 windy (not a season)
5 snow (not a transport verb)
6 sky (not a weather adjective)
7 forest (not an ordinal number)
8 tree (not a celebrity)

3 Sts read the sentences and choose the correct words to complete them. Check answers.

Answers
1 a
2 a
3 b
4 c
5 b
6 a
7 a
8 a
9 c
10 a

4 Sts read the sentences and complete them with the correct words. Check answers.

Answers
1 last
2 Friday
3 at
4 on
5 6.00
6 in
7 ago
8 May
9 yesterday
10 at
11 in
12 summer

3 x PRACTICE *SB page 77, exercise 4*

1 Do the exercise as normal. When you check the answers, put sts into pairs and ask them to choose five answers they are both confident about. Read out each sentence in turn and ask a pair who are confident about that answer to tell the class. Finish by discussing the answers that no students were confident about.

2 Ask sts to close their books. Write one key word for each sentence on the board, e.g. *holiday, friends, work*. In pairs, sts try to remember as many of the sentences as they can. They can check by looking in their books.

3 In pairs, ask sts to write four questions to ask their classmates, using the ideas in the sentences, e.g. *Where did you go on holiday last year? Did you meet your friends on Friday?* Ask some pairs to read their sentences to the class, and correct any errors. Then put pairs together into groups of four to ask and answer their questions. Ask some sts to tell the class something about their classmates.

Personal Best

At the end of each *Review and practice* double-page spread, there is a *Personal Best* section. The aim here is to provide a quick challenge to change the pace and allow for language recall and personalization.

These questions and prompts give sts the opportunity to revise a number of language and skills points from the preceding two units in a more productive way. The points being revised are referenced according to which lesson they appear in (e.g. Lesson 7A). They cover grammar, vocabulary, text builder language from reading and writing lessons, and conversation builder language from speaking lessons. Sts work individually, in pairs or in groups, according to the class dynamic and the time available. Set a time limit if you would like to add a competitive element. Encourage sts to refer back to the relevant lessons if they are having difficulties. The aim is for them to respond to the prompts and engage with the target language in a personal way. Their answers will vary. Monitor and help as necessary and get feedback on sts' answers.

WORKBOOK REVIEW AND PRACTICE

Students will find two pages of Review and Practice at the end of each unit of their Workbooks.
Unit 7, pages 44 and 45
Unit 8, pages 50 and 51

UNIT 9

Shopping

LANGUAGE present continuous ■ clothes

9A Street style

1 Match the words in the box with the clothes in the picture.

belt jeans jacket T-shirt hat

1 ________ 2 ________ 3 ________ 4 ________ 5 ________

Go to Vocabulary practice: clothes, page 128

2 Discuss the questions in pairs.

1 What do you usually wear ...
   a at home? b at work/in class? c on holiday?
2 Where do you usually buy your clothes? What's your favourite shop?
3 Do you buy second-hand clothes? Why/Why not?

3 Read the text and answer the questions.

1 Where is Sukanya from?
2 What type of clothes does she wear?
3 Why does she buy these clothes?
4 Where does she take Mark?

Fashion Diary with Mark Ashcroft

This week, I'm in Thailand with local fashion blogger Sukanya Tanasan. Sukanya only wears second-hand clothes, but she looks amazing!

'There are some great places to buy clothes in Bangkok,' she says. 'If I need a new dress, a T-shirt or shoes, I always go to the markets. You can find really cool clothes there and they're cheap too!'

Today, Sukanya takes me to the Chatuchak market in Bangkok on a shopping trip.

PLAY DOWNLOAD

4 9.2 Listen and tick (✓) the things Sukanya buys.

T-shirt ☐ dress ☐ shoes ☐ hat ☐ skirt ☐

5 **A** 9.2 Complete the sentences with the words in the box. Listen again and check.

getting buying taking eating leaving doing

1 We're ________ the train to Chatuchak market.
2 A lot of people are ________ out here.
3 She's ________ the dress!
4 What's this man ________ ?
5 Sukanya, you aren't ________ the rice!
6 We're ________ the market now.

B Look at sentences 1–6 again and answer the questions. Then read the Grammar box.

1 What are the sentences about? *things happening now / regular events*
2 Which three letters are at the end of the main verbs? ________
3 Which verb do we use before the main verb? *be / do*

Shopping

UNIT 9

UNIT 9 OVERVIEW: The topic for this unit is shopping. Sts read about shopping for clothes in Thailand, and practise describing people and saying what they are doing now. In *Learning Curve*, Ethan and Penny talk to people about the clothes they wear, and how different colours make them feel. Sts talk about how often they go shopping and write their own email describing a photo.

LANGUAGE

Grammar	Vocabulary	Pronunciation
Present continuous: *how often* + expressions of frequency	Clothes; feelings; shopping	*-ing* endings; sentence stress

SKILLS

Listening	Writing
Identifying key points; filler words	Describing a photo; describing position

LANGUAGE 9A

9A Street style

Sts read a text about shopping for clothes in Thailand, and listen to part of a radio documentary about clothes shopping in Thailand. They then practise describing people by talking about what they are wearing and what they are doing now.

Grammar	Vocabulary	Pronunciation	Communication
Present continuous	Clothes (*belt, boots, coat, dress, hat, jacket, jeans, jumper, shirt, shoes, skirt, socks, suit, T-shirt, trousers*)	*-ing* endings	Describing people and what they are doing now

WARMER

Point to one or two items of clothing that sts are wearing and elicit the words for them by asking: *What's this? (a T-shirt), What are these? (jeans)*. Teach the word *clothes* and ask: *Are clothes important to you? Do you buy a lot of new clothes?* Find out who is interested in clothes, and who isn't. Tell sts that in this unit they are going to practise talking about clothes and shopping.

1 Sts work in pairs and match the clothes with the items in the picture. Model and drill pronunciation of the words.

Answers
1 hat 2 jacket 3 T-shirt 4 belt 5 jeans

Go to Vocabulary practice: clothes, SB page 128/TB page 269.
Sts will find more language presentation and practice for clothes here. Do these exercises with the class, or set them for homework, before continuing with exercise 2 of lesson 9A.

PB Remind sts to go to the app for further self-study vocabulary practice of clothes vocabulary.

2 Allow sts time to read the questions and prepare their ideas individually. Sts then discuss the questions in pairs. Ask some sts to tell the class something about their partner.

3 Read out the title of the text and elicit the meaning of *diary*. Pre-teach *second-hand, market* and *cheap*. Sts read the text and find the answers to the questions. Allow sts time to compare their answers in pairs, then check with the class.

Answers
1 Thailand
2 second-hand clothes
3 Because they are cool and cheap.
4 the Chatuchak Market in Bangkok

4 9.2 Explain to sts that they are going to hear part of a radio programme with Sukanya, and they have to listen for the things that she buys. Play audio recording 9.2. See TB page 313 for audio script. Sts listen and tick. Allow sts time to compare their answers in pairs, then check answers with the class.

Answers
dress, hat

5 A 9.2 Read out the first gapped sentence and elicit the correct verb (*taking*). Sts then complete the remaining sentences. Check answers.

Answers
1 taking 2 getting 3 buying 4 doing 5 eating
6 leaving

B Ask sts to read the sentences in 5A again, then read through the rules with the class and elicit the answers.

Answers
1 things happening now 2 -ing 3 be

Grammar present continuous

Things that are happening now

Positive:	Negative:	Questions and short answers:
*I'**m going** to the market.*	*She **isn't having** a drink.*	***Are** you **working** today?*
*We'**re getting off** the bus.*	*They **aren't wearing** glasses.*	*Yes, I **am**. No, I'**m not**.*

Go to Grammar practice: present continuous, page 104

6 Complete the phone messages with the present continuous form of the verbs in brackets.

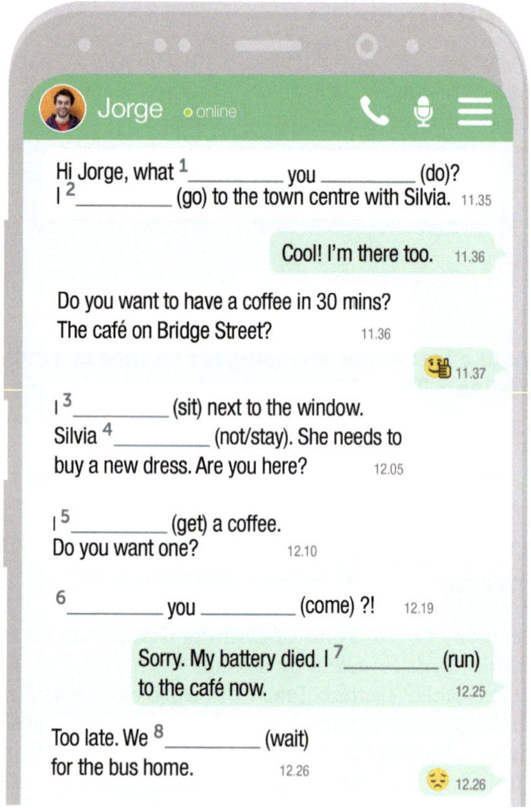

7 **A** 9.4 **Pronunciation:** *-ing* endings Listen and repeat. Pay attention to the /ɪŋ/ sound in **bold**.

com**ing** go**ing** do**ing** runn**ing** wait**ing** stay**ing**

B 9.5 Say the questions and sentences. Then listen, check and repeat.

1 Where are you going?
2 She's running for her bus.
3 I'm not doing any work.
4 Are you staying?
5 He's coming to the café.
6 We're waiting for a taxi.

Go to Communication practice: Student A page 150, Student B page 149

8 In pairs, ask and answer the question *What is/are … doing?* about the people in the pictures.

A *What's David doing?*
B *I think he's having lunch in a restaurant.*

David

Emilia

Megan and Yasmina

Yoshi

Anya

Jenny and Stefan

9 In pairs, describe a classmate. Your partner guesses the person.

A *She's wearing a blue dress and she's sitting next to Leon.*
B *Is it Malika?*
A *Yes, it is!*

Personal Best Think of six people you know. Write sentences about what they're doing at the moment.

 EXTRA PRACTICE Workbook page 52; photocopiable activity 9A Grammar

Grammar

Read the Grammar box with sts about the present continuous. Reinforce the point that we use the present continuous for things that are happening now, not things that happen regularly. Give a contrasting example, e.g. *I work every day. I'm working now*. Point out that there are two parts to the present continuous: the correct form of *be* and the *-ing* form of the verb: *I + am + eating. Ana + is + waiting*. Point out the word order in questions: *Are you coming?* NOT ~~*You are coming?*~~ Ask questions to check concept.

Concept check questions:
I often wear jeans – is this happening now? (no). *I'm wearing jeans – is this happening now?* (yes). *She working today – correct?* (no – *she's working* today). *Can you make the sentence negative?* (she isn't working today). *You're have a drink – correct?* (no – *you're having* a drink) *Can you make it into a question?* (*Are you having* a drink?).

Go to Grammar practice: present continuous, SB page 104/TB page 221
Sts will find more language reference, presentation and practice for the present continuous here. Do these exercises with the class, or set them for homework, before continuing with exercise 6 of lesson 9A.

PB Remind sts to go to the app for further self-study grammar practice of the present continuous.

6 Focus attention on the phone messages on the right. Read out the first message and elicit the correct form. Sts then complete the messages, individually or in pairs. Check answers.

Answers
1 are, doing
2 'm going
3 'm sitting
4 isn't staying
5 'm getting
6 Are, coming
7 'm running
8 're waiting

3 x PRACTICE *SB page 79, exercise 6*

1 Do the exercise as normal. To check answers, read out each message in turn with three possible answers, one correct and two incorrect. Sts identify the correct answer.
2 In pairs, sts cover the messages. They try to remember each message in turn, then uncover it to check.
3 With books closed, write prompts for the messages on the board, e.g. *Jorge / what / do? town / Silvia*. In pairs, sts try to write the messages again from memory. Ask some pairs to read their messages to the class. Other sts can help out if they have forgotten parts. See if, as a class, you can re-create the complete message sequence.

7 A 9.4 Play audio track 9.4 once for sts to listen to the verbs. See SB page opposite for audio script. Play the audio again for sts to listen and repeat, paying attention to the *-ing* sound.

B 9.5 In pairs, sts practise saying the questions and sentences. Play audio track 9.5. See SB page opposite for audio script. Sts listen to check their pronunciation. Play the audio again for sts to repeat.

Go to Communication practice
Divide the class into Student A and Student B. All 'Student A' sts should go to SB page 150. All 'Student B' sts should go to SB page 149. Go to TB page 295 for the teacher notes. Do the activity, then continue with exercise 8 of lesson 9A.

8 Read out the example question and answer. Ask a question in the plural, e.g. *What are Megan and Yasmina doing?* Elicit the answer. Sts work in pairs to ask and answer the questions. Elicit answers from individual sts.

Answers
What's Emilia doing? I think she's getting off a train.
What are Megan and Yasmina doing? I think they're singing.
What's Yoshi doing? I think he's playing the guitar.
What's Anya doing? I think she's cooking.
What are Stefan and Jenny doing? I think they're riding a motorbike.

9 Read out the example description, then give a similar description of someone in the class. Sts guess the person. Allow sts time to prepare their descriptions individually. They then work in pairs to describe their classmates and guess the people. Ask some sts to say their descriptions for the class.

PERSONAL BEST

Sts can practise talking about things happening now further. They think of six people they know and write sentences about what they are doing now. Encourage them to write some negative sentences, as well as positive ones. They can compare their sentences in pairs.

Weaker sts could write two sentences about themselves, and two sentences about one of their classmates. Ask some sts to read their sentences to the class.

9B How do you feel?

1 Match the words in the box with pictures a–f.

angry calm excited hungry thirsty tired

Go to Vocabulary practice: feelings, page 129

2 9.7 Complete the text with four feelings from exercise 1. Listen and check.

Colours and feelings

Colours can sometimes change how we feel. For example, orange can make us feel happy and [1]________ . A lot of restaurants, for example McDonald's and KFC, use red because it can make us feel [2]________ . Offices often use blue because it makes us [3]________ . But grey isn't a popular colour for offices because it can make us feel sad or [4]________ .

3 **A** Look at the picture of Ethan. How does his shirt make you feel?

B 9.8 Match the colours in the box with sentences 1–4. Watch or listen to the first part of *Learning Curve* and check.

orange blue white black yellow

1 Doctors often wear this colour. ________
2 Firefighters usually wear these colours. ________ or ________
3 The police in the USA wear this colour. ________
4 People wear this colour when they're sad. ________

Skill **identifying key points**

When people speak, try to listen for the important things they say.

- We often emphasize or repeat the most important ideas.
- We sometimes give examples or more information.

4 9.8 Read the Skill box. Then watch or listen again. Tick (✓) the **two** key points Ethan talks about.

a Colours can change how we feel. ☐
b Colours are important in festivals all around the world. ☐
c Orange is a popular colour for clothes. ☐
d Workers sometimes wear uniforms of the same colour. ☐

5 Discuss the questions in pairs.

1 Do you wear a uniform for work?
2 Did you wear a uniform at school?
3 What colours are/were the uniforms?
4 How do/did they make you feel?

80

 EXTRA PRACTICE Workbook page 53; photocopiable activity 9B Vocabulary

Learning Curve

9B How do you feel?

Sts learn adjectives for feelings, then listen to people talking about what colours they like wearing, and how different colours make them feel. They end by talking about the colours they like, and how different colours make them feel.

Listening	Skill	Listening builder	Vocabulary
Sts watch a video or listen to a recording about the colours we choose the wear.	Identifying key points	Filler words	Feelings (*angry, bored, calm, excited, happy, hungry, sad, scared, surprised, thirsty, tired, worried*)

WARMER

Ask: *How many colours can you see in this room?* Put sts into pairs and give them two minutes to write down all the colours they can see. Bring all the colour words together on the board and check that sts understand them all. See which pair spotted the most different colours.

1 Read through the words in the box with the class and elicit or teach the meanings. Sts then match the words with the pictures. Check answers.

Answers
a hungry b calm c excited d thirsty e tired f angry

Go to Vocabulary practice: Feelings, SB page 129/TB page 271.
Sts will find more language presentation and practice for adjectives for feelings here. Do these exercises with the class, or set them for homework, before continuing with exercise 2 of lesson 9B.

PB Remind sts to go to the app for further self-study vocabulary practice of adjectives for feelings.

2 9.7 Sts read the text and complete it with the correct feelings. Play audio track 9.7. See SB page opposite for audio script. Sts listen and check their answers. Ask: *Are you surprised by anything in the text? Do you think colours change the way you feel?* Elicit a few ideas.

Answers
1 excited 2 hungry 3 calm 4 tired

3 A Focus on Ethan's shirt. Use the picture to teach the meaning of *Hawaiian shirt*. Ask: *How does it make you feel? Happy? Tired? Calm?*

B 9.8 In this episode of *Learning Curve*, Ethan and Penny talk about how different colours make us feel. They then interview people about the colours they are wearing. Sts read through the sentences and match them with the colours. Pre-teach the following words if necessary from the video: *firefighters, fast food*, and the phrase *See you in a bit* (= see you soon). Play video/audio track 9.8. See TB page 313 for video/audio script. Sts listen and check their ideas. Check answers, and discuss whether sts agree or disagree with the ideas.

Answers
1 white 2 orange, yellow 3 blue 4 black

Skill

Read the Skill box with sts about identifying key points. Point out that it is often very difficult to understand every single word that someone says, so listening to identify key points is an important skill.

4 9.8 Allow sts time to read through the sentences. Check they understand *festival* and *uniform*. Play video/audio track 9.8. Sts watch/listen and tick the two key points. Check answers, playing the video/audio again and referring back to the skill box to show why these are the key points.

Answers
a, d

5 Sts discuss the questions in pairs. Ask some pairs to tell the class which things they agreed and disagreed about.

6 ▶ 9.9 Watch or listen to the rest of the show. Match the feelings in the box with the people.

bored excited scared hungry thirsty

1 ________

2 ________

3 ________

4 ________ and ________

7 ▶ 9.9 Watch or listen again. Choose the correct options to complete the key points.

1 Udo ____ .
 a makes his own clothes b buys expensive clothes c only wears bright colours
2 Akiko ____ .
 a doesn't like *Learning Curve* b doesn't like Ethan's shirt c is late for class
3 Bob ____ .
 a loves the colour yellow b wears a uniform for work c wants to eat something

8 Ask and answer the questions in the boxes.

What are you wearing today? | What colours are the clothes? | How do they make you feel?

9 ▶ 9.10 Read the two extracts. Can you understand them without the missing words? Listen and write the missing words.

1 ________ Penny, what are people wearing today? Do you see a lot of colours on the streets of New York?

2 ________, people are leaving work at the moment. Let's see what they're wearing.

Listening builder filler words

When people speak, they often say short words while they are thinking of what to say. You can ignore these words – they don't really mean anything.

__So__, what are you, __er__, wearing today?

__Well__, I'm wearing blue jeans and, __um__, this red T-shirt.

10 ▶ 9.11 Read the Listening builder. Then listen to the description of the photo. Tick (✓) the sentences the speaker says.

1 a This photo is of a young girl in a school. ☐
 b In this photo, there's a young girl at school. ☐
 c The photo shows a young girl in school. ☐
2 a And she's wearing a grey uniform and glasses. ☐
 b And she has a long grey uniform and glasses. ☐
 c And she's wearing a uniform and some glasses. ☐
3 a She's standing near the teacher's desk. ☐
 b In the class, there aren't any teachers. ☐
 c I think she's waiting for the teacher. ☐

11 Discuss the questions in pairs.

1 What are your favourite colours?
2 How do they make you feel?
3 Which colours don't you like?
4 How do they make you feel?

Personal Best Describe the colours in the rooms in your house and say how they make you feel.

6 9.9 Focus attention on the photos and ask sts to guess which feelings they think match each person. Pre-teach the following words if necessary from the video: *amazing, style, fashion school, a mistake and fast food cart* (= a truck on a street that sells fast food). Play video/audio track 9.9. See TB page 313 for video/audio script. Sts watch/listen and match the feelings with the people. Check answers. Play the video/audio track again if necessary, pausing for sts to hear the answers.

Answers
1 excited 2 scared 3 hungry 4 thirsty, bored

7 9.9 Allow sts time to read all the options. Point out that in order to choose the correct options, they need to focus on listening for the key points. Play video/audio track 9.9 again. Sts listen and choose the correct options. Check answers.

Answers
1 a 2 b 3 b

8 Sts ask and answer the questions in pairs. Ask some sts to tell the class about their partner's clothes.

9 9.10 Sts read the two speech bubbles. Ask: *Can you understand them without the missing words?* Elicit that you can understand them, so the missing words don't have any important meaning. Play audio track 9.10. See SB page opposite for audio track. Sts listen and write the missing words. Check answers.

Answers
1 So 2 Well

Listening builder

Read the Listening builder box with sts about filler words. Point out that everyone uses filler words, and individuals often have personal preferences about which words they use. Point out that the words have no meaning, so sts can learn to ignore them and focus on the words with meaning. Ask questions to check concept.

Concept check questions:
When do we use filler words? (when we are thinking about what to say). *What meaning do filler words have?* (no meaning). *Should we listen carefully for these words?* (no – we can ignore them).

10 9.11 Allow sts time to read the sentences. Point out that they will hear one of each pair of sentences, with some filler words around it. Explain that they should ignore the filler words and tick the sentence they hear. Play audio track 9.11. See SB page opposite for audio script. Sts listen and tick the correct sentences. Check answers.

Answers
1 b 2 a 3 c

11 As a round-up, sts discuss their own opinions and responses to colours. They discuss the questions in pairs. Ask some sts to tell the class something they learned about their partner.

PERSONAL BEST

Sts can practise talking about colours and feelings further. In pairs, they describe the colours in the rooms in their house or flat, and say how they make them feel. Get feedback on their discussions.

Weaker sts can work in new pairs. They ask and answer the questions in exercise 11 again, then write their partner's answers. Ask some sts to read their sentences to the class.

EXTRA PRACTICE

Sts work in groups of three. They take turns to use their phones to film their classmates discussing the questions in exercise 11. They can swap roles and practise again. Allow sts time to watch the films of themselves. Watching themselves on film will help sts to evaluate how naturally and fluently they can speak.

9C Love it or hate it?

1 Complete phrases 1–5 with the words in the box.

buy pay shop sell try on

1 ________ shoes 2 ________ by credit card 3 ________ fruit 4 ________ online 5 ________ a new car

Personal Best

Go to Vocabulary practice: shopping, page 130

2 Do the questionnaire in pairs. Write down your partner's answers. Then go to page 147 and look at the results.

Shopping – do you love it or hate it?

1 How often do you go to a shopping centre?
- a Never! I hate shopping centres.
- b I only go when I need some new clothes.
- c I go there every week. I love it!

2 Do you spend a lot of money on clothes and shoes?
- a No, I don't. I usually buy second-hand clothes.
- b When I have a special occasion – once or twice a year.
- c Yes, I do. Clothes are very important to me.

3 How often do you shop online?
- a Not often. Maybe once a year.
- b A few times a month.
- c Very often. Three or four times a week.

4 How do you feel if you need to buy a present for someone?
- a Bored. I prefer to give cash as a present.
- b Happy. I can find something in a local shop.
- c Really excited! I can go shopping all day on Saturday!

5 How do you usually pay when you go shopping?
- a I pay with cash. I never spend money that I don't have.
- b I sometimes pay with cash and sometimes by card.
- c I usually pay by credit card.

3 A Complete the questions and sentences from the questionnaire with the words in the box.

how every times twice often once

1 How ________ do you go to a shopping centre?
2 I go there ________ week.
3 Once or ________ a year.
4 ________ often do you shop online?
5 Maybe ________ a year.
6 Three or four ________ a week.

B Which tense do we use to talk about the frequency of events? *present simple / present continuous* Read the Grammar box.

 EXTRA PRACTICE Workbook page 54; photocopiable activity 9C Vocabulary

9C Love it or hate it

Sts do a quiz about their shopping habits. They then ask and answer questions about how often they go shopping, and how often they do other activities.

Grammar	Vocabulary	Pronunciation	Communication
How often + expressions of frequency	Shopping (*buy, department store, go shopping, local shops, market, pay by credit card, pay with cash, sell, shop online, shopping centre, spend money, try on*)	Sentence stress	Talking about how often you do things

WARMER

Write on the board: *I love ...* and *I hate ...* . Ask: *What do you love doing? What do you hate doing?* Give a few examples of things that you love and hate doing, e.g. *I love watching movies. I hate doing exams*. Ask sts individually to write three sentences about things they love doing, and three about things they hate doing. Put sts into small groups to compare their ideas. Ask groups to report back on the most popular answers, and see what sts love and hate doing the most in the class. Elicit how many people included *shopping* as something they love or hate.

1 Point to each picture in turn and ask questions to elicit the meaning, e.g. *Is she in a shop? Does she want to buy some new shoes? What's she doing?* Elicit or say the correct word to complete each phrase.

Answers
1 try on 2 pay 3 sell 4 shop 5 buy

Go to Vocabulary practice: shopping, SB page 130/TB page 273
Sts will find more language presentation and practice for shopping vocabulary here. Do these exercises with the class, or set them for homework, before continuing with exercise 2 of lesson 9C.

PB Remind sts to go to the app for further self-study vocabulary practice of shopping vocabulary.

2 Allow sts time to read through the questionnaire first. Explain any vocabulary they don't understand. Sts then do the questionnaire in pairs and look at the results. Discuss who in the class agrees with the results, and who disagrees.

3 A Read out the first gapped question and ask sts to find it in the questionnaire. Elicit the missing word. Sts then complete the remaining sentences and questions. Check answers, and check that sts understand all the sentences and questions.

Answers
1 often 2 every 3 twice 4 How 5 once 6 times

B Read out the question and explain that frequency refers to how often you do something. Elicit the answers to the question.

Answer
present simple

Grammar *how often* + expressions of frequency

How often *do you go shopping?*

I go shopping	***once a*** ***twice a*** ***three/four times a*** ***every***	***day/week/month/year.***

Personal Best

Go to Grammar practice: *how often* + expressions of frequency, page 104

4 A 9.14 **Pronunciation:** sentence stress Listen and repeat the expressions of frequency. Pay attention to the underlined stressed words.

1 once a day
2 twice a year
3 three times a month
4 every day and every night

B 9.15 Say the sentences. Pay attention to the sentence stress. Listen, check and repeat.

1 I call my girlfriend twice a day.
2 We go to the cinema every month.
3 They shop online three times a week.
4 My grandparents visit every year.

Go to Communication practice: Student A page 141, Student B page 149

5 A Write the questions.

1 How often / you buy someone a present?
______
______
______

4 How often / it snow in your town?
______
______
______

2 How often / your teacher give homework?
______
______
______

5 How often / you go to bed after midnight?
______
______
______

3 How often / you wash your hair?
______
______
______

6 How often / you pay by credit card?
______
______
______

B In pairs, ask and answer the questions.

A *How often do you buy someone a present?*
B *I buy someone a present once or twice a month. How about you?*

6 A Write three true sentences and three false sentences about you with expressions of frequency.

B Read your sentences to your partner. Guess if they are true or false.

A *I go to Singapore twice a year.*
B *I think that's false.*
A *No, it's true! My sister lives there.*

Personal Best Write some more questions about shopping for a questionnaire.

Grammar

Read the Grammar box with sts about *how often* + expressions of frequency. Point out that expressions of frequency tell us how often something happens, and they usually go at the end of a sentence, e.g. *I buy new shoes once a month/three times a year*. Point out the use of *a* in some of the expressions, e.g. *once a day, three times a week*. Point out that we say *twice*, NOT ~~two times~~: *I play football twice a week*. NOT ~~two times a week~~. Ask questions to check concept.

Concept check questions:
What do expressions of frequency tell us? (how often something happens). *What tense do we use when we ask about frequency?* (the present simple). *Where do expressions of frequency usually go in a sentence?* (at the end). *I'm drinking coffee once a day – correct?* (no – *I drink* coffee once a day). *I play tennis three times the week – correct?* (no – three times *a* week). *I see my friends every a week – correct?* (no – *every week*). *I go on holiday two times a year – correct?* (no – *twice a year*).

Go to Grammar practice: *how often* + expressions of frequency, SB page 104/TB page 221. Sts will find more language reference, presentation and practice for *how often* + expressions of frequency here. Do these exercises with the class, or set them for homework, before continuing with exercise 4A of lesson 9C.

PB Remind sts to go to the app for further self-study grammar practice of *how often* + expressions of frequency.

4 A 9.14 Remind sts that in sentences some words are stressed and some are unstressed. Elicit or remind them that stressed words are slightly louder and spoken more clearly than unstressed ones. Play audio track 9.14 once for sts to listen and notice the pronunciation of the stressed words. See SB page opposite for audio script. Play the audio again for sts to listen and repeat.

B 9.15 In pairs, sts practise saying the sentences, paying attention to the stressed words. Play audio track 9.15 once for sts to listen and check the pronunciation. See SB page opposite for audio script. Play the audio again for them to listen and repeat.

Go to Communication practice
Divide the class into Student A and Student B. All 'Student A' sts should go to SB page 141. All 'Student B' sts should go to SB page 149. Go to TB page 295 for the teacher notes. Do the activity, then continue with exercise 5A of lesson 9C.

5 A Read out the first set of prompts and elicit the correct question form. Sts then write the questions. Check answers.

Answers
1 How often do you buy someone a present?
2 How often does your teacher give homework?
3 How often do you wash your hair?
4 How often does it snow in your town?
5 How often do you go to bed after midnight?
6 How often do you pay by credit card?

3 x PRACTICE *SB page 83, exercise 5A*

1 Do the exercise as normal. To check answers, say the first word of each question, then go around the class, asking sts in turn to say the next word. Other sts can interrupt if they think a word is incorrect. Ask the final student in the chain to say the completed question.

2 In pairs, sts cover the prompts. They look at the pictures and try to remember each question. They can look at the prompts and their answers again to check.

3 With books closed, write the verb from each set of prompts on the board, e.g. *buy, give, wash*. Divide the class into teams. Teams take turns to choose a verb and say a new sentence using the verb, e.g. *How often do you buy clothes?* If the question is correct, they get a point and the verb is crossed off the board. If the sentence is not correct, don't correct it, but move on to the next team. Continue until all the verbs are crossed off. See which team has the most points.

B Allow sts time to prepare their answers individually. Encourage them to use a range of expressions of frequency in their answers. Sts then ask and answer the questions in pairs. Ask some pairs which of their answers were similar, and which were very different.

6 A Give one or two examples of sentences about yourself, and get sts to guess if they are true or false, e.g. *I watch TV every day. I go on holiday three times a year*. Sts write three true sentences and three false ones about themselves. Encourage them to use a range of different expressions of frequency.

B In pairs, sts read their sentences to their partner, and their partner guesses if they are true or false. Get feedback on who guessed correctly.

PERSONAL BEST

Sts can practise talking about shopping further. They write more questions about shopping for a questionnaire. They could work in pairs for this. They can then ask and answer their questions in pairs or small groups.

For weaker sts, brainstorm some more questions with the class, e.g. *How often do you buy new shoes? What's your favourite department store?* Sts can write the questions, then ask and answer them in pairs or small groups.

9D Garage sale

1 A What do you do with things you don't use any more?

a Throw them away.

b Take them to a second-hand shop.

c Sell them online.

d Have a garage sale.

B Discuss the questions in pairs.

1 How often do you buy second-hand things?
2 What type of second-hand things do you buy?
3 Do people have garage sales in your country?
4 Do you think they're a good idea? Why/Why not?

2 A Read the email quickly. What relationship is the writer to Patrick?

B Read the email again. Match the names in the box with the people in the picture.

Bill Sandra Evie Eddie

Hi Patrick,

How are you?

a We had a garage sale yesterday. It was at our house and we sold some old clothes, books and other things.

b Here's a photo. The man on the right is our friend, Bill. He's looking at our old things. His wife Sandra is on the left, and the girl in the middle is their daughter, Evie. She's trying on my old hat. There's an old skateboard at the bottom of the photo – I think it's your dad's. The man at the top of the picture is our neighbour, Eddie. He's looking at a pair of Grandpa's old trousers!

c We made about £100! We bought some new chairs for the garden with the money.

Email me soon with your news.

Grandma

3 A Match paragraphs a–c with the parts of the email 1–3.

1 description of photo ____ 2 what happened after ____ 3 introduction ____

B What tenses are the verbs in paragraphs a–c? Read the Skill box.

Skill describing a photo

When we describe a photo, we:
- explain who the people are: *The man on the right is our friend, Bill.*
- use the present continuous to say what they are doing: *She's trying on my old hat.*
- use *there is/are* to say what things are in the picture: *There's an old skateboard ...*

9D Garage sale

Sts read an email in which someone describes a photo. They study language for describing a photo and learn phrases for describing position, then write their own email in which they describe a photo.

Writing	Skill	Text builder
Describing a photo	Describing a photo	Describing position

WARMER

Ask: *Do you take a lot of photos? What do you take photos of? Your friends? Places you visit?* Elicit a range of answers, then ask: *Do you sometimes share your photos with friends? How do you share them? On your phone? In an email? On social media?* Elicit a range of answers. Tell sts they are going to practise describing a photo they want to share with someone.

1 A Read out the question and the four possible answers. Explain the meaning of *garage sale* if necessary (= an informal sale in your garden or outside your house, of things you no longer need). Sts discuss the question in pairs. Find out who in the class does each of the things in the pictures. Ask more questions to find out more details. e.g. *What things do you throw away? What do you take to second-hand shops?*

B Allow sts time to read the questions and prepare their answers individually. Sts then discuss the questions in pairs. Discuss the questions briefly as a class, encouraging sts to join in and talk about their experiences and opinions.

2 A Sts read the email quickly to answer the question. Check the answer.

Answer
She is his grandmother.

B Sts read the email again and match the names with the people in the picture. Check answers.

Answers
1 Sandra 2 Eddie 3 Evie 4 Bill

3 A Point out the three paragraphs a–c in the email. Sts match the paragraphs with the parts of the email. Check answers.

Answers
1 b 2 c 3 a

B Sts look at the email again and focus on the tenses. Check answers and elicit one or two examples of each tense from the email.

Answers
a past simple
b present simple and present continuous
c past simple

Skill

Read the Skill box with sts about describing a photo. Check that sts understand everything, and elicit one or two more possible sentences using each tense, e.g. *The man at the top of the picture is Eddie. He's looking at a pair of trousers. There are some books at the bottom of the photo. We sold everything.*

4 Complete Patrick's reply with the correct form of the verbs in brackets.

Dear Grandma,

I'm very well, thanks. That's great about the garage sale!

I [1]________ (go) to Bristol last Saturday with some friends. We [2]________ (take) the train in the morning and we [3]________ (explore) the city.

Here's a photo. The girl on the left is Sara and the girl in the middle is Lisa. They [4]________ (be) my classmates from university. They [5]________ (try) to find the Clifton Suspension Bridge on the map. Lisa's boyfriend, Shaun, is on the right. He [6]________ (take) a photo of some street art.

It was a fun day out, but we [7]________ (be) all really tired when we [8]________ (get) home!

Love Patrick x

5 Match the halves to make sentences. Check your answers in the emails.

1 The man on
2 The girl in
3 There's an old skateboard at
4 The man at
5 The girl on

a the left is Sara.
b the middle is their daughter, Evie.
c the right is our friend, Bill.
d the top of the picture is our neighbour, Eddie.
e the bottom of the photo.

Text builder describing position

on the right *at the top* *in the middle*
on the left *at the bottom* *in the corner*

6 A Read the Text builder. Then write sentences.

1 that / my brother / right *That's my brother on the right.*
2 my friend Casey / middle ________
3 there / a cat / corner ________
4 that / my cousin / top ________
5 there / more people / left ________

B In pairs, take a photo of some of your classmates. Describe the photo using phrases from the Text builder.
That's Nacho on the left and Lourdes is on the right. There's a blue bag in the corner. It's Nacho's bag.

7 A **PREPARE** Choose one of the photos. Imagine that you took it. Make notes to answer the questions.

1 When and where did you take the photo?
2 Who are the people in the photo?
3 What are they doing?
4 What happened after you took the photo?

B **PRACTISE** Write an email. Introduce the photo, describe it and say what happened after you took it.

C **PERSONAL BEST** Swap emails with your partner and read it. Check the tenses of the verbs and prepositions for describing position. Can you improve anything?

Personal Best Write an email describing one of your own photos.

4 Sts read the email and complete it with the correct verb forms. Remind them to think about whether the verbs in brackets are regular or irregular in the past simple. Allow sts time to compare their answers in pairs, then check with the class.

Answers
1 went
2 took
3 explored
4 are/'re
5 are/'re trying
6 is/'s taking
7 were
8 got

5 Sts try to match the sentence halves from memory, then check their answers in the emails. Check answers, and check that sts understand all the sentences.

Answers
1 c 2 b 3 e 4 d 5 a

3 x PRACTICE *SB page 85, exercise 5*

1 Do the exercise as normal. To check answers, read out each sentence beginning in turn and ask sts to call out the correct letter (a–e) all at the same time. Ask a student who gave the correct answer to read out the full sentence. Check that sts understand all the sentences.

2 In pairs, sts cover the sentence endings. They look at the sentence beginnings and try to remember the endings. They can uncover the endings and look at their answers to check.

3 In pairs, sts look at the photos on pages 84 and 85 again and write three more sentences about them, similar to the ones in exercise 5, e.g. *The man on the right is Shaun. The girl in the middle is Lisa*. Ask pairs in turn to read their sentences to the class.

Text builder

Read the Text builder box with sts about describing position. Explain that position refers to where someone or something is. Point out the different prepositions in the phrases, e.g. ***on** the right/left*, ***at** the top/bottom*, ***in** the middle/corner*. Point out that all the expressions use *the*, e.g. *on the left* NOT ~~*on left*~~. Ask questions to check concept.

Concept check questions:
What does describing position mean? (saying where someone or something is). *The man at the left is my brother – correct?* (no – the man *on* the left). *There's a skateboard on the bottom of the picture – correct?* (no – *at* the bottom). *The girl in middle is Alice – correct?* (no – *in* the middle).

6 A Sts write sentences using the phrases for describing position. Check answers.

Answers
2 That's my friend Casey in the middle.
3 There's a cat in the corner.
4 That's my cousin at the top.
5 There are more people on the left.

B In pairs, sts use one of their phones to take a photo of their classmates. Make sure all sts are happy to have their photo taken in this way. Sts then describe the photo, saying where the different people and things are in the photo. Ask some sts to show their photo to the class and describe it.

7 Sts follow the steps to describe a photo and write an email to a friend.

A PREPARE Sts look at the photos and read the questions, then prepare their ideas. Monitor while they are working, and help with vocabulary if necessary.

B PRACTISE Sts write their email. Refer them back to the Skill box to remind them of the tenses to use when describing a photo, and refer them to the Text builder box to remind them of phrases for describing position.

C PERSONAL BEST Sts work in pairs. They swap their emails with a partner to check that their partner has used tenses correctly and has used the phrases for describing position correctly. Encourage them to correct any mistakes, and also to give positive feedback.

PERSONAL BEST

Sts can practise describing a photo further. They write an email describing one of their own photos. Sts can share their emails in small groups and ask more questions about the photos.

Refer weaker sts to the photo in the questionnaire on page 82. In pairs, sts imagine they took the photo and write an email to a friend answering the questions in exercise 7A. Ask some pairs to read their email to the class.

EXTRA PRACTICE

Write the following gapped sentences on the board:

1 We had ______ garage sale yesterday.
2 Here's ______ photo.
3 There's ______ old skateboard.
4 We bought some new chairs for ______ garden.
5 That's great about ______ garage sale.
6 They are my classmates from ______ university.

Explain to sts that the missing words are all articles (*a/an/the* or no article). In pairs, sts complete the sentences, then read the two emails again to check. Check answers, and discuss as a class why each article is used in each sentence. Point out that we use *a* when we mention something for the first time, and *the* when we mention it for the second time (*a garage sale/the garage sale*). Point out that we use *the* when it is clear which one we are talking about (*the garden*). Point out that with some nouns, we don't usually use an article (*classmates from university*).

Answers
1 a 2 a 3 an 4 the 5 the 6 –

UNIT 10

Time out

LANGUAGE present continuous for future plans ■ free-time activities

10A What are you doing at the weekend?

1 **A** Look at the poster for a music festival. Discuss the questions in pairs.

1 Do you know this music festival?
2 Where and when is the festival?
3 Do you like music festivals? Why/Why not?
4 What can you see in the pictures?

B Complete the text with the words in the box.

visit go watch have stay

COACHELLA
Music and Arts
Festival

Win tickets for an incredible Coachella experience

Call 08081 570000 and tell us why you want to go.

1 ________ to all the concerts
2 ________ in a luxury tent
3 ________ the art area and see amazing sculptures
4 ________ films at night
5 ________ a good time!

April 14–16
Coachella Valley, California

Personal Best

Go to Vocabulary practice: free-time activities, page 131

2 10.2 Read and listen to the conversation between two friends. Where is Alex going this weekend?

Alex Guess what I'm doing this weekend.
Dan I don't know. Are you visiting your family again?
Alex No, I'm not. I'm going to a music festival – Coachella! I won tickets in a competition.
Dan Coachella? No way! Which bands are playing?
Alex Radiohead are playing on Friday and Lady Gaga on Saturday.
Dan That's amazing. Are you going on your own?
Alex No, the prize was for two tickets.
Dan Two tickets? You know, I'm not doing anything this weekend ...
Alex Sorry, Dan. I'm going with my mother.
Dan Your mother?
Alex Yeah, she loves Lady Gaga. We're driving there tonight and then we're staying in a tent all weekend!
Dan Well, have a good time. Tell me all about it on Monday, OK?

3 Are the sentences true (T) or false (F)? Check your answers in the conversation.

1 Dan's going to Coachella with Alex. ____
2 Lady Gaga's playing on Saturday. ____
3 They're driving to the festival tonight. ____
4 They're staying in a hotel all weekend. ____

Time out

UNIT 10

UNIT 10 OVERVIEW: **This unit focuses on free time. Sts read a poster and listen to a conversation about a music festival then practise talking about their own plans for the weekend. Sts discuss the kinds of music, films and events that they enjoy, then review and practise asking and answering questions about their own hobbies. In *Learning Curve* Ethan, Penny, Taylor and Marc visit a tourist attraction.**

LANGUAGE			SKILLS	
Grammar	**Vocabulary**	**Pronunciation**	**Reading**	**Speaking**
Present continuous for future plans; question review	Free-time activities; types of music and film; sports and games	Sentence stress; intonation in questions	Scanning for information; the imperative	Showing interest; asking about a tourist attraction

LANGUAGE 10A

10A What are you doing at the weekend?

Sts read a poster for a music festival, then read and listen to a conversation about the festival. They practise using the present continuous to talk about future plans, and then talk about their own plans for the weekend.

Grammar	**Vocabulary**	**Pronunciation**	**Communication**
Present continuous for future plans	Free-time activities (*go to a concert/festival, go to the beach, have a barbecue/good time/party, stay at home, stay in a hotel/tent, visit an art gallery/a museum, visit family/friends, watch a film/football match/video*)	Sentence stress	Talking about free-time activities and future plans

WARMER

Ask: *What do you usually do at the weekend?* Elicit a few ideas, e.g. *do sport, meet friends*, etc. Make notes of useful vocabulary on the board, then ask: *What are your favourite free-time activities?* Put sts into pairs to discuss the question, then ask pairs in turn to tell the class which activities they both enjoy.

1 A Sts look at the poster and discuss the questions in pairs. Discuss the answers briefly as a class. Explain if necessary that the Coachella Festival takes place each year in California, and is one of the largest music festivals in the USA. Focus on the picture of the truck sculpture, and remind sts of the word *sculpture*.

B Sts read the poster and complete it with the correct verbs. Check answers.

> **Answers**
> 1 Go 2 Stay 3 Visit 4 Watch 5 Have

3 x PRACTICE *SB page 86, exercise 1B*

1 Do the exercise as normal. To check answers, write the gapped phrases on the board. Invite sts in turn to come and complete one of the phrases they feel confident about. Confirm the answers with the class.

2 In pairs, sts cover the gapped phrases. They look at the words in the wordpool box and try to remember the phrases. They can look at the phrases again to check.

3 Focus on the poster again and point out the phone number and the instruction to call the number and say why you want to go to the festival. In pairs, sts take turns to role-play a conversation in which they call the number and say why they want to go to the festival. Encourage them to give reasons, e.g. *I want to go to all the concerts because I love music.* Ask some sts to perform their conversation for the class.

Go to Vocabulary practice: free-time activities, SB page 131/TB page 275.
Sts will find more language presentation and practice for free-time activities here. Do these exercises with the class, or set them for homework, before continuing with exercise 2 of lesson 10A.

PB Remind sts to go to the app for further self-study vocabulary practice of free-time activities.

2 10.2 Check that sts understand *on your own*. Play audio track 10.2. See SB page opposite for audio script. Sts read and listen to the conversation, and answer the question. Check the answer.

> **Answer**
> He's going to the Coachella Festival.

3 Sts read the conversation again and decide if the sentences are true or false. Check answers.

> **Answers**
> 1 F 2 T 3 T 4 F

4 A Look at the sentences in exercise 3 again. Answer the questions.

1 Which tense are the verbs? *present simple / past simple / present continuous*
2 When do the actions happen? *in the past / now / in the future*

B Find more examples of this tense in the conversation in exercise 2. Then read the Grammar box.

Grammar **present continuous for future plans**

Positive:
*I'm **going** to a music festival this weekend.*
*We're **visiting** a museum tomorrow.*

Negative:
*Sue **isn't going** to the concert tonight.*
*They **aren't staying** in a hotel.*

Questions and short answers:
***Are** you **having** a party in the summer?*
*Yes, I **am**. No, I'**m not**.*

Personal Best

Go to Grammar practice: present continuous for future plans, page 105

5 A 10.5 **Pronunciation:** sentence stress Listen and repeat the questions and answers from the conversation in exercise 2. Pay attention to the underlined stressed words.

1 Are you <u>visiting</u> your <u>family</u>? <u>No</u>, I'm <u>not</u>.
2 <u>Which</u> <u>bands</u> are <u>playing</u>? <u>Radiohead</u> are <u>playing</u> on <u>Friday</u>.

B 10.6 Match the questions with answers a–c. Ask and answer the questions in pairs with the correct stress. Listen, check and repeat.

1 What are you doing this weekend?
2 How are you getting there?
3 Are you staying with friends?

a I'm taking the bus.
b Yes, I am.
c I'm going to the beach.

6 Look at Rosie's diary on her smartphone. In pairs, ask and answer the question *What's she doing ...?* with the times in the box.

~~this morning~~ on Friday tomorrow at the weekend
the day after tomorrow this evening

A *What's she doing this morning?*
B *She's having coffee with Kate.*

Go to Communication practice:
Student A page 141, Student B page 149

7 A 10.7 Use the words to write questions in the present continuous. Listen to the conversation and check.

1 What / you / do / at the weekend?
____
2 Who / you / go / with?
____
3 How / you / get / there?
____
4 When / you / leave?
____
5 Where / you / stay?
____

B 10.7 Listen again and write Cheryl's answers to the questions.

8 A Make notes about your plans for the weekend. They can be real or imaginary.

B In pairs, ask and answer the questions in exercise 7 about your plans.

A *What are you doing at the weekend?* B *I'm having a barbecue with my friends.*

Personal Best Write a paragraph about your 'perfect' weekend.

4 A Sts look at the sentences in exercise 3 again and discuss the questions in pairs. Discuss the answers with the class.

Answers
1 present continuous 2 in the future

B Sts find more examples of the present continuous tense. Check answers.

Answers
I'm doing, Are you visiting, I'm going, are playing, Are you going, I'm not doing, We're driving, we're staying

Grammar

Read the Grammar box with sts about the present continuous for future plans. Remind sts that they have already studied this tense for talking about things happening now. Explain that this is a different use of the tense, but is formed in the same way. Explain that we use the present continuous to talk about definite plans in the future, not just ideas or hopes for the future. Point out that, for this use of the present continuous, we use it with future time expressions, e.g. *this weekend, tomorrow, tonight, in the summer*. NOT ~~*didn't thought about this*~~. Ask questions to check concept.

Concept check questions:
Which tense can we use to talk about future plans? (present continuous). *I'm studying English today – is this about the future?* (no – it's something happening now). *I'm going shopping tomorrow – is this about the future?* (yes). *Is it just an idea, or is it a plan?* (it's a plan).

Go to Grammar practice: present continuous for future plans, SB page 105/TB page 223. Sts will find more language reference, presentation and practice for the present continuous for future plans here. Do these exercises with the class, or set them for homework, before continuing with exercise 5A of lesson 10A.

PB Remind sts to go to the app for further self-study grammar practice of the present continuous for future plans.

5 A 10.5 Play audio track 10.5. See SB page opposite for audio script. Point out that the unstressed words are often pronounced with the weak vowel /ə/. Play the audio again for sts to repeat.

B 10.6 Sts match the questions and answers. Check answers, then put sts into pairs to practise asking and answering the questions. Play audio track 10.6. See SB page opposite for audio script. Sts listen to check the pronunciation and repeat.

Answers
1 c 2 a 3 b

6 Allow sts time to read through the diary. Make sure they understand *the day after tomorrow*. In pairs, sts ask and answer the questions. Check answers.

Answers
A What's she doing on Friday?
B She's having a party.
A What's she doing tomorrow?
B She's meeting Sandra.
A What's she doing at the weekend?
B She's visiting her mum and dad.
A What's she doing the day after tomorrow?
B She's visiting the Picasso exhibition.
A What's she doing this evening?
B She's going to the cinema with Malika.

Go to Communication practice
Divide the class into Student A and Student B. All 'Student A' sts should go to SB page 141. All 'Student B' sts should go to SB page 149. Go to TB page 295 for the teacher notes. Do the activity, then continue with exercise 7A of lesson 10A.

7 A 10.7 Read out the first set of prompts and elicit the question. Sts then write the remaining questions. Play audio track 10.7 for sts to check. See TB page 314 for audio script. Check answers.

Answers
1 What are you doing at the weekend?
2 Who are you going with?
3 How are you getting there?
4 When are you leaving?
5 Where are you staying?

B 10.7 Play audio track 10.7 again, pausing to allow sts time to write the answers. Allow sts time to compare their answers in pairs. Check answers.

Answers
1 I'm going to a film festival in Cambridge.
2 I'm going with my boyfriend.
3 We're taking the train.
4 We're leaving tomorrow morning.
5 We're staying with some friends.

8 A Sts work individually and make notes about their plans for the weekend. Suggest that they make a diary, like the one in exercise 6.

B Demonstrate the activity by asking a confident student questions about their plans. Sts then ask and answer questions in pairs. Ask some sts to tell the class about their partner's plans.

PERSONAL BEST

Sts can practise talking about future plans further. They imagine their 'perfect' weekend next weekend, and write a paragraph about it. Sts can compare their paragraphs in small groups and decide whose weekend sounds fun.

With weaker sts, brainstorm some ideas for a 'perfect' weekend, and make notes on the board. Sts then use the ideas to write three or four sentences about their perfect weekend. Ask some sts to read their sentences to the class.

10B What's on?

1 10.8 Listen and match the words in the box with the types of music and film.

classical science-fiction action jazz electronic romance

1 ________ 2 ________ 3 ________ 4 ________ 5 ________ 6 ________

Personal Best

Go to Vocabulary practice: types of music and film, page 132

2 Look at the webpage on page 89. What type of website is it? Do you use websites like this?

Skill scanning for information

'Scanning' means looking quickly at a text to find specific information.
- Underline the key word(s) in the question.
- Look for the word(s) in the text quickly. Use your finger to help you.
- When you find the word, read the information to answer the question.

3 A Read the Skill box. Then read questions 1–4 and scan the text for the answers. The key words are underlined.

1 What time does the concert start? ________
2 Where is the art exhibition? ________
3 How much is a cinema ticket for children? ________
4 Which event is free to enter? ________

B Read questions 1–4 and underline the key words. Then scan the text for the answers.

1 What's the name of the theatre in the city? ________
2 How old do you need to be to try speed dating? ________
3 Which event costs less if you buy tickets online? ________
4 Who's playing electronic music tonight? ________

4 Look at the text and discuss the questions in pairs.

1 Which events do you want to go to? Why?
2 Which events aren't you interested in? Why?

5 Complete the sentences from the text with the correct words.

1 Don't ________ it!
2 ________ to our Speed Dating night!
3 ________ all night.
4 ________ very scared!

Text builder the imperative

We use the imperative to give instructions.
***Book** early!* ***Open** the window!* ***Don't be** late!* ***Don't forget** about the party!*

6 Read the Text builder. Then complete the sentences with the positive or negative imperative of the verbs in the box.

call listen talk sit open be

1 ________ down, please. I can't see the film.
2 The concert starts at 7.45, so ________ late.
3 ________ to this great song. I love it!
4 ________ the window, please. It's very hot.
5 Please ________ in the library. I'm trying to read.
6 ________ me today because I'm working.

7 Discuss the questions in pairs.

1 What's your favourite type of music?
2 When do you listen to music?
3 How often do you go to concerts/nightclubs?
4 What type of films do you like?
5 What was the last film you saw?
6 How often do you go to the cinema?

10B What's on?

Sts read a web page about upcoming events, and discuss the kinds of music, films and events that they enjoy.

Vocabulary	Reading	Skill	Text builder
Types of music and film (*classical music, electronic music, hip-hop music, jazz music, pop music, rock music; action film, comedy, drama, horror film, romance, science-fiction film*)	Sts read a 'What's On' web page about upcoming events in a particular area.	Scanning for information	The imperative

WARMER

Ask: *What's your favourite film? Why?* Elicit a few ideas, and see who in the class likes similar films. Ask: *How do you find out what films are on at the cinema in your area? How do you find out about other events, like concerts or festivals?* Elicit a few answers, including the idea of looking for information online.

1 10.8 Read through the words in the box with the class and teach the meanings if necessary. Explain to sts that they are going to hear six pieces of music or parts of films. Play audio track 10.8. See TB page 314 for audio script. Sts listen and match. Check answers.

Answers
1 jazz
2 romance
3 classical
4 electronic
5 action
6 science fiction

Go to Vocabulary practice: types of music and film, SB page 132/TB page 277.
Sts will find more language presentation and practice for types of music and film here. Do these exercises with the class, or set them for homework, before continuing with exercise 2 of lesson 10B.

PB Remind sts to go to the app for further self-study vocabulary practice of types of music and film.

2 Sts look at the web page and discuss the questions in pairs. Discuss the answers as a class, and explain the meaning of *What's On* (a list of events that are currently on or will be coming soon in a particular area).

Answers
It's a What's On website; Students' own answers.

Skill

Read the Skill box with sts about scanning for information. Explain that when you are scanning, you don't read the text, but just look at it quickly, in order to spot key words, numbers, dates, etc. Explain to sts that it is the skill you use when you look at a train timetable, for example, or when you look for your name in a list of names. Focus on the questions 1–4 in exercise 3A and point out the underlined key words.

3 A Sts scan the text to find the answers. Check answers.

Answers
1 8.00 p.m. 2 Trinidad Gallery 3 £8
4 the book reading with Joe Arnott

B Check that sts understand *speed dating* in question 2. Sts read the questions and underline the key words, then scan the text for the answers. Check answers.

Answers
1 key word: theatre; King's Theatre
2 key word: speed dating; 21
3 key word: online; Hot Potato
4 key word: electronic; DJ Octopus

4 Allow sts time to prepare their answers individually. Sts then discuss their answers in pairs. Ask pairs in turn which events they both want to go to, and which they aren't interested in.

5 Read out the first gapped sentence and ask sts to read the first part of the web page again and find the missing word. Sts then complete the remaining sentences. Check answers.

Answers
1 miss 2 Come 3 Dance 4 Be

Text builder

Read the Text builder box with sts about the imperative. Point out that we use the imperative to give instructions, or to make strong recommendations. Explain that the imperative form is the same if we are speaking to one person or more than one, and it is the base form of the verb. Point out the negative form with *don't*, and that we don't use a pronoun with the imperative: *Come with me!* NOT ~~*You come with me!*~~ Ask questions to check concept.

Concept check questions:
When do we use the imperative? (to give instructions, or to make strong recommendations). *What form of the verb is the imperative?* (the base form). *Does it change for singular or plural?* (no). *You come in – correct?* (no – *Come in*). *Can you make it negative?* (Don't come in).

6 Sts complete the sentences with the correct imperatives. Check answers.

Answers
1 Sit 2 don't be 3 Listen 4 Open 5 don't talk
6 Don't call

7 Sts discuss the questions in pairs. Ask pairs to tell the class which questions they agree on, and which they disagree on.

What's On

Events in your area: Saturday 9 June — Sort by: Date

Visitors

Science-fiction adventure. When aliens arrive on Earth, do they want to help people – or start a war?
ABC Cinema, 6.30 p.m. 9.00 p.m. 11.30 p.m.
Tickets £10. Under-16s: £8

Buy Tickets

Anderson .Paak in concert

Anderson .Paak brings his mix of jazz, hip-hop and rock to the city. Don't miss it!
Royal Arena, 8.00 p.m.
Tickets £17.50

Sold Out

Romeo and Juliet

William Shakespeare's great love story. A boy and a girl find love on the streets of Verona.
King's Theatre, 7.15 p.m.
Tickets £18.00

Sold Out

Underwater garden

Dance all night as DJ Octopus plays the latest in electronic music from around the world.
Club Infinity, 10.00 p.m.–late **Entry** £8.00 (Over-18s only)

Buy Tickets

Hot Potato

Enjoy an evening of comedy with Sally Quentin. 'Really funny' *The Daily Times*. Book online and save £5.
Comedy Club, 7.00 p.m.
Tickets £15 on the door

Buy Tickets

Looking for love?

Are you single? Do you want to find that special person? Come to our Speed Dating night – the fun way to meet new people!
Union Café, 6.30 p.m.
Admission £15. **Minimum age** 21

Buy Tickets

Book reading with Joe Arnott

Joe Arnott reads from his new horror story, *Play With Fire*. Be scared, be very scared!
Forest Hill Library, 8.00 p.m.
Admission free. Over-16s only.

Reserve

Picasso's portraits

Exhibition of paintings and sculptures from one of the most popular artists of the twentieth century.
Trinidad Gallery
Tickets £12.50

Buy Tickets

Personal Best Write information about three events in your town or city. Use imperatives.

PERSONAL BEST

Sts can practise talking about music and films further. They write information about three events in their town or city, using imperatives to give instructions or make strong recommendations. They can compare their events in small groups and decide which ones they would all like to go to.

With weaker sts, brainstorm some ideas for events in the sts' own town or city, and make notes on the board. In pairs, sts choose one and write information about it, using an imperative. Ask some sts to read their information to the class.

EXTRA PRACTICE

Write the following adjectives and definitions on the board:

1 single	a different to all the others, and better
2 special	b the smallest number or amount that is possible
3 minimum	c frightened
4 popular	d not married
5 scared	e liked by a lot of people

Sts find the adjectives in the text and match them with the meanings. Check answers, and check that sts understand all the adjectives.

Answers
1 d 2 a 3 b 4 e 5 c

EXTRA PRACTICE

Ask sts to imagine they are going to one of the events on the web page next weekend, and they want to invite a friend. Ask: *What can I say to my friend?* Elicit a few ideas, e.g. *I'm going to a concert next weekend. Would you like to come with me?* Ask: *What questions might my friend ask?* Elicit a few ideas, e.g. *Who's playing in the concert? Where is it? What time does it start? How much are the tickets?* Refer sts back to the conversation in exercise 2 on page 86 to help with useful phrases. In pairs, sts then prepare a conversation. Monitor and help while they are working. Tell them they can use information in the text, and they can also use their own ideas. Allow sts time to practise their conversations in pairs, then ask some pairs to perform their conversations for the class.

10C Royal hobbies

1 Complete the sports and games with the verbs *go*, *play* and *do*.

1 ________ tennis 2 ________ karate 3 ________ running 4 ________ rock climbing 5 ________ videogames 6 ________ yoga

Personal Best

Go to Vocabulary practice: sports and games, page 133

2 In pairs, ask and answer the question *Do you …?* with the correct verbs and the sports and games in the box.

A *Do you go cycling?* **B** *Yes, I do. I usually go cycling once a week.*

cycling	swimming	football	Pilates	gymnastics	basketball	chess	karate	skiing

3 **A** Who are the people in the picture? Read the text and check. What do you know about them?

B 10.11 Guess which three activities in exercise 1 the people do. Listen to the interview and check.

4 **A** 10.11 Complete the interviewer's questions with the words in the box. Listen again and check.

was	where	how	does	is	what

1 ________ does he relax?
2 ________ is his favourite game?
3 ________ did she go to university?
4 ________ she good at sports?
5 ________ William do lots of exercise too?
6 ________ he training for a marathon now?

B Look at questions 1–6 again.

1 Which questions do you answer with *yes* or *no*? ____ ____ ____
2 Which questions do you answer with specific information? ____ ____ ____

7.00 p.m.

Relaxing with the Royals

What do Prince Harry, Prince William and his wife Kate, the Duchess of Cambridge, do in their free time? Royal expert Jenny Brown joins us to talk about how the young royals relax.

5 **A** Match the tenses in the box with the questions in 4A.

past simple	present continuous	present simple (x2)	present simple of *be*	past simple of *be*

1 ________ 2 ________ 3 ________ 4 ________ 5 ________ 6 ________

B Match the words in the box with the parts of the question 1–4. Then read the Grammar box.

subject	question word	main verb	auxiliary verb

1 What ________ 2 do ________ 3 they ________ 4 do ________ in their free time?

10C Royal hobbies

Sts talk about activities that they do in their free time, then listen to an interview about the hobbies of some members of the British Royal Family. They guess information about the hobbies of three more famous people, and listen to check the information. They then ask and answer questions about their own hobbies.

Grammar	Vocabulary	Pronunciation	Communication
Question review	Sports and games (*do gymnastics/karate/Pilates/yoga, go cycling/ rock climbing/running/skiing/swimming/walking, play basketball/ chess/football/hockey/ rugby/tennis/videogames/volleyball*)	Intonation in questions	Asking and answering questions about your hobbies

WARMER

Ask: *Do you like sports? What sports do you do? What sports do you like watching? What's your favourite sport? Why?* Encourage sts to join in and talk about their likes and dislikes. Teach the word *hobby*, and tell sts they are going to talk about hobbies in this lesson.

1 Focus on the pictures and use them to teach the words for the sports. Sts complete the sports and games with the correct words. Check answers.

Answers
1 play 2 do 3 go 4 go 5 play 6 do

3 x PRACTICE *SB page 90, exercise 1*

1 Do the exercise as normal. To check answers, point to each picture in turn and say the three possibilities, e.g. *go tennis, play tennis, do tennis?* Elicit the correct answer.

2 In pairs, sts cover the words below the pictures. They look at the pictures again and try to remember the full phrase for each sport or game. They can look at the words and their answers again to check.

3 With books closed, mime one of the sports or games and ask: *What am I doing?* Elicit the answer: *You're (doing karate)*. Invite other sts to mime one of the sports or games. Ask: *What's (Maria) doing?* Elicit the answer each time. You could repeat this activity once sts have done the exercises in the Vocabulary practice section.

Go to Vocabulary practice: sports and games, SB page 133/TB page 279.
Sts will find more language presentation and practice for sports and games here. Do these exercises with the class, or set them for homework, before continuing with exercise 2 of lesson 10C.

PB Remind sts to go to the app for further self-study vocabulary practice of sports and games.

2 Read out the example question and answer, then ask individual sts one or two more questions. Revise adverbs of frequency and expressions of frequency. Sts ask and answer questions in pairs. Ask some sts to tell the class about their partner's hobbies.

3 A Focus on the picture and read out the question. Elicit a few ideas. Sts then read the text to check their ideas. Check the answer.

Answers
Prince Harry, Kate, the Duchess of Cambridge and Prince William.
Note: Princes William and Harry are the two sons of Prince Charles, and grandsons of Queen Elizabeth II. William is married to Kate, and, as the older of the two brothers, is second in line to the throne after his father.

B 10.11 In pairs, sts guess which activity in exercise 1 each person does. Elicit a few possible answers, but don't confirm them. Play audio track 10.11. See TB page 314 for audio script. Sts listen and note down the activity that each person does. Check answers with the class.

Answers
Prince Harry plays videogames, Kate does yoga, Prince William goes running.

4 A 10.11 Sts complete the questions with the correct words. Play audio track 10.11 again for them to check their answers. Check answers with the class and check that sts understand all the questions.

Answers
1 How 2 What 3 Where 4 Was 5 Does 6 Is

B In pairs, sts look at the questions in 4A again and decide which you answer with *yes* or *no*, and which you answer with specific information. Check answers.

Answers
1 4, 5, 6 2 1, 2, 3

5 A In pairs, sts look at the questions in 4A again and match them with the tenses. Check answers.

Answers
1 present simple
2 present simple of *be*
3 past simple
4 past simple of *be*
5 present simple
6 present continuous

B Focus on each part of the question in turn and elicit which word in the box it matches. Check that sts understand the meaning of *subject* and *auxiliary* verb.

Answers
1 question word 2 auxiliary verb 3 subject
4 main verb

Grammar question review

Most verbs: (question word) + auxiliary verb + subject + main verb:

Where do you live? *What are you doing?* *When did they arrive?*
Does Carla play tennis? *Is he watching TV?* *Did you go running yesterday?*

The verb *be*: (question word) + *be* + subject:

How old are you? *Where was Antonio yesterday?*
Is the milk in the fridge? *Were you worried about the exam?*

Personal Best

Go to Grammar practice: question review, page 105

6 A 10.14 **Pronunciation:** Intonation in questions Listen and repeat the questions. Pay attention to the intonation that goes up (↗) or down (↘).

questions with question words	***yes/no* questions**
1 Which films do you like? ↘	3 Is she from Japan? ↗
2 Where are they going? ↘	4 Did you stay in a hotel? ↗

B 10.15 Say the questions with the correct intonation. Listen, check and repeat. Then ask and answer the questions in pairs.

1 What are you doing tonight?
2 Did you cook dinner yesterday?
3 Where were you at 7.00 this morning?
4 How often do you take the bus?
5 Is it raining at the moment?
6 Does our teacher like pop music?

Go to Communication practice: Student A page 141, Student B page 150

7 A 10.16 Order the words to make questions 1–6. Listen and check.

B 10.16 In pairs, ask and answer the questions. Listen again and check.

Estonian fashion model Carmen Kass plays chess.

1 start / did / when / she
______________________?
2 she / how / did / learn
______________________?

American singer Elvis Presley did karate.

3 karate / at / was / good / he
______________________?
4 where / do / did / it / he
______________________?

American actor Lucy Liu goes rock climbing.

5 go / how / rock climbing / she / does / often
______________________?
6 dangerous / is / it
______________________?

8 Choose a sport or game that you do. In pairs, ask and answer the questions in the boxes.

What's your hobby? | When did you start? | Where do you do it? | How often do you do it?
Are you doing it this weekend? | Is it difficult? | Is it expensive?
How did you learn? | Who do you do it with? | What do you need to do it?

Personal Best Write a paragraph about a sport or game you enjoy.

…RA PRACTICE Workbook page 60; photocopiable activity 10C Grammar

Grammar

Read the Grammar box with sts. Point out to sts that in questions in all tenses, the auxiliary verb comes before the subject: ***Do** you play football? **Did** you play football? **Are** you playing football?* This word order stays the same if there is a question word: *Where **do** you work? Where **did** you work? Where **are** you working?* Point out that the verb *be* is different because it does not use an auxiliary verb, and always comes before the subject: ***Are** you at home? **Were** you at home?* Ask questions to check concept.

Concept check questions:
you – doing – what – are: Can you put the words together to make a question? (What are you doing?). *In questions with most verbs, what comes before the subject?* (the auxiliary verb). *What comes after the subject?* (the main verb). *Is this order the same if there is a question word?* (yes). *Where you do live? – correct?* (no – *where do* you live?). *What happens in questions with the verb 'be'?* (the verb *be* comes before the subject). *You are good at football? – correct?* (no – *Are you* good at football?).

Go to Grammar practice: question review, SB page 105/TB page 223. Sts will find more language reference, presentation and practice for the question review here. Do these exercises with the class, or set them for homework, before continuing with exercise 6A of lesson 10C.

PB Remind sts to go to the app for further self-study grammar practice of the question review.

6 A 10.14 Demonstrate rising and falling intonation by saying the same question with both intonation patterns and indicating with your hand how the intonation goes up or down. Play audio track 10.14 once for sts to listen and notice the intonation. See SB page opposite for audio script. Elicit or point out that when there is a question word, the intonation goes down, but for yes/no questions, the intonation goes up. Play the audio again for sts to repeat, paying attention to the intonation.

B 10.15 In pairs, sts practise saying the questions. Play audio track 10.15. See SB page opposite for audio script. Sts listen and check their pronunciation. Play the audio again for them to listen and repeat. Sts then ask and answer the questions in pairs. Ask some sts to tell the class something they learned about their partner.

Go to Communication practice
Divide the class into Student A and Student B. All 'Student A' sts should go to SB page 141. All 'Student B' sts should go to SB page 150. Go to TB page 295 for the teacher notes. Do the activity, then continue with exercise 7A of lesson 10C.

7 A 10.16 Focus on the pictures of the three famous people and ask sts which ones they recognize. Sts read about each person's hobby, then put the words in the correct order to make questions. Play audio track 10.16. See TB page 314 for audio script. Sts listen to check their answers. Check answers with the class.

Answers
1 When did she start?
2 How did she learn?
3 Was he good at karate?
4 Where did he do it?
5 How often does she go rock climbing?
6 Is it dangerous?

B 10.16 Sts ask and answer the questions from memory. Play audio track 10.16 again for them to listen and check. Check answers with the class.

Answers
1 When she was a young girl.
2 Her father taught her.
3 Yes, he was.
4 Memphis, the USA.
5 When she has time.
6 No, it isn't.

8 Allow sts time to read through all the questions. Make sure they understand them all. Demonstrate the activity by asking a confident student about a sport or game that they do, using a selection of the questions. Sts then ask and answer questions in pairs. Ask some sts to tell the class about a sport or game that their partner does.

PERSONAL BEST

Sts can practise talking about sports and games further by writing a paragraph about a sport or game they enjoy. Encourage them to include a range of tenses, and to give their opinion. Sts can share their paragraphs in small groups and decide which sports are the most difficult.

Weaker sts can choose four questions from exercise 8 and write answers to the questions, using full sentences. Ask some sts to read their sentences to the class.

Learning Curve

10D Where are we going now?

1 Look at the pictures and answer the questions.

1 Which tourist attractions can you see?
2 Which countries are they in?
3 Do you want to visit them? Why/Why not?
4 What tourist attractions are there in your town/city?

2 A 10.17 Watch or listen to the first part of *Learning Curve*. Where is Ethan? Who does he meet?

B 10.17 Choose the correct options to complete the sentences. Watch or listen again and check.

1 Flushing Meadows is famous for its *football stadium / tennis stadium*.
2 There were two World's Fairs in the park – in 1939 and in *1964 / 1974*.
3 There is a *science museum / design museum* in the park.
4 Ethan, Penny and Taylor are meeting Marc in *half an hour / an hour*.
5 Marc and Taylor *know / don't know* each other.

3 10.18 Listen and complete the questions in the conversation.

Taylor So what time [1]________ the Hall of Science ________ ?
Ethan It opens at 10.00 a.m.
Penny What [2]________ ________ to do if it rains?
Ethan Well, we can stay inside and look at exhibits all day.
Penny OK. Sounds good. When [3]________ it ________ ?
Ethan 6.00 p.m.
Taylor OK, great. So, what [4]________ we ________ now?
Ethan We're meeting our friend Marc from *Learning Curve*, at the Information Desk.

Conversation builder asking about a tourist attraction

What time does it open/close?
Which days is it open?
How do you get there?
Is there a café/restaurant/gift shop?
What is there to do if it rains?
Are there any special events?

4 A Read the Conversation builder. Then look at the information about a tourist attraction on page 93. Ask and answer questions in pairs.

A *What time does it open?* **B** *It opens at 9.30 a.m.*

B Do you want to visit this attraction? Why/Why not?

Learning Curve

10D Where are we going now?

Sts watch or listen to people talking about tourist attractions. They then practise asking and answering questions about invented tourist attractions, using expressions and intonation to show interest.

Speaking	Skill	Conversation builder
Sts watch a video or listen to a recording of people talking about tourist attractions. They then practise asking and answering questions about tourist attractions.	Showing interest	Asking about a tourist attraction

WARMER

Ask: *What kinds of places do you visit when you go to a new town or city?* Elicit a few ideas, e.g. museums, famous buildings, ancient monuments. Teach the word *tourist attraction*, and explain that museums, famous buildings, etc. are all different kinds of tourist attractions. Ask: *What tourist attractions did you visit last year? Which ones do you want to visit?* Put sts into pairs to talk about the tourist attractions they visited last year, and ones they want to visit in the future. Get feedback on their discussions.

1 Sts look at the pictures and answer the questions in pairs. Discuss the answers with the class and ask sts which attractions they want to visit and why.

Answers
a the Louvre Museum, Paris, France
b Stonehenge, UK
c the Taj Mahal, India
d Chichen Itza, Mexico
e the Terracotta Army, China
f the Golden Gate Bridge, San Francisco, USA

2 A 10.17 In this episode of *Learning Curve*, Ethan, Penny, Taylor and Marc visit Flushing Meadows Park in New York. Pre-teach the words exhibition and exhibit. Read out the questions, then play video/audio track 10.17. See TB page 314 for video/audio script. Sts watch/listen and answer the questions. Check answers.

Answers
Flushing Meadows Park; Penny, Taylor and Marc

B 10.17 Sts read the sentences. Pre-teach the following words if necessary from the video: *stadium*, and *World's Fair* (= an exhibition of culture, food, etc. from around the world). Sts choose the correct options to complete the sentences. Teach the words *Information Desk*, *Observation Tower* and *research*, then play video/audio track 10.17 again. Sts watch/listen and check their answers. Check answers, and check that sts understand all the sentences.

Answers
1 tennis stadium 2 1964 3 science museum
4 half an hour 5 know

3 10.18 Allow sts time to read through the gapped conversation. Ask: *What tourist attraction is Taylor asking about?* (the Hall of Science). Play audio track 10.18. Sts listen and complete the conversation. Check answers.

Answers
1 does, open 2 is there 3 does, close 4 are, doing

3 x PRACTICE *SB page 92, exercise 3*

1 Do the exercise as normal. To check the answers, invite different pairs of sts to read out each completed question and answer. Ask other sts if they agree, then play that part of the audio for sts to check.

2 Ask sts to close their books. Write prompts for the conversation on the board, e.g. *What time / open? 10 a.m.* In pairs, sts try to remember the conversation, using the prompts. They can open their books again to check.

3 In pairs, sts role-play the conversation. Tell them they can make a few notes to help them remember their lines, and then they should close their books. Ask some pairs to perform the conversation for the class.

Conversation builder

Read the Conversation builder box with sts about asking about a tourist attraction. Make sure they understand all the questions. Point out the word order in the questions, e.g. *Which days is it open?* NOT ~~*Which days it is open?*~~ Point out the use of *is there* in *What is there to do if it rains?* Ask questions to check concept.

Concept check questions:
How can I ask about the opening or closing time of a tourist attraction? (What time does it open/close?). *I want to know about transport to the attraction – what can I ask?* (How do you get there?). *How can I ask about a gift shop?* (Is there a gift shop?). *I want to know what will happen if it rains – what can I ask?* (What is there to do if it rains?). *How can I ask about special events?* (Are there any special events?).

4 A Allow sts time to read the information about *Legoland* on page 93. Check they understand that the New Year's Eve Firework show is a special event. Read out the example question and elicit the answer. Sts then ask and answer questions in pairs. They can swap roles and practise again.

B Discuss with the class whether sts would like to visit *Legoland*, and why.

Fun days out

Legoland > Plan your trip — Week: 13–19 September

Monday	Tuesday	Wednesday	Thursday	Friday	Saturday	Sunday
9.30 a.m. – 5.00 p.m. (£30)	9.30 a.m. – 5.00 p.m. (£30)	Closed	9.30 a.m. – 5.00 p.m. (£30)	9.30 a.m. – 5.00 p.m. (£30)	9.30 a.m. – 6.00 p.m. (£35)	9.30 a.m. – 6.00 p.m. (£35)

Weather: Most attractions are outside. Umbrellas are available from the gift shop. Inside attractions include: LEGO 4D Movie Theatre, Imagination Centre and the Exploratorium workshops.

Food & drink: City Walk Pizza and Pasta, Hill Top Café and many more.

Getting there:
By car: Legoland is on the B3022 road (parking available).
By bus: Take the number 200 bus from Windsor Theatre Royal.

31 December: Kids' New Year's Eve firework show

5 A ▶ 10.19 Watch or listen to the second part of the show. How many exhibits do Penny, Marc, Ethan and Taylor see in the Hall of Science?

B ▶ 10.19 Are the sentences true (T) or false (F)? Watch or listen again and check.

1 Tickets for the Hall of Science cost $15. ____
2 There are almost 450 exhibits. ____
3 Marc and Ethan buy tickets for a 3D film. ____
4 Taylor doesn't like flying. ____
5 Taylor wants a flying car. ____
6 They decide to eat pizza. ____

6 ▶ 10.20 Match the sentences with the responses. Listen, check and repeat the responses.

1 It costs $15, but we paid for you.
2 What about *Journey into Space*? It's a 3D film.
3 We're hungry and we're eating a very large pizza.

a OK. Sounds good.
b Oh really? Thanks!
c That sounds interesting.

Skill showing interest

When people speak to you, it's important to show that you're listening.
- Use expressions: *Oh really? That sounds good. Great.*
- Use intonation to sound interested.

7 A ▶ 10.21 Read the Skill box. Then listen to conversations 1–4. Which response sounds more interested: *a* or *b*?

1 I'm visiting my family this weekend. ____
2 My sister goes rock climbing every week. ____
3 There's a new comedy at the cinema. ____
4 We went to the beach yesterday. ____

B ▶ 10.22 Listen and repeat the interested responses.

Go to Communication practice: Students A and B, page 150

8 A PREPARE In pairs, invent a tourist attraction and write information about it. Include:
- the days and times it is open
- the price of tickets
- what you can do
- how to get there
- shops and restaurants
- special events

B PRACTISE Swap your information with another pair. Then ask and answer questions about the tourist attraction. Remember to show you're interested.

A *What time does the museum open?* B *It opens at 9.30 a.m.* A *OK, great.*

C PERSONAL BEST Listen to the other pair. Do they ask questions well? Do they show interest?

Personal Best Write about a tourist attraction in your town/city.

5 A 10.19 Read out the question, then play video/audio track 10.19. See TB page 315 for video/audio script. Sts watch/listen and answer the question. Check the answer with the class.

> **Answer**
> two

B 10.19 Allow sts time to read through the sentences. Pre-teach the following words if necessary from the video: *tickets, 3D film, pilot* and the phrase *Our pleasure* (= we are happy to do this for you). Play video/audio 10.19 again. Sts watch/listen and decide if the sentences are true or false. Check answers.

> **Answers**
> 1 T 2 T 3 F 4 F 5 T 6 T

6 10.20 Sts read the sentences and responses, and match them. Play audio track 10.20. See SB page opposite for audio script. Sts listen and check their answers. Check that sts understand all the sentences and responses.

> **Answers**
> 1 b 2 c 3 a

Skill

Read through the Skill box with the class about showing interest. Point out that intonation is very important, and demonstrate the point by saying the expressions in the Skill box in a bored way first, then in an interested way.

7 A 10.21 Explain to sts that they will hear two responses in each conversation, one not interested and one interested. Play audio track 10.21. See TB page 315 for audio script. Sts listen and choose the more interested response. Play the audio track again, pausing to check answers.

> **Answers**
> 1 b 2 a 3 a 4 a

B 10.22 Play audio track 10.22. See TB page 315 for audio script. Pause the recording after each expression for sts to repeat. Encourage sts to copy the intonation on the recording.

Go to Communication practice

Divide the class into Student A and Student B. All sts (A & B) should go to SB page 150. Go to TB page 295 for the teacher notes. Do the activity, then continue with exercise 8 of lesson 10D.

8 Sts follow the steps to have a conversation in which they ask about a tourist attraction.

A PREPARE Allow sts time to plan their ideas in pairs. Alternatively, you could brainstorm a few ideas for tourist attractions as a class first. Sts could then use one of the ideas and make notes about it.

B PRACTISE Sts swap their information with another pair, then ask and answer questions about the attraction, using the information they are given. Encourage them to use a range of questions from the Conversation builder box to ask for information, and remind them to show interest by using expressions from the Skill box and intonation. They can swap roles and practise again.

C PERSONAL BEST Pairs work together in groups of four. They listen to each other and give feedback on how well they ask questions and how well they show interest. Remind sts that it is important to give positive feedback as well as negative.

PERSONAL BEST

Sts can practise talking about tourist attractions further. They write an information leaflet about a tourist attraction in their town or city, giving information about opening times, etc. Refer them back to the information about *Legoland* to use as a model. Sts could share their leaflets in small groups. Ask groups in turn to tell the class which tourist attraction they like visiting or would like to visit in the future.

Weaker sts could work in pairs. Write some headings on the board for them to use, e.g. *Days open, Opening times, Food and drink, Getting there*. They choose a tourist attraction they both know and complete the information about it using the headings. They can compare their information in small groups and discuss which they want to visit.

EXTRA PRACTICE

Sts work in groups of four. One pair repeats their conversation from part C of exercise 8 while a student from the other pair films them on their phone. They then swap roles and practise again. Watching themselves on film will help sts to evaluate how well they can ask about a tourist attraction and show interest.

Grammar

1 Tick (✓) the correct sentences.

1 a I can't talk now. I'm doing my homework. ☐
b I can't talk now. I do my homework. ☐
c I can't talk now. I did my homework. ☐

2 a They not working at the moment. ☐
b They aren't working at the moment. ☐
c They don't working at the moment. ☐

3 a What often do you go to the gym? ☐
b How often do you go to the gym? ☐
c How much often do you go to the gym? ☐

4 a I see my brother three times at year. ☐
b I see my brother three times for year. ☐
c I see my brother three times a year. ☐

5 a What are you doing tomorrow? ☐
b What do you do tomorrow? ☐
c What you are doing tomorrow? ☐

6 a He not is coming to the party tonight. ☐
b He isn't coming to the party tonight. ☐
c He doesn't come to the party tonight. ☐

7 a What time did the train leave? ☐
b What time the train did leave? ☐
c What time left the train? ☐

8 a They were at work yesterday? ☐
b Did they be at work yesterday? ☐
c Were they at work yesterday? ☐

2 Complete the questions and sentences with the correct form of the verbs in the box.

cost finish spend go have meet
not be not study can buy wear

1 How often ________ you ________ a shower?
2 Carlos ________ some new boots today. Look – they're really nice.
3 What time ________ you ________ work last night?
4 We ________ shopping in London next Tuesday.
5 How much ________ your new coat ________ ? Was it expensive?
6 She's in the library, but she ________ . She's texting a friend.
7 ________ you ________ your friends next weekend?
8 He ________ at work yesterday. I think he was ill.
9 Where ________ I ________ some good shoes?
10 How much money ________ you ________ on clothes every month?

3 Complete the text with the correct form of the verbs in brackets.

The Kinderkook Café

The Kinderkook Café in Amsterdam is a café with a difference – the chefs and waiters are all children! Parents take their children to the café in the afternoon and the children cook a meal. Then, in the evening, the parents return to eat it. Matt Baker talked to one of the parents, Sonja Kroes.

Matt When [1] ________ the café ________ (start)?
Sonja It started in 1981. It's very popular.
Matt What [2] ________ the children ________ (cook)?
Sonja They cook pasta, curry, pizza and lots more. The food is healthy and delicious.
Matt How often [3] ________ you ________ (come) here with your daughter?
Sonja We come once a month. Lotte loves it!
Matt [4] ________ she ________ (work) here today?
Sonja Yes, she is. She [5] ________ (make) a cake. Look, she's over there. She [6] ________ (wear) a pink jumper. And her friend, Stijn, is helping her. They [7] ________ (have) a good time!
Matt [8] ________ you ________ (eat) here tonight?
Sonja Yes, I am. I [9] ________ (come) with my husband and my parents. It was Lotte's birthday yesterday, and she wanted to have a small party here with the family.
Matt That's nice. How old [10] ________ (be) she?
Sonja She's seven.

Vocabulary

1 Put the words in the box in the correct columns.

volleyball a museum videogames an art gallery
a suit shopping cycling gymnastics karate
trousers walking tennis yoga my family a belt

go	do	visit	wear	play

Grammar

1 Sts read the sentences and tick the correct one in each group. Check answers and discuss as a class why the other sentences are incorrect.

Answers
1 a
2 b
3 b
4 c
5 a
6 b
7 a
8 c

2 Sts read the questions and sentences and complete them with the correct verb forms. Check answers.

Answers
1 do, have
2 is wearing
3 did, finish
4 are going
5 did, cost
6 isn't studying
7 Are, meeting
8 wasn't
9 can, buy
10 do, spend

3 Focus on the picture and read out the title of the text. Ask: *What do you think is special about the Kinderkook Café?* Elicit a few ideas, then ask sts to read the text quickly to check their ideas. Discuss the answer with the class. Sts then read the text again and complete it with the correct verb forms. Check answers.

Answers
1 did, start
2 do, cook
3 do, come
4 Is, working
5 's making
6 's wearing
7 're having
8 Are, eating
9 'm coming
10 is

3 x PRACTICE *SB page 94, Grammar exercise 3*

1 Do the exercise as normal. To check answers, read out the text with five correct and five incorrect answers. Ask sts to note down the incorrect answers. Put sts into small groups to compare their lists. Discuss as a class which answers were incorrect, and what the correct answers should be.

2 Put sts into pairs and ask them to close their books. Read out each question from the text. Sts work in their pairs to remember the answers to the questions and make notes. They can look at their books again to check.

3 In pairs, sts think of two or three more questions that Matt could ask Sonja about the Kinderkook Café. You could brainstorm a few ideas with the class first, e.g. *Is the food nice? What did Lotte cook last time she came? When did Lotte start coming here?* Sts can then think of Sonja's answers and role play their conversation. Ask some pairs to perform their conversations for the class.

Vocabulary

1 Sts put the words in the correct columns. As an extension, sts could add one or two more words to each column.

Answers

go	do	visit	wear	play
shopping cycling walking	gymnastics karate yoga	a museum an art gallery my family	a suit trousers a belt	volleyball videogames tennis

2 Circle the word that is different. Explain your answers.

1	angry	happy	hockey	thirsty
2	skirt	beach	jacket	dress
3	festival	concert	suit	party
4	tent	pay	spend	buy
5	pop	rock	jazz	coat
6	socks	boots	shoes	trousers
7	museum	art gallery	jumper	department store
8	money	comedy	romance	drama

3 Choose the correct options to complete the sentences.

1 Can I try ________ this shirt, please?
a in b off c on

2 That shop ________ really nice T-shirts.
a sells b spends c pays

3 Let's stay ________ home tonight. I'm really tired.
a in b at c on

4 Do you want to ________ a video?
a go b look c watch

5 I don't have any money. Can I pay ________ card?
a with b by c for

6 I usually shop ________ . I don't have time to go to the supermarket.
a online b by card c by cash

7 We're ________ a barbecue at the weekend. Would you like to come?
a having b staying c spending

8 We don't accept credit cards here. Can you pay with ________ , please?
a chess b cash c calm

4 Complete the conversation with the words in the box.

hungry	excited	time	scared
horror	bored	happy	tired

Bella What did you do last night, Ruby?
Ruby Tim and I went to the cinema. We watched that new [1]________ film, *Black Night*.
Bella Were you [2]________ ?
Ruby No, we were [3]________ . It wasn't very good.
Bella That's a pity. Did you do anything after the film?
Ruby We were really [4]________ , so we went to a restaurant.
Bella How was the food?
Ruby It was excellent, so we were [5]________ ! What about you? What did you do?
Bella We went to a concert – the Foo Fighters. They're Nick's favourite band. He was very [6]________ when he got tickets.
Ruby Did you have a good [7]________ ?
Bella Yes, it was great. The concert finished at 1.00 in the morning, so I'm really [8]________ today!

Personal Best

Lesson 9A Name five types of clothes.

Lesson 10A Name three activities a tourist can do in your town or city.

Lesson 9A Write what three friends or family members are doing now.

Lesson 10A Write about your plans for two days next week. Use the present continuous.

Lesson 9B Name three positive feelings.

Lesson 10B Write three instructions using the imperative.

Lesson 9C Write a sentence about shopping.

Lesson 10C Name six sports or games. Use the verbs *go*, *play* and *do*.

Lesson 9C Write three questions with *How often ...?* Then answer the questions.

Lesson 10C Write questions with *What*, *When* and *Where* in three different tenses.

Lesson 9D Describe a photo on your phone or in a magazine.

Lesson 10D Write three questions to ask about a tourist attraction.

2 Sts circle the word that is different in each set. Check answers, and ask sts to explain in each case why the word is different. As an extension, sts could write two or three sentences using some of the words.

Answers
1 hockey (not a feeling)
2 beach (not clothes)
3 suit (not an event)
4 tent (not a money verb)
5 coat (not a type of music)
6 trousers (not for feet)
7 jumper (not a place)
8 money (not a type of film)

3 Sts read the sentences and choose the correct options to complete them. Check answers.

Answers
1 c
2 a
3 b
4 c
5 b
6 a
7 a
8 b

3 x PRACTICE *SB page 95, exercise 3*

1 Do the exercise as normal. To check the answers, read out the sentences, some with correct answers and some with incorrect ones. Ask sts to call out 'no' when you say an incorrect one. Elicit the correct answers.

2 Put sts into pairs and ask them to close their books. Tell them you are going to read out each sentence, word by word, and they should put their hand up as soon as they can remember the full sentence. Read out each sentence word by word, pausing after each word. Sts race to say the full sentence.

3 Sts work in pairs. They write a conversation using as many of the words and phrases from this exercise as they can. Encourage them to use some of the words which are incorrect answers too, e.g. *spend, pay, look*. Monitor and help while they are working, and encourage them to use their imagination! Ask some sts to perform their conversations for the class. See which pair managed to use the most words and created the most interesting conversation.

4 Sts read the conversation and complete it with the correct words in the box. Check answers.

Answers
1 horror
2 scared
3 bored
4 hungry
5 happy
6 excited
7 time
8 tired

Personal Best

At the end of each *Review and practice* double-page spread, there is a *Personal Best* section. The aim here is to provide a quick challenge to change the pace and allow for language recall and personalization.

These questions and prompts give sts the opportunity to revise a number of language and skills points from the preceding two units in a more productive way. The points being revised are referenced according to which lesson they appear in (e.g. Lesson 9A). They cover grammar, vocabulary, text builder language from reading and writing lessons, and conversation builder language from speaking lessons. Sts work individually, in pairs or in groups, according to the class dynamic and the time available. Set a time limit if you would like to add a competitive element. Encourage sts to refer back to the relevant lessons if they are having difficulties. The aim is for them to respond to the prompts and engage with the target language in a personal way. Their answers will vary. Monitor and help as necessary and get feedback on sts' answers.

WORKBOOK REVIEW AND PRACTICE

Students will find two pages of Review and Practice at the end of each unit of their Workbooks.
Unit 9, pages 56 and 57
Unit 10, pages 62 and 63

GRAMMAR PRACTICE

Hello The verb *be* (*I, you*)

We use the verb *be* to give information about people.

I'm Carlos and I'm a teacher.

We usually use contractions in positive and negative forms.

You're a student. = You are a student.
I'm not in Class 3. = I am not in Class 3.

1.4	I	you
+	I'**m** a student.	You'**re** a teacher.
–	I'**m not** a teacher.	You **aren't** a student.
?	**Am** I in Class 2?	**Are** you in my class?
Y/N	Yes, I **am**. / No, I'**m not**.	Yes, you **are**. / No, you **aren't**.

1 Choose the correct words to complete the sentences and questions.

1 I *'m / 're* Harry.
2 You *'m / 're* Lola.
3 *Am / Are* you a student?
4 *Am I / I'm* in Room 3.
5 *Are you / You are* late?
6 No, I *'m not / aren't*.
7 *Am / Are* I in this class?
8 Yes, you *am / are*.

◄ Go back to page 4

1A The verb *be* (*he, she, it*)

We use *he*, *she* and *it* to talk about a person or a thing.

The teacher is Mexican. He's from Puebla.
The car isn't from Germany. It's from Japan.

We usually use contractions in positive and negative forms.

Akemi isn't Chinese. = Akemi is not Chinese.
She's Japanese. = She is Japanese.

1.14	he	she	it
+	Leo'**s** from Peru.	Lucía'**s** Colombian.	The book'**s** Chinese.
–	He **isn't** from Chile.	She **isn't** Argentinian.	It **isn't** Italian.
?	**Is** Ravi from India?	**Is** Ayla Turkish?	**Is** the car German?
Y/N	Yes, he **is**. / No, he **isn't**.	Yes, she **is**. / No, she **isn't**.	Yes, it **is**. / No, it **isn't**.

1 Complete the sentences with the correct words.

1 This is my friend Daniel. He _________ from Spain.
2 Anna isn't in class today. _________'s at home.
3 Sophie _________ a student. She's the teacher.
4 This is my car. _________'s a Toyota.
5 A Where _________ Leonardo DiCaprio from?
B He _________ from the USA.
6 A What's the capital of Australia? Is _________ Sydney?
B No, it _________ . It's Canberra.
7 A _________ María from Colombia?
B No, she _________ . She's from Mexico.
8 A Is sushi from Japan?
B Yes, _________ is.

◄ Go back to page 7

1C The verb *be* (*we, you, they*)

We use *we*, *you* and *they* to talk about people and things in the plural.

The engineers are here. They're from India.
Susan and I aren't happy. We're sad.

We usually use contractions in positive and negative forms.

You're in Class 3. = You are in Class 3.
The pizzas aren't expensive. = The pizzas are not expensive.

1.29	we	you	they
+	We'**re** 25 years old.	You'**re** doctors.	They'**re** French.
–	We **aren't** old.	You **aren't** chefs.	Ana and Bea **aren't** here.
?	**Are** we sad?	**Are** you happy?	**Are** they in Class 4?
Y/N	Yes, we **are**. / No, we **aren't**.	Yes, you **are**. / No, you **aren't**.	Yes, they **are**. / No, they **aren't**.

1 Rewrite the sentences. Change the words in **bold** to *we*, *you* or *they*.

1 **Elsa and Lucy** are police officers.
____
2 **Maite and I** are 21 years old.
____
3 Are **you and Wei** from China?
____
4 **The doctors** aren't from India.
____
5 Where are **Maggie and Jake Gyllenhaal** from?
____
6 How old are **you and your friend**?
____

2 Choose the correct words to complete the questions and sentences.

1 We *isn't / aren't* doctors.
2 *Is / Are* Ismail from Turkey?
3 Sam and I *am / are* in London.
4 I *'m not / aren't* your teacher.
5 Where *is / are* the actor from?
6 Ana and Rosa *is / are* from Spain.

◄ Go back to page 11

Hello The verb *be* (*I*, *you*)

1 1.4 Read through the information with the class, or allow sts time to read it on their own. Play audio track 1.4 for sts to listen and repeat. Sts read the sentences and choose the correct words to complete them. Check answers.

Answers
1 'm
2 're
3 Are
4 I'm
5 Are you
6 'm not
7 Am
8 are

Refer sts back to page 4 if they want to revise *I* and *you* forms of the verb be further, or see more examples of it in context.

1A The verb *be* (*he*, *she*, *it*)

1 1.14 Read through the information with the class, or allow sts time to read it on their own. Play audio track 1.14 for sts to listen and repeat. Sts read the sentences and complete them with the correct verb forms. Check answers.

Answers
1 's
2 She
3 isn't
4 It
5 is, 's
6 it, isn't
7 Is, isn't
8 it

Refer sts back to page 7 if they want to revise *he, she* and *it* forms of the verb be further, or see more examples of it in context.

1C The verb *be* (*we*, *you*, *they*)

1 1.29 Read through the information with the class, or allow sts time to read it on their own. Play audio track 1.29 for sts to listen and repeat. Sts rewrite the sentences using *we*, *you* or *they*. Check answers.

Answers
1 They are police officers.
2 We are 21 years old.
3 Are you from China?
4 They aren't from India.
5 Where are they from?
6 How old are you?

2 Sts choose the correct words to complete the sentences. Check answers.

Answers
1 aren't
2 Is
3 are
4 'm not
5 is
6 are

3 x PRACTICE *SB page 96, exercise 2*

1 Do the exercise as normal. To check answers, read out each completed sentence twice, once with each verb form. Ask sts to shout 'yes' for the correct sentence and 'no' for the incorrect one. Discuss any answers where there is disagreement.

2 Ask sts to close their books. Read out a prompt for each sentence in turn, e.g. *doctors*. Sts race to remember the correct sentence. You could give clues if they are struggling, e.g. *plural form, negative*.

3 Sts work in pairs. They change each sentence so that the incorrect answer becomes correct, e.g. *Sam isn't a doctor*. Ask some sts to read their sentences to the class.

Refer sts back to page 11 if they want to revise the verb *be* (*we*, *you they*) further, or see more examples of it in context.

2A Singular and plural nouns

We use *a* and *an* with singular nouns. We use *a* with nouns that start with consonants (*b*, *d*, *f*, *g*, etc.) and we use *an* with nouns that start with vowels (*a*, *e*, *i*, *o*, *u*).

It's a book. *She's an actor.*

To make a noun plural, we usually add *-s* or *-es*.

a key ⇨ three keys *a watch ⇨ two watches*

2.3	Singular	Plural
	It's **an** umbrella.	They're umbrella**s**.
	I'm **a** waitress.	We're waitress**es**.

Spelling rules for plurals

We usually add ***-s*** to nouns to make a plural.
bag ⇨ bags

When a noun ends in a consonant + ***y***, we remove the ***y*** and then add ***-ies***.
country ⇨ countries

When a noun ends in ***ch***, ***sh***, ***s*** or ***x***, we add ***-es***.
watch ⇨ watches

Some plurals are irregular.
child ⇨ children *man ⇨ men* *woman ⇨ women* *person ⇨ people*

1 Complete the sentences with singular or plural nouns and *a* or *an*, if necessary.

	Singular	Plural
1	It's a city.	They're ________ .
2	She's ________ .	They're actors.
3	Are you a waitress?	Are you ________ ?
4	He isn't ________ .	They aren't children.
5	It's a watch.	They're ________ .
6	It isn't ________ .	They aren't umbrellas.
7	I'm a woman.	We're ________ .
8	He's ________ .	They're people.

2 Match the parts to make sentences and questions.

1 Alice is an ____
2 It's an ____
3 He's a ____
4 Jo and I are ____
5 Are you a ____
6 Where are my ____

a tour guide.
b IT worker.
c umbrella.
d engineers.
e sunglasses?
f chef?

◀ Go back to page 14

2A *this, that, these, those*

We use *this* and *these* + the verb *be* to identify things that are near us.

This is my bag and these are my sunglasses.

We use *that* and *those* + the verb *be* to identify things that aren't near us.

That's my school and those are my friends.

2.4	Things that are near	Things that aren't near
Singular	**This** is my wallet.	**That**'s my teacher.
Plural	**These** are my books.	**Those** are my classmates.

Look! We can also use *this/that/these/those* + noun. *That book is new.*

1 Choose the correct words to complete the sentences.

1 *This* / *These* is my room.
2 Excuse me. Are *that* / *those* your glasses?
3 Look! Is *this* / *that* your phone over there?
4 Are *these* / *this* your keys?
5 Is *that* / *those* your pen, or is it my pen?
6 Are *these* / *this* your credit cards?

◀ Go back to page 15

2C Possessive adjectives, *'s* for possession

We use possessive adjectives before nouns to say that something belongs to someone.

Joseph is my brother. *This is our house.*

We use the same possessive adjectives for singular and plural nouns.

Is that your key? *Are those your keys?*

2.11	Possessive adjectives
my	I'm French. **My** wife is Spanish.
your	Are **you** sad? **Your** boyfriend isn't here.
his	**He**'s a teacher. **His** students are young.
her	**She**'s an actor. **Her** house is big.
its	**It**'s a small restaurant. **Its** pizzas are good.
our	**We**'re late. **Our** boss isn't happy.
their	**They**'re tour guides. **Their** jobs are interesting.

If we talk about possession with a name or a noun, we add *'s* to the name or noun.

Is that the teacher's book? *Are you Rob's sister?*

1 Complete the sentences with the correct possessive adjectives.

1 Hello. ________ name's Kate.
2 We're from Lima. This is a photo of ________ house.
3 He's French. ________ name is Olivier.
4 They're British, but ________ parents are from Peru.
5 Hi, I'm Tom. What's ________ name?
6 This is Luisa and ________ husband, Sven.

2 Complete the sentences with *'s* for possession so they mean the same as the first sentences.

1 She's Olivia. Those are her sunglasses.
Those are *Olivia's sunglasses* .
2 He's my son. That's his credit card.
That's ________________ .
3 This is my daughter. Her name is Ruby.
My ________________ .
4 She's our doctor. Her phone number is 665342.
Our ________________ .

◀ Go back to page 19

2A Singular and plural nouns

1 ▶2.3 Read through the information about singular and plural forms with the class, or allow sts time to read it on their own. Play audio track 2.3 for sts to listen and repeat. Sts read the sentences and complete them with the correct singular or plural nouns. Check answers.

Answers
1 cities
2 an actor
3 waitresses
4 a child
5 watches
6 an umbrella
7 women
8 a person

2 Sts match the beginnings and ends of the sentences and questions. Check answers.

Answers
1 b
2 c
3 a
4 d
5 f
6 e

Refer sts back to page 14 if they want to revise singular and plural forms further, or see more examples of them in context.

2A *this, that, these, those*

1 ▶2.4 Read through the information about *this*, *that*, *these* and *those* with the class, or allow sts time to read it on their own. Play audio track 2.4 for sts to listen and repeat. Sts read the sentences and choose the correct words to complete them. Check answers.

Answers
1 This
2 those
3 that
4 these
5 that
6 these

Refer sts back to page 15 if they want to revise *this*, *that*, *these*, *those* further, or see more examples of them in context.

2C Possessive adjectives, *'s* for possession

1 ▶2.11 Read through the information about possessive adjectives with the class, or allow sts time to read it on their own. Play audio track 2.11 for sts to listen and repeat. Sts read the sentences and complete them with the correct possessive adjectives. Check answers.

Answers
1 My
2 our
3 His
4 their
5 your
6 her

3 x PRACTICE *SB page 97, 2C exercise 1*

1 Do the exercise as normal. To check answers, elicit each answer from an individual student, then elicit the examples from the table in the grammar explanation which support the answer, e.g. *Hello. My name's Kate. I'm French. My wife is Spanish*. Reinforce the meaning and use of each possessive adjective.
2 Ask sts to close their books. Write prompts for the sentences on the board, e.g. *Hello/ Kate, we/Lima/ house*. Sts work in pairs and try to rewrite the sentences using the prompts. They can look in their books to check.
3 Sts work in pairs and use some of the sentences, or similar sentences, to prepare a short dialogue in which people introduce themselves and each other. Sts can practise their dialogues in pairs. Ask some sts to perform their dialogues for the class.

2 Read through the information about *'s* for possession with the class, or allow sts time to read it on their own. Sts read the sentences and complete the second sentences using *'s* for possession. Check answers.

Answers
2 my son's credit card
3 daughter's name is Ruby
4 doctor's phone number is 665342

Refer sts back to page 19 if they want to revise possessive adjectives and *'s* for possession further, or see more examples of them in context.

3A Present simple (*I, you, we, they*)

We use the present simple to talk about facts and routines.

I drink coffee for breakfast.
We eat a lot of fruit.

We form negatives with *don't* (*do not*) + the infinitive of the verb.

My parents don't like tea.
They don't eat meat.

We form questions with *do* + subject + the infinitive of the verb.

Do you like fish?
Do they have breakfast?

3.3	I / you / we / they
+	I **have** a big breakfast. You **eat** a lot of fruit.
–	We **don't drink** coffee. They **don't like** cheese.
?	**Do** you **have** a big breakfast? **Do** they **eat** fish?
Y/N	Yes, I **do**. / No, I **don't**. Yes, they **do**. / No, they **don't**.

1 Complete the sentences with the correct form of the verbs in brackets.

1 I ________ pizza. (like)
2 We ________ eggs or cheese. (not eat)
3 They ________ lunch at home. (not have)
4 You ________ tea. (drink)
5 Our children ________ green vegetables. (not like)
6 My husband and I ________ a lot of fruit. (eat)
7 I ________ coffee at night. (not drink)
8 You ________ breakfast. (not have)

2 Order the words to make questions. Then complete the short answers.

1 you / meat / eat / do
________________? No, I ________ .
2 you / do / food / like / Indian
________________? Yes, we ________ .
3 potatoes / they / like / do
________________? Yes, they ________ .
4 drink / do / you and Anna / coffee
________________? No, we ________ .

◀ Go back to page 25

3C Present simple (*he, she, it*)

For *he, she* and *it*, we often add *-s* to the infinitive to make the positive form.

I drink tea for breakfast. ⇨ *He drinks tea for breakfast.*

Spelling rules for present simple verbs with *he, she, it*

We usually add ***-s*** to the infinitive.
work ⇨ *works*

When a verb ends in a consonant + ***y***, we remove the ***y*** and then add ***-ies***.
study ⇨ *studies*

When a verb ends in ***ch***, ***sh***, ***s*** or ***x***, we add ***-es***.
watch ⇨ *watches*

Some verbs are irregular.
go ⇨ *goes*   *do* ⇨ *does*   *have* ⇨ *has*

We form negatives with *doesn't* (*does not*) + the infinitive of the verb.

My sister doesn't speak English.

We form questions with *does* + subject + the infinitive of the verb.

Does our teacher work at the weekend?

3.14	he / she / it
+	Kevin **does** exercise in the morning. She **lives** in Scotland.
–	He **doesn't want** a new car. My house **doesn't have** a garden.
?	**Does** he **live** in London? **Does** Sandra **go** to the gym?
Y/N	Yes, he **does**. / No, he **doesn't**. Yes, she **does**. / No, she **doesn't**.

1 Write the present simple *he*, *she*, *it* form of the verbs.

1 like ________
2 have ________
3 play ________
4 eat ________
5 go ________
6 try ________
7 drink ________
8 wash ________

2 Rewrite the sentences. Use positive (+), negative (–) or question (?) forms.

1 My father makes good cakes.
________________ (?)
2 Anna doesn't study at university.
________________ (+)
3 Mark works on Tuesday.
________________ (–)
4 Does she have two children?
________________ (+)
5 Sam thinks about football all day.
________________ (?)
6 My sister doesn't watch TV in the evening.
________________ (+)

◀ Go back to page 29

3A present simple (*I, you, we, they*)

1 3.3 Read through the information about the present simple with the class, or allow sts time to read it on their own. Play audio track 3.3 for sts to listen and repeat. Sts read the sentences and complete them with the correct verb forms. Check answers.

Answers
1 like
2 don't eat
3 don't have
4 drink
5 don't like
6 eat
7 don't drink
8 don't have

2 Sts put the words in the correct order to make questions, then complete the short answers. Check answers.

Answers
1 Do you eat meat? don't
2 Do you like Indian food? do
3 Do they like potatoes? do
4 Do you and Anna drink coffee? don't

3 x PRACTICE *SB page 98, 3A exercise 2*

1 Do the exercise as normal. To check answers, say the first word of each question, then ask individual sts in turn to say the next word, building up each question in turn. Repeat the full question, then elicit the short answer.

2 In pairs, ask sts to cover the question prompts and just look at the short answers. They try to remember the question for each short answer. They can look at the question prompts and their answers again to check.

3 In pairs, sts ask and answer the questions, changing the questions where necessary so that they all use *you*. Ask pairs to write some sentences using we, about things that are true for both of them, e.g. *We eat meat. We don't like potatoes*.

Refer sts back to page 25 if they want to revise the present simple (*I, you, we, they*) further, or see more examples of it in context.

3C Present simple (*he, she, it*)

1 3.14 Read through the information about the present simple (*he, she, it*) with the class, or allow sts time to read it on their own. Play audio track 3.14 for sts to listen and repeat. Sts write the *he, she, it* forms of the verbs. Check answers, writing the correct forms on the board for sts to check their spellings.

Answers
1 likes
2 has
3 plays
4 eats
5 goes
6 tries
7 drinks
8 washes

2 Elicit the first question as an example. Sts then rewrite the sentences using the correct forms. Check answers.

Answers
1 Does your/my father make good cakes?
2 Anna studies at university.
3 Mark doesn't work on Tuesday.
4 She has two children.
5 Does Sam think about football all day?
6 My sister watches TV in the evening.

Refer sts back to page 29 if they want to revise the present simple (*he, she, it*) further, or see more examples of it in context.

4A Adverbs of frequency

We use adverbs of frequency with the present simple to talk about routines.

They always go to the gym on Friday.
I sometimes play football at the weekend.

Adverbs of frequency come before most verbs, but we put adverbs of frequency after the verb *be*.

I usually have lunch at work.
I'm always at home in the evening. NOT ~~*I always am at home in the evening.*~~

4.3	Adverbs of frequency	
always	He **always** has a shower in the morning.	100%
usually	Julia **usually** gets up early.	
often	You **often** get home after 9.00 p.m.	
sometimes	I'm **sometimes** late for class.	
never	My parents **never** drink coffee.	0%

Look! *never* has a negative meaning, but we use a positive form.
My children never get up early. NOT ~~*My children don't never get up early.*~~

1 Order the words to make sentences.

1 brother / never / my / up / gets / early
______________________.

2 office / I / have / usually / lunch / at / the
______________________.

3 trains / late / always / the / night / at / are
______________________.

4 always / the / morning / a / have / I / in / shower
______________________.

5 dressed / I / get / usually / breakfast / before
______________________.

6 friendly / very / is / teacher / my / always
______________________.

7 never / we / dinner / before / have / 9.00 p.m.
______________________.

8 videos / watch / sometimes / in / we / class
______________________.

◄ Go back to page 33

4C Present simple: *wh-* questions

We ask questions with question words to ask for specific information.

A day / time of day – ***When** does your brother go to the gym?*
A time – ***What time** does the class start?*
A thing – ***What** do you drink at work?*
A person – ***Who** do you work with?*
A place – ***Where** do you live?*
A reason – ***Why** do you get up early on Saturday?*
A number – ***How many** keys do you have?*
An age – ***How old** is Julian?*
A manner – ***How** do you get to work?*

The word order in questions with most verbs is question word + *do/does* + subject + main verb + rest of question.

4.8	Question word	*do*/*does*	Subject	Main verb	Rest of question
	What	do	you	have	for breakfast?
	When	does	she	see	her friends?
	Where	do	his parents	work?	

With the verb *be*, the word order in questions is question word + *am/is/are* + subject + rest of question.

4.9	Question word	am/is/are	Subject	Rest of question
	Why	am	I	cold?
	What time	is	the bus?	
	How	are	you	today?

1 Complete the questions with the question words in the box.

How many What What time When Where Why

1 ________ does your brother do?
He's a taxi driver.
2 ________ do you usually play tennis?
I usually play at the weekend.
3 ________ does your sister work?
She works at the hospital.
4 ________ do you like your job?
Because I meet a lot of people and it's interesting.
5 ________ does your English class start?
At 7.30 p.m.
6 ________ cousins do you have?
I have eight cousins.

2 Write questions.

1 What / you / want for dinner?
____

2 Why / he / cycle to work?
____

3 Who / be / your favourite actors?
____

4 How / they / know that man?
____

5 Where / your mum / go shopping?
____

6 What time / the lesson / finish?
____

◄ Go back to page 37

4A Adverbs of frequency

1 4.3 Read through the information about adverbs of frequency with the class, or allow sts time to read it on their own. Play audio track 4.3 for sts to listen and repeat. Sts put the words in the correct order to make sentences. Check answers.

Answers
1 My brother never gets up early.
2 I usually have lunch at the office.
3 The trains are always late at night.
4 I always have a shower in the morning.
5 I usually get dressed before breakfast.
6 My teacher is always very friendly.
7 We never have dinner before 9.00 p.m.
8 We sometimes watch videos in class.

Refer sts back to page 33 if they want to revise adverbs of frequency further, or see more examples of them in context.

4C Present simple: *wh-* questions

1 4.8 Read through the information about *wh-* questions in the present simple with the class, or allow sts time to read it on their own. Play audio track 4.8 for sts to listen and repeat. Read through the *wh-* words in the box with the class and elicit the type of answer for each one (a number, a place, etc.). Sts read the questions and answers, and complete the questions with the correct words. Check answers.

Answers
1 What
2 When
3 Where
4 Why
5 What time
6 How many

2 Remind sts that we use *do* with *I, you, we* and *they*, and we use *does* with *he, she* and *it*. Remind sts also that questions with the verb *be* are different, because they don't use *do/ does*. Sts write the questions. Check answers.

Answers
1 What do you want for dinner?
2 Why does he cycle to work?
3 Who are your favourite actors?
4 How do they know that man?
5 Where does your mum go shopping?
6 What time does the lesson finish?

3 x PRACTICE *SB page 99, 4C exercise 2*

1 Do the exercise as normal. To check answers, read out each question with one mistake, e.g. *What you want for dinner? Why do he cycle to work?* Ask: *Correct or incorrect?* Elicit the correct questions.

2 Ask sts to close their books. Read out each question one word at a time, pausing after each word. Ask sts to guess each question as soon as they recognize it. You could do this as a game, awarding a point to the first student to say each question correctly.

3 In pairs, sts write answers to the questions. Monitor and help while they are working. Put pairs together into groups of four. They take turns to read one of their answers to each other, in a random order. The other pair must guess the question it answers.

Refer sts back to page 37 if they want to revise *wh-* questions in the present simple, or see more examples of them in context.

5A *can* and *can't*

We use *can* and *can't* (*cannot*) to talk about ability.

I can play the piano. *My grandmother can't drive.*

To make questions with *can*, we put *can* before the subject.

Can you speak Portuguese? *What can he cook?*

We use the same form for all people and things.

I/You/He/She/It/We/They can swim.

5.3	I / you / he / she / it / we / they
+	I **can speak** Italian.
–	You **can't play** the violin.
?	**Can** he **cook** Chinese food?
Y/N	Yes, he **can**. / No, he **can't**.

Look! We use *can*/*can't* with *well* to say we are good/bad at something.
She can speak English well.
They can't swim well.

1 Write positive (+) or negative (–) sentences with *can*.

1 My sister / drive. (–)
____

2 Dogs / swim. (+)
____

3 Her son / use a computer. (–)
____

4 My dad / cook well. (+)
____

2 Complete the questions. Use *can* and the verbs in brackets. Then write the short answers.

1 A ________ Sarah ________ 10 km? (run)
B Yes, ________ .

2 A ________ you and Jo ________ salsa? (dance)
B No, ________ .

3 A ________ your son ________ Italian food? (cook)
B Yes, ________ .

4 A ________ you ________ well? (sing)
B No, ________ .

◀ Go back to page 43

5C Object pronouns

The object of a sentence is the noun which comes after the verb.

I like biscuits. (*biscuits* are the object of the sentence)

Ana calls her sister every week. (*her sister* is the object of the sentence)

We use object pronouns instead of nouns when we know what the noun is.

Emily is a really nice person. I like her. (*her = Emily*)

Fruit juice is good for you. I drink it for breakfast. (*it = fruit juice*)

5.14	Subject pronouns	Object pronouns	
	I	me	I'm here. Can you see **me**?
	you	you	You're friendly. I like **you**.
	he	him	Paul's a doctor. We work with **him**.
	she	her	Who is Karen? I don't know **her**.
	it	it	I love walking. Do you like **it**?
	we	us	We're at work. Call **us** if you have a problem.
	you	you	You and Ben are only 12 years old. Your parents look after **you**.
	they	them	I have three cats. I love **them**!

Look! We always use object pronouns, not subject pronouns, after prepositions.
Can you come with me?
Where's Paul? I want to talk to him.

1 Replace the underlined words with object pronouns.

1 I love <u>books</u>. ________
2 My sister has <u>the car</u>. ________
3 He doesn't like <u>Maria</u>. ________
4 They cook for <u>my wife and me</u>. ________
5 Give the book to <u>John</u>. ________
6 Can he help <u>you and Abdul</u>? ________

2 Choose the correct words to complete the sentences.

1 Ivan's a waiter. I see *he* / *him* at work.
2 Lucy lives in France, but *she* / *her* isn't French.
3 I hate cleaning. Why do I do *me* / *it*?
4 Your children are quiet. Where are *they* / *them*?
5 This bike is very fast. Do you want *it* / *them*?
6 Can you look after my plant? *It* / *Her* needs water every day.

◀ Go back to page 47

5A *can* and *can't*

1 5.3 Read through the information about *can* and *can't* with the class, or allow sts time to read it on their own. Play audio track 5.3 for sts to listen and repeat. Sts write the positive and negative sentences. Check answers.

Answers
1 My sister can't drive.
2 Dogs can swim
3 Her son can't use a computer
4 My dad can cook well

2 Sts complete the questions with *can* and the verbs in brackets, then write the short answers. Check answers.

Answers
1 Can, run, she can
2 Can, dance, we can't
3 Can, cook, he can
4 Can, sing, I can't

3 x PRACTICE *SB page 100, 5A exercise 2*

1 Do the exercise as normal. To check answers, invite pairs of sts in turn to read out each question and answer. Ask other sts: *Correct or incorrect?*

2 Put sts into pairs. One student in each pair reads questions 1 and 2, and tries to remember them. They also try to remember the answers to questions 3 and 4. The other student tries to remember the answers to questions 1 and 2, and the questions 3 and 4. With books closed, they try to remember the questions and answers together. They can look in their books again to check.

3 Sts work in pairs and ask and answer questions about themselves, using the ideas in the exercise, e.g. *Can you run 10km?* Ask some sts to tell the class what their partner *can* and *can't* do.

Refer sts back to page 43 if they want to revise *can* and *can't* further, or see more examples of them in context.

5C Object pronouns

1 5.14 Read through the information about object pronouns with the class, or allow sts time to read it on their own. Play audio track 5.14 for sts to listen and repeat. Sts read the sentences and replace the underlined parts with the correct pronouns. Check answers.

Answers
1 them
2 it
3 her
4 us
5 him
6 you

2 Point out that in this exercise sts have to choose between subject and object pronouns. Sts read the sentences and choose the correct pronouns to complete them. Check answers.

Answers
1 him
2 she
3 it
4 they
5 it
6 It

Refer sts back to page 47 if they want to revise object pronouns further, or see more examples of them in context.

6A *there is/are*

We use *there's* (*there is*) + *a/an* with singular nouns to say that something exists.

There's a beautiful park near my house.
There's an umbrella on the table.

We use *there are* with plural nouns to say that something exists.

There are five hotels in my city.
There are six people on the bus.

We often use *some* in positive sentences with plural nouns. We use *any* in negative sentences and questions with plural nouns.

There are some good cafés in the town centre.
There aren't any museums.
Are there any hotels near here?

6.2	Singular	Plural
+	**There's** a school. **There's** an airport.	**There are some** schools. **There are** two airports.
–	**There isn't** a cinema.	**There aren't any** cinemas.
?	**Is there** a restaurant?	**Are there any** restaurants?
Y/N	Yes, **there is**. / No, **there isn't**.	Yes, **there are**. / No, **there aren't**.

1 Complete the sentences with the correct forms of *there is/are*.

1 ________ a great museum in town.
2 ________ a school near your house?
3 I'm sorry, but ________ a chemist near here.
4 ________ some cheap hotels near the train station.
5 ________ any parks, so children play in the street.
6 ________ any good restaurants at the shopping centre?

2 Complete the sentences with *a/an, some* or *any*.

1 There aren't ________ supermarkets in this area.
2 There's ________ good hospital near here.
3 There are ________ police officers in the street.
4 There isn't ________ Italian restaurant in our village.
5 Are there ________ pens in your bag?
6 Is there ________ police station near here?

◀ Go back to page 51

6C Prepositions of place

We use prepositions of place to say where an object or person is.

There's a table next to the bed.
My brother is in the kitchen.
Your keys are behind the sofa.
Simon is next to Amy.

6.9 Prepositions of place			
on	 The phone is **on** the table.	next to	 The chair is **next to** the table.
in	 The phone is **in** the bag.	in front of	 The table is **in front of** the chair.
above	 The shelves are **above** the table.	between	 The chair is **between** the window and the table.
under	 The bag is **under** the table.	behind	 The lamp is **behind** the sofa.

1 Look at the picture. Write sentences saying where the things are with prepositions of place.

1 fridge / cooker
____
2 shelves / bed
____
3 cat / table
____
4 laptop / desk
____
5 window / sofa
____
6 table / sofa
____

◀ Go back to page 55

6A *there is/are*

1 6.2 Read through the information about *there is/are* with the class, or allow sts time to read it on their own. Play audio track 6.2 for sts to listen and repeat. Point out the use of *there are* + *some* and *there aren't* + *any*. Sts read the sentences and complete them with the correct words. Check answers.

Answers
1 There's
2 Is there
3 there isn't
4 There are
5 There aren't
6 Are there

2 Sts read the sentences and complete them with the correct words. Check answers.

Answers
1 any
2 a
3 some
4 an
5 any
6 a

Refer sts back to page 51 if they want to revise *there is/are* further, or see more examples of it in context.

6C Prepositions of place

1 6.9 Read through the information about prepositions of place with the class, or allow sts time to read it on their own. Play audio track 6.9 for sts to listen and repeat. Focus on the picture, then read out the first prompt and elicit the correct sentence. Sts write the remaining sentences. Check answers.

Answers
1 The fridge is next to the cooker.
2 The shelves are above the bed.
3 The cat is under the table.
4 The laptop is on the desk.
5 The window is behind the sofa.
6 The table is in front of the sofa.

3 x PRACTICE *SB page 101, 6C exercise 1*

1 Do the exercise as normal. To check answers, ask questions about each of the things in the prompts, e.g. *Is the fridge behind the cooker? Is it in front of the cooker?* Elicit the correct answer.
2 Give sts one minute to look at the picture, then ask them to close their books. Write the objects from the exercise on the board in a jumbled order, e.g. *fridge, lamp, desk, cat*, etc. In pairs, sts try to remember the sentences and write them. They can open their books again and look at their answers to check.
3 In pairs, sts write three more sentences about the picture, two true and one false. Put pairs together into groups of four. With books closed, they read their sentences to each other and try to remember the picture, to decide which of their classmates' sentences is false. Ask who guessed correctly.

Refer sts back to page 55 if they want to revise prepositions of place further, or see more examples of them in context.

7A Past simple: *be*

We use the past simple of the verb *be* to talk about situations in the past.

Marilyn Monroe was an actor. She was American.

The positive past simple forms of the verb *be* are *was and were*.

I was in New York yesterday. The people were very friendly.

The negative past simple forms of the verb *be* are *wasn't* (*was not*) and *weren't* (*were not*).

I wasn't at home last night.
The Beatles weren't from Manchester.

We form questions with *was*/*were* + subject.

Was the teacher late for class?
Were you cold at work today?

7.2	I / he / she / it	you / we / they
+	I **was** happy.	They **were** singers.
–	It **wasn't** a good film.	We **weren't** at home yesterday.
?	**Was** she at school?	**Were** they Mexican?
Y/N	Yes, she **was**. / No, she **wasn't**.	Yes, they **were**. / No, they **weren't**.

1 Choose the correct words to complete the sentences.

1 My father *was* / *were* an artist.
2 Enrique and Javier *wasn't* / *weren't* at work on Monday.
3 How *was* / *were* your holiday?
4 This book *wasn't* / *weren't* very interesting.
5 My grandparents *was* / *were* both musicians.
6 What *was* / *were* the answer to this question?
7 *Were* / *Was* you and your sister at home yesterday?
8 We *wasn't* / *weren't* happy with our exam results.

2 Complete the conversations with the correct form of *was* or *were*.

1 A ________ you at home yesterday?
B No, I ________ . I ________ at the hospital.
2 A ________ the film good?
B Yes, it ________ . The actors ________ amazing.
3 A ________ your parents teachers?
B No, they ________ . They ________ writers.
4 A ________ Akira Kurosawa a photographer?
B No, he ________ . He ________ a film director.
5 A ________ you late for school today?
B Yes, I ________ . I ________ 30 minutes late.
6 A ________ you and Nico at the same school?
B Yes, we ________ , but we ________ in the same class.

◀ Go back to page 61

7C Past simple: regular verbs

We use the past simple to talk about completed actions in the past. We usually add *-ed* to the infinitive to form the past simple of regular verbs.

cook ⇨ cooked *I cooked pasta yesterday.*

Spelling rules for regular positive past simple *verbs*
We usually add ***-ed*** to the infinitive. *cook ⇨ cooked*
When a verb ends in ***-e***, we add ***-d***. *dance ⇨ danced*
When a verb ends in consonant + ***y***, we change the ***y*** to ***i*** and then we add ***-ed***. *study ⇨ studied*
When a verb ends in vowel + consonant, we usually double the consonant and add ***-ed***. *stop ⇨ stopped*

We form the negative with *didn't* (*did not*) + infinitive.

I didn't want coffee for breakfast. *My parents didn't like the food.*

We form questions with *did* + subject + infinitive.

Did she play the piano yesterday? *Did your brother live in Canada?*

7.12	I / you / he / she / it / we / they
+	He **worked** in London.
–	They **didn't live** in this house.
?	**Did** you **study** Spanish at university?
Y/N	Yes, I **did**. / No, I **didn't**.

1 Rewrite the sentences and questions in the past simple.

1 My grandfather lives in this street.
____
2 I cook paella for dinner.
____
3 She doesn't cycle home.
____
4 The train doesn't stop in Paris.
____
5 Liam studies Science at university.
____
6 Does she dance with her friends?
____
7 Do they live in Ecuador?
____
8 Elise doesn't want ice cream.
____

◀ Go back to page 65

7A Past simple: *be*

1 7.2 Read through the information about the past simple of *be* with the class, or allow sts time to read it on their own. Play audio track 7.2 for sts to listen and repeat. Point out that we use *was/wasn't* with *I, he, she* and *it*, and we use *were/weren't* with *you, we* and *they*. Sts read the sentences and choose the correct words to complete them. Check answers.

Answers
1 was
2 weren't
3 was
4 wasn't
5 were
6 was
7 Were
8 weren't

2 Sts read the conversations and complete them with the correct words. Check answers.

Answers
1 Were, wasn't, was
2 Was, was, were
3 Were, weren't, were
4 Was, wasn't, was
5 Were, was, was
6 Were, were, weren't

3 x PRACTICE *SB page 102, 7A exercise 2*

1 Do the exercise as normal. To check answers, put sts into pairs and ask them to compare their answers. Ask them to choose one conversation where they are confident about the answers. Invite a pair who are confident about each conversation to read it out. Check the answers.

2 In pairs, sts cover the exercise. They then uncover each question in turn and try to remember the answer. They can uncover the answer to check.

3 In pairs, sts write two more questions using *Were you ...?* to ask their classmates. Elicit a few examples from the class first, e.g. *Were you at school yesterday? Were you at work last week? Were you at home on Saturday?* In groups of four, sts can ask and answer their questions. Ask some sts to tell the class something they learned about their classmates.

Refer sts back to page 61 if they want to revise the past simple of *be* further, or see more examples of it in context.

7C Past simple: regular verbs

1 7.12 Read through the information about regular verbs in the past simple with the class, or allow sts time to read it on their own. Play audio track 7.12 for sts to listen and repeat. Sts read the sentences and questions and rewrite them in the past simple. Elicit an example answer from the class first if necessary. Check answers.

Answers
1 My grandfather lived in this street
2 I cooked paella for dinner.
3 She didn't cycle home.
4 The train didn't stop in Paris.
5 Liam studied Science at university.
6 Did she dance with her friends?
7 Did they live in Ecuador?
8 Elise didn't want ice cream.

Refer sts back to page 65 if they want to revise the past simple of regular verbs further, or see more examples of them in context.

8A Past simple: irregular verbs

A lot of common verbs have an irregular past simple form (for a full list of irregular verbs see page 151).

take ⇨ took	*I took a taxi to the airport.*
go ⇨ went	*We went to the park yesterday.*
buy ⇨ bought	*I bought a new bag.*

Only the positive forms are irregular. We form the negative with *didn't* + infinitive.

We didn't take the train.
They didn't go to the party.
My sister didn't buy coffee.

We form questions with *did* + subject + infinitive.

Did they take the train?
Did you go to the supermarket?
Did we buy any vegetables?

8.2	I / you / he / she / it / we / they
+	He **went** to university in Edinburgh.
–	She **didn't have** breakfast yesterday.
?	**Did** you **see** Carly at the party?
Y/N	Yes, I **did**. / No, I **didn't**.

1 Complete the sentences with the past simple form of the verbs in brackets.

1 They ________ to work by car. (go)
2 She ________ to Hong Kong. (fly)
3 I ________ on the 11.30 bus to Newcastle. (get)
4 Paula ________ her daughter a lot of stories. (tell)
5 Richard ________ coffee and toast for breakfast. (have)
6 Clarissa ________ 'Hi'. (say)
7 I ________ pasta for dinner. (make)
8 My mum ________ to work yesterday. (drive)

2 Complete the questions and answers with the correct form of the verbs in brackets.

1 A What time ________ her train ________ ? (leave)
B It ________ at 8.00 p.m.
2 A ________ you ________ a dress to the party? (wear)
B No, I ________ a dress. I ________ jeans.
3 A ________ he ________ a bus to the station? (take)
B No, he ________ a bus. He ________ the underground.
4 A ________ you ________ well last night? (sleep)
B No. I ________ at all!
5 A ________ you ________ a big lunch? (have)
B No, I ________ . I ________ a sandwich.
6 A ________ you ________ to your dad yesterday? (speak)
B No, but I ________ to my mum.

◀ Go back to page 69

8C *there was/were*

We use *there was/were* and *a/an* with singular nouns to say that something existed in the past.

There was a big school here 50 years ago.
There was an egg in the fridge yesterday.

We use *there were* with plural nouns to say that something existed in the past.

There were lots of fields here in the past.
There were two books on my desk.

We often use *some* in positive sentences with plural nouns. We use *any* in negative sentences and questions.

There were some people in the shop.
There weren't any children.
Were there any cakes in the supermarket?

8.9	Singular	Plural
+	**There was** a road. **There was** an old house.	**There were** two shops. **There were some** trees.
–	**There wasn't** a supermarket.	**There weren't any** restaurants.
?	**Was there** a school?	**Were there any** tall buildings?
Y/N	Yes, **there was**. / No, **there wasn't**.	Yes, **there were**. / No, **there weren't**.

1 Look at the picture of Fairfield 100 years ago. Complete the sentences with the correct form of *there was/were* and *a/an* or *some/any*.

1 ________ supermarket, but ________ shops.
2 ________ cars in the village, but ________ bikes.
3 ________ cinema, but ________ nightclub.
4 ________ old tree and ________ flowers.

◀ Go back to page 73

8A Past simple: irregular verbs

1 ▶ 8.2 Read through the information about irregular verbs in the past simple with the class, or allow sts time to read it on their own. Play audio track 8.2 for sts to listen and repeat. Sts read the sentences and complete them with the correct verb forms. Check answers.

Answers
1 went
2 flew
3 got
4 told
5 had
6 said
7 made
8 drove

2 Sts complete the questions and answers with the correct verb forms. Check answers.

Answers
1 did leave, left
2 Did, wear, didn't wear, wore
3 Did, take, didn't take, took
4 Did, sleep, didn't sleep
5 Did, have, didn't, had
6 Did, speak, spoke

3 x PRACTICE *SB page 103, 8A exercise 2*

1 Do the exercise as normal. To check answers, say the three missing words from each question and answer in a random order, e.g. *leave, left, did*. Invite a student to read out the correct question and answer.
2 Ask sts to close their books. Read out the answers to the questions in turn, e.g. *It left at 8.00 p.m.* Sts race to remember the questions.
3 Sts work in pairs and write two more questions to ask their classmates, using the verbs in exercises 1 and 2. Put pairs together into groups of four to ask and answer their questions. Ask some sts to tell the class something about their classmates.

Refer sts back to page 69 if they want to revise the past simple of irregular verbs further, or see more examples of them in context.

8C *there was/were*

1 ▶ 8.9 Read through the information about there *was/were* with the class, or allow sts time to read it on their own. Play audio track 8.9 for sts to listen and repeat. Remind them of the use of *there were* + *some* and *there weren't* + *any*. Sts look at the picture and complete the sentences with the correct words. Check answers.

Answers
1 There wasn't a, there were some
2 There weren't any, there were some
3 There was a, there wasn't a
4 There was an, there were some

Refer sts back to page 73 if they want to revise there *was/were* further, or see more examples of it in context.

9A Present continuous

We use the present continuous to talk about actions that are happening now. We often use time expressions like *at the moment* and *now* with the present continuous.

I'm wearing my new jeans today.
We aren't working at the moment.
What are you doing now?

We form the present continuous with the verb *be* + the *-ing* form of the main verb.

Spelling rules for the *-ing* form
We usually add **-ing** to the infinitive of the verb. *cook ⇨ cooking watch ⇨ watching*
When the verb ends in a consonant + **e**, we usually remove the **e** and then add **-ing**. *take ⇨ taking dance ⇨ dancing*
When the verb ends in a consonant + a vowel + a consonant, we double the consonant and then add **-ing**. *begin ⇨ beginning get ⇨ getting*

9.3	I	he / she / it	you / we / they
+	I'**m listening** to music.	He'**s reading** a book.	You'**re singing**.
–	I'**m not watching** TV.	She **isn't working**.	We **aren't stopping** here.
?	**Am** I **sleeping**?	**Is** he **studying**?	**Are** they **going**?
Y/N	Yes, I **am**. / No, I'**m not**.	Yes, he **is**. / No, he **isn't**.	Yes, they **are**. / No, they **aren't**.

1 Write the *-ing* form of the verbs.

1 buy ________
2 drive ________
3 sit ________
4 go ________
5 leave ________
6 look ________
7 make ________
8 stop ________
9 swim ________
10 watch ________

2 Write positive (+) sentences, negative (–) sentences or questions (?) in the present continuous.

1 George / listen to / music / now (+)
____
2 you / wear / a new coat (?)
____
3 she / listen to / me (–)
____
4 they / do / their homework (–)
____
5 we / have dinner / at the moment (+)
____
6 it / rain / today (?)
____

◄ Go back to page 79

9C *How often* + expressions of frequency

We use *How often ... ?* + the present simple or the verb *be* to ask about frequency.

How often do you go shopping?
How often does Tim go to London?
How often are you late for class?

We can answer the question *How often ...?* with expressions of frequency.

How often are your English classes?
I have a class once or twice a week. (*once* = one time, *twice* = two times)

9.13	Expressions of frequency
every day/week/month/year	I go to the gym **every day**.
once a day/week/month/year	John has a holiday **once a year**.
twice a day/week/month/year	Ali has a coffee with his friends **twice a week**.
three/four times a day/week/month/year	They play football **three or four times a month**.

Look! We can also answer questions with *How often ...?* with adverbs of frequency (*always, usually, often, sometimes, never*).
How often do you walk to work?
I never walk to work. I usually get the bus.

1 Complete the questions and answers. Use the words in brackets.

1 How often ________ your bike? (you / ride)
I ________ my bike ________ day.
2 How often ________ in your city? (it / snow)
It only ________ once ________ year.
3 How often ________ his grandparents? (Luis / see)
He ________ his grandparents three ________ a month.
4 How often ________ tennis? (you / play)
We ________ tennis ________ weekend.
5 How often ________ their friends? (they / meet)
They ________ their friends twice ________ week.

◄ Go back to page 83

9A Present continuous

1 9.3 Read through the information about the present continuous with the class, or allow sts time to read it on their own. Play audio track 9.3 for sts to listen and repeat. Focus especially on the information about spelling rules. Sts write the *-ing* form of the verbs. Check answers.

Answers
1 buying
2 driving
3 sitting
4 going
5 leaving
6 looking
7 making
8 stopping
9 swimming
10 watching

3 x PRACTICE *SB page 104, 9A exercise 1*

1 Do the exercise as normal. To check answers, read out each verb in turn and ask: What's the rule for this verb? Elicit which of the spelling rules applies, then elicit the correct *-ing* form.

2 In pairs, sts cover their answers and the rules. They look at the verbs again and try to remember the *-ing* forms. They can look at their answers again to check.

3 Ask sts to close their books, and put them into teams. Write the verbs from exercise 1 on the board. Ask teams in turn to choose a verb and say a correct sentence using the present continuous. If their sentence is correct, award a point and cross the verb off the board. If their sentence is not correct, don't correct it, but move on to the next team. Continue until all the verbs are crossed off. See which team has the most points.

2 Sts write the sentences in the present continuous. Check answers.

Answers
1 George is listening to music now.
2 Are you wearing a new coat?
3 She isn't listening to me.
4 They aren't doing their homework.
5 We're having dinner at the moment.
6 Is it raining today?

Refer sts back to page 79 if they want to revise the present continuous further, or see more examples of it in context.

9C *How often* + expressions of frequency

1 9.13 Read through the information about *How often* + expressions of frequency with the class, or allow sts time to read it on their own. Play audio track 9.13 for sts to listen and repeat. Sts read the questions and answers and complete them with the correct words. Check answers.

Answers
1 do you ride, ride, every
2 does it snow, snows, a
3 does Luis see, sees, times
4 do you play, play, every
5 do they meet, meet, a

Refer sts back to page 83 if they want to revise *How often* + expressions of frequency further, or see more examples of them in context.

10A Present continuous for future plans

We use the present continuous to talk about plans and arrangements in the future (for spelling rules of *-ing* forms see page 104).

I'm going to the dentist next week.

10.3	I	he / she / it	you / we / they
+	I'**m meeting** friends tonight.	She'**s taking** the bus tomorrow.	You'**re working** next Tuesday.
–	I'**m not going** to school tomorrow.	He **isn't watching** a film tonight.	We **aren't playing** tennis later.
?	**Am** I **working** this weekend?	**Is** she **staying** at home tonight?	**Are** they **going** to the gym?
Y/N	Yes, I **am**. / No, I'**m not**.	Yes, he **is**. / No, he **isn't**.	Yes, they **are**. / No, they **aren't**.

We often use a future time expression to talk about future plans and arrangements. Time expressions usually go at the end of the sentence.

10.4	Future time expressions
this morning/afternoon/evening	We're taking the train **this afternoon**.
tonight	What are you having for dinner **tonight**?
tomorrow	Sven isn't coming to the party **tomorrow**.
next week/month/year	We're going on holiday **next week**.
later	Are you meeting Jorge **later**?

1 Complete the sentences and questions with the present continuous form of the verbs in the box.

take not visit meet not come stay watch

1 We ________ our friends for dinner later.
2 ________ you ________ the football match tonight?
3 They ________ the 7.30 train to Edinburgh tomorrow.
4 He ________ with some friends in Lima at the weekend.
5 Maria is ill. She ________ to the concert this evening.
6 We ________ the museum next week. It's closed.

2 Write sentences and questions in the present continuous.

1 I / meet / my friends this weekend
________.
2 My brother / not visit / us this month
________.
3 They / not go / on holiday this summer
________.
4 What / you / cook / for dinner on Saturday
________?

◄ Go back to page 87

10C Question review

Questions can be *yes/no* questions or they can ask for specific information with a question word (*where*, *when*, *who*, etc.).

Do you live in Japan? Yes, I do./No, I don't.
Where are you from? I'm from Turkey.

For most verbs, the word order in questions is: (question word +) auxiliary verb + subject + main verb + rest of question.

10.12	(Question word)	Auxiliary verb	Subject	Main verb	Rest of question
Present simple		Does	Chris	speak	English?
	What	do	you	have	for breakfast?
Past simple		Did	Lucy	call	you yesterday?
	When	did	you	arrive	at the airport?
Present continuous		Is	it	snowing	now?
	Where	are	they	going	next week?

For the verbs *be* and *can*, the word order in questions is: (question word +) verb + subject + rest of question.

10.13	(Question word)	Verb	Subject	Rest of question
be (present simple)		Is	Julia	here?
	Where	are	you	from?
be (past simple)		Were	you	late for work?
	Who	was	Philip	with?
can		Can	you	ride a motorbike?
	What sports	can	they	do?

1 Order the words to make questions.

1 rock climbing / does / go / how often / he
________?
2 you / what / for / lunch / are / having
________?
3 homework / when / she / did / do / her
________?
4 can / instrument / you / play / an
________?
5 you / crying / why / are
________?
6 did / where / he / on / go / holiday
________?
7 they / were / home / night / last / at
________?
8 what / is / she / time / leaving
________?

◄ Go back to page 91

10A Present continuous for future plans

1 10.3 Read through the information about the present continuous for future plans with the class, or allow sts time to read it on their own. Play audio track 10.3 for sts to listen and repeat. Sts read the sentences and complete them with the correct verb forms. Check answers.

Answers
1 're meeting
2 Are, watching
3 are/'re taking
4 's staying
5 isn't coming
6 aren't visiting

2 10.4 Read through the information about future time expressions with the class, or allow sts time to read it on their own. Play audio track 10.4 for sts to listen and repeat. Sts write the sentences and questions in the present continuous. Check answers.

Answers
1 I'm meeting my friends this weekend.
2 My brother isn't visiting us this month.
3 They aren't going on holiday this summer.
4 What are you cooking for dinner on Saturday?

Refer sts back to page 87 if they want to revise the present continuous for future plans further, or see more examples of it in context.

10C Question review

1 10.12/10.13 Read through the information about questions with the class, or allow sts time to read it on their own. Play audio tracks 10.12/10.13 for sts to listen and repeat. Elicit a few answers to the questions in the tables as examples. Sts put the words in the correct order to make questions. Check answers.

Answers
1 How often does he go rock climbing?
2 What are you having for lunch?
3 When did she do her homework?
4 Can you play an instrument?
5 Why are you crying?
6 Where did he go on holiday?
7 Were they at home last night?
8 What time is she leaving?

3 x PRACTICE *SB page 105, 10C exercise 1*

1 Do the exercise as normal. To check answers, say the first word of each question, then ask individual sts in turn to say the next word, building up each question in turn. Repeat the full question to confirm it.

2 Ask sts to close their books. Read out each question, one word at a time, pausing after each word. Ask sts to guess each question as soon as they recognize it. You could do this as a game, awarding a point to the first student to say each question correctly.

3 In pairs, sts write answers to the questions. Monitor and help while they are working. Put pairs together into groups of four. They take turns to read one of their answers to each other, in a random order. The other pair must guess the question it answers. As an extra activity, sts could work in pairs and change three of the questions slightly so they can ask their classmates, e.g. *How often do you go to the gym? What are you having for dinner tonight?* In groups of four, sts can ask and answer their questions.

Refer sts back to page 91 if they want to revise questions further, or see more examples of them in context.

Hello Classroom language

1 1.7 Listen and repeat.

1 Open your books.

2 Close your books.

3 Go to page 5.

4 Look at the picture.

5 Listen and repeat.

6 Work in pairs.

7 Excuse me, what does 'nice' mean?

8 Sorry, I don't understand.

9 How do you say 'bom dia' in English?

10 Can you repeat that, please?

11 How do you spell that?

12 Sorry I'm late.

2 Complete the conversation with the words in the box.

go	open	listen	~~late~~	look	spell	work	close	mean	repeat

Norio Hello. Sorry I'm 1 *late* .
Teacher Hello. Are you Norio?
Norio Yes, I am.
Teacher I'm your teacher. My name's Helen.
Norio Hi.
Teacher 2 _______ your book and go to page 6, please.
Norio Sorry, can you 3 _______ that?
Teacher Yes. 4 _______ to page 6 in your book.
Norio OK.
Teacher 5 _______ at the picture of a family.
Norio Excuse me, what does 'family' 6 _______ ?
Teacher Your mother, father, brothers, sisters ...
Norio I understand. How do you 7 _______ 'family'?
Teacher F-A-M-I-L-Y.
Norio Thank you.
Teacher 8 _______ and repeat – 'family'.
Norio Family.
Teacher Very good. Now, 9 _______ your books and 10 _______ in pairs ...

◀ Go back to page 5

Hello Classroom language

1 1.7 Play audio track 1.7 once for sts to listen and look at the pictures. Play the audio again, pausing after each phrase for sts to repeat. See SB page opposite for audio script.

3 x PRACTICE *SB page 106, exercise 1*

1 Do the exercise as normal. After sts have repeated the phrases, point to each picture in turn and invite a student to say the phrase individually. Play the audio for that phrase again to confirm their pronunciation, and get the class to repeat again if necessary.

2 Ask sts to cover the pictures and phrases. In pairs, they uncover each row of pictures in turn and try to remember the phrases. They can uncover the phrases to check.

3 Ask sts to close their books, and put them into teams. Write one word from each phrase on the board, e.g. *open, close, page, picture, listen, pairs, mean, understand*. Invite teams in turn to choose a word from the board and say the full phrase. If the phrase is correct, give the team a point and add the full phrase to the board. If the phrase is not correct, don't give the correct phrase, but move on to the next team. Continue until all the phrases are on the board. See which team has the most points.

2 Sts complete the conversation with the correct words. Check answers. Sts could then practise the conversation in pairs.

Answers
1 late
2 Open
3 repeat
4 Go
5 Look
6 mean
7 spell
8 Listen
9 close
10 work

Refer sts back to page 5 if they want to revise classroom language further, or see more examples in context.

1A Countries and nationalities

1 1.12 Listen and repeat.

1 Argentina
Argentinian

2 Brazil
Brazilian

3 Canada
Canadian

4 Chile
Chilean

5 China
Chinese

6 France
French

7 Germany
German

8 India
Indian

9 Italy
Italian

10 Japan
Japanese

11 Mexico
Mexican

12 Peru
Peruvian

13 Poland
Polish

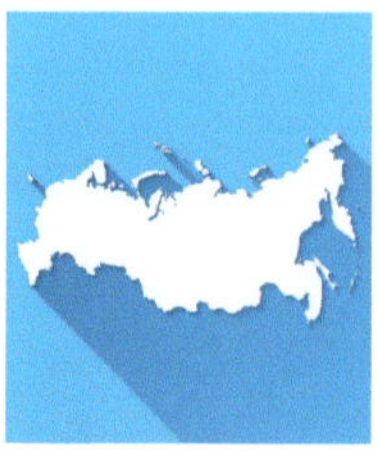
14 Russia
Russian

15 Spain
Spanish

16 Turkey
Turkish

17 the UK
British

18 the USA
American

2 Look at the pictures. Complete the sentences with the correct country or nationality.

1 Lionel Messi is _________ .

2 Paris is in _________ .

3 A kimono comes from _________ .

4 Pasta is _________ food.

5 A panda is an animal from _________ .

6 Washington D.C. is the capital of _________ .

7 Machu Picchu is in _________ .

8 These are _________ dolls.

9 The Taj Mahal is in _________ .

10 Warsaw is a _________ city.

◀ Go back to page 6

1A Countries and nationalities

1 1.12 Play audio track 1.12, pausing after each country and nationality for sts to repeat. See SB page opposite for audio script.

2 Sts look at the pictures and complete the sentences with the correct countries and nationalities. Encourage sts to guess if they aren't sure about the answers. They could work in pairs for this. Check answers. See who got the most answers right.

Answers
1 Argentinian
2 France
3 Japan
4 Italian
5 China
6 the USA
7 Peru
8 Russian
9 India
10 Polish

3 x PRACTICE *SB page 107, exercise 2*

1 Do the exercise as normal. When you check the answers, ask individual sts to give each answer. Ask: *Does anyone have a different answer?* Ask for a show of hands on each of the suggested answers, then confirm the correct answer.

2 Ask sts to close their books. Read out each country or nationality from the exercise in turn, e.g. *Argentinian, France*. Sts race to say the correct sentence for each one.

3 Sts work in pairs. They write three more sentences about countries or nationalities, using words from exercise 1, e.g. *Berlin is in Germany*. Put pairs together into groups of four. They take turns to read their sentences to each other, omitting the country or nationality, e.g. *Berlin is in …* . Their classmates guess the missing countries and nationalities. Ask who guessed all the answers correctly.

Refer sts back to page 6 if they want to revise countries and nationalities further, or see more examples in context.

1B Jobs

1 1.19 Listen and repeat.

1 an actor

2 a chef

3 a doctor

4 an engineer

5 an IT worker

6 an office worker

7 a police officer

8 a receptionist

9 a shop assistant

10 a singer

11 a student

12 a taxi driver

13 a teacher

14 a tour guide

15 a TV presenter

16 a waiter/a waitress

Look! We use *an* with jobs that begin with vowels (*a, e, i, o, u*) and *a* with jobs that begin with consonants (*b, c, d, f*, etc.).
*I'm **a** teacher.*
*Are you **an** office worker?*

2 Match the jobs in the box with objects 1–8. Use *a* or *an*.

waiter	shop assistant	engineer	singer	receptionist	doctor	chef	actor

1 ______________

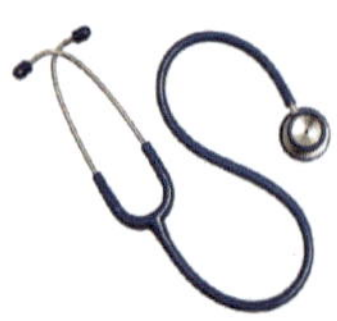
2 ______________

3 ______________

4 ______________

5 ______________

6 ______________

7 ______________

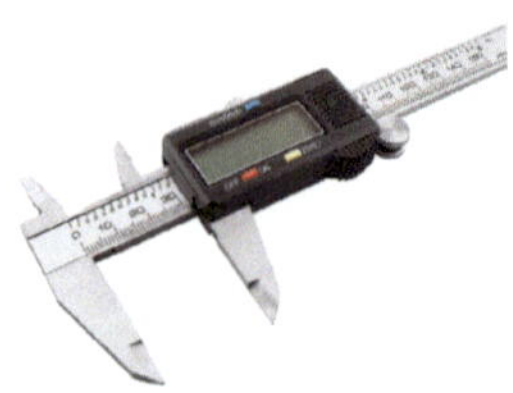
8 ______________

◀ Go back to page 8

1B Jobs

1 1.19 Play audio track 1.19, pausing after each job for sts to repeat. See SB page opposite for audio script. Read through the information in the *Look!* box with the class.

3 x PRACTICE *SB page 108, exercise 1*

1 Do the exercise as normal. After sts have repeated the words, point to each picture in turn and invite a student to say the word for the job individually. Play the audio for that job again to confirm their pronunciation, and get the class to repeat again if necessary.

2 Ask sts to cover the pictures and words. In pairs, they uncover each row of pictures in turn and try to remember the word for each job. They can uncover the words to check.

3 Mime one of the pictures, e.g. mime being a receptionist, holding a phone to your ear. Sts race to say the correct job. Make sure they include *a/an* in their answer. Invite sts in turn to mime one of the pictures. Other sts race to say the correct word, using *a/an* correctly.

2 Sts match the jobs with the objects. Check answers, making sure sts have used *a/an* correctly in their answers.

Answers
1 a singer
2 a doctor
3 a chef
4 a shop assistant
5 an actor
6 a receptionist
7 a waiter/waitress
8 an engineer

Refer sts back to page 8 if they want to revise jobs vocabulary further, or see more examples in context.

1C Adjectives (1)

1 1.32 Listen and repeat.

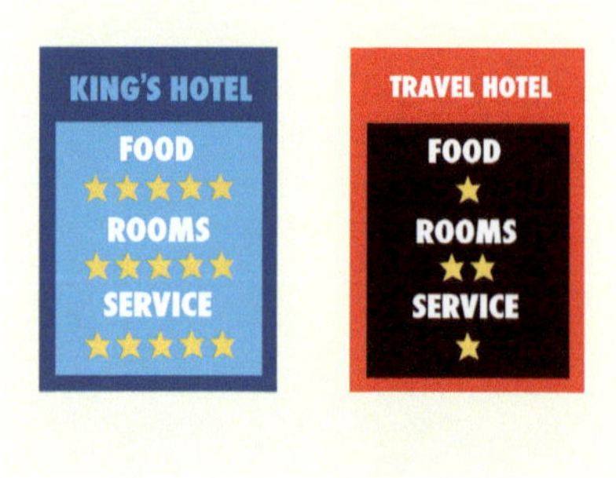

1 good 2 bad

3 beautiful 4 ugly

5 big 6 small

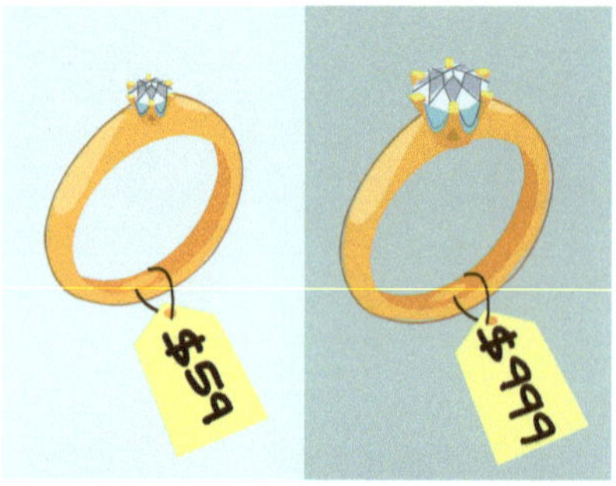

7 cheap 8 expensive

9 interesting 10 boring

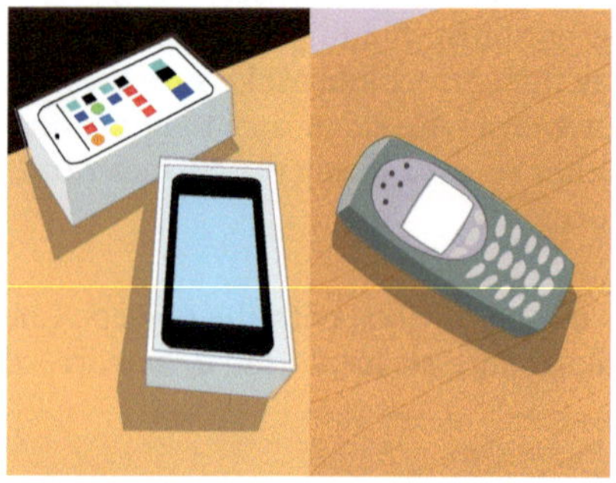

11 new 12 old

13 happy 14 sad

15 easy 16 difficult

17 old 18 young

2 Choose the correct words to complete the conversations.

A This phone is [1] *cheap / boring*. It's only £50.
B Yes, but it isn't [2] *difficult / good*. Look at this phone.
A It's £695! It's very [3] *expensive / new*.

A How [6] *good / old* is Michael?
B He's [7] *new / young*. He's three years old today!
A He's very [8] *happy / sad*.

A Hi, Sara. Do you understand Italian?
B Yes. I'm Spanish, but Italian is [4] *big / easy* for me.
A Oh, that's [5] *interesting / ugly*.

A Wow – this painting is [9] *beautiful / difficult!*
B Yes, but it's very [10] *bad / small*.
A My house is small, too!

◀ Go back to page 11

1C Adjectives (1)

1 1.32 Play audio track 1.32, pausing after each adjective for sts to repeat. See SB page opposite for audio script.

2 Sts read the conversations and complete them with the correct words. Check answers, and check that sts understand all the sentences.

Answers
1 cheap
2 good
3 expensive
4 easy
5 interesting
6 old
7 young
8 happy
9 beautiful
10 small

3 x PRACTICE *SB page 109, exercise 2*

1 Do the exercise as normal. To check answers, invite pairs of sts in turn to read out each conversation. When they have finished, ask other sts if they think any of the answers are wrong. Elicit the correct answers.

2 Ask sts to cover the conversations and look at the pictures. In pairs, they try to remember each conversation. They can read the conversation and look at their answers again to check.

3 In pairs, sts choose one of the conversations to learn. They can change some of the details if they want, e.g. *This TV is cheap*. Tell them they can each write down four words to help them learn their part of the conversation. Sts then practise their conversations in pairs, referring to the words they have noted down. Ask some sts to perform their conversation for the class.

Refer sts back to page 11 if they want to revise adjectives further, or see more examples in context.

2A Personal objects

1 2.2 Listen and repeat.

1 a bag

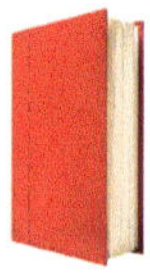
2 a book

3 a camera

4 a credit card

5 glasses

6 keys

7 a mobile phone

8 a pen

9 a pencil

10 a purse

11 sunglasses

12 a tablet

13 an umbrella

14 a wallet

15 a watch

2 Write the objects you can see in the pictures.

1 ________
2 ________
3 ________
4 ________
5 ________
6 ________

◀ Go back to page 14

2B Colours

1 2.8 Listen and repeat.

1 black

2 blue

3 brown

4 gold

5 green

6 grey

7 orange

8 pink

9 purple

10 red

11 silver

12 white

13 yellow

2 Write the colours.

1 red + blue = ________
2 red + white = ________
3 blue + yellow = ________
4 black + white = ________
5 red + yellow = ________
6 red + blue + yellow = ________

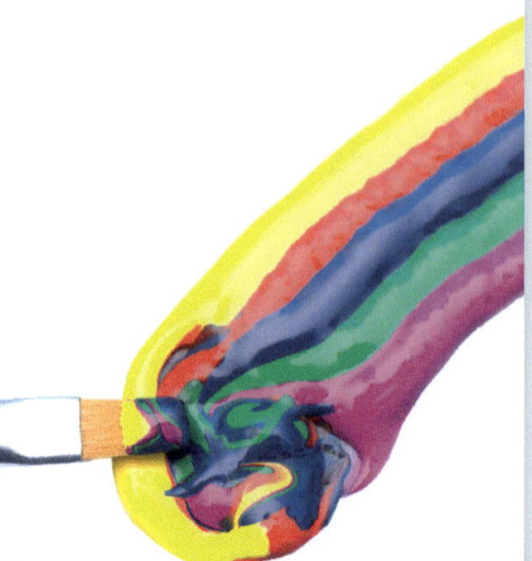

◀ Go back to page 16

2A Personal objects

1 2.2 Play audio track 2.2, pausing after each word for sts to repeat. See SB page opposite for audio script.

3 x PRACTICE *SB page 110, 2A, exercise 1*

1 Do the exercise as normal. After sts have repeated the words, say the number of each picture in turn and ask: *What is number (1)?* Invite a student to say the word individually. Get other sts to repeat again if necessary.

2 Ask sts to cover the pictures and words. In pairs, they uncover each row of pictures in turn and try to remember the word for each object. They can uncover the words to check.

3 With books closed, divide the class into two teams and invite one person from each team to come to the board. Show these two sts one of the objects in exercise 1. They race to draw the object on the board for their team mates to guess. The first team to say the correct word gets a point. Change the sts at the front from time to time, and continue until all the objects have been drawn and guessed. See which team has the most points.

2 Sts look at the picture and write the objects they can see. You could do this as a race, or with exercise 1 covered, to make it more challenging. Check answers.

Answers
1 umbrella
2 watch
3 camera
4 keys
5 bag
6 pen

Refer sts back to page 14 if they want to revise personal objects further, or see more examples in context.

2B Colours

1 2.8 Play audio track 2.8, pausing after each word for sts to repeat. See SB page opposite for audio script.

2 Sts read the clues and write the colours. Sts could work in pairs for this, or you could do it as a race to make it more challenging. Check answers.

Answers
1 purple
2 pink
3 green
4 grey
5 orange
6 brown

Refer sts back to page 16 if they want to revise colours further, or see more examples in context.

1C Numbers 0–100

1 1.26 Listen and repeat.

0 zero/oh	5 five	10 ten	15 fifteen	20 twenty	50 fifty	100 a hundred/ one hundred
1 one	6 six	11 eleven	16 sixteen	21 twenty-one	60 sixty	
2 two	7 seven	12 twelve	17 seventeen	22 twenty-two	70 seventy	
3 three	8 eight	13 thirteen	18 eighteen	30 thirty	80 eighty	
4 four	9 nine	14 fourteen	19 nineteen	40 forty	90 ninety	

2 Write the numbers as words or digits.

1 34 ________
2 ____ seventy-two
3 63 ________
4 ____ ninety-one
5 88 ________
6 ____ fifty-seven
7 29 ________
8 ____ forty-four
9 12 ________
10 ____ a hundred

◀ Go back to page 10

2C Family and friends

1 2.10 Listen and repeat.

1 grandfather 2 grandmother
3 grandparents

4 mother 5 father
6 parents
7 son 8 daughter
9 children

10 husband 11 wife

12 sister 13 brother

14 boyfriend 15 girlfriend

2 Look at the family tree. Read the sentences and write the names.

1 My brother is Liam. ________
2 Julia is my wife. ________
3 My sister is Julia and my brother is George. ________
4 My girlfriend is Molly. ________
5 My parents are George and Gloria, and my sister is Molly. ________
6 Bob is my father, and Mark and George are my brothers. ________
7 My wife is Judith. ________
8 My husband's brother is Mark. ________
9 Our children are Julia, Mark and George. ________ and ________
10 Our parents are Judith and Bob. ________ , ________ and ________

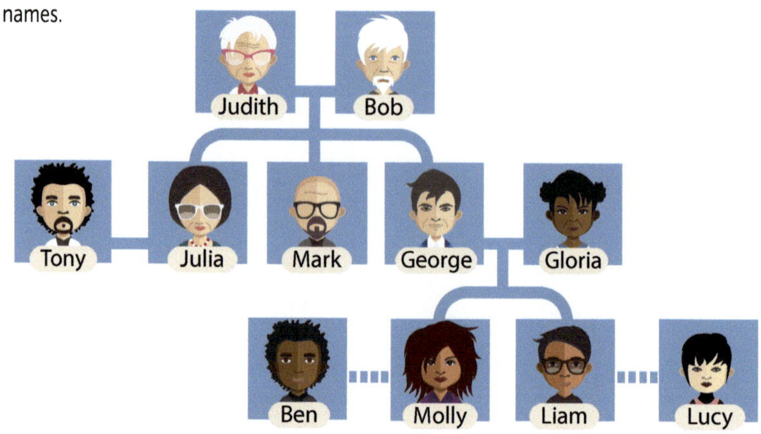

◀ Go back to page 18

1C Numbers 0–100

1 1.26 Play audio track 1.26, pausing after each number for sts to repeat. See SB page opposite for audio script. Point out the hyphens in the compound numbers, e.g. *twenty-one, twenty-two*.

2 Sts write the numbers or digits. Check answers.

Answers
1 thirty-four
2 72
3 sixty-three
4 91
5 eighty-eight
6 57
7 twenty-nine
8 44
9 twelve
10 100

3 x PRACTICE *SB page 111, 1C, exercise 2*

1 Do the exercise as normal. To check the answers, write the answers on the board in a random order. Point to each answer on the board in turn and elicit which number it matches in the exercise.

2 Ask sts to close their books. Say each number from the exercise in turn. In pairs, sts write the words and digits for each number they hear. They can open their books again to check their answers.

3 In pairs, sts write four more numbers in words and digits. Monitor while they are working, and make sure all their numbers are correct. Put pairs together into groups of four. They take turns to say one of their numbers. The other pair must write the number in words and digits. Sts can check their answers together.

Refer sts back to page 10 if they want to revise numbers 0–100 further, or see more examples in context.

2C Family and friends

1 2.10 Allow sts time to read through the words and look at the pictures. Play audio track 2.10, pausing after each word for sts to repeat. See SB page opposite for audio script.

2 Sts look at the family tree, then read the sentences and write the names. Check answers.

Answers
1 Molly
2 Tony
3 Mark
4 Ben
5 Liam
6 Julia
7 Bob
8 Gloria
9 Judith, Bob
10 Julia, Mark, George

Refer sts back to page 18 if they want to revise vocabulary for family and friends further, or see more examples in context.

3A Food and drink

1 3.2 Listen and repeat.

Food

1 biscuits

2 bread

3 cake

4 cheese

5 chicken

6 chips

7 chocolate

8 crisps

9 eggs

10 fish

11 fruit

12 ice cream

13 meat

14 pasta

15 pizza

16 potatoes

17 rice

18 salad

19 sandwich

20 vegetables

Drinks

21 coffee

22 milk

23 orange juice

24 tea

25 water

Look! If we want to talk about the food and drink that we eat and drink at breakfast, lunch and dinner, we can use the verb *have*.
*What do you **have** for breakfast/lunch/dinner?*
*I **have** coffee for breakfast. I **have** a sandwich for lunch. I **have** fish for dinner.*

08.00

have breakfast

13.00

have lunch

18.30

have dinner

2 Choose the correct words to complete the sentences.

1 Ice cream has *milk* / *cheese* in it.
2 Potatoes are *fruit* / *vegetables*.
3 Cake, biscuits and *chocolate* / *salad* are bad for you.
4 Crisps and chips come from *potatoes* / *pasta*.
5 British people have *rice* / *milk* in their tea.
6 Spaghetti is a type of *bread* / *pasta*.
7 I have *breakfast* / *lunch* at 8.00 a.m.
8 Vegetarians don't eat *meat* / *salad*.
9 I drink *orange juice* / *fish* in the morning.
10 I have *chocolate* / *meat* and vegetables for dinner.

◀ Go back to page 24

3A Food and drink

1 3.2 Allow sts time to read through the words and look at the pictures. Play audio track 3.2, pausing after each word for sts to repeat. See SB page opposite for audio script. Read through the information in the *Look!* box with the class. Ask individual sts: *What do you have for breakfast/lunch/dinner?*

2 Sts read the sentences and choose the correct words to complete them. Check answers.

Answers
1 milk
2 vegetables
3 chocolate
4 potatoes
5 milk
6 pasta
7 breakfast
8 meat
9 orange juice
10 meat

3 x PRACTICE *SB page 112, exercise 2*

1 Do the exercise as normal. To check answers, read out each sentence in turn, some with the correct answer and some with the incorrect answer. Ask sts to all call out 'yes' (correct) or 'no' (incorrect) after each sentence.

2 Ask sts to cover the exercise. Write a clue for each sentence on the board, e.g. *ice cream, milk; potatoes; cake, bad*. In pairs, they try to remember the sentences. They can look at the exercises again to check.

3 In pairs, sts choose three sentences and change them so they are about different foods, e.g. *Cake has eggs in it. Chicken is meat. Chips and crisps are bad for you*. Tell sts that two of their sentences should be true, and one should be false. Ask pairs in turn to read their sentences to the class. Ask other sts to call out 'yes' (true) or 'no' (false) for each sentence.

Refer sts back to page 24 if they want to revise food and drink vocabulary further, or see more examples in context.

3C Common verbs (1)

1 3.12 Listen and repeat.

1 **change** money

2 **do** exercise

3 **go** to school

4 **have** two children

5 **know** the answer

6 **live** in a flat

7 **make** coffee

8 **say** 'goodbye'

9 **study** German

10 **think** (about ...)

11 **use** a tablet

12 **want** a drink

13 **watch** a film

14 **work** in an office

Look! We use *make* for food and drink:
They make very good cakes.
We use *do* for activities:
We do exercise in the morning.
We use *think* for thoughts and opinions:
I think about work. (thought)
We think it's a good idea. (opinion)

2 Choose the correct words to complete the sentences.

1 After work, I *know* / *go* / *use* to the gym.
2 I *study* / *say* / *live* English and Spanish at university.
3 My daughter and I *make* / *do* / *work* cakes at the weekend.
4 I *think* / *know* / *work* in a restaurant – I'm a waitress!
5 A Do you like that book?
B No, I *think* / *watch* / *use* it's boring.
6 My boyfriend and I *watch* / *say* / *live* TV in the evening.
7 Do you *make* / *do* / *go* exercise at the weekend?
8 Do they *use* / *know* / *live* in a big house?
9 I *study* / *live* / *say* 'good morning' to people at work.
10 My mobile phone is old. I *watch* / *want* / *work* a new one.
11 A What's the capital of China?
B I don't *go* / *use* / *know*.
12 My children *use* / *say* / *make* the internet a lot.

◀ Go back to page 28

3C Common verbs (1)

1 ⊙3.12 Allow sts time to read through the words and look at the pictures. Play audio track 3.12, pausing after each phrase for sts to repeat. See SB page opposite for audio script. Read through the information in the *Look!* box with the class. Ask individual sts: *Do you make cakes? Do you sometimes make dinner for friends? Do you do exercise in the morning? When do you do your homework?*

2 Sts read the sentences and complete them with the correct verbs. Check answers.

Answers
1 go
2 study
3 make
4 work
5 think
6 watch
7 do
8 live
9 say
10 want
11 know
12 use

3 x PRACTICE *SB page 113, exercise 2*

1 Do the exercise as normal. To check answers, invite individual sts in turn to read out one of their completed sentences that they feel confident is correct. Continue until all the sentences have been checked.

2 Ask sts to cover the sentences and look at the verbs. In pairs, they try to remember the sentence for each verb. They can look at the sentences again to check.

3 Ask sts to close their books, and put them into teams. Say a verb from exercise 2, e.g. *work*. Teams race to write a correct sentence using that verb and bring it to you. They can use the sentences from exercise 2 or their own ideas. The team that brings the first correct sentence to you gets a point. Continue until all the verbs have been used. See which team has the most points.

Refer sts back to page 28 if they want to revise common verbs further, or see more examples in context.

4A Daily routine verbs

1 4.2 Listen and repeat.

1 get up

2 have a shower

3 get dressed

4 leave home

5 start work

6 go shopping

7 listen to the radio

8 do housework / homework

9 finish work

10 get home

11 go to bed

12 read a book

2 Complete the text with the correct form of the verbs in the box.

do (x2)	get (x3)	go (x2)	leave	finish	listen	start	have

I'm Miranda and this is my typical day. I 1________ up at 7.00 in the morning and 2________ a shower. Then I have breakfast with my son, Leon. He 3________ dressed and then we 4________ home at about 8.30 a.m. Leon goes to school and I'm an office worker. I 5________ work at 9.00 a.m.
I 6________ work at 3.00 p.m. and go to Leon's school. We 7________ shopping and 8________ home at about 4.00 in the afternoon. In the evening, Leon 9________ his homework and I make dinner. After dinner, Leon 10________ to bed at 8.00 p.m. and I 11________ the housework and 12________ to the radio. I go to bed at 11.00 p.m. … and the next day, we do it all again!

◀ Go back to page 32

4A Daily routine verbs

1 4.2 Allow sts time to look at the pictures and read the verbs. Play audio track 4.2, pausing after each verb for sts to repeat. See SB page opposite for audio script.

2 Sts read the text and complete it with the correct verbs. Check answers. Ask: *What things about Miranda are also true for you?* Elicit a range of answers.

Answers
1 get
2 have
3 gets
4 leave
5 start
6 finish
7 go
8 get
9 does
10 goes
11 do
12 listen

3 x PRACTICE *SB page 114, exercise 2*

1 Do the exercise as normal. To check the answers, tell sts you are going to read out the completed text with some correct answers and some incorrect ones. Ask sts to bang on their desk when you say an incorrect answer. Read out the completed text, including a mixture of correct and incorrect answers. Elicit the correct answers.

2 Ask sts to cover the text, but not the verbs in the wordpool box. Write the times from the text on the board: *7.00, 8.30, 9.00, 3.00, 4.00, 8.00, 11.00*. In pairs, sts look at the times on the board and the verbs on page 114, and try to remember as much as they can about Miranda's day. They can look at the text again to check.

3 Sts write five sentences about their own daily routines, saying what time they do different things, e.g. *I get up at 7.30*. Tell sts they now need to find other sts whose sentences are the same as theirs. Sts move around the class and compare their sentences. If some of their sentences are the same, they write the name of the student next to the sentence. Stop the activity after a few minutes and see who has the most names next to their sentences.

Refer sts back to page 32 if they want to revise daily routine verbs further, or see more examples in context.

4B Transport

1 4.6 Listen and repeat.

1 by bike

2 by boat

3 by bus

4 by car

5 by ferry

6 by lorry

7 by motorbike

8 by plane

9 by taxi

10 by train

11 on foot

12 on the subway/underground/ metro

Look! Different cities have different names for their underground trains.
In New York, I go on the ***subway****.* *In London, I go on the* ***underground****.* *In Sydney, I go on the* ***metro****.*

2 Match the types of transport in the box with the pictures.

lorry taxi underground ferry train plane boat motorbike

3 Complete the sentences with the correct types of transport and *by* or *on*.

1 I go ________  to the train station. Then I go ________  to the city. After that, I go ________  to the office.

2 Lucia goes ________  to the airport. Then she goes ________  to New York. After that, she goes ________  to the city centre.

3 We go ________  to Dover, but my brother goes ________ . Then we all go ________  to France.

◀ Go back to page 34

4B Transport

1 4.6 Allow sts time to look at the pictures and read the words. Play audio track 4.6, pausing after each phrase for sts to repeat. See SB page opposite for audio script.

2 Sts match the forms of transport with the pictures. Check answers.

Answers
lorry, taxi, motorbike
underground, train
ferry, boat
plane

3 Sts complete the sentences with the correct forms of transport and prepositions. Check answers.

Answers
1 by bike, by train, on foot
2 by taxi, by plane, on the subway
3 by car, by motorbike, by ferry

3 x PRACTICE *SB page 115, exercise 3*

1 Do the exercise as normal. To check the answers, tell sts you will read out each sentence with one mistake. Read out the sentences, including one mistake in each, e.g. *I go on bike to the train station*. Ask sts to correct the sentences.

2 Ask sts to cover the sentences. Write clues for the sentences on the board, e.g. *train station, city, office; airport, New York, city centre; Dover, brother, France*. In pairs, sts look at the clues and try to remember the sentences. They can look at the sentences and their answers again to check.

3 Ask a student to say a sentence saying how they travel somewhere, e.g. I go to work by car. The next student repeats this and adds another sentence, e.g. *(Ana) goes to work by car and I go shopping by bus*. Continue around the class, with sts repeating all the previous sentences and adding one more. Continue until there are too many sentences to remember!

Refer sts back to page 34 if they want to revise transport vocabulary further, or see more examples in context.

3B Days and times of day

1 3.7 Listen and repeat.

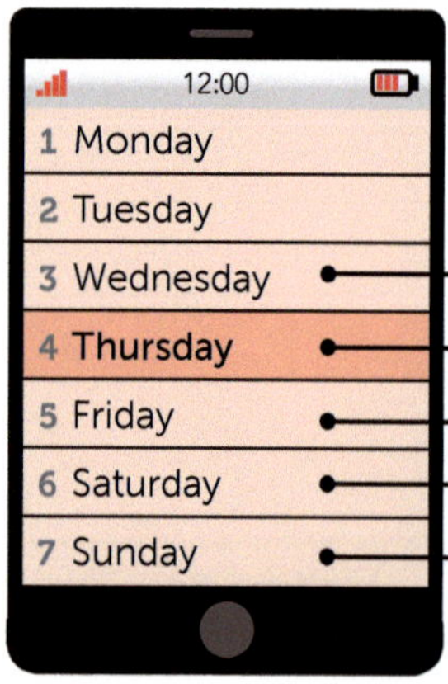

8 yesterday
9 today
10 tomorrow
11 the weekend

12 morning

13 afternoon

14 evening

15 night

Look! We use the preposition *on* with days of the week, *in* with *the morning*, *the afternoon* and *the evening* and *at* with *the weekend* and *night*.
I eat fish ***on*** *Friday.*
I have breakfast ***in*** *the morning.*
I drink milk ***at*** *night.*
We also say *on* + day and time of day:
on Wednesday morning, on Friday afternoon, etc.

2 Chose the correct words to complete the sentences and questions.

1 My birthday is *on / in / at* Sunday.
2 I have dinner *on / in / at* the evening.
3 We don't drink coffee at *afternoon / evening / night*.
4 I have lunch with Emma on *the weekend / Friday / the morning*.
5 Is your English lesson *on / in / at* Thursday evening?
6 They have breakfast at 9.00 in *the weekend / Wednesday / the morning*.
7 Is Marcus on holiday *on / in / at* Thursday?
8 They aren't at university *on / in / at* Wednesday afternoon.
9 What do you have for lunch at *the afternoon / the weekend / Monday*?
10 On Sunday, I have chicken for lunch *on / in / at* the afternoon.

◀ Go back to page 26

4C Adjectives (2)

1 4.7 Listen and repeat.

1 cold 2 hot

3 clean 4 dirty

5 fast 6 slow

7 friendly 8 unfriendly

9 nice 10 horrible

11 large 12 small

13 long 14 short

15 noisy 16 quiet

2 Complete the text with the adjectives in the box.

noisy cold quiet hot short friendly dirty large

Hi, I'm Matt. I'm a student in Edinburgh, Scotland. I always get up at 8.30 and I have a [1]________ tea for breakfast. Then I go to the university on foot. It's sometimes [2]________ in the mornings, but that's OK – it's only a [3]________ walk.

I live in a [4]________ house with eight students. They're really [5]________ . We always make dinner together, and sometimes there are a lot of [6]________ dishes when we finish! My housemates play music and the house is sometimes [7]________ , so I usually work in the library – it's always [8]________ there.

◀ Go back to page 36

3B Days and times of day

1 3.7 Allow sts time to look at the pictures and read through the words. Play audio track 3.7, pausing after each word or phrase for sts to repeat. See SB page opposite for audio script. Check that sts understand all the words and phrases.

2 Sts complete the sentences with the correct words. Check answers.

Answers
1 on
2 in
3 night
4 Friday
5 on
6 the morning
7 on
8 on
9 the weekend
10 in

3 x PRACTICE *SB page 116, 3B, exercise 2*

1 Do the exercise as normal. To check answers, invite individual sts in turn to read out one of their completed sentences that they feel confident is correct. Continue until all the sentences have been checked.

2 In pairs, ask sts to read the sentence without the preposition. Their partner tries to remember the correct preposition for each sentence. They can look at the sentences again to check.

3 Ask sts to write five questions for their partner, e.g. *When is your birthday? What do you like doing at the weekend?* They ask and answer each other's questions.

Refer sts back to page 26 if they want to revise days and times of day further, or see more examples in context.

4C Adjectives (2)

1 4.7 Play audio track 4.7, pausing after each word for sts to repeat. See SB page opposite for audio script. Check that sts understand all the adjectives.

2 Sts read the text and complete it with the correct adjectives. Check answers.

Answers
1 hot
2 cold
3 short
4 large
5 friendly
6 dirty
7 noisy
8 quiet

Refer sts back to page 36 if they want to revise adjectives further, or see more examples in context.

5A Common verbs (2)

1 5.1 Listen and repeat.

1 **arrive** at the airport

2 **call** my mother

3 **cook** fish

4 **dance** salsa

5 **drive** a car

6 **give** a present

7 **help** my grandmother

8 **look after** my daughter

9 **meet** friends

10 **play** football

11 **play** the piano

12 **sing**

13 **speak** Italian

14 **swim** in the sea

15 **travel** by bus

2 Complete the sentences with the correct form of the verbs in the box.

cook meet give arrive help drive speak play (x2) travel sing call look after

1 Simon _________ Portuguese.
2 I _________ dinner at the weekend.
3 Sharon often _________ basketball.
4 My father _________ a bus.
5 I always _________ my son with his homework.
6 We usually _________ by train.
7 I sometimes _________ my friend's dog.
8 We _________ in Lima at 9.15 a.m.
9 I always _________ Lucy for a coffee after work.
10 You never _________ me flowers.
11 Jo likes music. She _________ and _________ the guitar.
12 My parents live in India, so I _________ them on Skype.

◀ Go back to page 42

5A Common verbs (2)

1 5.1 Allow sts time to look at the pictures and read through the words. Play audio track 5.1, pausing after each phrase for sts to repeat. See SB page opposite for audio script. Check that sts understand all the phrases.

3 x PRACTICE *SB page 117, exercise 1*

1 Do the exercise as normal. After sts have repeated the phrases, call out the numbers of the pictures in a random order and invite students to say the phrase individually. Get other sts to repeat again if necessary.

2 Ask sts to cover the pictures and phrases. In pairs, they uncover each row of pictures in turn and try to remember the phrases. They can uncover the phrases again to check.

3 Ask sts to close their books, and put them into teams. Write one word from each phrase on the board, e.g. *airport, mother, fish*. Invite teams in turn to choose a word from the board and say the full phrase. If the phrase is correct, give the team a point and add the full phrase to the board. If the phrase is not correct, don't give the correct phrase, but move on to the next team. Continue until all the phrases are on the board. See which team has the most points.

2 Sts read the sentences and complete them with the correct verbs. Check answers.

Answers
1 speaks
2 cook
3 plays
4 drives
5 help
6 travel
7 look after
8 arrive
9 meet
10 give
11 sings, plays
12 call

Refer sts back to page 42 if they want to revise common verbs further, or see more examples in context.

5B Electronic devices

1 5.8 Listen and repeat.

1 desktop computer

2 DVD player

3 DVR (digital video recorder)

4 earphones

5 headphones

6 laptop

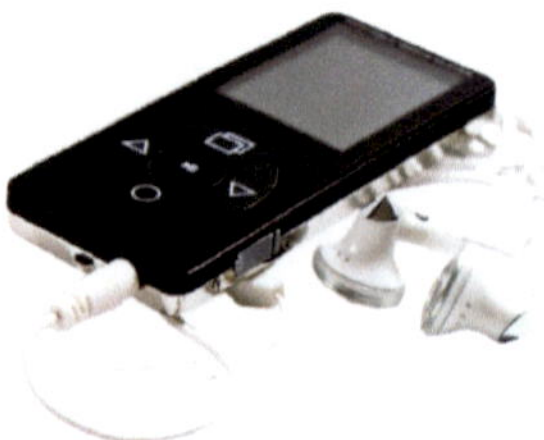
7 MP3 player

8 radio

9 remote control

10 Sat Nav

11 smartphone

12 TV (television)

2 ~~Cross out~~ the word which is incorrect in each sentence.

1 A Listen to this song on my phone – it's great!
B One moment – I need some *earphones / remote control / headphones*.

2 A Can I check my emails?
B Yes. You can use my *radio / laptop / smartphone*.

3 A My friend lives on Bridge Street, but I don't know where that is.
B It's OK. I have *a smartphone / a Sat Nav / an MP3 player*. We can use that.

4 A Do you want to watch a film tonight?
B We can't, sorry. I don't have a *remote control / TV / DVD player*.

5 A I work at home. I have a *laptop / TV / desktop computer* and that's all I need.
B At home? What a nice job!

6 A It's quiet. Why don't we listen to some music?
B OK ... where is the *radio / Sat Nav / MP3 player*?

7 A The news is on at 12.00.
B OK, the *DVD player / TV / radio* is over there.

8 A Do you have a TV?
B No, I don't. I watch TV shows on my *laptop / radio / smartphone*.

◀ Go back to page 44

5B Electronic devices

1 5.8 Allow sts time to look at the pictures and read through the words. Play audio track 5.8, pausing after each word for sts to repeat. See SB page opposite for audio script.

2 Sts read the sentences and cross out the word which is incorrect in each one. Check answers and check that sts understand all the sentences.

Answers
1 remote control
2 radio
3 an MP3 player
4 remote control
5 TV
6 Sat Nav
7 DVD player
8 radio

3 x PRACTICE *SB page 118, exercise 2*

1 Do the exercise as normal. To check the answers, read out each sentence three times, once with each possible answer. Ask sts to put up their left hand for each correct sentence, and their right hand for the incorrect one. Elicit why that sentence is incorrect.

2 Sts work in pairs. They take turns to read out the first line of each dialogue to their partner. Their partner tries to remember the response, without looking at the exercise. Sts can help each other with clues, mimes, etc. if necessary.

3 Sts work in pairs. They write two more mini-dialogues, using some of the words for electronic devices. Ask pairs in turn to read out the first lines of their dialogues to the class. Other sts try to guess the response before the sts give it.

Refer sts back to page 44 if they want to revise words for electronic devices further, or see more examples in context.

5C Activities

1 5.13 Listen and repeat.

1 cleaning

2 cooking

3 cycling

4 dancing

5 going out

6 listening to music

7 meeting friends

8 reading

9 running

10 shopping

11 sleeping

12 swimming

13 walking

14 watching TV/films

Look! We can use activities that end in *-ing* or nouns with the verbs *like*, *love* and *hate*.
I like shopping. I love clothes!
I don't like cycling. I hate bikes.

2 Match the activities in the box with pictures 1–8.

swimming	reading	running	cooking	cycling	cleaning	shopping	sleeping

1 ______________

2 ______________

3 ______________

4 ______________

5 ______________

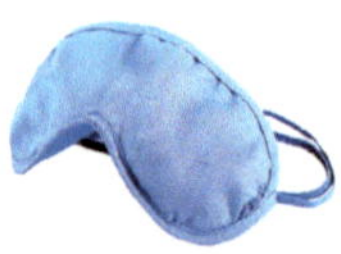
6 ______________

7 ______________

8 ______________

◀ Go back to page 46

5C Activities

1 5.13 Allow sts time to look at the pictures and read through the words. Play audio track 5.13, pausing after each word for sts to repeat. See SB page opposite for audio script. Read through the information in the *Look!* box with the class. Elicit a few more examples, e.g. *I like dancing. I don't like running.*

3 x PRACTICE *SB page 119, exercise 1*

1. Do the exercise as normal. After sts have repeated the words, call out the numbers of the pictures in a random order and invite a student to say the word individually. Get other sts to repeat again if necessary.
2. Ask sts to cover the pictures and words. In pairs, they uncover each row of pictures in turn and try to remember the word for each activity. They can uncover the words to check.
3. With books closed, divide the class into two teams and invite one person from each team to come to the front of the class. Show these two sts one of the pictures in exercise 1. They race to mime the activity for their team mates to guess. The first team to say the correct word gets a point. Change the sts at the front from time to time, and continue until all the activities have been mimed. See which team has the most points.

2 Sts match the objects with the activities. Check answers.

Answers
1 cycling
2 cooking
3 cleaning
4 running
5 swimming
6 sleeping
7 shopping
8 reading

Refer sts back to page 46 if they want to revise vocabulary for activities further, or see more examples in context.

6A Places in a town

1 6.1 Listen and repeat.

1 bank

2 bus stop

3 café

4 cinema

5 hospital

6 hotel

7 museum

8 nightclub

9 park

10 police station

11 post office

12 restaurant

13 school

14 shopping centre

15 supermarket

16 train station

Look!

a village

a town

a city

A village is small.
A town is medium-sized.
A city is big.

2 Match the places in the box with jobs 1–5.

hospital police station school restaurant shopping centre

1 waiter ________
2 police officer ________
3 shop assistant ________
4 teacher ________
5 doctor ________

3 Complete the sentences with the places in the box.

bank nightclub train station park post office supermarket bus stop café cinema museum

1 You can send a letter at a ________ .
2 You can get a train at a ________ .
3 You wait for a bus at a ________ .
4 You drink tea or coffee at a ________ .
5 You can dance at a ________ .
6 You watch a film at a ________ .
7 You see interesting things at a ________ .
8 You get money at a ________ .
9 You walk, play games or relax in a ________ .
10 You can buy food and drink at a ________ .

◀ Go back to page 50

6A Places in a town

1 6.1 Allow sts time to look at the pictures and read through the words. Play audio track 6.1, pausing after each word for sts to repeat. See SB page opposite for audio script. Read through the information in the *Look!* box with the class.

2 Sts match the places in the box with the jobs. Check answers.

Answers
1 restaurant
2 police station
3 shopping centre
4 school
5 hospital

3 Sts read the sentences and complete them with the correct places. Check answers.

Answers
1 post office
2 train station
3 bus stop
4 café
5 nightclub
6 cinema
7 museum
8 bank
9 park
10 supermarket

3 x PRACTICE *SB page 120, exercise 3*

1 Do the exercise as normal. To check answers, read out each word from the box in turn. Elicit the correct sentence using that word.

2 Ask sts to cover the sentences. In pairs, sts look at the places in the box again and try to remember the sentence for each place. They can look at the sentences and their answers again to check.

3 Write on the board the six places from exercise 1 that are not used in exercise 3: *hospital, hotel, police station, restaurant, school, shopping centre*. In pairs, sts write a sentence for each place, like the sentences in exercise 3. Ask some sts to read their sentences to the class, omitting the place. Other sts can listen and guess the places.

Refer sts back to page 50 if they want to revise places in a town further, or see more examples in context.

6B Parts of the body

1 6.7 Listen and repeat.

Look! The plural of *tooth* is *teeth*. The plural of *foot* is *feet*.

2 Put the parts of the body in the box in the correct columns.

arms body ears face feet hands head knees legs mouth nose teeth

I have one …	I have two …	I have more than two …

◀ Go back to page 52

6B Parts of the body

1 6.7 Allow sts time to look at the picture and read through the words. Play audio track 6.7, pausing after each word for sts to repeat. See SB page opposite for audio script. Read the information in the *Look!* box with the class.

3 x PRACTICE *SB page 121, exercise 1*

1 Do the exercise as normal. After sts have repeated the words, say each part of the body again and get sts to point to it on their own body. Get them to repeat each word again as they point to it.

2 Ask sts to copy the picture on page 121, without the labels, then close their books. Tell sts that there are 14 words for body parts on page 121. In pairs, sts look at their drawings and try to remember the 14 words and add them to their drawings. They can look at the picture on page 121 again to check. See who remembered all the words correctly.

3 With books closed, put sts into pairs. They write clues for five of the words in exercise 1, e.g. *You can cut it* (hair), *You put food in it* (mouth). Put pairs together into groups of four. They take turns to read their clues to each other and guess the body parts. See who guessed all the words correctly.

2 Sts add the parts of the body from the box to the table. Check answers.

Answers

I have one ...	I have two ...	I have more than two ...
body	arms	teeth
face	ears	
head	feet	
mouth	hands	
nose	knees	
	legs	

Refer sts back to page 52 if they want to revise vocabulary for parts of the body further, or see more examples in context.

6C Rooms and furniture

1 6.8 Listen and repeat.

2 Complete the sentences with the rooms and furniture in the box.

fridge	bath	table	sofa	desk	window	bedroom	cooker	wardrobe	shelves

1 Let's have dinner in the living room. We can sit on the _________ and watch a film.
2 Shona has a big white _________ for all her clothes.
3 My favourite room is the _________ . I sleep there and it's very quiet.
4 After they make dinner, the _________ is very hot.
5 My bathroom is small, so I have a shower, but I don't have a _________ .
6 Ken needs a lot of _________ because he has hundreds of books!
7 It's hot in here. Can you open the _________ ?
8 Please put the milk and orange juice in the _________ .
9 I have a _________ in my bedroom where I do homework and use my laptop.
10 Dinner is ready. The food is on the _________ !

◀ Go back to page 54

6C Rooms and furniture

1 6.8 Allow sts time to look at the picture and read through the words. Play audio track 6.8, pausing after each word for sts to repeat. See SB page opposite for audio script.

2 Sts read the sentences and complete them with the correct words. Check answers.

Answers
1 sofa
2 wardrobe
3 bedroom
4 cooker
5 bath
6 shelves
7 window
8 fridge
9 desk
10 table

3 x PRACTICE *SB page 122, exercise 2*

1 Do the exercise as normal. To check answers, read out each word in the box in turn and ask sts to find it in the picture in exercise 1. Then elicit the correct sentence.

2 Ask sts to cover the sentences. In pairs, they look at the words in the box and try to remember the sentences. They can look at the sentences and their answers again to check.

3 Sts work in pairs. They write a short conversation about someone's home, and try to include as many words for rooms and furniture as possible. Ask pairs in turn to perform their conversation for the class. Other sts can listen and count the words for rooms and furniture that they use. See who managed to use the most words.

Refer sts back to page 54 if they want to revise vocabulary for rooms and furniture further, or see more examples in context.

7A Celebrities

1 7.1 Listen and repeat.

1 artist

2 athlete

3 dancer

4 DJ

5 fashion model

6 film director

7 footballer

8 journalist

9 king

10 musician

11 photographer

12 politician

13 queen

14 racing driver

15 tennis player

16 writer

2 Look at the pictures and complete the sentences with the words in the box.

fashion model writer queen musician tennis player dancer king film director artist footballer politician athlete

1 Shelly-Ann Fraser-Pryce is a Jamaican ________ .

2 Gisele Bündchen is a Brazilian ________ .

3 Emmanuel Macron is a French ________ .

4 Isabel Allende is a Chilean ________ .

5 Thomas Müller is a German ________ .

6 Margrethe II is the ________ of Denmark.

7 Salvador Dalí was a Spanish ________ .

8 Beyoncé is an American ________ .

9 Sofia Coppola is an American ________ .

10 Venus Williams is an American ________ .

11 Felipe VI is the ________ of Spain.

12 Rudolf Nureyev was a Russian ________ .

◀ Go back to page 60

7A Celebrities

1 7.1 Allow sts time to look at the pictures and read through the words. Play audio track 7.1, pausing after each word for sts to repeat. See SB page opposite for audio script.

2 Sts look at the pictures and complete the sentences with the correct words. Check answers.

Answers
1 athlete
2 fashion model
3 politician
4 writer
5 footballer
6 queen
7 artist
8 musician
9 film director
10 tennis player
11 king
12 dancer

3 x PRACTICE *SB page 123, exercise 2*

1 Do the exercise as normal. To check answers, read out each celebrity word from the box in turn and ask: *Which picture? What's the full sentence?* Elicit the answers from individual sts.

2 Ask sts to cover the pictures and sentences. In pairs, they uncover each row of pictures in turn and try to remember who the people are and why they are celebrities. They can look at the sentences and their answers again to check.

3 Sts work in pairs. They write three clues for celebrities that they know, using words from exercises 1 and 2, e.g. *He's a Swiss tennis player* (Roger Federer). Ask pairs in turn to read their clues to the class. Other sts can guess the celebrities.

Refer sts back to page 60 if they want to revise vocabulary for celebrities further, or see more examples in context.

VOCABULARY PRACTICE

7B Months and ordinals

1 7.5 Listen and repeat.

1 January	2 February	3 March	4 April
5 May	6 June	7 July	8 August
9 September	10 October	11 November	12 December

2 7.6 Listen and repeat.

1st	first	7th	seventh	13th	thirteenth	19th	nineteenth
2nd	second	8th	eighth	14th	fourteenth	20th	twentieth
3rd	third	9th	ninth	15th	fifteenth	21st	twenty-first
4th	fourth	10th	tenth	16th	sixteenth	22nd	twenty-second
5th	fifth	11th	eleventh	17th	seventeenth	30th	thirtieth
6th	sixth	12th	twelfth	18th	eighteenth	31st	thirty-first

Look! In British English the ordinal comes before the month.
2 February = the second of February
16 June = the sixteenth of June
But in American English, the ordinal comes after the month.
February 2 = February second
June 16 = June sixteenth

3 Look at the dates in brackets and complete the sentences with the words.

1 St Valentine's Day is the _________ of _________ . (14/02)
2 Independence Day in the USA is the _________ of _________ . (04/07)
3 New Year's Day is the _________ of _________ . (01/01)
4 Halloween is the _________ of _________ . (31/10)
5 My birthday is the _________ of _________ . (25/07)
6 Mother's Day in the UK this year is the _________ of _________ . (11/03)

◀ Go back to page 62

7C Time expressions

1 7.14 Listen and repeat.

1 last — last night, last week, last year
2 ago — two days ago, three weeks ago, four years ago
3 yesterday — yesterday morning, yesterday afternoon, yesterday evening
4 times — at 9.00, at 11.30, at midnight
5 days — on Monday, on Tuesday, at the weekend
6 dates — on 1 January, on 24 April, on 11 December
7 years — in 1985, in 2001, in 2018
8 decades — in the 1960s, in the 1990s, in the 2010s

Look! We say *yesterday morning/afternoon/evening*, but ***last*** *night*, NOT ~~yesterday~~ night.

2 Complete the sentences with the words in the box.

on (x2) in ago last (x2) yesterday at

1 I studied English _________ morning. Then I watched TV.
2 We enjoyed your party _________ night. It was great!
3 Slavska meets her friends _________ 6.30 after work.
4 I lived in Madrid _________ the 1980s. It was an interesting time.
5 My brother travelled to South America _________ year.
6 I started my new job _________ 4 November.
7 My grandfather played football for Arsenal 50 years _________ .
8 I usually finish work early _________ Friday.

◀ Go back to page 65

7B Months and ordinals

1 7.5 Play audio track 7.5 once for sts to listen and look at the calendar. Play the audio again, pausing for them to repeat.

2 7.6 Allow sts time to read through the numbers. Play audio track 7.6, pausing for sts to repeat.

3 Read through the information in the *Look!* box with the class. Focus on the sentences and elicit that they use the British English form of dates. Sts read the sentences and complete them with the correct dates. Check answers.

Answers
1 fourteenth, February
2 fourth, July
3 first, January
4 thirty-first, October
5 twenty-fifth, July
6 eleventh, March

Refer sts back to page 62 if they want to revise months and ordinals further, or see more examples in context.

7C Time expressions

1 7.14 Play audio track 7.14, pausing for sts to repeat. After each group of expressions, pause and ask concept questions to check understanding, e.g. *What was the date on Monday last week? What year was it last year? What day was it two days ago?* Check that sts understand all the time expressions. Read through the information in the *Look!* box with the class.

2 Sts read the sentences and complete them with the words in the box. Check answers.

Answers
1 yesterday
2 last
3 at
4 in
5 last
6 on
7 ago
8 on

3 x PRACTICE *SB page 124, 7C, exercise 1*

1 Do the exercise as normal. To check answers, tell sts you are going to read out all the answers, but there will be three mistakes. Read out the sentences, including three incorrect answers. Sts listen and note down the incorrect answers. They can compare their ideas in pairs. Elicit the correct answers from the class.

2 Ask sts to close their books and put them into pairs. Read out every other word of each sentence in turn, e.g. *studied, yesterday, then, watched*. Sts race to write the complete sentence. You can give them one or two extra words if they are struggling.

3 Sts work individually and rewrite some of the sentences so they are true for them, e.g. *I played tennis yesterday morning. Then I met some friends*. Sts can compare their sentences in pairs. Ask some sts to read their sentences to the class. Ask if any other sts have similar sentences.

Refer sts back to page 65 if they want to revise time expressions further, or see more examples in context.

8A Travel verbs

1 8.1 Listen and repeat.

1 **book** a flight

2 **fly**

3 **get in** a taxi

4 **get lost**

5 **get off** a bus

6 **get on** a train

7 **get out of** a taxi

8 **miss** the bus

9 **ride** a bike

10 **sail**

11 **take** the underground

12 **walk**

2 Tick (✓) the verbs we can use with each type of transport.

	a taxi	a bike	a boat	a plane	a bus	a train
ride						
take						
miss						
get in / out of						
get on / off						
sail						

3 Choose the correct words to complete the sentences.

1 Anne needs to *walk* / *book* a ticket for her trip to Los Angeles.
2 This is our bus stop. Quick, *get off* / *get out* now!
3 Let's *walk* / *get out* home. It's a nice warm evening.
4 Juan decided to *sail* / *fly* to Spain because he hates planes.
5 When the train arrived, a lot of people tried to *get lost* / *get on*.
6 There aren't any trains. We need to *ride* / *take* a taxi home.
7 They *missed* / *booked* their bus, so they arrived really late.
8 I can drive you home if you want. *Get in* / *Get out*!
9 Stuart *drives* / *rides* a motorbike because it's fast.
10 You can *take* / *ride* the number 35 bus to the city centre.

◀ Go back to page 68

8A Travel verbs

1 8.1 Allow sts time to look at the pictures and read through the words. Play audio track 8.1, pausing after each word or phrase for sts to repeat. See SB page opposite for audio script.

3 x PRACTICE *SB page 125, exercise 1*

1 Do the exercise as normal. After sts have repeated the words and phrases, say the numbers of the pictures in a random order and invite a student to say the word or phrase individually. Get other sts to repeat individually.

2 Ask sts to cover the pictures and words. In pairs, they uncover each row of pictures in turn and try to remember the word or phrase for each picture. They can uncover the words to check.

3 With books closed, divide the class into two teams and invite one person from each team to come to the front of the class. Show these two sts one of the pictures in exercise 1. They race to mime the travel verb for their team mates to guess. The first team to say the correct travel verb gets a point. Change the sts at the front from time to time, and continue until all the travel verbs have been mimed. See which team has the most points.

2 Sts tick the verbs that we can use with each form of transport. Check answers.

Answers

	a taxi	a bike	a boat	a plane	a bus	a train
ride		✓				
take	✓			✓	✓	✓
miss				✓	✓	✓
get in/ out of	✓		✓			
get on/ off		✓		✓	✓	✓
sail			✓			

3 Sts read the sentences and choose the correct words to complete them. Check answers. Ask sts questions using some of the travel verbs, e.g. *When did you last book a ticket online? Do you ever walk home? Would you prefer to sail or fly to England? Why?* Elicit a range of answers.

Answers

1 book
2 get off
3 walk
4 sail
5 get on
6 take
7 missed
8 Get in
9 rides
10 take

Refer sts back to page 68 if they want to revise travel verbs further, or see more examples in context.

8B Weather and seasons

1 8.6 Listen and repeat.

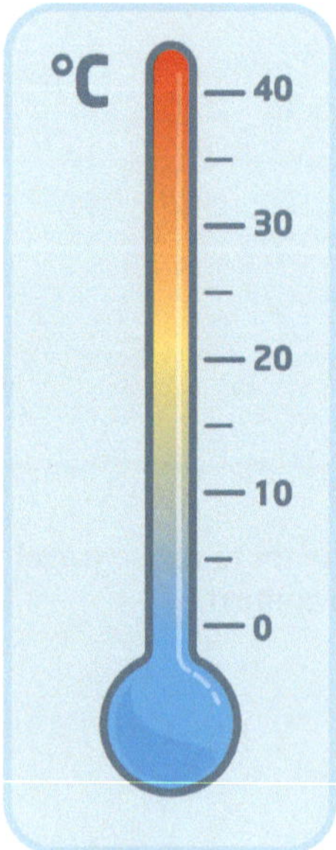

1 hot

2 warm

3 cold

4 cloudy 5 sunny

6 wet 7 dry

8 windy 9 foggy

10 rain 11 snow

12 spring 13 summer 14 autumn 15 winter

> **Look!** *rain* and *snow* are verbs. To talk about the weather now, we say *It's raining*/ *It's snowing*. To talk about the weather in general, we say *It rains*/*It snows*.

2 Look at the weather map and complete the sentences.

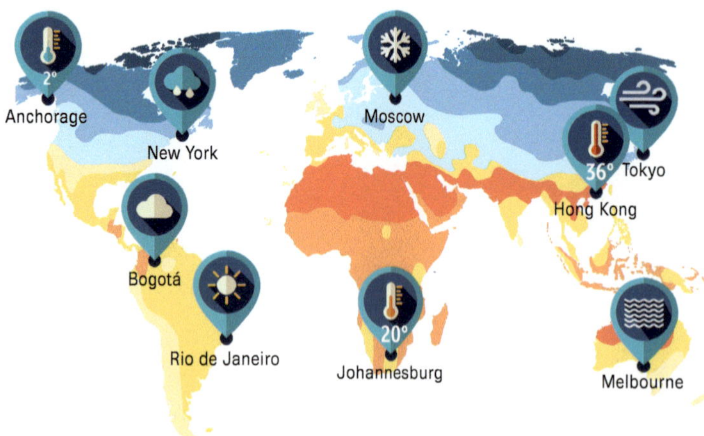

1 It's ________ in Moscow.
2 It's ________ in Bogotá.
3 It's ________ in Rio de Janeiro.
4 It's ________ in New York.
5 It's ________ in Tokyo.
6 It's ________ in Hong Kong.
7 It's ________ in Anchorage.
8 It's ________ in Johannesburg.
9 It's ________ in Melbourne.

◀ Go back to page 70

8B Weather and seasons

1 8.6 Allow sts time to look at the pictures and read through the words. Play audio track 8.6, pausing after each word for sts to repeat. See SB page opposite for audio script. Read through the information in the *Look!* box with the class. Elicit or give some longer examples to show the use of the two present tenses, e.g. *It often snows here in winter. Look, it's snowing now!*

2 Sts look at the map and complete the sentences with the correct words. Check answers.

Answers
1 snowing
2 cloudy
3 sunny
4 raining
5 windy
6 hot
7 cold
8 warm
9 foggy

3 x PRACTICE *SB page 126, exercise 2*

1 Do the exercise as normal. To check answers, ask questions using the adjectives and present participles in the answers in a random order, e.g. *Where is it windy? Where is it cold?* Elicit the answers in this way.

2 Ask sts to close their books. Write the nine answers from the exercise on the board, and the nine places in a random order. In pairs, sts try to remember the weather in each place and write the sentences. They can look at the map and sentences again to check.

3 Sts work in pairs. They use their phones, tablets or laptops to check the weather in another city around the world. Ask them to check what it is usually like in winter and summer, and what it is like today. Ask pairs in turn to tell the class what they learned, e.g. *In New York it's usually cold in winter. It's sunny today*. Ask: *Which city would you like to live in? Why?*

Refer sts back to page 70 if they want to revise vocabulary for weather and seasons further, or see more examples in context.

8C Nature

1 8.7 Listen and repeat.

1 beach

2 cloud

3 field

4 flower

5 forest

6 grass

7 mountain

8 river

9 sea

10 sky

11 sun

12 tree

2 Choose the correct words to complete the sentences.

1 Kilimanjaro is a *beach* / *mountain* in Tanzania.
2 The Nile is a *river* / *field* in Africa.
3 The Amazon is a type of *forest* / *mountain* in South America.
4 The rose is a *cloud* / *flower* that can be different colours.
5 Jamaica is in the Caribbean *Sea* / *River*.
6 Copacabana is a *beach* / *forest* in Brazil.
7 Apples are a fruit that come from a *grass* / *tree*.
8 The temperature of the *sun* / *sky* is 15 million °C.
9 Cumulus, Cirrus and Stratus are *clouds* / *trees*.
10 Animals like horses and rabbits eat *trees* / *grass*.

◀ Go back to page 72

8C Nature

1 8.7 Allow sts time to look at the pictures and read through the words. Play audio track 8.7, pausing after each word for sts to repeat. See SB page opposite for audio script.

2 Sts read the sentences and choose the correct words to complete them. Check answers.

Answers
1 mountain
2 river
3 forest
4 flower
5 Sea
6 beach
7 tree
8 sun
9 clouds
10 grass

3 x PRACTICE *SB page 127, exercise 2*

1 Do the exercise as normal. To check answers, ask a question about each sentence first, e.g. *Kilimanjaro – a beach or a mountain?* Elicit the answer, then invite a student to read out the full sentence.

2 Ask sts to close their books. Write one or two key words for each sentence on the board, e.g. *Kilimanjaro, Tanzania; Amazon, South America; rose, colours*. In pairs, sts try to remember the sentences. They can look at the exercise and their answers again to check.

3 Put sts into teams. Write the following words on the board: *hot, the USA, eat, high, sail, play, swim, blue*. In their teams, sts try to write a sentence using each of the words on the board and one of the nature words from exercises 1 and 2. Tell them they can only use each nature word once. Stop the activity after a few minutes and ask teams in turn to read their sentences to the class. Award a point for each correct sentence. See which team managed to use the most nature words correctly.

Refer sts back to page 72 if they want to revise nature vocabulary further, or see more examples in context.

9A Clothes

1 9.1 Listen and repeat.

1 belt

2 boots

3 coat

4 dress

5 hat

6 jacket

7 jeans

8 jumper

9 shirt

10 shoes

11 skirt

12 socks

13 suit

14 T-shirt

15 trousers

2 Write the clothes from exercise 1 in the correct places.

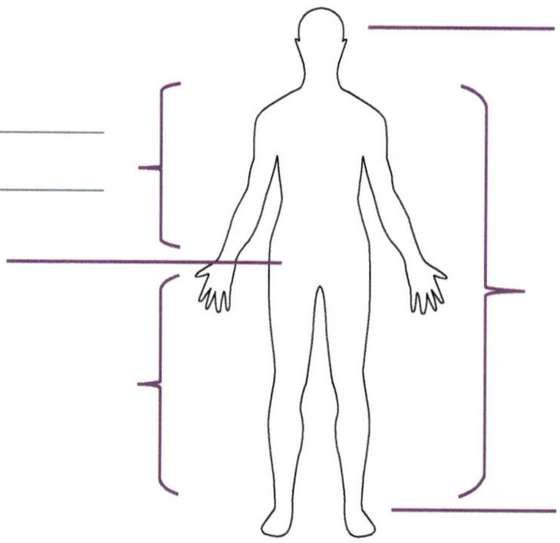

1 ______________ 3 ______________
2 ______________ 4 ______________

5 ______________
6 ______________
7 ______________
8 ______________

9 ______________

10 ______________
11 ______________
12 ______________

13 ______________ 15 ______________
14 ______________

◀ Go back to page 78

9A Clothes

1 9.1 Allow sts time to look at the picture and read through the words. Play audio track 9.1, pausing after each word for sts to repeat. See SB page opposite for audio script.

2 Sts write the clothes from exercise 1 in the correct places. Check answers.

Answers
1–4 jacket, jumper, shirt, T shirt
5 belt
6–8 jeans, skirt, trousers
9 hat
10–12 coat, suit, dress
13–15 socks, boots, shoes

3 x PRACTICE *SB page 128, exercise 2*

1 Do the exercise as normal. To check answers, copy the drawing onto the board. Invite sts in turn to come and add one word to the drawing. Discuss any differences of opinion and make sure all the answers on the board at the end are correct.

2 Ask sts in pairs to copy the drawing from exercise 2 (but not the words) onto a piece of paper. With books closed, they try to remember the 15 clothes words and add them to the drawing in the correct place. They can look at their books and their answers again to check.

3 Ask sts individually to copy the drawing from exercise 2 and then dress it, using clothes from exercise 1. Encourage them to use different colours for the different clothes they add. Sts then work in pairs, with books closed. They take turns to describe their drawing to their partner, e.g. *He has a red jumper, blue jeans, and black boots*. Their partner listens and draws the person. Sts can compare their drawings to see if they have listened and understood correctly.

Refer sts back to page 78 if they want to revise clothes vocabulary further, or see more examples in context.

9B Feelings

1 9.6 Listen and repeat.

1 angry

2 bored

3 calm

4 excited

5 happy

6 hungry

7 sad

8 scared

9 surprised

10 thirsty

11 tired

12 worried

2 Choose the correct adjective to complete the sentences.

1 Can I have a drink of water? I'm really *hungry* / *thirsty*.
2 He's *surprised* / *worried* about money because he doesn't have a job.
3 I'm *bored* / *scared*. This film isn't very interesting.
4 It's Louisa's birthday tomorrow – she's very *excited* / *tired*.
5 I like yoga because it makes me feel *calm* / *sad*.
6 Are you *angry* / *hungry*? Do you want a sandwich?
7 You're very *scared* / *tired*. Why don't you go to bed?
8 Tim is *angry* / *hungry* with me because I broke his computer.
9 I was *bored* / *surprised* that John ran a marathon because he doesn't like sport.
10 Suzie doesn't like horror films. They make her feel *scared* / *surprised*.

3 Match the feelings in the box with the messages.

tired	sad	worried	angry	surprised

1 **Julia** I get my exam results today!
2 **Ying-Li** I arrived in London today after a 10-hour flight.
3 **Saanvi** I won the Science competition. I can't believe it!
4 **Dave** All my friends are in Cuba on holiday. I'm at work.
5 **Hans** I lost my wallet on the train today ... and I was late for work.

◀ Go back to page 80

9B Feelings

1 9.6 Allow sts time to look at the pictures and read through the words. Play audio track 9.6, pausing after each word for sts to repeat. See SB page opposite for audio script. Ask questions to check that sts understand all the words, e.g. *You want a drink. Are you hungry or thirsty? You're watching a bad TV programme. Are you bored or happy?*

2 Sts read the sentences and choose the correct adjectives to complete them. Check answers.

Answers
1 thirsty
2 worried
3 bored
4 excited
5 calm
6 hungry
7 tired
8 angry
9 surprised
10 scared

3 Sts read the messages and match the correct feeling with each one. Check answers.

Answers
1 worried
2 tired
3 surprised
4 sad
5 angry

3 x PRACTICE *SB page 129, exercise 3*

1 Do the exercise as normal. To check answers, ask questions using each adjective, e.g. *Who is sad? Why? Who is surprised? Why?* Elicit the answers in this way.

2 Ask sts to cover the words in the box in exercise 3, and the pictures in exercise 1. In pairs, they look at the messages again and try to remember the correct adjective for each one. They can look at the words in the box and their answers again to check.

3 Sts work in pairs. They write two more messages and add their own emoticons to show some of the other feelings in exercise 1. Monitor and help while they are working. Pairs can swap messages with another pair and try to guess the correct feelings. Ask who guessed correctly, and who drew good emoticons.

Refer sts back to page 80 if they want to revise adjectives for feelings further, or see more examples in context.

9C Shopping

1 9.12 Listen and repeat.

1 buy a car

2 go shopping

3 pay by credit card

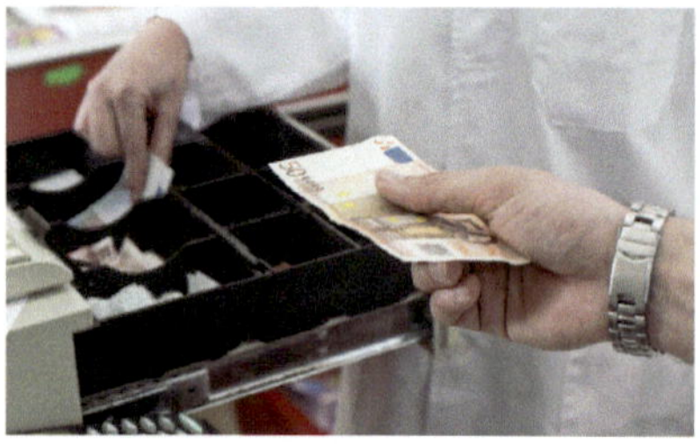
4 pay with cash

5 sell ice cream

6 shop online

7 spend money

8 try on clothes

9 department store

10 local shops

11 market

12 shopping centre

2 Match the halves to make sentences.

1 I always pay by	_____	a	these jeans, please?
2 We usually spend	_____	b	a new laptop.
3 Can I try on	_____	c	fish in the market.
4 I never shop	_____	d	shopping for food.
5 Jorge sells	_____	e	£100 every weekend.
6 Malika wants to buy	_____	f	credit card. It's easy!
7 You can only pay with	_____	g	cash in this shop.
8 We need to go	_____	h	online. I like real shops.

3 Choose the correct words to complete the sentences.

1 I don't *go* / *buy* shopping on Saturdays. There are lots of people.
2 My brother works for a technology company. He *spends* / *sells* computers.
3 Sharon lives in a small village. There are only three or four *department stores* / *local shops*.
4 Carla *spends* / *buys* all her money on clothes.
5 When we go on holiday, we usually pay *with* / *by* credit card.
6 The *shopping centre* / *market* near us has a cinema and lots of restaurants.
7 I always *try* / *shop* on clothes before I buy them.
8 My mobile phone is broken. I need to *buy* / *pay* a new one.

◀ Go back to page 82

9C Shopping

1 9.12 Allow sts time to look at the pictures and read through the words. Play audio track 9.12, pausing after each word or phrase for sts to repeat. See SB page opposite for audio script.

2 Sts match the sentence halves. Check answers.

Answers
1 f
2 e
3 a
4 h
5 c
6 b
7 g
8 d

3 x PRACTICE *SB page 130, exercise 2*

1 Do the exercise as normal. To check answers, read out each sentence beginning. Ask sts to put up their left hand if they are confident about the ending, and their right hand if they are not confident. Ask a confident student to complete the sentence with the correct ending.

2 Ask sts to cover the second half of the sentences. In pairs, they read the sentence beginnings and try to remember the endings. They can look at the endings to check. They can repeat this, looking this time at the sentence endings and trying to remember the beginnings.

3 Sts work in pairs. They look at the sentence beginnings again and write a new ending for each one. Monitor and help while they are working. Put pairs together into groups of four. They take turns to read out one of their endings, in a random order. The other pair tries to guess which beginning it matches. Ask who guessed all the sentences correctly.

3 Sts read the sentences and choose the correct words to complete them. Check answers.

Answers
1 go
2 sells
3 local shops
4 spends
5 by
6 shopping centre
7 try
8 buy

Refer sts back to page 82 if they want to revise vocabulary for shopping further, or see more examples in context.

10A Free-time activities

1 10.1 Listen and repeat.

1 go to a concert

2 go to a festival

3 go to the beach

4 have a barbecue

5 have a good time

6 have a party

7 stay at home

8 stay in a hotel

9 stay in a tent

10 visit a museum

11 visit an art gallery

12 visit family/friends

13 watch a film

14 watch a football match

15 watch a video

2 Match the activities in the box with the people.

visit family	go to the beach	have a barbecue	watch a film
have a party	stay at home	visit a museum	stay in a tent

1 Erica likes hot weather and swimming. She has two new books to read. ____________
2 It's a nice sunny day. Paul is hungry and he has some meat and fish. ____________
3 It's Lucia's birthday tomorrow and she wants to celebrate with her friends. ____________
4 The weather isn't good and Samuel has an exam next week. ____________
5 Marek and Kasia are in London for the weekend. They're interested in history. ____________
6 Sonia loves nature. She wants to go on holiday, but she doesn't want to spend a lot of money. ____________
7 Cristian is going to San Francisco. His parents and brothers and sisters live there. ____________
8 Natalia is at home tonight. She bought a new 102 cm TV last week. ____________

◀ Go back to page 86

10A Free-time activities

1 10.1 Allow sts time to look at the pictures and read through the phrases. Play audio track 10.1, pausing after each phrase for sts to repeat. See SB page opposite for audio script.

2 Sts read the sentences and match the activities with the people. Check answers.

Answers
1 go to the beach
2 have a barbecue
3 have a party
4 stay at home
5 visit a museum
6 stay in a tent
7 visit family
8 watch a film

3 x PRACTICE *SB page 131, exercise 2*

1 Do the exercise as normal. To check answers, read out each activity in the box in turn and ask: *Which person matches this activity? Why?* Elicit the answers in this way.

2 Sts work in pairs. They take it in turns to close their books, while their partner chooses two sentences to read to them. They try to remember the correct activity for each person. Their partner can confirm the answers.

3 Individually, sts look at the activities in exercise 1 again and choose two that they like. They then write sentences about themselves, e.g. *I love sport and I love watching my team.* (Watch a football match). Monitor and help while they are working. Sts then work in small groups. They take turns to read out their sentences. The other sts in the group race to say the correct activities.

Refer sts back to page 86 if they want to revise vocabulary for free-time activities further, or see more examples in context.

10B Types of music and film

1 10.9 Listen and repeat.

1 classical music

2 electronic music

3 hip-hop music

4 jazz music

5 pop music

6 rock music

7 an action film

8 a comedy

9 a drama

10 a horror film

11 a romance

12 a science-fiction film

2 Look at the pictures and write the types of music and films.

1 ____________

2 ____________

3 ____________

4 ____________

5 ____________

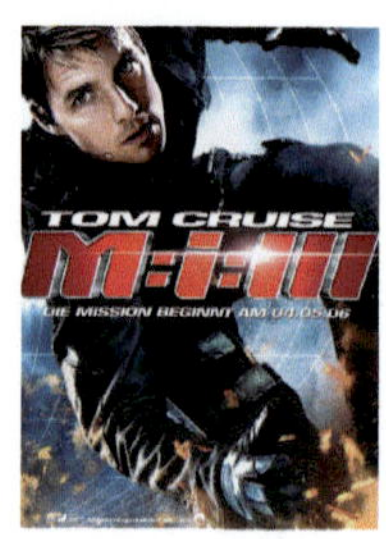

6 ____________

◀ Go back to page 88

10B Types of music and film

1 10.9 Allow sts time to look at the pictures and read through the words. Play audio track 10.9, pausing after each type of music or film for sts to repeat. See SB page opposite for audio script.

3 x PRACTICE *SB page 132, exercise 1*

1. Do the exercise as normal. After sts have repeated the words, say the numbers of the pictures in a random order and invite individual sts to say the type of music or film individually. Get other sts to repeat again if necessary.
2. Ask sts to cover the pictures and words. In pairs, they uncover each row of pictures in turn and try to remember the word for each type of music or film. They can uncover the words to check.
3. Give an example of the name of a type of film, or a person or band associated with a type of music, e.g. *Mozart* (classical music), *Titanic* (a romance). In pairs, sts write the names of four more examples of different types of music or film. Put pairs together into groups of four to read their examples to each other and guess the types of music or film.

2 Sts look at the pictures and write the types of music and films. Check answers.

Answers
1 hip-hop music
2 science-fiction film
3 jazz music
4 rock music
5 romance
6 action film

Refer sts back to page 88 if they want to revise types of music and film further, or see more examples in context.

10C Sports and games

1 10.10 Listen and repeat.

1 do gymnastics

2 do karate

3 do Pilates

4 do yoga

5 go cycling

6 go rock climbing

7 go running

8 go skiing

9 go swimming

10 go walking

11 play basketball

12 play chess

13 play football

14 play hockey

15 play rugby

16 play tennis

17 play videogames

18 play volleyball

Look!

We use *play* with sports that use a ball and with games.
I play golf.

We use *go* with activities that end in *-ing*.
I go sailing.

We use *do* with individual activities and sports that don't use a ball.
I do judo.

2 Complete the sentences with the correct form of *go*, *play* or *do*.

1 He usually _________ tennis at the weekend.
2 It's a lovely sunny day. Why don't we _________ walking?
3 They _________ gymnastics every Monday after school.
4 Do you want to _________ chess later?
5 Did you _________ cycling last weekend?
6 She often _________ Pilates to relax.
7 I _________ skiing with my parents every winter.
8 Do your children _________ a lot of videogames?

◀ Go back to page 90

10C Sports and games

1 10.10 Allow sts time to look at the pictures and read through the phrases. Play audio track 10.10, pausing after each phrase for sts to repeat. See SB page opposite for audio script.

3 x PRACTICE *SB page 133, exercise 1*

1 Do the exercise as normal. After sts have repeated the words, say the numbers of the pictures in a random order and invite individual sts to repeat the correct phrase individually. Get other sts to repeat again if necessary.

2 Ask sts to cover the pictures and words. In pairs, they uncover each row of pictures in turn and try to remember the phrase for each sport or game. They can uncover the words to check.

3 With books closed, mime one of the pictures, e.g. mime *cycling*. Sts race to say the correct sport or game, including the correct verb. Invite sts in turn to look at their book again and choose one of the sports or games to mime. Other sts race to guess the sport or game.

2 Read through the information in the *Look!* box with the class. Elicit one or two more examples with each verb, e.g. *play volleyball, go skiing, do yoga*. Sts read the sentences and complete them with the correct verbs. Check answers.

Answers

1 plays
2 go
3 do
4 play
5 go
6 does
7 go
8 play

Refer sts back to page 90 if they want to revise sports and games vocabulary further, or see more examples in context.

Hello Student A

1 Look at the labels. Ask Student B for the name of the city.

A *What's LHR?*
B *I think it's London.*
A *How do you spell that?*
B *L-O-N-D-O-N.*

1 ____________

2 ____________

3 ____________

4 ____________

5 ____________

2 Listen to Student B's airport codes. Tell him/her the correct city for the letters.

New Delhi Cape Town Barcelona New York Amsterdam

1A Student A

1 You are Mehmet. Answer Student B's questions with the information.

B *What's your name?*
A *I'm Mehmet Guliyev.*
B *How do you spell that?*
A *M-E-H-M-E-T ...*

Name:	Mehmet Guliyev
Nationality:	Turkish
Phone:	90 312 213 2965

2 Ask Student B the questions and write down his/her answers.

1 What's your name?

____

2 Where are you from?

____

3 What's your phone number?

____

1C Student A

1 Ask Student B questions about the Antarctic Zebras to complete the information.

Where are they from? *How old is Bev?* *What is her job?*

The Antarctic Zebras are from ____________________ .

	age	job
Bev		
Angela		
Sammy		

2 Now look at the information about the Rocking Stones. Answer Student B's questions.

The Rocking Stones are from Portland, in the USA.

	age	job
Kevin	44	police officer
Rob	40	engineer
Nick	41	chef

Hello

Ask sts to read through the instructions for the activity. Explain that they each have some airport codes. These will be in exercise 1 for A sts and exercise 2 for B sts. They also each have some country names. These will be in exercise 2 for A sts and exercise 1 for B sts. Allow sts time to read through all the information they have. Make sure they understand everything. With weaker classes, you could briefly revise how to say the letters of the alphabet. Read out the model questions and answers and make sure sts understand what they have to do. Sts then work in pairs and take turns to ask about their airport codes. Monitor while they are working and note down any errors with the target language. Get feedback on which airport codes were difficult to guess. Elicit any other airport codes that sts know. Correct any errors you noticed in a feedback session at the end.

Answers
LHR: London
MEX: Mexico City
IST: Istanbul
LAX: Los Angeles
HGK: Hong Kong
JFK: New York
BCN: Barcelona
CPT: Cape Town
DEL: New Delhi
AMS: Amsterdam

1A

Ask sts to read through the instructions for the activity. Explain that they each have some information about a person. This will be in exercise 1 for A sts and exercise 2 for B sts. They also each have some questions with missing answers. This will be in exercise 2 for A sts and exercise 1 for B sts. Allow sts time to read through all the information they have. Make sure they understand everything, and suggest that they think about how to spell their name, and how to say the phone number. Sts then work in pairs and take turns to ask questions and write down the missing information about their person. They can look at each other's sheets to check the spelling of the names and the phone numbers. Monitor while they are working and note down any errors with the target language. Get feedback on who managed to transfer all the information correctly.

1C

Ask sts to read through the instructions for the activity. Explain that they each have some information about a band. This will be in exercise 2 for A sts and exercise 1 for B sts. They also each have some incomplete information about another band. This will be in exercise 1 for A sts and exercise 2 for B sts. Allow sts time to read through all the information they have. Make sure they understand everything, and suggest that they think about how to say the ages of their band members. Read out the example questions and elicit the question sts need to ask about jobs, e.g. *What does he do?/What's his job?* Sts then work in pairs and take turns to ask questions and write down the missing information. They can look at each other's sheets to check their answers. Monitor while they are working and note down any errors with the target language. Get feedback on who managed to transfer all the information correctly.

2A Students A and B

1 Look at the picture. In pairs, ask about the objects.

What's this/that? *What are these/those?*

2 Now go to page 143 and check your ideas.

2C Student A

Ask and answer questions with Student B to complete David and Victoria Beckham's family tree.

A *What's David's mother's name?*
B *Her name is ...*

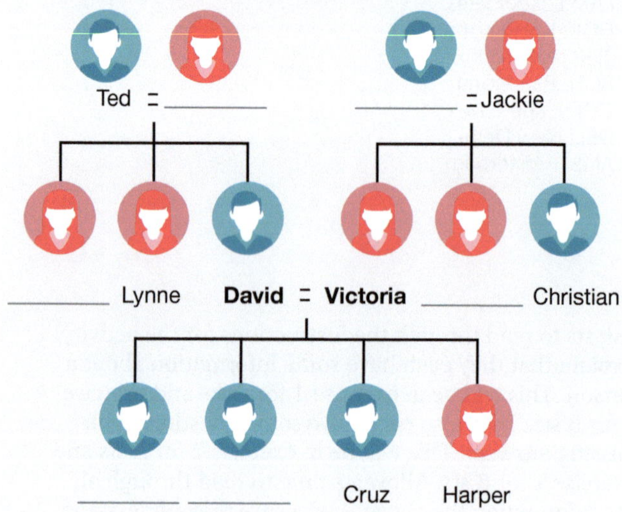

2D Student A

1 Ask Student B the questions and write down the answers. Remember to be polite.

A *Excuse me, what time's the next train to Boston, please?*
B *It's at quarter to twelve.*
A *Thanks.*

1 What time's the next train to Boston? ________
2 What's Lucy's phone number? ________
3 Where's the teacher from? ________
4 How old are you? ________
5 What's the name of the café? ________

2 Answer Student B's questions with the answers in the box.

He's 28. She's from Mexico. You're in Room 48. It's F-O-S-T-E-R. It's at 6.40.

2A

Ask sts to read through the instructions for the activity. Explain that they should try to guess the words for the objects first and write down their ideas. When they have guessed all the words, they can look on page 143 to check their answers and discuss if they were right or wrong. Get feedback on who guessed all the objects correctly.

2C

Focus on the photo and elicit who it shows. Ask sts what they know about David and Victoria Beckham. Ask sts to read through the instructions for the activity. Explain that they each have some information about David and Victoria Beckham's family tree, and they also each have some gaps. Explain that they need to ask their partner for their missing information. Read out the example questions, then allow sts time to prepare the questions they need to ask. You could put them into AA and BB pairs for this. Monitor while they are working, and make sure all their questions are correct. Sts then work in AB pairs and take turns to ask questions and write down the missing information. They can look at each other's sheets to check their answers. Monitor while they are working and note down any errors with the target language. Get feedback on who managed to transfer all the information correctly.

2D

Ask sts to read through the instructions for the activity. Explain that they each have some questions to ask. These will be in exercise 1 for A sts and exercise 2 for B sts. They also each have some answers to questions. These will be in exercise 2 for A sts and exercise 1 for B sts. Allow sts time to read through all the information they have. Make sure they understand everything, and suggest that they think about each of their questions and the kind of answer each question needs, e.g. a number, a place, a time, etc. You could discuss this with the class if necessary. Sts then work in pairs and take turns to ask questions and write down the answers their partner gives them. Monitor while they are working and note down any errors with the target language. Get feedback on who managed to transfer all the information correctly.

Answers

Student A

1 It's at 11.45.
2 It's 07700900638.
3 He's from Canada.
4 I'm 39.
5 The Oak Tree Cafe.

Student B

1 It's at 6.40.
2 He's 28.
3 She's from Mexico.
4 You're in Room 48.
5 It's F-O-S-T-E-R.

3A Student A

1 Ask Student B questions to complete the information.

A *What do you have for breakfast?*
B *For breakfast, I eat …*

breakfast	lunch	dinner

2 Look at the information. Answer Student B's questions about your breakfast, lunch and dinner.

breakfast	lunch	dinner

3C Student A

1 Ask Student B questions about Magda to complete the information in the table.

A *Does Magda live in a city?*
B *Yes, she does. She lives in Gdansk.*

	Magda	Antonio

work in an office?		✗ (he / work / in a school)
live in a city?		✓
have children?		✓ (he / have / two daughters)
watch TV in the morning?		✗ (he / work)
use public transport every day?		✓
go to the gym after work?		✗ (he / make / dinner)
study in the evening?		✗ (he / watch / TV)
do sport at the weekend?		✓

2 Look at the information about Antonio. Answer Student B's questions and give extra information when you can.

B *Does Antonio work in an office?* A *No, he doesn't. He works in a school.*

4A Student A

1 Write sentences in the present simple with the adverbs of frequency in brackets. Then read them to Student B.

1 Leila / watch / films on her phone. (sometimes)
____
2 Dean / wake up / before 6.00 a.m. (often)
____
3 Paulo / read / in bed. (usually)
____
4 Marta / be / late for work. (never)
____
5 Shaun / cook / dinner for his family. (always)
____

2 Listen to Student B. Match the names in the box with the people.

Danny Nina Eric Claire Tom

1 ________

I usually finish work after 7.00 p.m.

2 ________

I'm often in the library at night.

3 ________

I always drink tea for breakfast.

4 ________

I never have a bath in the morning.

5 ________

I sometimes go to the gym on Saturday.

3A

Ask sts to read through the instructions for the activity. Explain that they each have some information about what they eat for breakfast, lunch and dinner. This will be in exercise 2 for A sts and exercise 1 for B sts. They also each have a table to complete about their partner's meals. Ask sts to look at the table about their food and make sure they know all the words. They could work in AA and BB pairs for this. Read out the example question and answer. Sts then work in AB pairs to ask and answer questions about what they eat and complete the table about their partner. They can look at each other's tables to check their answers. Monitor while they are working and note down any errors with the target language. Correct any errors you noticed in a feedback session at the end. Sts could repeat the activity with information about themselves.

3C

Ask sts to read through the instructions for the activity. Explain that they each have some information about a person. This will be in exercise 2 for A sts and exercise 1 for B sts. They also each have some incomplete information about this person. This will be in exercise 1 for A sts and exercise 2 for B sts. Allow sts time to read through all the information they have. Make sure they understand everything. Read out the example question and answer, then elicit a few more of the questions sts need to ask, e.g. *Does he/she have children? Does he/she watch TV in the morning?* Elicit some possible positive and negative answers, e.g. *Yes, he/she does./No, he/she doesn't.* Sts then work in pairs and take turns to ask questions and write down the missing information about their person. They can look at each other's sheets to check their answers. Monitor while they are working and note down any errors with the target language.

4A

Ask sts to read through the instructions for the activity. Explain that they each have some sentence prompts. These will be in exercise 1 for A sts and exercise 2 for B sts. They also each have some pictures of people, with information about them. These will be in exercise 2 for A sts and exercise 1 for B sts. Ask sts to read the sentence prompts and write their sentences. They could work in AA and BB pairs for this. Monitor and help while they are working, and make sure their sentences are completed correctly. Put sts into their AB pairs, then model the activity by asking an A student to read out their first sentence. Elicit from a B student which of their pictures it matches, and ask them to write the name next to the picture. Point out that they have the names in a wordpool box above the pictures. Sts then work in pairs to read their sentences and note down the names. Monitor while they are working and note down any errors with the target language. Correct any errors you noticed in a feedback session at the end.

4C Student A

1 Ask Student B questions about Ella. Write his/her answers.

A *Where does Ella live?* **B** *She lives in Manchester.*

Ella

Questions

- Where / live?
- What / do?
- Where / work?
- What time / get up?
- What time / finish work?
- Why / like her job?
- How / relax in the evening?
- What / do at the weekend?

2 Read Zain's profile. Listen to Student B and answer his/her questions.

Zain

Hi, I'm Zain. I live in Los Angeles. I'm a waiter at a big hotel in Hollywood. I get up at 8.00 a.m. and before work I usually go to the gym. I start work at 11.00 and I finish at 9.00 p.m. I like my job because I meet interesting people. To relax in the evening, I play the guitar. I usually work at the weekend.

4D Student A

1 You are a customer. Ask Student B for the things on your shopping list. Then ask how much each thing is. Remember to be polite.

A *Good morning. Can I have a cheese sandwich, please?*
B *Here you are.*
A *Thank you. How much is it?*
B *£1.99. Anything else?*

Shopping list
1 cheese sandwich
6 eggs
some orange juice
some coffee
some pasta
Total price = ?

2 You are a shop assistant. Serve Student B. Remember to be polite.

2x bottles water	$1.60
fish	$5.80
1x pizza (4 cheese)	$3.99
1 box salad	$1.50
1 chocolate cake	$3.85
Total	$16.74

5A Student A

1 Look at the table. Ask questions with *can* to guess which person Student B has.

A *Can she drive?*
B *Yes, she can.*

	Annie	Mona	Sara	Lucy	Hana	Kim
Can / drive?	✗	✓	✓	✓	✓	✓
Can / speak Spanish?	✗	✓	✓	✗	✓	✗
Can / play the guitar?	✓	✗	✓	✗	✓	✗
Can / cook Chinese food?	✓	✓	✗	✓	✗	✗
Can / dance salsa?	✗	✗	✓	✗	✗	✓

2 Answer Student B's questions about Mark. You can only say *Yes, he can* or *No, he can't*.

MARK

He can swim well and write computer programs.
He can't look after children, play the piano or speak French.

4C

Ask sts to read through the instructions for the activity. Explain that they each have some information about a person. This will be in exercise 2 for A sts and exercise 1 for B sts. They also each have some question prompts to ask about their partner's person. This will be in exercise 1 for A sts and exercise 2 for B sts. Allow sts time to read through all the information they have. Make sure they understand everything. Read out the example question and answer, then ask sts to prepare the questions they need to ask their partner. They could work in AA and BB pairs for this. Monitor while they are working, and make sure their questions are formed correctly. Sts then work in pairs and take turns to ask questions about their partner's person and write down the answers. They can look at each other's sheets to check their answers. Monitor while they are working and note down any errors with the target language.

4D

Ask sts to read through the instructions for the activity. Explain that they each have a shopping list of things they want to buy. This will be in exercise 1 for A sts and exercise 2 for B sts. They also each have a list of prices of the things their partner wants to buy. This will be in exercise 2 for A sts and exercise 1 for B sts. Allow sts time to read through all the information they have. Make sure they understand everything. Write a pound sign (£) and a dollar sign ($) on the board and elicit how to say the words. Read out the model conversation and elicit how sts can ask about the total price (*How much is that?*). Sts then work in pairs and take turns to role-play asking for the items on their list and then asking about the price. They can look at each other's sheets to check their answers. Monitor while they are working and note down any errors with the target language. Get feedback on how easy or difficult they found the task.

5A

Ask sts to read through the instructions for the activity. Explain that they each have some information about a person. This will be in exercise 2 for A sts and exercise 1 for B sts. They also each have information about what lots of different people can and can't do. This will be in exercise 1 for A sts and exercise 2 for B sts. Allow sts time to read through all the information they have. Make sure they understand everything. Read out the example question and answer, and elicit one or two more questions from the tables using *can*, e.g. *Can she speak Spanish? Can he look after children?* Explain to sts that they have to ask their partner questions, then decide from their answers which person they are talking about. Sts then work in pairs and take turns to ask questions about their partner's person and guess which person their partner is talking about. They can look at each other's sheets to check their answers. Monitor while they are working and note down any errors with the target language. Get feedback on who managed to guess correctly.

5C Student A

1 Look at the profiles for a website called *New Friends*. Ask and answer questions with Student B to complete the information.

A *What does Daniela think about cooking?* B *She likes it.*

☺☺ = love, ☺ = like, ☹ = not like, ☹☹ = hate

Daniela	
	cooking
	cats and dogs
	early mornings

Bill	
	walking
	housework
	books

Monica	
	going out
	cycling
	the cinema

Miguel	
☹	cleaning
☺☺	reading
☹☹	sport

Claudio	
☺	swimming
☺☺	watching films
☹	dancing

Lucy	
☺	sleeping
☺	animals
☺☺	food and drink

2 Look at the profiles again. Find the best new friend for each person.

6A Student A

Look at the picture. Ask and answer questions with Student B to find six differences.

A *Are there any hotels?*
B *Yes, there are. There are two hotels.*
A *In my picture, there's one hotel.*
B *Is there a cinema?*

6C Student A

1 Describe your picture to Student B. He/She will draw it.

A *There's a bed. Next to the bed, there's a small table.*

2 Listen to Student B and draw the room.

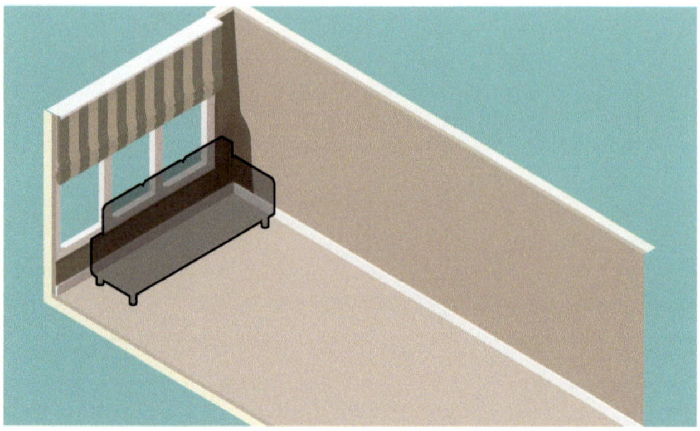

5C

Ask sts to read through the instructions for both exercises in the activity. Explain that they each have some information about what people like and don't like doing, and they each have some incomplete tables. Point out the symbols box, showing what the different symbols mean. Read out the example question and answer and ask: *What should we add to the table for Daniela?* Elicit that it should be one smiley face. Elicit another question from a B student, and the answer from an A student. Sts then work in pairs and take turns to ask and answer questions and complete their tables. They can look at each other's sheets to check their answers and discuss who would be the best new friend for each person. Monitor while they are working and note down any errors with the target language. Discuss as a class who would be the best new friend for each person and why. Correct any errors you noticed in a feedback session at the end.

Suggested answers

Monica and Claudio because they both like watching films.

Daniela and Lucy because Daniela likes cooking and Lucy loves food and drink. They also both like animals.

Bill and Miguel because they both like reading books.

6A

Ask sts to read through the instructions for the activity. Explain that they each have a picture showing places in a town, but there are six differences between their pictures. Ask sts to look at their picture and think about how to talk about what there is in the town. They could work in AA and BB pairs for this. Read out the example questions and answers. Sts then work in pairs and take turns to ask questions about their pictures and find the differences. Monitor while they are working and note down any errors with the target language. Sts can compare their pictures to check their answers. Get feedback on the differences sts noticed, and the ones they missed. Correct any errors you noticed in a feedback session at the end.

6C

Ask sts to read through the instructions for the activity. Explain that they each have a picture showing a room. This will be in exercise 1 for A sts and exercise 2 for B sts. Point out that they also have an incomplete drawing of another room. This will be in exercise 2 for A sts and exercise 1 for B sts. Read out the example sentence, then ask sts to look at their completed picture and think about how to describe it. They could work in AA and BB pairs to prepare their descriptions. Sts then work in pairs and take turns to describe their pictures for their partner to draw. Monitor while they are working and note down any errors with the target language. Sts can compare their pictures to check their answers. Get feedback on how accurately they managed to draw their partner's room, and which parts they found difficult. Correct any errors you noticed in a feedback session at the end.

6D Student A

1 Ask Student B for directions to the places in the box. Listen and mark on the map where they are. Check the information if you need to.

post office   bank   Internet café

A *Excuse me, is there a post office near here?*
B *Yes, there is. You go down Market Street ...*
A *Could you repeat that, please?*

2 Listen to Student B. Look at the map and give directions.

7A Student A

1 Ask Student B questions with *was* to match the celebrities with their jobs and where they were from.

A *Was Federico Fellini an artist?*
B *No, he wasn't.*

1 Federico Fellini	writer	South Africa
2 Janis Joplin	politician	the USA
3 Nelson Mandela	film director	Colombia
4 Greta Garbo	artist	Japan
5 Katsushika Hokusai	singer	Italy
6 Gabriel García Márquez	actor	Sweden

2 Answer Student B's questions about the celebrities. You can only say *Yes, he/she was* or *No, he/she wasn't*.

1 Frida Kahlo was an artist from Mexico.
2 Johan Cruyff was a footballer from the Netherlands.
3 Celia Cruz was a singer from Cuba.
4 Jane Austen was a writer from the UK.
5 Paco de Lucía was a musician from Spain.
6 Jawaharlal Nehru was a politician from India.

7C Student A

1 Ask Student B questions. Find one incorrect piece of information for each person.

A *Did Luke visit his grandparents last week?*
B *No, he didn't. He visited his grandparents last month.*

1 Luke / visit / his grandparents / last ~~week~~ *month*
2 Kenny / travel / to Brazil / three years ago
3 Clara / play / volleyball / yesterday
4 Debbie / cook / noodles / last night
5 Steve / work / as a teacher / in the 1980s
6 Amelia / watch / a TV show / yesterday morning

2 Listen to Student B's questions. Correct the information.

1 Zoe stayed in a hotel in the city centre last year.
2 Jim studied Spanish at university in the 1990s.
3 Antonia walked 30 kilometres yesterday.
4 Leandro watched a football match three days ago.
5 Rachel started a new job in London last month.
6 Tom finished work one hour ago.

7A London's famous houses: answers

1 Mahatma Gandhi

2 Bob Marley

3 Agatha Christie

4 Vincent van Gogh

6D

Ask sts to read through the instructions for the activity. Explain that they each have a map of a town with some places labelled and some places not labelled. Explain that they need to ask directions to find out where the other places are. Read out the example dialogue and briefly revise phrases for giving directions. Point out the place where all directions should start from. Ask sts to look at their map and think about how to give directions to the places that are already labelled. They could work in AA and BB pairs for this. Monitor while they are working, and make sure all their directions are correct. Sts then work in AB pairs to ask for directions and label the places on their map. Monitor while they are working and note down any errors with the target language. Sts can look at each other's maps to check their answers. Get feedback on how well they managed to give directions and understand their partner's directions. Correct any errors you noticed in a feedback session at the end.

7A

Ask sts to read through the instructions for the activity. Explain that they each have some information about famous people from the past. This will be in exercise 2 for A sts and exercise 1 for B sts. Explain that they have some jumbled information about some more famous people from the past. This will be in exercise 1 for A sts and exercise 2 for B sts. Allow sts time to read through all the information. Make sure they understand everything. Read out the example question and answer, and elicit a question and answer about where Federico Fellini was from. Point out to sts that when they answer, they should just answer *yes* or *no*, and shouldn't give any more information. Sts then work in pairs and take turns to ask and answer questions. Monitor while they are working and note down any errors with the target language. Sts can look at their partner's sheet to check their answers at the end. Ask who guessed all the answers first in each pair, and elicit what sts know about some of the people. Correct any errors you noticed in a feedback session at the end.

7C

Ask sts to read through the instructions for the activity. Explain that they each have some information about some people. This will be in exercise 2 for A sts and exercise 1 for B sts. Allow sts time to read through their information and make sure they understand everything. Explain that they also have some prompts to ask questions about some more people. This will be in exercise 1 for A sts and exercise 2 for B sts. Allow sts time to read through the prompts. Make sure they understand everything. Read out the example question and answer and point out that one piece of information is wrong in each question, and their partner will give them the correct information. With weaker classes you could allow sts time to prepare their questions in AA and BB pairs before they work in AB pairs. Sts then work in pairs and take turns to ask and answer questions. They can look at each other's sheets to check their answers. Monitor while they are working and note down any errors with the target language. Correct any errors you noticed in a feedback session at the end.

8A Student A

1 Ask Student B questions to find out what Lola did yesterday.

A *Where did Lola go?*
B *She went to her dad's birthday party.*

Lola

- Where / go?
- What time / leave / the house?
- she / take / the bus?
- What / wear?
- What / buy / for her dad?
- she / have / a good time?
- Where / sleep / last night?

2 Read the information and answer Student B's questions about what Mateo did yesterday.

Mateo

- He / go / Rome
- He / fly
- He / take / taxi to the airport
- His flight / leave at 11.00 a.m.
- He / go / with friends
- He / sleep / on a plane for 20 minutes
- He / have / a good journey

8C Student A

1 Look at the picture for one minute. Then close your book and answer Student B's questions.

2 Give Student B one minute to look at his/her picture. Ask him/her questions with *Was/Were there a/an/any ...?* and the words in the box. If he/she answers *Yes, there were*, ask *How many were there?*

boats	hospital	cars	flowers
birds	shops	beach	river

A *Were there any boats?* B *Yes, there were.*
A *How many were there?* B *There was one boat.*

8D Student A

1 Read the situation in the box, then look at the flowchart. You are the receptionist. Student B calls you. Have the conversation.

A *Hello, Green Lane Medical Centre. Jorge speaking. How can I help you?*
B *Hello, my name's Anna Lopez. I'd like to see the doctor.*

You work at the Green Lane Medical Centre. Answer the phone. Ask the person what the problem is.

Receptionist	Patient/Customer
Answer the phone. Give the name of the medical centre/sports centre and your name. →	Introduce yourself and say why you are calling.
← Ask more detailed questions. →	Answer.
← Ask for the caller's contact details. →	Answer.
← Finish the call.	

2 Read the situation in the box, then look at the flowchart again. You are the customer. Call Student B and have the conversation.

You want to join a sports centre. You're interested in swimming and tennis. Your phone number is 07700 900382.

8A

Ask sts to read through the instructions for the activity. Explain that they each have some information about what someone did yesterday. This will be in exercise 2 for A sts and exercise 1 for B sts. Allow sts time to read through their information and make sure they understand everything. Explain to sts that they also have some question prompts to ask questions about another person. This will be in exercise 1 for A sts and exercise 2 for B sts. Allow sts time to read through the prompts and make sure they understand everything. Read out the example question and answer and point out that the question and answer use the past simple tense. Allow sts time to prepare their questions and answers in the past simple. They could work in AA and BB pairs for this. Monitor while they are working, and make sure they can form their sentences and questions correctly. Sts then work in pairs and take turns to ask and answer questions, and note down the answers. They can look at each other's sheets to check their answers. Monitor while they are working and note down any errors with the target language. Correct any errors you noticed in a feedback session at the end.

8C

Ask sts to read through the instructions for the activity. Explain that this activity will test their memory. Explain that they each have a picture which they need to try to memorize and then answer questions on. Read out the example questions and answers and point out the form of the questions using *Was there ...? and Were there ...?* Sts then take turns to look at their picture and try to answer their partner's questions on it. Monitor while they are working and note down any errors with the target language. Sts can look at their picture again to see how well they remembered. Get feedback on who had the best memory in each pair. Correct any errors you noticed in a feedback session at the end.

8D

Ask sts to read through the instructions for the activity and the two situations. Explain that they are going to role-play some conversations between a receptionist and a patient or customer. Put sts into AA and BB pairs and allow them time to read through all their prompts and think about what they should say, and what questions they should ask in each of their role-plays. Monitor and help while they are working, and make sure they feel confident about the role-plays. Sts then work in AB pairs to role-play their conversations. You could get them to sit back to back, to create the feeling that they are talking on the phone. Monitor while they are working and note down any errors with the target language. Get feedback on which parts of the role-play sts found difficult. They could repeat the activity with a different partner if they need more practice. Correct any errors you noticed in a feedback session at the end.

9C Student A

Ask and answer the question *How often do/does ...?* with Student B to complete the table.

A *How often do Jon and Andy go to the cinema?*
B *They go to the cinema three or four times a year.*

Laura	have dinner in a restaurant	twice a month
Jon and Andy	go to the cinema	
Carlota	shop online	once or twice a week
Ahmed	ride a motorbike	
Hope and Sara	check their emails	four or five times a day
Igor	read a new book	
Luisa and Raul	go swimming	every week
Yannis	go on holiday	

10A Student A

Look at your diary. Try to find a time when you can meet Student B. Ask and answer the question *What are you doing on ...?* for the different days.

A *What are you doing on Monday morning?*
B *I'm going to the gym. What about Monday afternoon?*

	Monday	Tuesday	Wednesday	Thursday	Friday
Morning			travel to the city		
Afternoon	see doctor	have lunch with parents	visit National Museum		
Evening	watch film at cinema		stay with friends		have dinner with Carl

10C Student A

Ask Student B questions about his/her hobby in the correct tense. Write down his/her answers. Then guess what the hobby is.

A *How often do you do your hobby?*
B *I do it twice a week.*

	Student B's hobby	Your hobby: rock climbing

1 How often / you / do / your hobby?		Every weekend.
2 When / you / start?		When I was 14.
3 it / be / expensive?		No, it isn't.
4 it / be / dangerous?		It can be.
5 you / play / it in a team?		No, but I always go with another person.
6 How many people / be there / in your team?		–
7 Where / you / do / your hobby?		Sometimes at a sports centre, sometimes in the mountains.
8 you / do / your hobby next weekend?		Yes, I'm driving to the beach on Friday night.

9A

(NB: The activity for Student A is on page 150 in the Student Book.)

Ask sts to read through the instructions for the activity. Explain that they each have a picture of a market, but there are six differences between their pictures. Ask sts to look at their picture and think about how to describe the people and say what they are doing. Sts could work in AA and BB pairs for this. Read out the example questions and answers. Sts then work in pairs and take turns to describe their pictures and find the differences. Monitor while they are working and note down any errors with the target language. Sts can compare their pictures to check their answers. Get feedback on the differences sts noticed, and the ones they missed. Correct any errors you noticed in a feedback session at the end.

9C

Ask sts to read through the instructions for the activity. Explain that they each have some information about how often people do different activities, but they also each have some information missing. Explain that they are going to ask their partner for the missing information. Allow sts time to read through all the information. Make sure they understand everything. Read out the example question and answer, and elicit another example using a singular form: *How often does …?* Sts then work in pairs and take turns to ask and answer the questions, and complete their information. Sts can look at each other's sheets to check their answers. Monitor while they are working and note down any errors with the target language. Elicit all the completed sentences, then correct any errors you noticed in a feedback session at the end. Sts could then ask and answer questions about how often they do the activities.

10A

Ask sts to read through the instructions for the activity. Explain that they each have a diary to show when they are doing things and when they are free. Explain that their partner also has some activities and some free time in their diary, and they must ask and answer questions to find out when they are both free so they can meet. Read out the example question and answer and elicit that they use the present continuous tense for future plans. Sts then work in pairs to ask and answer questions about what they are doing at different times, and agree a time to meet. Monitor while they are working and note down any errors with the target language. Ask some pairs to tell the class how quickly they agreed a time. As an extension, sts could complete the diary with seven activities using their own ideas. They could then work with a new partner and repeat the activity, to see if they can find a time to meet.

10C

Ask sts to read through the instructions for the activity. Explain that they each have some information about their own hobby, and they need to complete the information about their partner's hobby. Allow sts time to read through the question prompts and the information about their hobby, and make sure they understand everything. Read out the example question and answer and point out that the questions and answers use different tenses, so sts need to think about which tense to use for each question. Allow sts time to prepare the questions. You could elicit all the questions from the class if necessary, and allow sts time to write the completed questions. Sts then work in pairs to ask and answer questions and complete the information. They can look at each other's sheets to check their answers. Monitor while they are working and note down any errors with the target language. Correct any errors you noticed in a feedback session at the end.

10D

(NB: The activity for both Student A and Student B is on page 150 in the Student Book.)

Ask sts to read through the instructions for the activity. Explain that they are going to tell each other some information about themselves, and respond with interest to what their partner tells them. Allow sts time to read through the sentence beginnings and complete them with information about themselves. Point out that they can invent the information if they prefer. Read through the words in the box with the class and model pronunciation to sound interested and enthusiastic. Read out the example sentence and response. Sts then work in pairs to ask and exchange information and respond with interest. Monitor while they are working and note down any errors with the target language. Encourage sts to use intonation to sound interested and enthusiastic. Correct any errors you noticed in a feedback session at the end.

Hello Student B

1 Listen to Student A's airport codes. Tell him/her the correct city for the letters.

Hong Kong Los Angeles Mexico City London Istanbul

A *What's LHR?*
B *I think it's London.*
A *How do you spell that?*
B *L-O-N-D-O-N.*

2 Look at the labels. Ask Student A for the name of the city.

FINAL DEST. JFK
1 ______

FINAL DEST. BCN
2 ______

FINAL DEST. CPT
3 ______

FINAL DEST. DEL
4 ______

FINAL DEST. AMS
5 ______

1A Student B

1 Ask Student A the questions and write down his/her answers.

1 What's your name?
______

2 Where are you from?
______

3 What's your phone number?
______

2 You are Saori. Answer Student A's questions with the information.

A *What's your name?*
B *I'm Saori Arakawa.*
A *How do you spell that?*
B *S-A-O-R-I ...*

Name:	Saori Arakawa
Nationality:	Japanese
Phone:	81 90 1790 1357

1C Student B

1 Look at the information about the Antarctic Zebras. Answer Student A's questions.

The Antarctic Zebras are from Liverpool, in the UK.

	age	job
Bev	19	student
Angela	24	IT worker
Sammy	25	tour guide

2 Now ask Student A questions about the Rocking Stones to complete the information.

Where are they from? *How old is Kevin?* *What is his job?*

The Rocking Stones are from ______ .

	age	job
Kevin		
Rob		
Nick		

2A Students A and B

Look at the picture. In pairs, discuss if you were right or wrong.

A *This is a pen.*
B *You're right.*

2C Student B

Ask and answer questions with Student A to complete David and Victoria Beckham's family tree.

B *What's Victoria's mother's name?*
A *Her name is ....*

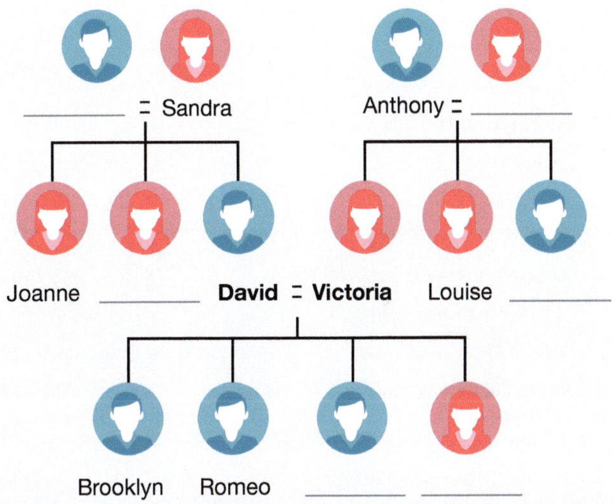

2D Student B

1 Answer Student A's questions with the answers in the box.

I'm 39. It's 07700 900638. The Oak Tree Café. It's at 11.45. He's from Canada.

2 Ask Student A the questions and write down the answers. Remember to be polite.

B *Excuse me, what time's the flight to Los Angeles, please?*
A *It's at twenty to seven.*
B *Thanks.*

1 What time's the flight to Los Angeles? _____
2 How old is the teacher? _____
3 Where's María from? _____
4 What room am I in? _____
5 How do you spell your surname? _____

3A Student B

1 Look at the information. Answer Student A's questions about your breakfast, lunch and dinner.

breakfast	lunch	dinner

2 Ask Student A questions to complete the information.

B *What do you have for breakfast?*
A *For breakfast, I eat ...*

breakfast	lunch	dinner

3C Student B

1 Look at the information about Magda. Answer Student A's questions and give extra information when you can.

A *Does Magda live in a city?*
B *Yes, she does. She lives in Gdansk.*

	Magda	Antonio

work in an office?	✓	
live in a city?	✓ (she / live / in Gdansk)	
have children?	✗ (she / have / two cats)	
watch TV in the morning?	✗	
use public transport every day?	✗ (she / walk / to work)	
go to the gym after work?	✓	
study in the evening?	✓ (she / study / English)	
do sport at the weekend?	✗ (she / make / cakes)	

2 Ask Student A questions about Antonio to complete the information in the table.

B *Does Antonio work in an office?* A *No, he doesn't. He works in a school.*

4A Student B

1 Listen to Student A. Match the names in the box with the people.

Marta Shaun Leila Dean Paulo

1 ________

I often wake up before 6.00 a.m.

2 ________

I'm never late for work.

3 ________

I usually read in bed.

4 ________

I sometimes watch films on my phone.

5 ________

I always cook dinner for my family.

2 Make sentences in the present simple with the adverbs of frequency in brackets. Then read them to Student A.

1 Claire / drink / tea for breakfast. (always)
____

2 Tom / go / to the gym on Saturday. (sometimes)
____

3 Eric / have / a bath in the morning. (never)
____

4 Danny / be / in the library at night. (often)
____

5 Nina / finish / work after 7.00 p.m. (usually)
____

4C Student B

1 Read Ella's profile. Listen to Student A and answer his/her questions.

A *Where does Ella live?* B *She lives in Manchester.*

Ella

Hi, I'm Ella. I live in Manchester. I'm a teacher at a school in the city centre. I usually get up at 6.00 a.m. I start work at 8.30 and I finish at 5.00 p.m. I love my job because I like children. To relax in the evening, I watch TV with my family. At the weekend, I do a lot of sport.

2 Ask Student A questions about Zain. Write his/her answers.

Zain

Questions

Where / live?
What / do?
Where / work?
What time / get up?
What time / finish work?
Why / like his job?
How / relax in the evening?
What / do at the weekend?

4D Student B

1 You are a shop assistant. Serve Student A. Remember to be polite.

A *Good morning. Can I have a cheese sandwich, please?*
B *Here you are.*
A *Thank you. How much is it?*
B *£1.99. Anything else?*

1 sandwich (cheese)	£1.99
6 eggs	£2.50
orange juice	£1.80
coffee	£3.29
pasta	£1.50
Total	£11.08

2 You are a customer. Ask Student A for the things on your shopping list. Then ask how much each thing is. Remember to be polite.

Shopping list
2 bottles of water
some fish
1 four-cheese pizza
1 box of salad
1 chocolate cake
Total price = ?

5A Student B

1 Answer Student A's questions about Hana. You can only say *Yes, she can* or *No, she can't*.

A *Can she drive?*
B *Yes, she can.*

HANA

She can drive, speak Spanish and play the guitar.
She can't cook Chinese food or dance salsa.

2 Look at the table. Ask questions with *can* to guess which person Student A has.

	 Sergio	 Tom	 Mark	 Andy	 Pete	 Dennis
Can / look after children?	✓	✗	✗	✗	✓	✗
Can / swim well?	✗	✓	✓	✗	✓	✓
Can / play the piano?	✗	✗	✗	✗	✓	✗
Can / speak French?	✓	✓	✗	✓	✗	✗
Can / write computer programs?	✗	✗	✓	✗	✓	✗

5C Student B

1 Look at the profiles for a website called *New Friends*. Ask and answer questions with Student A to complete the information.

B *What does Miguel think about cleaning?* A *He doesn't like it.*

☺☺ = love, ☺ = like, ☹ = not like, ☹☹ = hate

Daniela	
☺	cooking
☺☺	cats and dogs
☹	early mornings

Bill	
☹	walking
☹☹	housework
☺	books

Monica	
☹	going out
☹	cycling
☺	the cinema

Miguel	
	cleaning
	reading
	sport

Claudio	
	swimming
	watching films
	dancing

Lucy	
	sleeping
	animals
	food and drink

2 Look at the profiles again. Find the best new friend for each person.

6A Student B

Look at the picture. Ask and answer questions with Student A to find six differences.

B *Are there any hotels?*
A *Yes, there are. There's one hotel.*
B *In my picture, there are two hotels.*
A *Is there a cinema?*

6C Student B

1 Listen to Student A and draw the room.

A *There's a bed. Next to the bed, there's a small table.*

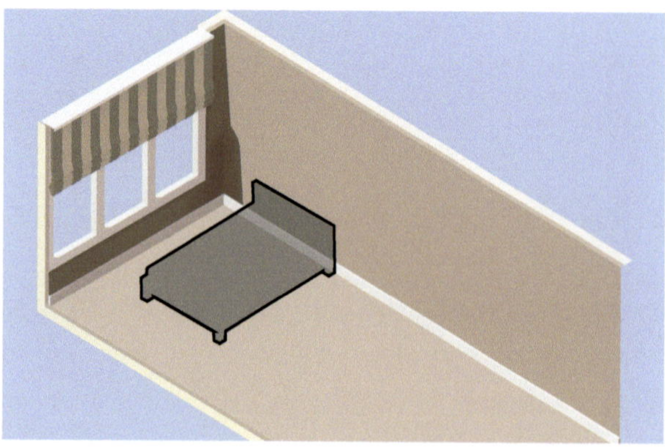

2 Describe your picture to Student A. He/She will draw it.

B *There's a sofa in front of the window.*

6D Student B

1 Listen to Student A. Look at the map and give directions.

A *Excuse me, is there a post office near here?*
B *Yes, there is. You go down Market Street ...*
A *Could you repeat that, please?*

2 Ask Student A for directions to the places in the box. Listen and mark on the map where they are. Check the information if you need to.

restaurant
tourist information office
supermarket

7A Student B

1 Answer Student A's questions about the celebrities. You can only say *Yes, he/she was* or *No, he/she wasn't.*

A *Was Federico Fellini an artist?*
B *No, he wasn't.*

1 Federico Fellini was a film director from Italy.
2 Janis Joplin was a singer from the USA.
3 Nelson Mandela was a politician from South Africa.
4 Greta Garbo was an actor from Sweden.
5 Katsushika Hokusai was an artist from Japan.
6 Gabriel García Márquez was a writer from Colombia.

2 Ask Student A questions with *was* to match the celebrities with their jobs and where they were from.

1 Frida Kahlo	footballer	India
2 Johan Cruyff	musician	Spain
3 Celia Cruz	politician	Mexico
4 Jane Austen	singer	the Netherlands
5 Paco de Lucía	writer	Cuba
6 Jawaharlal Nehru	artist	the UK

7C Student B

1 Listen to Student A's questions. Correct the information.

A *Did Luke visit his grandparents last week?*
B *No, he didn't. He visited his grandparents last month.*

1 Luke visited his grandparents last month.
2 Kenny travelled to Brazil six years ago.
3 Clara played basketball yesterday.
4 Debbie cooked rice last night.
5 Steve worked as a teacher in the 1970s.
6 Amelia watched a film yesterday morning.

2 Ask Student A questions. Find one incorrect piece of information for each person.

1 Zoe / stay / in a hotel near the beach / last year
2 Jim / study / German at university / in the 1990s
3 Antonia / walk / 30 kilometres / two days ago
4 Leandro / watch / a football match / last week
5 Rachel / start / a new job in Paris / last month
6 Tom / finish / work / half an hour ago

9C Questionnaire results

Mostly as: You don't like shopping and you hate shopping centres. You prefer to spend money on other things. What do you do and how often do you do it?

Mostly bs: You like shopping, but you also like doing other things. A shopping centre is a good place to meet friends. How often do you go there?

Mostly cs: You love shopping – it's your life. You go shopping two or three times a week and you shop online almost every day ... but do you really need to buy all those things?

8A Student B

1 Read the information and answer Student A's questions about what Lola did yesterday.

A *Where did Lola go?* B *She went to her dad's birthday party.*

Lola

She / go / her dad's birthday party
She / leave / the house at 7.00 p.m.
She / take / the train
She / wear / a new dress
She / buy / a book
She / have / a good time
She / sleep / on her dad's sofa

2 Ask Student A questions to find out what Mateo did yesterday.

Mateo

Where / he / go?
he / go / by train?
he / take / a taxi to the airport?
what time / his flight / leave?
he / go / with friends?
he / sleep / on the plane?
he / have / a good journey?

8C Student B

1 Give Student A one minute to look at his/her picture. Ask him/her questions with *Was/Were there a/an/any ...?* and the words in the box. If he/she answers *Yes, there were*, ask *How many were there?*

people clouds forest trees
bus houses cars river

B *Were there any people?* A *Yes, there were.*
B *How many were there?* A *There were four people.*

2 Look at the picture for one minute. Then close your book and answer Student A's questions.

8D Student B

1 Read the situation in the box, then look at the flowchart. You are the patient. Call Student A and have the conversation.

A *Hello, Green Lane Medical Centre. Jorge speaking. How can I help you?*
B *Hello, my name's Anna Lopez. I'd like to see the doctor.*

You don't feel well and want to see the doctor. Your head hurts. Your phone number is 01632 960785.

Receptionist	Patient/Customer
Answer the phone. Give the name of the medical centre/sports centre and your name.	Introduce yourself and say why you are calling.
Ask more detailed questions.	Answer.
Ask for the caller's contact details.	Answer.
Finish the call.	

2 Read the situation in the box, then look at the flowchart again. You are the receptionist. Student A calls you. Have the conversation.

You work at a sports centre called The Fitness Factory. Answer the phone. Ask the person what sports they want to do.

9A Student B

Look at the picture. Describe James, Grace and Kara to Student A. Try to find six differences.

B *Grace is wearing a red dress and boots.*
A *In my picture, she's wearing shoes.*

9C Student B

Ask and answer the question *How often do/does ...?* with Student A to complete the table.

B *How often does Laura have dinner in a restaurant?*
A *She has dinner in a restaurant twice a month.*

Laura	have dinner in a restaurant	
Jon and Andy	go to the cinema	three or four times a year
Carlota	shop online	
Ahmed	ride a motorbike	every day
Hope and Sara	check their emails	
Igor	read a new book	four or five times a year
Luisa and Raul	go swimming	
Yannis	go on holiday	once a year

10A Student B

Look at your diary. Try to find a time when you can meet Student A. Ask and answer the question *What are you doing on ...?* for the different days.

A *What are you doing on Monday morning?*
B *I'm going to the gym. What about Monday afternoon?*

	Monday	Tuesday	Wednesday	Thursday	Friday
Morning	go to the gym	meet Simon for coffee		take bus to city	see dentist
Afternoon				visit art gallery	
Evening		go to a concert		stay in hotel	

9A Student A

Look at the picture. Describe Aziz, Oscar and Petra to Student B. Try to find six differences.

A *Aziz is looking at a white hat.*
B *In my picture, he's looking at some sunglasses.*

10C Student B

Ask Student A questions about his/her hobby in the correct tense. Write down his/her answers. Then guess what the hobby is.

B *How often do you do your hobby?*
A *I do it every weekend.*

	Student A's hobby	Your hobby: basketball

1 How often / you / do / your hobby?		Twice a week.
2 When / you / start?		Last year.
3 it / be / expensive?		No, it isn't.
4 it / be / dangerous?		No, it isn't.
5 you / play / it in a team?		Yes, I do.
6 How many people / be there / in your team?		12 (but only five play at the same time).
7 Where / you / do / your hobby?		At the sports centre.
8 you / do / your hobby next weekend?		Yes, we're going to Los Angeles for a match.

10D Students A and B

1 Complete the sentences. You can use real information or invent it.

About me
In my free time, I often ______.
My favourite type of music is ______.
Last weekend
I went shopping on Saturday and I bought ______ ______.
Last weekend, I ______.

My holidays
Last summer, I went to ______.
When I'm on holiday, I usually ______.
My plans
Next weekend, I'm meeting ______.
For my next holiday, I'm ______.

2 Read your sentences in pairs. Respond with interest using the words in the box.

Oh really?	That's interesting.	That sounds good.	Wow, that's amazing!	Cool!	Great!

A *In my free time, I often go skiing in the mountains.*
B *Wow, that's amazing!*

AUDIO/VIDEO TRACK LISTING

Tracks in red are for *Learning Curve* (available as video and audio)

CD 1 Units 1–2

UNIT 1

CD track	Audio track	Content
1	1.1	page 4 Exercise 1
2	1.2	page 4 Exercise 3A
3	1.3	page 4 Exercise 4B
4	1.4	page 96 Grammar Practice
5	1.5	page 5 Exercise 5A
6	1.6	page 5 Exercise 7
7	1.7	page 106 Vocabulary Practice
8	1.8	page 5 Exercise 8
9	1.9	page 5 Exercise 9
10	1.10	page 6 Exercise 1B
11	1.11	page 6 Exercise 2A
12	1.12	page 107 Vocabulary Practice
13	1.13	page 6 Exercise 4
14	1.14	page 96 Grammar Practice
15	1.15	page 7 Exercise 6A
16	1.16	page 7 Exercise 6B
17	1.17	page 7 Exercise 8A
18	1.18	page 7 Exercise 8B
19	1.19	page 108 Vocabulary Practice
20	1.20	page 8 Exercise 2A
21	1.21	page 8 Exercise 3 and 4
22	1.22	page 9 Exercise 5 and 6
23	1.23	page 9 Exercise 8
24	1.24	page 9 Exercise 9
25	1.25	page 9 Exercise 10
26	1.26	page 111 Vocabulary Practice
27	1.27	page 10 Exercise 2B
28	1.28	page 11 Exercise 4
29	1.29	page 96 Grammar Practice
30	1.30	page 11 Exercise 6A
31	1.31	page 11 Exercise 6B
32	1.32	page 109 Vocabulary Practice
33	1.33	page 12 Exercise 2B

UNIT 2

CD track	Audio track	Content
34	2.1	page 14 Exercise 1
35	2.2	page 110 Vocabulary Practice
36	2.3	page 97 Grammar Practice
37	2.4	page 97 Grammar Practice
38	2.5	page 15 Exercise 6A
39	2.6	page 15 Exercise 6B
40	2.7	page 15 Exercise 8A and B
41	2.8	page 110 Vocabulary Practice
42	2.9	page 16 Exercise 6A
43	2.10	page 111 Vocabulary Practice
44	2.11	page 97 Grammar Practice
45	2.12	page 19 Exercise 7A
46	2.13	page 19 Exercise 7B
47	2.14	page 19 Exercise 8
48	2.15	page 20 Exercise 1A
49	2.16	page 20 Exercise 1B
50	2.17	page 20 Exercise 2A and B
51	2.18	page 21 Exercise 4 and 5A
52	2.19	page 21 Exercise 6

CD 2 Units 3–5

UNIT 3

CD track	Audio track	Content
1	3.1	page 24 Exercise 1
2	3.2	page 112 Vocabulary Practice
3	3.3	page 98 Grammar Practice
4	3.4	page 25 Exercise 6
5	3.5	page 25 Exercise 7A
6	3.6	page 25 Exercise 8A
7	3.7	page 116 Vocabulary Practice
8	3.8	page 26 Exercise 4A and B
9	3.9	page 27 Exercise 5 and 6
10	3.10	page 27 Exercise 8
11	3.11	page 27 Exercise 9
12	3.12	page 113 Vocabulary Practice
13	3.13	page 28 Exercise 3
14	3.14	page 98 Grammar Practice
15	3.15	page 29 Exercise 6A
16	3.16	page 29 Exercise 6B
17	3.17	page 29 Exercise 7

UNIT 4

CD track	Audio track	Content
18	4.1	page 32 Exercise 1A
19	4.2	page 114 Vocabulary Practice
20	4.3	page 99 Grammar Practice
21	4.4	page 33 Exercise 5A
22	4.5	page 33 Exercise 7B
23	4.6	page 115 Vocabulary Practice
24	4.7	page 116 Vocabulary Practice
25	4.8	page 99 Grammar Practice
26	4.9	page 99 Grammar Practice
27	4.10	page 37 Exercise 5
28	4.11	page 37 Exercise 6A
29	4.12	page 37 Exercise 6B
30	4.13	page 38 Exercise 1A
31	4.14	page 38 Exercise 3
32	4.15	page 38 Exercise 4 and 5
33	4.16	page 39 Exercise 6B
34	4.17	page 39 Exercise 7
35	4.18	page 39 Exercise 8

UNIT 5

CD track	Audio track	Content
36	5.1	page 117 Vocabulary Practice
37	5.2	page 42 Exercise 3 and 4A
38	5.3	page 100 Grammar Practice
39	5.4	page 43 Exercise 5
40	5.5	page 43 Exercise 6A
41	5.6	page 43 Exercise 7B
42	5.7	page 43 Exercise 8
43	5.8	page 118 Vocabulary Practice
44	5.9	page 44 Exercise 3 and 4
45	5.10	page 45 Exercise 5 and 6
46	5.11	page 45 Exercise 7
47	5.12	page 45 Exercise 8A and B
48	5.13	page 119 Vocabulary Practice
49	5.14	page 100 Grammar Practice
50	5.15	page 47 Exercise 5A
51	5.16	page 47 Exercise 5B
52	5.17	page 47 Exercise 6

CD 3 Units 6–8

UNIT 6

CD track	Audio track	Content
1	6.1	page 120 Vocabulary Practice
2	6.2	page 101 Grammar Practice
3	6.3	page 51 Exercise 6
4	6.4	page 51 Exercise 7A
5	6.5	page 51 Exercise 7B
6	6.6	page 51 Exercise 8A and B
7	6.7	page 121 Vocabulary Practice
8	6.8	page 122 Vocabulary Practice
9	6.9	page 101 Grammar Practice
10	6.10	page 55 Exercise 6
11	6.11	page 55 Exercise 7B
12	6.12	page 55 Exercise 8A and B
13	6.13	page 56 Exercise 2 and 3
14	6.14	page 56 Exercise 4B
15	6.15	page 57 Exercise 5 and 6
16	6.16	page 57 Exercise 7A and B

UNIT 7

CD track	Audio track	Content
17	7.1	page 123 Vocabulary Practice
18	7.2	page 102 Grammar Practice
19	7.3	page 61 Exercise 5A
20	7.4	page 61 Exercise 6
21	7.5	page 124 Vocabulary Practice
22	7.6	page 124 Vocabulary Practice
23	7.7	page 62 Exercise 5 and 6
24	7.8	page 63 Exercise 7 and 8
25	7.9	page 63 Exercise 10
26	7.10	page 63 Exercise 11
27	7.11	page 64 Exercise 3
28	7.12	page 102 Grammar Practice
29	7.13	page 65 Exercise 6
30	7.14	page 124 Vocabulary Practice
31	7.15	page 65 Exercise 8A
32	7.16	page 65 Exercise 8B

UNIT 8

CD track	Audio track	Content
33	8.1	page 125 Vocabulary Practice
34	8.2	page 103 Grammar Practice
35	8.3	page 69 Exercise 7A
36	8.4	page 69 Exercise 7B
37	8.5	page 69 Exercise 8A
38	8.6	page 126 Vocabulary Practice
39	8.7	page 127 Vocabulary Practice
40	8.8	page 72 Exercise 4 and 5A
41	8.9	page 103 Grammar Practice
42	8.10	page 73 Exercise 7A
43	8.11	page 73 Exercise 7B
44	8.12	page 74 Exercise 2A and B
45	8.13	page 74 Exercise 3
46	8.14	page 75 Exercise 5A and B
47	8.15	page 75 Exercise 6
48	8.16	page 75 Exercise 7

CD 4 Units 9–10

UNIT 9

CD track	Audio track	Content
1	9.1	page 128 Vocabulary Practice
2	9.2	page 78 Exercise 4 and 5A
3	9.3	page 104 Grammar Practice
4	9.4	page 79 Exercise 7A
5	9.5	page 79 Exercise 7B
6	9.6	page 129 Vocabulary Practice
7	9.7	page 80 Exercise 2
8	9.8	page 80 Exercise 3B and 4
9	9.9	page 81 Exercise 6 and 7
10	9.10	page 81 Exercise 9
11	9.11	page 81 Exercise 10
12	9.12	page 130 Vocabulary Practice
13	9.13	page 104 Grammar Practice
14	9.14	page 83 Exercise 4A
15	9.15	page 83 Exercise 4B

UNIT 10

CD track	Audio track	Content
16	10.1	page 131 Vocabulary Practice
17	10.2	page 86 Exercise 2
18	10.3	page 105 Grammar Practice
19	10.4	page 105 Grammar Practice
20	10.5	page 87 Exercise 5A
21	10.6	page 87 Exercise 5B
22	10.7	page 87 Exercise 7A and B
23	10.8	page 88 Exercise 1
24	10.9	page 132 Vocabulary Practice
25	10.10	page 133 Vocabulary Practice
26	10.11	page 90 Exercise 3B and 4A
27	10.12	page 105 Grammar Practice
28	10.13	page 105 Grammar Practice
29	10.14	page 91 Exercise 6A
30	10.15	page 91 Exercise 6B
31	10.16	page 91 Exercise 7A and B
32	10.17	page 92 Exercise 2A and B
33	10.18	page 92 Exercise 3
34	10.19	page 93 Exercise 5A and B
35	10.20	page 93 Exercise 6
36	10.21	page 93 Exercise 7A
37	10.22	page 93 Exercise 7B

UNIT 1

1.9 page 5, exercise 9

R = Receptionist, K = Kenan, C = Camila, H = Hiro

1

R: Good morning. Welcome to ABC School of English. What's your name, please?
K: My name's Kenan Zorlu.
R: How do you spell that?
K: Kenan – K-E-N-A-N, Zorlu – Z-O-R-L-U.
R: Thank you.

2

C: Hello.
R: Good morning. What's your name?
C: I'm Camila Bernardi.
R: How do you spell that, please?
C: Camila– C-A-M-I-L-A, Bernardi – B-E-R-N-A-R-D-I.
R: Thank you. Welcome to the school.

3

H: Hi, I'm a new student at the school.
R: Hello. What's your name, please?
H: Hiro Matsumoto.
R: How do you spell that?
H: Hiro-H-I-R-O, Matsumoto-M-A-T-S-U-M-O-T-O
R: Nice to meet you, Hiro.

1.13 page 6, exercise 4

The Countries Quiz!

1 What nationality is Lewis Hamilton?
a) He's British. He's from Stevenage in the UK.

2 Where is Mount Fuji?
b) It's in Japan.

3 Is this elephant from India or Africa?
a) It's from India. Its ears are small.

4 Is Elsa Pataky Russian?
b) No, she isn't. She's Spanish.

5 Which sentence is correct?
b) Sydney isn't the capital of Australia. Canberra is the capital of Australia.

6 Is *ceviche* Mexican or Peruvian?
b) It's Peruvian.

7 Where is the Bosphorus?
a) It's in Turkey.

8 What nationality is Paulo Coelho?
b) He's Brazilian. He's from Rio de Janeiro in Brazil.

1.18 page 7, exercise 8B

1

A: What's the international dialling code for China?
B: It's 8 6.

2

A: What's the dialling code for Colombia?
B: It's 5 7.

3

A: Is the dialling code for India 1 9?
B: No it isn't. The code is 9 1.

4

A: What's the dialling code for Mexico?
B: It's 5 2.

5

A: Is the dialling code for Spain 4 4?
B: No, that's the code for the UK. The code for Spain is 3 4.

6

A: Is the international dialling code for Turkey 9 0?
B: Yes, it is. It's 9 0.

1.21 page 8, exercises 3 and 4

Learning Curve

C = Cameraman, S = Simon, E = Ethan, P = Penny, K = Kate

C: Action!
S: Hello and welcome! I'm Simon Collins. This is *Learning Curve* and I'm one of the hosts in the UK. *Learning Curve* is an English language internet programme about interesting things from around the world. Our studios are in London, in the UK, and New York City in the US. *Learning Curve* is for everyone. This is the *Learning Curve* team! Meet Ethan Moore! He's a co-host at *Learning Curve* in New York. He's American and he's from Connecticut. It's near New York.
E: Hello! I'm Ethan!
S: Ethan's co-host in New York is Penny Abernathy. Penny's family is from England and Argentina. Hello, Penny! Are you there?
P: Hello, Simon! I'm here. How are you? You're right, I'm English and Argentinian.
S: Nice to see you. Penny, how's New York?
P: It's great here! Where's Kate?
S: Oh, yes, Kate. Our new co-host. She's on the street. This is our receptionist, Marina. She's at our office in London. Marina is Russian. She's from Moscow. Today's show is about people, places and jobs. What jobs are popular in your country? In the US, jobs in technology are very popular. Mohammed is an office worker in our Technology Department at the New York studio. Hey, Mo! And Marc is an Internet Technology Specialist. Technology specialists are doctors for computers! California, in the US, is a great place for IT jobs. But IT jobs are also popular in cities like Boston, Massachusetts; Seattle, Washington; and Austin, Texas. There are also lots of technology jobs in cities like Cambridge and Glasgow here in the UK, Berlin, Germany and other countries like China and India. What about doctors for people? The statistics are 590 doctors for every 100,000 people in Cuba. Wow! And in France, Germany and Spain, it's about 330 doctors for every 100,000 people. Kate? Are you there?
K: Hi Simon!
S: Kate, er, where are you from?
K: I'm Kate McRea and I'm from the United States. I'm American. I'm from Los Angeles, California, but London is my home now.

1.22 page 9, exercises 5 and 6

Learning Curve

K = Kate, V = Viktor, Sa = Sarah, Si = Simon, P = Pedro

K: This is Viktor. Viktor, I'm from *Learning Curve*. We're an Internet show.
V: Hi, Kate. Nice to meet you. Yes, *Learning Curve* is excellent!
K: Are you familiar with the show? Are you a fan?
V: Yes, I am! A big fan!
K: Great. And Viktor, where are you from?
V: I'm from Warsaw. I'm Polish.
K: And are you a taxi driver?
V: Yes, on Saturday and Sundays, I'm a taxi driver in London. But I'm also an engineer. I'm busy!
K: Wow, two jobs! Thanks, Viktor! Have a nice day. Excuse me. Hi, I'm Kate from *Learning Curve*. What's your name?
Sa: Hi, I'm Sarah.
K: Where are you from, Sarah?
Sa: I'm from Vancouver, Canada.
K: Oh! So, are you a tourist?
Sa: Yes. I'm a tourist this week. But I'm here in London for a teachers' meeting next week. Then it's just work!
K: Oh. So, are you a teacher?
S: Yes, an English teacher.
K: Wow! That's wonderful. Thanks, Sarah.
Sa: Bye! Your show is great! My students love it!
K: Thanks!
Si: Thanks, Kate. On video chat is Pedro. Pedro, where are you from?
P: Hi, Simon! I'm from Santiago, Chile!
Si: And what's your job?
P: I'm a police officer in Alaska!
Si: Wow! How's Alaska?
P: It's cold here. But it's very nice.
Si: Thanks, Pedro! Brrr! Well, that's all for today. So, where are you from and what's your job? See you next time on *Learning Curve*!

1.25 page 9, exercise 10

1
B: Who's that?
A: That's my friend Jia. She's an office worker.
B: Great photo! Where is she?
A: She's in New York at the moment, in the USA.
B: Where is she from? Is she Chinese?
A: Yes, she is.
2
A: Who's Luis?
B: He's my friend. He's in the UK at the moment.
A: Is he a student?
B: Yes, he is. And he's a waiter, too!
A: Is he from Venezuela?
B: No, he's from Colombia.

1.27 page 10, exercise 2B

I = Interviewer, K = Kyle, M = Martin, L - Lorna

I: Hi Kyle. How old are you?
K: I'm forty-two.
K: And Martin, how old are you?
M: I'm fourteen.
I: And Lorna ... are you twenty-one?
L: No, I'm not! I'm sixty-five!

1.31 page 11, exercise 6B

1 He isn't sixteen.
2 She's eighty.
3 We aren't seventy.
4 They're nineteen.

1.33 page 12, exercise 2B

R = Receptionist, C = Customer

R: Good morning sir, how are you?
C: Hello. I'm very well, thanks. I'd like to rent a car.
R: Yes, of course. I need to complete a form for you. What's your surname?
C: It's Martin. That's M-A-R-T-I-N.
R: And what's your first name?
C: It's Louis – L-O-U-I-S.
R: Where are you from, Mr Martin?
C: I'm from France. I'm French.
R: OK, and what's your date of birth?
C: 17.06.1980
R: And, what's your address in France?
C: It's 35 Rue Pasteur, Paris.
R: How do you spell 'Pasteur', please?
C: It's P-A-S-T-E-U-R.
R: And what's your postcode?
C: It's 75009.
R: What's your email address, please?
C: It's louis.martin@mymail.com
R: And what's your phone number?
C: 33 1 80 26 58
R: Thank you. So our cars are...

UNIT 2

2.1 page 14, exercise 1

a It's a bag
b It's a camera.
c It's an umbrella.
d They're keys.
e It's a book.
f It's a watch.

2.7 page 15, exercises 8A and 8B

1
J = Jack, H = Helen
J: Hi Helen.
H: Hi Jack.
J: What's that?
H: This is my bag! It's new ... and expensive.
J: Oh, OK ... it's er ... interesting.
2
W = Woman, J = Jorge
W: Jorge, who's that over there?
J: That´s Sergio. He's a new teacher, and those are the students from the school.
W: Oh, OK.
3
M = Man, K = Karen
M: Hi, Karen. What are those?
K: These are my cameras.
M: Oh, right.
K: This is a small camera ... for holidays. That camera is new. It's Japanese. And this camera is my favourite ...

2.16 page 20, exercise 1B

1 It's eleven o'clock
2 It's quarter past three
3 It's half past twelve
4 It's twenty five to nine

2.17 page 20, exercises 2A and 2B

Learning Curve **K = Kate**

K: It's half past two in the morning! Hello? Hi, Mom. Hi, Dad. What time is it? Uh, it's half past two in the morning. Yes, asleep! That's OK. Oh, I'm fine. Just tired. Tomorrow at 5.30 p.m.? OK, that's good. Talk to you tomorrow. Bye. Oh, great. Now I'm awake! Oh, my parents are in California. It's 6.30 p.m. in Los Angeles. I'm so tired. Here are my parents. And those are my brothers. That's Mike. He's married. That's his wife, Samantha, and their daughter, Annie. And that's Tom. And this is my sister, Caroline. She's in Boston. That's her boyfriend, Raj. I'm so tired. Four and a half more hours until I get up for work! Good night! It's 7.00 a.m. It's time for a shower and breakfast, then, my new job! Today is day two at *Learning Curve*. So exciting! Here's my new photo ID card. These are my keys to the studio. And my tablet. OK. In the wallet ... this credit card, not that credit card. OK, time to go. Sunglasses? No, not today! An umbrella? Yes, that's good.

2.18 page 21, exercises 4 and 5A

Learning Curve **K = Kate, M1 = Man 1, W1 = Woman 1, W2 = Woman 2, M2 = Man 2, S = Simon**

M1: Excuse me. What time's the James Bond film?
K: Sorry? A James Bond film? Oh, wow! Um, the time is here. 11.00 a.m., 12.30, and one o'clock in the afternoon.
M1: Oh, good! Half past twelve! Thank you!
K: OK.
W1: Excuse me. What time is it, please?
K: It's 8.15. Quarter past.
W1: Oh! I'm late. Thank you very much. Thank you.
W2: Sorry, what time is the 67 bus?
K: Um ... next bus ... 8.45. It's in ten minutes.
W2: Oh, 8.45, not 8.35. Ten minutes. OK. Thanks. Wait. There's the bus. Where's the 67 bus?
K: It's in ten minutes.
W2: Oh, OK. Thanks.
M2: Oh, football! Manchester United versus Liverpool. When's the match?
K: This Saturday!
M2: What time?
K: Uh, 3.00 p.m.! It's exciting!
M2: Yeah, it is! Thank you.
S: Oh, Kate, you're here!
K: Yes.
S: Is that coffee?
K: Yes! Now it's cold ... blaaah.
S: No worries.
K: Oh, thank you! It's hot!
S: Two minutes. No waiting!
K: Mmm. That is good coffee! Thanks.
S: You're welcome. OK. What time is it?
K: Another question! It's nine o'clock, Simon! Time for work!

UNIT 3

3.8 page 26, exercises 4A and 4B

Learning Curve E = Ethan

E: It's 9.30. Time for our show! Do you drink coffee or tea? I have a coffee here from the café next door. Cafés are good places to meet friends and eat or drink. I go to my favourite café every morning for coffee and every Friday at six o'clock after work! When do people drink coffee or tea where you live, and what do they eat at cafés? All over the world from New York to Paris, from Rome to Rio or from London to Tokyo, people drink tea and coffee, sometimes in a café and sometimes at home. Some people only drink coffee at breakfast. Or, like me, they drink it at breakfast and later in the day! From Sunday through Saturday, about 54% of Americans drink coffee. Sixty-five percent of them drink it in the morning between six and eleven o'clock, and 35% drink it at lunch or later in the day! Some people drink thirteen cups a day! Woah! In the UK, people like tea. People there drink about 165 million cups of tea every day. They only drink about 70 million cups of coffee. But here in New York, at a tea café like this one, you can eat sandwiches and drink tea any time!

3.9 page 27, exercises 5 and 6

Learning Curve E = Ethan, K = Kate, J = Jolene, I = Ioan, C = Chan

E: Now, let's speak with Kate. She's on the street in London. Kate, when do people go to the café to eat or drink, and what do they have?

K: Hi, Ethan! It's 2.30 p.m. here and I'm with Jolene. Jolene, what's in your paper bag and what do you drink, coffee or tea?

J: Er, this is a meat and cheese sandwich, and I have a bag of crisps and a chocolate biscuit. And I drink tea!

K: But that's a pizza place.

J: Right. We come here every Tuesday. It's my husband's favourite café.

K: You have tea and sandwiches from a pizza place?

J: My husband likes pizza and I like sandwiches. And they make both here! And they have tea! I drink coffee every morning, but between 2.30 and 3.00, I drink tea. Every day. Sorry. Hungry. Crisp?

K: Oh. Thanks, but I don't eat chips, I mean, crisps! Enjoy your lunch, Jolene! Excuse me. I'm Kate from *Learning Curve*. What's your name?

I: Ioan. I'm from Wales.

K: So Ioan, where's your food from?

I: This shop, right here. I have biscuits and ice cream!

K: Oh. What kind of ice cream?

I: Chocolate. Today is my wife's birthday! Shh!

K: What about cake?

I: Oh, she doesn't like cake. But she eats chocolate ice cream!

K: So, what do you drink, coffee or tea?

I: Oh, we like coffee at 9.00 p.m. at night, after our dinner ... and tonight, with the ice cream!

K: Well, happy birthday to your wife! What time's the party?

I: The party's at 8.00 p.m.! Bye!

K: Well Ethan, people here like coffee and tea with their food. What about in New York?

E: Thanks, Kate. Yes, I'm in Chinatown. Excuse me?

C: Hello! Wow! Are you Ethan from *Learning Curve*? I'm Chan.

E: Yes, I am! And is that food from a café?

C: Yes. It's from my place! Happy Chan's Café. Uh, this is fish with rice and vegetables. Mm. And I have a hot tea.

E: And is that water?

C: Yes, I have two bottles of water. Here, please, this one's for you.

E: Oh, thank you very much!

C: We're open Monday through Friday from 11.00 a.m. until 10.00 p.m. And Saturday and Sunday from 10.00 a.m. until 11.00 p.m.! Please, come by any time!

E: Well, I do like fish and vegetables, but not in the morning! I have a coffee and cereal. Kate, back to you in London.

K: Well, it's half past three here and I have fish and chips from my favourite takeaway place! And a tea. Mmm. This food is good! So what do you eat at your favourite café or takeout place? Do you drink coffee or tea? See you next time on *Learning Curve*!

UNIT 4

4.5 page 33, exercise 7B

Hi, I'm Marcus.

I don't like mornings. I get up late and I always have breakfast in a café near our house. I often watch TV in the morning and later I have lunch. I usually work in the evening, but I don't work every day – I have Tuesday off.

I leave work late, so I'm tired ... but I sometimes see my friends after work, on Friday or at the weekend.

I get home late and I never go to bed before midnight. What's my job? I'm a chef in a restaurant!

4.12 page 37, exercise 6B

I = Interviewer, T = Tess

I: Tell me about your family, Tess. How many children do you have?

T: I have two children, Ben and Lucy. Lucy is six and Ben is four.

I: What time do they have breakfast?

T: They have breakfast at 7.30. My husband takes them to school.

I: What does your husband do?

T: He's a taxi driver.

I: When does he work?

T: He works in the afternoons and evenings. So I don't see him much!

I: What do you do at the weekend?

T: We often go to the park if the weather isn't cold. There's a large park near our house, so we go on foot. My husband doesn't want to use the car!

4.14 page 38, exercise 3

Learning Curve P = Penny

P: My day is usually long. But I have a great job at *Learning Curve*. I like my job a lot. But I don't really like food shopping. This is my routine. I always get up at seven. Then I have a shower, get dressed, have breakfast and a coffee, and I start work at 9.00 a.m. I don't like the underground in London or the subway in New York, but sometimes I take it. I usually walk to work. Anyway, I have a flatmate, um, a roommate. This is our apartment. Her name is Taylor. She's from the Midwest and she works at a gym. Taylor has a car. It's great! She drives everywhere. On Thursdays, we usually go shopping after work together. Today is Wednesday, and Taylor usually works until 7.00 p.m. When she comes home, she's tired, so she has a shower and then we cook dinner. She's in the bathroom now. But this morning? There's no food in the fridge and nothing to eat! And Thursday is tomorrow! Look. Coffee! This coffee is $7.99. That's about six pounds sterling. That isn't expensive. Food shopping in New York isn't easy when I go on foot. I shop at three or four stores because we don't have a supermarket in our neighbourhood. Then, I carry the food up 39 steps to our flat. This is why I'm tired today. At 6.00 p.m., I said goodbye to Ethan, my co-host, and then ...

4.15 page 38, exercises 4 and 5

Learning Curve

S1 = Shop assistant 1, P = Penny, S2 = Shop assistant 2, S3 = Shop assistant 3, T = Taylor

S1: Good evening!
P: Hello. Um, how much is the chicken?
S1: A whole chicken is $8.79. But a half chicken is $4.79.
P: OK. I'd like a whole chicken, please.
S1: Alright. Here you go.
P: Thank you!
S1: Ah, change! You're welcome.
P: Bye!
S1: Bye bye!
S2: Hello.
P: Hello. Can I have two pounds of this white cheese and a half pound of cheddar, um, the orange cheese, please? And a box of that salad? How much is that?
S2: $17.15.
P: OK.
S2: Here you are.
P: Wow! That's thirteen pounds sterling. That's expensive. Thank you.
S2: Thank you!
S3: Hello.
P: Hi. How much is it for that small shopping, er, trolley, er, I mean, cart?
S3: $20.
P: OK. Um, do you have it in black?
S3: Here's one in black. $21.77 with tax.
P: OK. Thank you! Here's $22.02.
S3: Here's your change. 25 cents – a quarter!
P: Thanks! Bye. OK. Just one more shop and that's all the groceries. $44.07 for all these groceries. That's good! OK. I have everything now. Time to go home. Wow, this is, urgh! Urgh! This is so heavy!
T: Penny? What? Is that you? Is that a new shopping cart?
P: Yes. It's OK on the street, but it's not good for the stairs.
T: Um, are those groceries?
P: Yes! Are those groceries in your bags, too?
T: There was no food in the fridge! Here, let me. I can help.
P: Thanks.
T: Oh, no! That's a lot of food. I also bought meat, bread, milk, and vegetables from the supermarket. And coffee.
P: Oh, coffee! Good. I don't have coffee. Well, it's a good thing our refrigerator is empty!
T: OK. I can cook dinner after my shower.
P: Well, what's on the telly? Mmm. Crisps!

4.18 page 39, exercise 8

C = Customer, W = Waiter, A = Assistant, R = Receptionist

C: Good morning.
W: Hi.
C: I'd like a coffee please, to take away.
W: OK. One coffee. That's £2.50.
C: Here you go. Thanks very much. Er, have a nice day.
W: Next.

2

A: Good afternoon, ma'am. Can I help you?
C: Yes, I'd like some bread, please, and one of those cakes.
A: Yes, of course. Here you are. That's $7.10, please.
C: Here you go. Thank you.
A: You're welcome. Have a nice day.
C: And you. Goodbye.

3

R: Good evening, sir. Can I help you?
C: I want a room for tonight.
R: Yes, of course. Can I have your passport, please.
C: Here.
R: Thank you. OK, so you're in Room 309. Here's your room card.
C: How much is the room?
R: It's £90 a night, with breakfast.
C: OK.
R: Have a nice evening, sir.

UNIT 5

5.2 page 42, exercises 3 and 4A

N = Nick, G = Georgia

N: Hello. Sydney City Tours. Nick speaking.
G: Hello Nick. My name's Georgia. I'm interested in the tour guide job.
N: OK great. Thanks for calling, Georgia. So, I need to ask you some questions. Is that OK?
G: Yes, of course.
N: OK, can you speak a foreign language? We have a lot of tourists from China and Japan. Some of the people can't speak English.
G: I can speak Chinese and I can speak Japanese. I study languages at university.
N: Oh wow, that's great. And when tourists arrive, we usually go to the airport. So, can you drive?
G: Yes, I can.
N: And can you work early in the morning?
G: No, I can't – sorry. I usually swim early in the morning. I can start at 10.00. Is that OK?
N: Yes, that's fine. So, can you swim well?
G: Yes, I can. I'm in the university's swimming team!
N: Oh, that's good! We sometimes go on boat trips with the tourists. I think you're perfect for the job, Georgia. Er, when can you start?

5.6 page 43, exercise 7B

E = Emily, L = Lisa, B = Ben

1

E: Hello?
L: Oh hello, is that Emily? This is Lisa Jones.
E: Yes, it's me. Hi Lisa, thanks for calling.
L: No problem. So can I ask you some questions?
E: Sure.
L: OK, first question. Can you cook?
E: Yes, I can. My family all say I'm a good cook.
L: Fantastic. And can you drive? The children's school is about 15 minutes from our house.
E: Yes, I can.
L: The job is in Madrid. Can you speak Spanish?
E: Er, no, I can't. But I can learn.
L: Yes, that's a good idea. Now the children both love tennis. Can you play tennis?
E: No, I can't play tennis, I'm afraid.
L: Can you swim? That's very important because we swim a lot here in the summer.
E: Yes, I can swim.
L: That's good. What about music? Max, our son, plays the piano, and Ava, our daughter, plays the guitar.
E: Well, I can play the piano a bit, but I can't play the guitar.
L: The children also go to singing lessons. Can you help them to practise?
E: I can't sing, I'm afraid.
L: OK, thanks very much Emily. I'll call you next week.
E: Thanks! Bye.

2

B: Hello, Ben Martinez.
L: Oh hello Ben, this is Lisa Jones, about the au pair job. Is now a good time to talk?
B: Hi, Lisa. Yes, now is perfect.
L: Great. So Ben, can you cook? The children are always hungry after school.
B: Yes, I can. I often cook for my little brother. He's 12 and he loves my food.
L: Very good. And can you drive?
B: No, I can't. Is that a problem?
L: Well no, not really. You can take the children to school by bus. What about the language? Can you speak Spanish?
B: Yes, I can speak Spanish. My father is Colombian.
L: Great. And what sports can you play?
B: Well, I love tennis and I can also swim.
L: And can you play a musical instrument? The children have piano and guitar lessons.
B: I can play the guitar, so I can help with that, but I can't play the piano.
L: OK, and can you sing?

B: I can sing. But I'm not very good!
L: That's OK. Well, thank you Ben. I'll call you next week. Good bye!
B: Thanks, Lisa. Bye.

5.7 page 43, exercise 8

V = Voicemail, L = Lisa, B = Ben

V: You have 1 new message. To listen to your messages, press 1. Message received today at 2.05 p.m.
L: Oh hello, it's Lisa Jones here – about the au pair job in Madrid. Well, I'm pleased to say we think you're the right person for the job. Can you call me? Thanks Ben. Bye!
B: Yes!

5.9 page 44, exercises 3 and 4

K = Kate, S = Simon

K: Hey, Simon!
S: Hi, Kate. Do you always go to the gym before work?
K: Always.
S: And what sports do you do?
K: Everything. I play basketball on Fridays with a women's team. I swim three days a week ...
S: I can't swim well.
K: Oh. Well, I do other sports, too. I run, I go rock climbing.
S: Wow! That's, wow! What's on your tablet? Can I see?
K: Yeah, sure. It's a French program. Look! I can learn French while I work out, too. I use my phone to do that. I listen and say the words.
S: Can you speak French now?
K: A little. 'Bonjour!'
S: Wow! That's great! Well, er, it's time for our show. I'm on the street today. See you.
K: Hello and welcome to *Learning Curve*. My name's Kate and my co-host, Simon, is on the street today. I can't live without my phone. Why? Because I can play games, listen to the radio or my MP3s, learn French, take a photo and do so many other things! Let's talk about electronic devices. The camera is something many people can't live without. Everywhere we go, we see people with a camera on a mobile phone or a tablet. Or a regular camera. About 123 million people in the U.S. have a digital camera! How many photos do people usually take? Just three photos per person every day can add up to about one trillion photos a year! Wow! That is a lot. So, what other things can't people live without? How many people own a television? TVs are very popular all over the world. Americans have about 116 million televisions. Some people have three in their home! In the UK, that number is about 26 million. Wow! But now, people have tablets, smartphones and laptops. We can watch TV shows on the Internet and take photos on the same device! Why have two devices when you can have just one? Let's talk to Simon and hear from our viewers. Simon, what do our fans say?

5.10 page 45, exercises 5 and 6

S = Simon, P = Parminder, V = Vincent

S: Well, Kate. I can't live without music on my mobile, and my headphones, or earphones. I don't like listening to other people's music. When you have earphones, it's good! Here comes someone now. Hello. I'm Simon from *Learning Curve*. And you are?
P: Parminder.
S: You have a lot of bags with you today. What technology can't you live without?
P: Well, I work for a big company and we use all the top technology. So I can't live without my laptop. It's in that bag. Um, and my tablet. I can use a computer and a tablet at the same time. I have everything I need for my presentations. I can't go anywhere without these things. I never do.
S: Wow! Is that heavy? So, do you carry these things every day?
P: Yes! Even at the weekend. Wherever I go, they're with me! These are for work, but also for a bit of fun. And I can exercise on my way to work.
S: Thanks, Parminder. Wow! She can work out, too!
V: Hey! You're Simon from that show!
S: Yes, I am. It's called *Learning Curve*. Hello! What's your name?
V: I'm Vincent. Um, I really like the show. You and um, Kate, is it?
S: Yes. Our question today is: What devices can't you live without?
V: Ah well, that's easy. My DVR.
S: Why is that?
V: Because I can record a show, like, right now! I can cook, play my guitar, or do my favourite thing – drive my car. And when I get home, I watch TV at night. Everything's recorded on the DVR.
S: That's very interesting. What kind of car do you have?
V: Um, I'll show you.
S: OK, but ...
V: I have a photo here. From 1972. Can't live without it. Nice meeting you.
S: That's all the time we have. Think about it. What technology can't you live without? I can live without a car. I take the underground! What about you? See you next time on *Learning Curve*!

UNIT 6

6.6 page 51, exercises 8A and 8B

C = Carmel, E = Erica

C: Hi, Erica. How's life in the big city?
E: Hi, Carmel! It's great. I love it here in Dublin.
C: So what's your area like?
E: Well, it's really nice. There's a big park – I sometimes go there at the weekend. There isn't a supermarket, but there are some small shops nearby. Oh, and there's a great café in my street. The coffee's really good, and they make amazing cakes!
C: That sounds great! So, do you live near the city centre?
E: Well, it's about twenty minutes by bus. There's a bus stop near my house.
C: Are there any good restaurants near you?
E: Mmm, no, there aren't. I usually eat at home, or I sometimes go into the city centre. Anyway, when can you come and visit me, Carmel?
C: Oh, I can't wait. What about next weekend? There's a flight that arrives at ...

6.12 page 55, exercises 8A and 8B

I really like my bedroom. It's quite small, but I have a big bed. Next to the bed there's a table with a clock on it and there's a picture on the wall, above the table. There are two windows, so there's lots of light in the room. There's a chair in front of my desk, and there are some shelves above it. I don't have a lot of clothes, so I only need a small wardrobe. It's opposite the desk. Anything else? Oh yes, my guitar. I usually put it between the wardrobe and the desk.

6.13 page 56, exercises 2 and 3

S = Simon, M = Man

S: I usually like helping people and talking to them. I often ask a lot of questions. It's my job at *Learning Curve*! But there are days when people ask me a lot of questions. This usually happens when I walk to the studio from the Underground station. Here's my day. I get up at 7.30 a.m., I have breakfast – the usual, eggs, toast and tea. I cycle to work when the weather is good. I don't have a car because I can't drive. But when it rains? Well, on those days, I take the underground train, and then walk for fifteen minutes. I don't like the Underground. But, I do like walking. There's one small problem. When I walk to or from the station, I'm Simon, the map! Look at me! Am I a map? OK. Time to go. There's the station! Kate always calls it 'the subway' because she's from the US. Here in London, it's often called 'the Tube'. I don't like taking it. No one speaks! People on the Tube don't like talking.

M: Excuse me. Is there a post office around here?

S: Yes, there is. It's down the street. Go straight on. It's on the left, near the car park.

M: Oh! Thank you very much.

S: No problem. See? Am I right? I'm Simon, the map!

6.14 page 56, exercise 4B

1

A: Excuse me, where's the bank?

B: OK ... Go straight on and the bank's on the left, in front of the supermarket.

2

A: Excuse me. Is there a post office near here?

B: Yes, there is. Go down this street ... and it's on the corner.

3

A: Excuse me, where's the museum, please?

B: The museum? Well, turn right here and it's on the left, next to a café.

4

A: Excuse me, is there a cinema around here?

B: Yes there is. Turn right, then turn left and the cinema is on the left.

6.15 page 57, exercises 5 and 6

Learning Curve W1= Woman 1, S = Simon, W2 = Woman 2, K = Kate

W1: Excuse me, excuse me ...

S: Yes?

W1: Um, is there a shopping centre near here?

S: Yes. It's near the supermarket. Go down this street, turn right on Bethnal Green Road. Don't stop at Ebor Street. Go straight on.

W2: Sorry, did you say near the supermarket?

S: Yes.

W1: Um, where are we? Can you show me on the map?

S: OK. We're here. And there's the cinema. And there's the supermarket. The shopping centre is next to the supermarket. See?

W2: Um, could you repeat that, please? Um, more slowly?

S: Sorry! OK. The cinema is here and there's the supermarket.

W2: Oh, it's OK. I understand! Thank you!

W1: Thank you!

S: You're welcome. Again! Oh wow! It's 8.45. Ah, time for a cup of tea. And no more questions about directions! Kate! Hello. What's up?

K: Today, it's what's down! Um, the Wi-Fi, the Internet is down. There's a problem, so there's no water in the kitchen or the bathroom. But there's water under the receptionist's desk! Poor Marina.

S: Sorry, did you say there's a problem on the street? You mean, a problem with the water?

K: Yes! There's water everywhere! Marina isn't happy, not at all. She's on her desk now!

S: There isn't any water in the kitchen? So, no tea?

K: Uh, is there a café near here?

S: Yes, there is. It's ... Just turn right at the corner. Simon the map, at your service!

6.16 page 57, exercises 7A and 7B

1

M: Excuse me, where's the station?

W: OK, go down this street. Turn right at the post office. Then turn left at the bank. It's a five-minute walk.

M: Sorry, could you speak more slowly, please?

W: Yes, of course. I'm sorry. You go down this street and turn right at the post office. Then turn left at the bank. It's a five-minute walk.

2

M: Hello, I'd like a room for the night, please.

W: Of course, can I take your email address?

M: It's david.jackson454@mail.com

W: Sorry, could you repeat that, please?

M: Sure. It's David – D-A-V-I-D – dot Jackson – J-A-C-K-S-O-N – 454 at mail dot com.

3

M: What's your phone number, Sally?

W: It's 70832 569411

M: Sorry, could you say that again, please?

W: Yes. It's 70832 569411.

4

M: Hello, how can I help you?

W: Hello, I'd like a black coffee, please.

M: One black coffee. Here you go. That's £3.50.

W: Sorry, did you say £3.15?

M: No, no. £3.50.

UNIT 7

7.7 page 62, exercises 5 and 6

Learning Curve S = Simon

S: Hello and welcome to *Learning Curve*! Do you like the theatre, or plays? Plays are a popular kind of entertainment. One of the first English playwrights – a writer of plays – was William Shakespeare! Do you know the plays *Romeo and Juliet* or *Hamlet*? Those are famous plays by William Shakespeare. There are many locations in his plays. *Romeo and Juliet* is about a boy and a girl in Italy. They're in love. *Hamlet* is about a prince in Denmark. The story of *Othello* is about a man from North Africa. The Globe Theatre was Shakespeare's first theatre. It was here in London during the 16th and 17th centuries, from 1599 to about 1642. This theatre looks just like the old Globe. Every year, from May to August, there's a Shakespeare festival in Central Park in New York City. It's called 'Shakespeare in the Park'. 1,800 people can see a Shakespeare play at the Delacorte Theatre for free! Shakespeare was the writer of 37 plays. People can read or perform the plays in translation into 80 different languages from around the world! That's a lot of languages.

7.8 page 63, exercises 7 and 8

Learning Curve S = Simon, P = Penny, M = Marty, E = Elizabeth, H = Henry, Z = Zhang

S: Let's ask our viewers about theatre, plays and Shakespeare! Penny, what do people in New York City say? Do they like theatre? Do they like Shakespeare?

P: Hi, Simon. A lot of people are here in the queue for theatre tickets! Let's ask. Um, excuse me. Do you enjoy plays?

M: Oh, yes, I do! I have two tickets! This is my tenth time in New York City! I'm here every spring, in March, and every autumn, in October!

P: Oh. Where do you live?

M: New Jersey. Not far. But I see two plays every time I visit. Last night, I was in the third seat in the front of the balcony, you know, high up in the theatre? They're cheap, but good seats.

P: So, do you like Shakespeare?

M: Oh, no. Um, he's too boring for me. No, I'm not a fan. I like plays with music and singers. I'm a musician!

P: Wow, you're good! Enjoy the show, or shows! Excuse me, can I ask you a question? Firstly, what are your names?

E: Yes. I'm Elizabeth, and this is my husband, Henry.

P: So, do you like Shakespeare?

E: Oh, yes! I was at the Cambridge Shakespeare Festival in England last year, in July. Oh, and at the Globe Theatre in London.

P: You were? That's great!

H: Uh, Beth? I was there, too!

E: He wasn't awake for all of it. Now, *Romeo and Juliet*. Ah, a love story! It is my favourite play! I also like *A Midsummer Night's Dream*, and ...

H: Right. She likes the plays about love and anything that's funny. Me? I like the plays about kings, like *The Winter's Tale*. Listen: 'I am a feather for each wind that ...'

E: 'To be, or not to be!'

H: Yeah, that's *Hamlet* though ...

E: This summer, we were at the play, *Twelfth Night*, in Central Park. It was free! Oh, it was so exciting!

P: Oh, at the Delacorte Theatre. Wow!

H: Now, I like the history plays, like *Henry V*. Or is that *Henry IV*? Or, *Henry VI*? Well, there are kings in all of them. So many Henrys.
P: Wait, isn't your name Henry?
H: It is! I'm the seventh Henry in my family!
P: Well, I'm glad he isn't Henry VIII! Back to you, Simon. Is there someone on videochat?
S: Yes, Penny, there is! Welcome to *Learning Curve*. So, do you like theatre?
Z: Hi, I'm Zhang and I work at a theatre in Beijing. I'm a stage manager. I love the theatre.
S: So, are there Shakespeare plays in China?
Z: Oh, yes. Shakespeare's play *A Midsummer Night's Dream* was here in Beijing in 2014! Henry IV was at the Hong Kong Arts Festival in July, last summer. Sometimes the plays are in English and Chinese!
S: Wow! That's amazing! Thanks, Zhang! 'I am a feather for each wind that ...' Oh, well! What kind of plays do you like? Do you like the theatre, or Shakespeare? Let us know! Thanks for watching *Learning Curve*.

7.10 page 63, exercise 11

1 Hi, my name's Lucas and I'm an actor.
2 In October, I was in New York City for the first time.
3 The play was about an old king.
4 She was born on the fourth of April, 1999.
5 I like *Hamlet*, but I don't understand all the story.

UNIT 8

8.5 page 69, exercise 8A

I = Interviewer, L = Leanne

I: So, Leanne. Tell me about your trip to Croatia.
L: It didn't start well. I was late and I missed the flight from Manchester. So I flew from London instead, but on the 25th of July – not the 24th.
I: Oh dear! And did you get to Dubrovnik OK?
L: Yes. It's a fantastic city – really fun!
I: And then, you went to Split, right?
L: Yes, but I didn't take a bus. I took a taxi. I shared it with three other people. After three hours we were all really good friends and we stayed together in Split.
I: And where did you go after that?
L: Well, I planned to go to Solta on the 5th of August, but I stayed an extra day in Split, and so we sailed to Solta on the 6th of August instead. It was so beautiful. I didn't want to leave, but on the 10th of August I took the train to Zagreb and flew home.
I: And what did you do on the holiday?
L: I ate lots of food – it was delicious – and I swam in the sea ...
I: Did you take lots of photos?
L: No, I didn't. I forgot my camera!
I: Oh no! And ... did you fall in love?
L: Yes – I did ... with Croatia! I want to go back next year.

8.8 page 72, exercises 4 and 5A

I = Interviewer, L = Liu

I: We're in Shenzhen, China. It's a very big, modern city – 12 million people live here. It's difficult to believe, but about 30 years ago it was a quiet fishing town. With me is the writer Liu Jiang.
L: Hello.
I: So, were you born here in Shenzhen?
L: Yes, I was, but when I was 12, we went to live in the USA. This is my first visit back to China in 30 years.
I: And why are you here now?
L: Well, I'm a writer, and I wanted to write a book about my childhood. So, I needed to see Shenzhen again. I arrived here yesterday.
I: I'm sure the city is very different from when you were a child.
L: Nothing is the same. Nothing. When I left, there were fields around the town and there was a forest where we played ... Now there are just tall buildings – everywhere! In the summer, we swam in the river. Look, you can't swim in that river today it's dirty ... And the cars! When I lived here, there weren't any cars – everyone had bicycles.
I: Just bicycles? Was there public transport to travel around the country? Were there any trains or buses?
L: Oh yes, there was a train station – a small one, but now there are six, I think – big and modern, with incredible fast trains. There's an airport too, and so many shops and shopping centres....
I: What about the people?
L: They're different too. There wasn't a university here before – everyone worked in the fields or went fishing. But this morning I saw lots of students, and business people from different countries – they were all very busy. It's an incredible city, but it isn't the Shenzhen I remember.
I: Let's talk about your book. Now that you're in Shenzhen, you can start to plan ...

8.12 page 74, exercises 2A and 2B

M = Marc, C = Clarisse

M: See my ID? It says, 'Marc Kim, Technology Specialist at *Learning Curve*.' Well, I'm good at my job. When people have problems with the internet, they call me! Ah, but I work a lot. My friends at *Learning Curve* think I need a vacation. So, I want to go somewhere interesting, but not far from New York. Maybe Canada! I heard it's cheap to travel in March. I don't like flying on long trips, but Ethan said you can take a train from New York to Canada. So, Penny gave me the phone number of her friend Clarisse. She's a travel agent. She said I can call Clarisse for help to plan my vacation. I usually buy my tickets online. Hmm. But I can try something new this time. OK, here goes.
C: Hello, Bon Voyage Travel. This is Clarisse.
M: Hello, my name is Marc Kim. I'm Penny's friend.
C: Oh, yes. Marc. Penny told me that you want to take a trip, eh? Where do you want to go?
M: Where can I go in the U.S. or Canada in March?
C: What about California? It's sunny!
M: No, no thanks. It's very hot. Urgh!
C: Well, they have air conditioning! Don't you like hot weather? Wearing sunglasses?
M: Uh, it's OK, but I don't like flying for five hours.
C: Hmm. Oh, so how about Montreal in Quebec, Canada? It's not far from New York. It's very cheap in the winter and you can visit many museums, sport events and parks.
M: Montreal? Oh, I don't mind cold weather. Can I take a train?
C: Oh, yes. You can go by train from New York to Montreal. Just give me your credit card information and we can send the train tickets to you by mail.
M: By mail? But I always buy my tickets online.
C: This will only take a few minutes.
M: Uh, OK!
C: Expiration April 2020. OK. When do you want to leave?
M: March 11.
C: And what kind of ticket would you like?
M: A round trip from New York to ...
C: Montreal? When would you like to return?
M: March 21. Um, what time does the train leave?
C: The train leaves from New York at 8.15 a.m.
M: And when does it arrive in Montreal?
C: 7.11 p.m.
M: Did you say 7.11 p.m.? Wow, that's a long day. Eleven hours? Is that right?
C: Ah, yes, it is. But you can read or use your laptop on the train.
M: Right. Right. OK, so, how much is it?
C: It's $138 for a return ticket. Um, round trip.
M: Great! That's very cheap! Where does the train arrive in Montreal?
C: Oh, the train from New York arrives at the centre platform of the Montreal station.
M: That's good.

8.14 page 75, exercises 5A and 5B

M = Marc, C = Clarisse

M: So, what about hotels there?
C: Oh. A lot of hotels have a discount of 20% because it's winter.
M: Sorry. Did you say that there's a discount at hotels in Montreal?
C: Yes. Good prices! Many hotels are close to the train and the bus station. You can go on foot everywhere. Or drive. Everything is nearby.
M: That sounds great. And is there good Wi-Fi at the hotels?
C: Uh, well, when it snows, the Wi-Fi is sometimes awful.
M: Hmm, really? Oh.
C: Oh, but don't worry, it doesn't snow very often in March. Only sometimes. OK! Finished. The tickets usually come in the mail in three days. Thanks for calling. Have a good trip!
M: Hmm. Thanks. Goodbye.
M: Thanks. Goodbye. I'm home! After ten days away on vacation ... and bad snow storms in March! Oh, good Wi-Fi! Hello, old friend. Well, at first, everywhere I went, the Wi-Fi was awful. At the library, at the café - the Wi-Fi was always down. Usually, it only worked on my smartphone. There was no Wi-Fi on the train! So, what did I do on my trip? I learned a little French. I made a lot of new friends. People gave me free coffee, free sandwiches ... even movie tickets! Why? Because when the Internet went down, I showed them this: my Learning Curve ID. And then, I fixed everyone's Wi-Fi for free!

UNIT 9

9.2 page 78, exercises 4 and 5A

P = Presenter, S = Sukanya

P: So here we are in Bangkok. We're taking the train to the Chatuchak market. It's 7.00 in the morning. Do you always come so early, Sukanya?
S: Yes. You find the best clothes early in the morning.
S: Oh, this is our stop.
P: A lot of people are getting out here. Are they going to the market too?
S: No, they aren't. They're going to work. The market is this way! OK, so this is my favourite shop in the market. I'm looking for a dress and some shoes for a party tonight. Oh, I love this blue and pink dress! It's only 200 baht.
P: So, that's about £4.50. Are you ... Oh, she's buying the dress! We're in another shop now.
S: I love these 1970s shoes. How much are they? Mmmm, 300 baht.
P: So, that's about £6.50 ...
S: They're cool, but they're quite expensive. I don't know. Maybe we can try another shop. It's 9.30. Time for some breakfast?
P: Good idea! I'm hungry.
S: Over here.
P: What's this man doing?
S: He's cooking meat. This is Khao Niew Gai Ping – it's rice with chicken in a sweet sauce. It's delicious.
P: OK, Can I try? Mmm! This is really good. Sukanya, you aren't eating the rice!
S: No, I prefer to have fruit for breakfast.
P: After a quick breakfast, we're in another shop now.
S: Look at this summer hat! What do you think?
P: It's perfect with your new dress.
S: I know! And it's only 100 baht.
P: She's buying the hat too. Well, It's 11 o'clock. Sukanya has some new clothes and we're leaving the market now. Thank you Sukanya.
S: Well, now you know a little about Bangkok fashion. I hope you liked it.
P: I loved it, thank you, Sukanya!

9.8 page 80, exercises 3B and 4

E = Ethan, P = Penny

E: Hello and welcome to *Learning Curve*!
P: Hello!
E: I like blue on you, Penny!
P: Aw, thanks, Ethan. Um, what are you wearing?
E: Look! My shirt has almost every color in it, except green!
P: Right. So, Ethan, why are you wearing that Hawaiian shirt?
E: Well, because we're talking about colors today, aren't we Penny?
P: Yes, we are. See you in a bit!
E: Do you wear some colors, but not others? Did you know that the colors you wear change how you feel? When I wear this Hawaiian shirt, people think it's funny and they think I'm happy. Why? Because these colors are very bright. I don't look bored or angry, do I? No! This is the shirt of a happy man. Let's look at the colors of uniforms, or clothes that people wear to do special jobs. In some jobs, workers wear uniforms of the same colors. Doctors wear white because it looks clean and makes us feel healthy! Firefighters wear orange or yellow on their uniforms so it's easy to see them. Police in the U.S. wear blue and, in many jobs, workers wear the colors of the company, like at a fast-food restaurant. How do you choose what colors to wear? When you're feeling angry, do you wear red or black? Does purple make you feel excited or important? Scientists say that some colors can change how you feel! When you wear red, it can make you look exciting and interesting. People wear black when they're sad or want to go to an evening party. And people don't wear orange often, but it's sometimes a popular color for sports uniforms. In India and Nepal, there is a spring festival called Holi. It's the festival of colors! For two days, people dress in many colors. They paint their faces and bodies, and use paint all over buildings in cities. Everything looks beautiful!

9.9 page 81, exercises 6 and 7

E = Ethan, P = Penny, U = Udo, A = Akiko, B = Bob

E: So Penny, what are people wearing today? Do you see a lot of colors on the streets of New York?
P: Well, people are leaving work at the moment. Let's see what they're wearing.
P: Hi, I'm Penny from *Learning Curve*.
U: Hey, I'm Udo.
P: Wow! That's an interesting hat you're wearing!
U: Yes, I'm a designer. I made this hat, T-shirt and I made my jeans, too.
P: That's amazing, Udo! How do those colors make you feel?
U: I feel excited about these colors. Yeah, I feel great!
P: Well, he has his own personal style! Thanks, Udo!
U: Thanks!
E: I'm standing near a popular fashion school here in New York. Students wear all styles and colors. Akiko, what do you think of my shirt?
A: Uh, hello. Uh, uh, I'm feeling a little scared ...
E: Scared? Does our web show make you feel scared?
A: No, I watch it five times a week! I love your show. But, um, I'm scared of that shirt! We call it, uh, a big fashion mistake!
E: But you're laughing!
A: Uh, time for class. Bye, Ethan!
E: OK, then! Back to you, Penny!
P: Was that a chicken?
B: What? Is someone speaking?
P: Excuse me. Do you wear a yellow chicken suit every day?
B: Ah, no, but three times a week I'm a big, yellow chicken. It's my uniform for work! Come on over to our fast-food cart! It's just down the street.
P: Wow, I'm feeling a bit hungry now.
B: Well, I'm thirsty. It's hot in here! Hey, thanks!
P: So, how do you feel when you wear yellow?
B: Right now, I feel a little bored. People aren't talking to me. They're scared.
P: Well, you are tall. Hmm.
B: Come on over! OK, where am I going?

P: Wow, he's one thirsty chicken! I think that's all the time we have today. Ethan?

E: So, what colors are you wearing now and how do they make you feel? I feel like dancing! Let us know on *Learning Curve*! See you next time!

UNIT 10

10.7 page 87, exercises 7A and 7B

D = Dan, C = Cheryl

D: What are you doing at the weekend, Cheryl?

C: I'm going to a film festival in Cambridge.

D: Really? That sounds interesting. Who are you going with?

C: I'm going with my boyfriend.

D: Cool. How are you getting there? Are you driving?

C: No, we're taking the train. My car's in the garage and my boyfriend can't drive.

D: I see. So, when are you leaving?

C: We're leaving tomorrow morning. Early, at about 8 o'clock.

D: And where are you staying in Cambridge?

C: We're staying with some friends. They're having a party on Saturday night.

D: Great – well, have a good time! See you on Monday.

10.8 page 88, exercise 1

2

S = Sharon, M = Mark

S: Mark, why are you here?

M: I came to see you.

S: But why?

M: Because ... because I ... because I love you, Sharon!

S: Oh Mark, I love you too!

5

O = Olga, J = James

O: You're driving so fast, James.

J: We only have seven minutes to save the world!

O: Look out! There's no bridge.

J: Don't worry. I have a plan.

6

C = Captain, L = Lieutenant

C: The year is 2152, we are travelling through space to find life on new planets. Yesterday, we received a signal from a small planet called Xanadu.

L: Captain, Captain, quickly, we need you. There's something on the planet ... something very strange.

10.11 page 90, exercises 3B and 4A

I = Interviewer, J = Jenny

I: Today we're talking about the young royals. That's right – Prince Harry, Prince William and his wife Kate – the Duchess of Cambridge. We all know who they are ... but what do they do in their free time? And with me today to answer this question is Jenny Brown. Welcome Jenny.

J: Thank you.

I: So, I imagine they go skiing and sailing ... expensive activities, like that.

J: Well, sometimes ... but many people are surprised at their favourite hobbies – they're actually quite ... normal.

I: OK, Prince Harry first. How does he relax?

J: Well, we know that he likes sports, like football and rugby, but, he also plays a lot of videogames.

I: Videogames? Really? What is his favourite game?

J: He loves the FIFA football games. He thinks he's really good at them, and says he usually wins!

I: Wow! What about William and Kate?

J: Well, Kate often goes walking, and she likes photography and painting. She studied those at university.

I: Oh right, er, where did she go to university?

J: In Scotland ... In fact, Prince William was a student at the same university. They met there.

I: I see! And ... Was she good at sports?

J: Yes, she was. She played hockey for the university. She doesn't play much now, but she does yoga and Pilates almost every day!

I: Right, and does William do lots of exercise too?

J: Er, yes, he sometimes goes running ... He wants to run a marathon.

I: Really? Is he training for a marathon now?

J: Well ... he promised to run in the Kenya Marathon ... but when a TV presenter asked Kate about it, she said 'I'll believe it when I see it'.

I: OK ... well I think we can all understand that! Thank you very much Jenny.

J: You're welcome.

I: Now, it's time to go to Peter Kuzmicki with the news and weather ...

10.16 page 91, exercises 7A and 7B

A: Estonian fashion model Carmen Kass plays chess.

1

B: When did she start?

A: She started when she was a young girl.

2

B: How did she learn?

A: Her father was a chess teacher and he taught her.

B: American singer Elvis Presley did karate.

3

A: Was he good at karate?

B: Yes, he was. He had a black belt.

4

A: Where did he do it?

B: He did karate in Memphis in the USA. He even opened a karate school there.

A: American actor Lucy Liu goes rock climbing

5

A: How often does she go rock climbing?

B: She goes rock climbing when she has time.

6

A: Is it dangerous?

B: No, it isn't dangerous, but Lucy is scared of heights!

10.17 page 92, exercises 2A and 2B

E = Ethan, P = Penny, T = Taylor, M = Marc

E: Wow. This is so exciting. I'm at Flushing Meadows Park today. It's my first time here. This area of New York City is famous for its big tennis stadium. My colleague Simon loves tennis! I'm sending him a photo and a message. OK. 'Hello, Simon. Here's a photo of me near the famous World's Fair and stadium. Too bad you're not here! Ethan.' I'm waiting for Penny and Taylor. They're coming in Taylor's car. Marc is on his way here by subway. We're going to the Hall of Science and seeing exhibits later. But, I'm meeting Penny and Taylor here. I read on the Internet that this park was the site of two World's Fairs. The first was in 1939 and the second in 1964. Millions of people from all over the world were right here. Look, you can still see some of the old buildings. That's the Tent of Tomorrow and those are the Observation Towers! And, we can walk through the park to the Hall of Science museum. This museum has really interesting exhibitions and films about science and the future of technology! Here they are now. Penny! Taylor! Over here!

P: Hey, Ethan!

T: Wow! I never knew this park was here!

P: Taylor doesn't like to leave Manhattan.

T: Funny! So what time does the Hall of Science open?

E: It opens at 10.00 a.m.

P: What is there to do if it rains?

E: Well, we can stay inside and look at exhibits all day.

P: OK. Sounds good. When does it close?

E: 6.00 p.m.

T: OK, great. So, what are we doing now?

E: We're meeting our friend Marc from *Learning Curve* at the Information Desk in half an hour.

P: And are we going to the exhibitions after that?

E: Yes. There are a lot of exhibits.
T: Ethan, Penny, are you doing research for a show?
P: Brilliant!
E: Good idea!
M: Hey, Penny, Ethan.
P: Marc, this is Taylor, my flatmate, um, roommate.
T: Hi. We met once.
M: Oh. Nice to see you again, Taylor. So, what are we doing?
E: Marc, you and I are buying the tickets and getting all the information about the Hall of Science.
M: Great.
P: OK. Taylor, let's wait here.

10.19 page 93, exercises 5A and 5B

Learning Curve **M = Marc, P = Penny, E = Ethan, T = Taylor**

M: It's cold in there. Here.
P: So, how much is it to get in?
E: It costs $15, but we paid for you!
T: Oh, really? Thanks!
P: That's very nice of you, thanks.
M: Here you go. Our pleasure.
P: So, what's there to do here?
E: Well, there are almost 450 exhibits. Where should we go?
M: What about Journey to Space? It's a 3D film.
T: That sounds interesting! I like anything about the future!
E: It costs $6. Come on, let's buy tickets.
P: Our turn!
T: Yes, we're buying these.
E: Wow! That was great. The technology was really interesting.
P: Where are we going next?
E: Over there. It's the Technology of Transport exhibit. Maybe we can do some research on airplanes and trains.
T: Oh, airplanes? I love flying!
M: Airplanes?
P: Oh! Good idea. Let's go.
E: So, what did you think?
P: Transport! That was amazing. Wow!
T: So exciting! I was an airplane pilot!
M: Right.
P: Well, Taylor, I'm telling you now, you're never flying us home in the future!
T: I'm buying a flying car as soon as I can!
E: So, Marc, what do you see happening in the future?
M: I see ... I see us in the future. We're hungry and we're eating a very large pizza.
P: Pizza? Really? OK. Sounds good.

10.21 page 93, exercise 7A

1
I'm visiting my family this weekend.
A Uh-huh.
B Oh great!
2
My sister goes rock climbing every week.
A Really?
B Right.
3
There's a new comedy at the cinema.
A That sounds good.
B Hmm, sorry what was that?
4
We went to the beach yesterday.
A Cool!
B OK.

10.22 page 93, exercise 7B

1 Oh great!
2 Really?
3 That sounds good.
4 Cool!

HELLO

Grammar

1

1 d 2 g 3 b 4 a 5 e 6 c 7 f

2

1 Are
2 am
3 are
4 I'm
5 Am
6 aren't
7 not
8 You're

Vocabulary

3

1 f 2 d 3 e 4 b 5 c 6 a

4

1 Open your books at page 8.
2 Close your books.
3 Go to page 7.
4 Look at the picture.
5 Listen and repeat.
6 Work in pairs.

Pronunciation

5

1 Jj, Kk
2 Dd, Ee, Gg, Pp, Tt, Vv
3 Ll, Mm, Nn, Ss, Xx, Zz
4 Ii, Yy
5 Oo
6 Uu, Ww
7 Rr

LESSON 1A

Grammar

1

1 A Is B it
2 A is B He's
3 A Is B It's
4 A isn't B She's
5 A are B I'm
6 A Where's B It's
7 A Is B isn't
8 A is B you're

2

1 am/'m
2 is/'s
3 isn't
4 Are
5 is, is/'s
6 am/'m
7 aren't, Are
8 is/'s

Vocabulary

3

1 Canada
2 Chinese
3 French
4 Germany
5 India
6 Italian
7 Peruvian
8 Polish
9 Russian
10 Britain
11 American
12 Turkish

4

1 *Turkey*
2 *Indian*
3 Japanese
4 China
5 Mexican
6 Chilean
7 Canada
8 Brazilian

Pronunciation

5

1 *S* 2 *D* 3 S 4 D 5 S 6 S
7 S 8 D

LESSON 1B

Listening

1

1 *first names*
2 nationalities
3 countries
4 numbers
5 surnames
6 jobs
7 addresses

2

In a language school

3

1 Sofya
2 Russian
3 tour guide
4 5
5 Teke
6 taxi driver
7 9
8 Gavin

4

1 A *What's* B *He's*
2 B aren't
3 A isn't, It's B Where's
4 A What's B She's
5 A You're B I'm
6 A I'm A It's

5

1 *actor*
2 engineer
3 student
4 IT worker
5 receptionist
6 shop assistant
7 singer
8 tour guide
9 TV presenter
10 waitress

LESSON 1C

Grammar

1

1 Are
2 are
3 are
4 Are
5 aren't
6 are
7 aren't
8 Are
9 aren't
10 are

2

1 *It's Marta.*
2 *They aren't American.*
3 I'm not a police officer.
4 Are they from Brazil?
5 Are you happy?
6 We're not old.
7 She's 25.
8 Is he in Italy?
9 They're from Japan.
10 Is it interesting?

Vocabulary

3

1 fifteen, sixteen
2 thirty, thirty-two
3 seventy, sixty
4 forty-four, fifty-five
5 eighty-five, ninety-one
6 fifty-seven, forty-three

4

1 small
2 beautiful
3 good
4 sad
5 interesting
6 cheap
7 difficult
8 old

Pronunciation

5

1 30
2 14

3 15
4 $60
5 17
6 80
7 £90
8 40
9 62 km
10 83

Writing

1

1 Dr
2 Noemí
3 Rios
4 28
5 Olive Road
6 Vancouver
7 V5K 1T3
8 nrios@standrews.hosp.ca
9 604-509-6995
10 Brazilian
11 doctor
12 18/05/1993

2

1 My name is Porfirio Cubillos.
2 I'm from Guadalajara in Mexico, but I am in France now.
3 My wife Claudine is French.
4 At home, we speak Spanish and French.

REVIEW and PRACTICE 1

Listening

1

a 5 b 4 c *1* d 3 e 2

2

1 c 2 d 3 b 4 e 5 a

3

1 F 2 F 3 T 4 T 5 F 6 T

Reading

1

1 b 2 c 3 a

2

1, 4, 9

3

1 China C
2 Spanish N
3 Poland C
4 France C
5 Canadian N
6 Russia C
7 German N
8 Japan C
9 Mexico C
10 Argentina C

LESSON 2A

Grammar

1

1 children
2 countries
3 beaches
4 people
5 nationalities
6 waitresses
7 women
8 boxes

2

1 That's
2 This
3 those
4 these
5 that
6 Those
7 This
8 Those

Vocabulary

3

1 wallet
2 sunglasses
3 credit card
4 tablet
5 camera
6 purse

4

1 glasses
2 umbrella
3 key
4 pencils
5 watch
6 mobile phones

Pronunciation

5

1 b 2 a 3 a 4 a 5 b 6 a 7 b
8 b 9 b 10 b

LESSON 2B

Reading

1

1 black, blue, brown
2 green, grey, gold
3 orange
4 pink, purple
5 red
6 silver
7 white
8 yellow

2

1 a 2 c 3 b

3

1 D 2 C 3 M 4 D 5 E 6 M
7 C 8 E

4

1 earrings are beautiful
2 his expensive glasses
3 old family photos
4 it is ugly
5 your prized object
6 isn't very difficult

LESSON 2C

Grammar

1

1 my
2 its
3 his
4 our
5 your
6 their
7 your
8 her
9 My
10 their

2

1 *the teacher's*
2 mother's
3 Anna's
4 tour guide's
5 Hugo's
6 engineer's
7 friend's
8 chef's

Vocabulary

3

1 husband
2 children
3 brother
4 grandfather
5 parents
6 father's
7 wife
8 grandparents
9 sister
10 boyfriend

4

1 mother
2 girlfriend
3 daughter
4 grandmother
5 brother
6 wife
7 son
8 parents

LESSON 2D

Speaking

1

1 c 2 a 3 b

2

Conversation 1: *Excuse me*, sorry, thanks
Conversation 2: Thank you
Conversation 3: Excuse me, please

3

Conversation 2

4

1 What time is it in Tokyo?
2 What time is the train to Birmingham?
3 What time is your flight?
4 What time is it now?
5 Excuse me, what is the time?
6 What time is the lesson?

5

1 It is four forty-five p.m. there. (c)
2 There's one in about ten minutes. (d)
3 It is almost twelve o'clock. (b)
4 It opens at ten a.m. on Saturdays. (a)

REVIEW and PRACTICE 2

Listening

1

a, d, e, h, j

2

1 F 2 F 3 T 4 F 5 T 6 T 7 F
8 T 9 T 10 F

Reading

1

Selma c
Nuria b

2

1 two
2 food
3 sisters
4 brothers and sisters
5 easy
6 presents
7 cousins

LESSON 3A

Grammar

1

1 A Do you like?
B do
2 A Do
B They play
3 A don't want
B I love
4 A Is
B don't like
5 A do you want
B don't have
6 A Do you
B I

2

1 *I don't eat an apple every day.*
2 We have lessons at eight o'clock.
3 Is he a taxi driver?
4 They don't watch TV.
5 Do they study English every day?
6 You have a credit card.
7 She isn't very happy.
8 Do you speak Italian?

Vocabulary

3

1 bread, sandwiches
2 coffee, milk
3 pasta
4 pizzas
5 meat, eggs
6 water, orange juice

4

Across
2 biscuits
5 ice cream
6 crisps
7 cake
8 salad
9 chocolate
10 fish

Down
1 potatoes
3 chips
4 vegetables
6 cheese

Pronunciation

5

1 Do you eat
2 Do I like
3 Do you like
4 Do they drink
5 What time do you have
6 What do you have

LESSON 3B

Listening

1

1 b 2 a 3 e

2

Conversation 1: today, Friday, 7.50
Conversation 2: Tuesday, 9.00
Conversation 3: Wednesday, 2.15

3

1 and
2 for
3 the, of
4 a, at
5 do, for
6 the

4

1 *yesterday*
2 tomorrow
3 Monday
4 Tuesday
5 Wednesday
6 Thursday
7 Friday
8 weekend
9 Sunday
10 afternoon
11 evening
12 night

LESSON 3C

Grammar

1

1 A Does Gabi live in Ciudad Juarez?
B No she doesn't. She lives in Monterrey.
2 A Where does Lionel study?
B He goes to the University of London.
3 A Naomi doesn't have any money.
B Does she need some today?
4 A Why doesn't your phone work?
B I don't know. It doesn't do anything.
5 A Does Halcon watch sports at the weekend?
B Yes. He likes watching tennis and rugby.

2

1 doesn't/does not go
2 watches
3 Does Yannick change
4 doesn't/does not work
5 speaks
6 studies
7 Does Vineet do
8 Does Nils want
9 doesn't/does not like
10 Do you have

Vocabulary

3

1 b 2 d 3 c 4 a 5 f 6 e 7 h
8 g

4

1 go
2 watch
3 use
4 make
5 do
6 have

Pronunciation

5

/s/ eats, makes, works
/z/ goes, knows, lives
/ɪz/ changes, uses, watches

Writing

1

c

2

1 Lucia is from Spain.
2 Carnival isn't in February.
3 In Carnival, people like singing, eating and seeing their friends.
4 People don't usually eat food in restaurants in Carnival.
5 Lucia thinks *erizos* are beautiful.
6 Lucia's favourite food isn't good for you.

3

1 T 2 F 3 T 4 T 5 F 6 T

4

1 f 2 a 3 b 4 c 5 e 6 d

REVIEW and PRACTICE 3

Listening

1

1 B
2 MP
3 B
4 EP

2

1 evening
2 actor
3 night/evening
4 student
5 friends
6 hospital
7 room
8 night
9 taxis

Reading

1

1 d 2 c 3 a 4 b

2

1 c 2 b 3 a 4 b 5 b 6 c 7 b

LESSON 4A

Grammar

1

1 a 2 b 3 b 4 a 5 b 6 a
7 b 8 c

2

1 *always does sport*
2 usually has
3 always works
4 often goes
5 never leaves
6 often studies
7 sometimes sees
8 usually watches

Vocabulary

3

1 get up
2 get dressed
3 leave home
4 start work
5 finish work
6 have a shower
7 go to bed

4

1 listens to music
2 do the housework
3 do our homework
4 get home
5 go shopping
6 read a book

LESSON 4B

Reading

1

1 underground
2 motorbike
3 ferry
4 taxi
5 bus
6 bicycle
7 plane
8 train

2

1 c
2 b, d, f
3 d
4 e
5 a

3

1 daily (paragraph 1)
2 boat (paragraph 2)
3 five hours (paragraph 3)
4 get home (paragraph 4)
5 plane (paragraph 5)
6 fast (paragraph 6)

4

1 Gary C
2 Henry P
3 Giovanna P
4 Lupita C
5 Jiang P
6 Venice P

LESSON 4A

Grammar

1

1 *How many (e)*
2 What (g)
3 Why (i)
4 What time (a)
5 How old (h)
6 Where (f)
9 Who (d)
8 How (b)
9 When (c)

2

1 What is your favourite film?
2 How do they know the answer?
3 Why does Casey go to school by car?
4 How old is your mother?
5 What time does Jerry finish work?
6 Where are my glasses?
7 How many people do you live with?
8 Where is the teacher this morning?
9 When does your brother get home?
10 Who do you know in the class?

Vocabulary

3

1 A hot
B cold
2 A noisy
B quiet
3 A long
B short
4 A nice
B horrible
5 A dirty
B clean

4

1 *small*
2 *friendly*
3 *slow*
4 *fast*
5 *large*
6 *unfriendly*

Pronunciation

5

1 When do you listen to the radio?
2 What books does he read?
3 How many films do they watch each week?
4 Who does she go to the cinema with?
5 Why do you like shopping?
6 What time do you study?

LESSON 4D

Speaking

1

c

2

1 b 2 a 3 c 4 a 5 b 6 c 7 a
8 b 9 b

3

1 c 2 b 3 a

4

a 2 b 3 c 1

REVIEW and PRACTICE 4

Listening

1

1 a, c, d, e, f, g, h, i

2

1 c 2 c 3 b 4 a 5 b 6 c

Reading

1

b

2

1 Y 2 N 3 N 4 N 5 N 6 Y
7 Y 8 N

3

1 e 2 b 3 g 4 a 5 h 6 c
7 f 8 d

LESSON 5A

Grammar

1

1 A *Can, watch*
B *can't*
2 A can start
3 A Can, have
B can
4 A can read
5 A can't study
6 A Can, eat
B can't

2

1 can make
2 I can
3 can't use/start, can, can
4 Can we change, we can't
5 can read, Can he drive
6 she can't

Vocabulary

3

1 call
2 look after
3 cook
4 helps
5 plays
6 drive
7 swim
8 meets

4

1 A arrive
B arrives
2 A dance
B dance
3 A speak
B speak
4 A travel
B travel
5 A give
B gives
6 A sing
B sing
7 A swim
B swim

Pronunciation

5

1 + 2 – 3 + 4 ? 5 – 6 ?
7 ? 8 +

LESSON 5B

Listening

1

1 b desktop computer, laptop
2 f television, players
3 d earphones, headphones
4 a Sat Nav, smartphone
5 c player, radio
6 e remote control, digital video recorder

2

a

3

1 *number*
2 person
3 number
4 place
5 thing
6 place

4

1 six
2 grandfather
3 four/4
4 internet
5 information
6 UK

5

1 My family comes from India but I live in Germany.
2 I can't buy the black laptop because it's too expensive.
3 That tablet is my sister's, not mine.
4 I study Spanish so I listen to Spanish radio online.

6

1 read books, tablet, go, bed.
2 often listens, music, car.
3 website, restaurant opens, seven

2

3

LESSON 5C

Grammar

1

1 it
2 them
3 me
4 it
5 him
6 her
7 us
8 it
9 you
10 it

2

1 it, it
2 I, me
3 We, us
4 you, you
5 She, her
6 them, they
7 He, him
8 her, she

Vocabulary

3

1 cooking
2 cleaning
3 running
4 walking
5 going out
6 meeting friends
7 listening to music
8 sleeping

4

1 cycling
2 Reading
3 shopping
4 Swimming
5 watching films
6 dancing

LESSON 5D

Writing

1

2 B 3 C 5 A 7 D

2

a 5 b 1 d 3 e 4 g 2

REVIEW and PRACTICE 5

Listening

1

1 drive
2 sing
3 swim
4 speak French

2

1 F 2 F 3 F 4 F 5 T 6 T 7 T 8 F

3

1 play
2 meet
3 sing
4 call
5 travel
6 look after
7 help
8 arrive

Reading

1

1 b 2 c 3 a

2

1 b 2 a 3 c 4 b 5 a 6 b

LESSON 6A

Grammar

1

1 *there are some*
2 There's a
3 Is there a
4 There are some
5 There aren't any
6 there's an
7 There isn't a
8 Are there any
9 there aren't
10 Is there a
11 There isn't a
12 there are some

2

1 *There's an*
2 there are some
3 There's a
4 there aren't any
5 there aren't any
6 There's a
7 there are a lot of
8 Is there an
9 Are there any
10 There are lots of

Vocabulary

3

1 post office
2 hospital
3 cinema
4 nightclub
5 police station
6 supermarket
7 train station
8 museum

4

1 shopping centre/department store
2 bus stop
3 café, restaurant
4 bank
5 hotel
6 airport
7 park
8 school

LESSON 6B

Reading

1

Lenny thinks the city is a good place to live; Ursula thinks the countryside is a good place to live.

2

1 *Y friends*
2 N … travelling an hour to work every day is not exciting.
3 Y There's lots to do in the city …
4 Y People are friendly in the countryside … Not like in cities!
5 Y … a place where you need a car …
6 N … there aren't many good jobs and the only social life is online.
7 Y … everything you need is right here.

3

1 e 2 f 3 c 4 a 5 d 6 b

4

1 eyes, face
2 ears, head
3 teeth, mouth
4 hands, feet
5 hair
6 nose
7 body
8 knees

LESSON 6C

Grammar

1

1 c 2 a 3 c 4 a 5 c 6 b 7 a 8 b

2

1 next
2 front
3 behind
4 in
5 under
6 between
7 above
8 on

Vocabulary

3

bedroom: *bed*, wardrobe
bathroom: shower, bath, toilet
kitchen: cooker
living room: sofa

4

1 study
2 desk
3 window
4 lamp
5 shelves
6 table
7 chair
8 fridge

Pronunciation

5

1 My desk is under the window.
2 The table is next to the shelves.
3 Their bathroom is above the kitchen.
4 The chair is between the bed and the wardrobe.
5 His keys are on the chair.
6 Our sofa is in the living room.

LESSON 6D

Speaking

1

1 park
2 police station
3 museum

2

Conversation 1
1 Excuse, where's
2 down, left
Conversation 2
3 there, here
4 Turn, behind, corner
Conversation 3
5 near
6 that, minutes, at

3

a

4

1 a 2 a 3 c 4 c 5 b 6 c

REVIEW and PRACTICE 6

Listening

1

a, c, d, g, h, i, j

2

1 T 2 F 3 NG 4 F 5 F 6 T
7 NG 8 F 9 F 10 T

Reading

1

b

2

1 b 2 a 3 c 4 c 5 b 6 a

3

1 post office
2 hospital
3 nightclub
4 supermarket
5 train station
6 hotel
7 shopping centre
8 police station
9 school
10 bank

LESSON 7A

Grammar

1

1 were
2 was
3 wasn't
4 was, were
5 were
6 weren't
7 weren't
8 was, was
9 Was, was
10 Were, wasn't

2

1 *I was a taxi driver.*
2 He wasn't with us. He was at the shopping centre.
3 Those students were not very friendly. They were unfriendly.
4 She wasn't at home. She was at the park.
5 'Were the pizzas cheap?' 'Yes, they were.'
6 'I wasn't very happy.' 'I was!'
7 'Were your exams difficult?' 'No, they weren't.'
8 'Was she your teacher?' 'No, she wasn't.'
9 Sam wasn't in class this week. He was on holiday.
10 'Was this question difficult to understand?' 'No, it wasn't.'

Vocabulary

3

1 a 2 b 3 a 4 a 5 b 6 a
7 b 8 a

4

1 fashion models
2 Politicians
3 journalist
4 king, queen
5 dancer
6 photographers
7 tennis player
8 artist

LESSON 7B

Listening

1

1 actor
2 sports player
3 travel writer

2

1 19th/nineteenth
2 1824, 1857
3 August 7th 1867
4 1893
5 16th July 1896
6 23
7 1856
8 73

3

1 I'm an
2 song, Queen of Artists
3 was an, was a shop
4 brother is a DJ
5 first of August
6 was at, in India

4

1 *March*
2 fifteenth
3 tenth
4 second
5 October
6 July
7 sixth
8 ninth

LESSON 7C

Grammar

1

1 Where did you live in the 2000s?
2 Did you listen to music then?
3 Who was your favourite singer?
4 What did they sing?
5 Did you play an instrument?
6 What was the name of your band?

2

1 visited
2 Did you travel, did
3 didn't watch
4 studied
5 Did he arrive, he didn't
6 listened
7 cooked
8 Did she use, she did
9 didn't like
10 stopped

Vocabulary

3

1 *morning*
2 the 10th of February
3 last year
4 2004
5 two fifteen
6 night
7 in
8 Wednesday

4

1 night
2 yesterday
3 in
4 last
5 at
6 ago
7 on/last
8 the
9 on
10 at

Pronunciation

5

1 b, c, e
2 d, g, i
3 a, f, h

LESSON 7D

Writing

1

a 5 b 1 c 2 d 4 e 3

2

1 c 2 b 3 b 4 a 5 b 6 a 7 c

3

Suggested answers

1 a2 b1 c3

1 *Nora got home at half past seven.*
First, she sat on the sofa/had a drink.
Then she cooked dinner.
After that, she studied/did her homework.

2 a1 b2 c3
First, he went to the supermarket with his mum.
Then he played football with his brother.
After that, he visited his grandmother.

REVIEW and PRACTICE 7

Listening

1

Speaker 1: live
Speaker 2: live
Speaker 3: TV
Speaker 4: live
Tom: TV
Sam: live

2

1 young
2 often
3 friends
4 music
5 hours
6 theatre
7 actors
8 pictures
9 days
10 boring

Reading

1

1 d 2 c 3 a 4 b

2

1 F
2 T
3 T
4 F
5 T
6 NG
7 T
8 NG
9 NG
10 F

3

1 film director
2 racing driver
3 footballer
4 athlete
5 fashion model
6 tennis player
7 writer
8 musician

LESSON 8A

Grammar

1

1 heard
2 spent
3 knew
4 taught
5 found
6 wrote
7 bought
8 chose

2

Across
1 cost
3 put
5 met
6 drove
7 gave
8 took

Down
1 came
2 sat
4 thought
6 did

Vocabulary

3

1 got on
2 car
3 bike
4 a car
5 got off
6 underground
7 ride
8 got lost

4

1 Get in
2 book
3 take
4 miss
5 walk
6 get lost
7 fly
8 ride
9 sail
10 get off

Pronunciation

5

1 /ɒ/
2 /əʊ/
3 /ɔː/
4 /ɔː/
5 /əʊ/
6 /ɒ/
7 /əʊ/

LESSON 8B

Reading

1

1 warm, cloudy
2 snowing
3 raining
4 foggy, sunny
5 autumn, spring
6 summer, winter

2

b

3

1 c 2 b 3 c 4 a 5 a 6 b

4

1 not very
2 really
3 not very
4 really
5 quite
6 not very
7 quite
8 really

LESSON 8C

Grammar

1

1 g 2 e 3 b 4 h 5 f 6 d
7 a 8 c

2

1 were there
2 there were
3 there was
4 there were
5 there weren't
6 Was there
7 there wasn't
8 there was
9 Was there
10 there was
11 there weren't
12 there wasn't

Vocabulary

3

1 sea (b)
2 tree (a)
3 sky (b)
4 grass (a)
5 river (a)
6 sun (b)

4

1 cloud
2 field
3 flowers
4 mountain
5 beach
6 forest

Pronunciation

5

1 'Was there a television in your room?' 'No, there wasn't.'
2 'Was there an evening meal?' 'Yes, there was.'
3 'Were there any nightclubs?' 'Yes, there were.'
4 'Were there good restaurants?' 'No, there weren't.'
5 'Was there any music?' 'Yes, there was.'
6 'Were there many nice people?' 'No, there weren't!'
7 'Were there any shops?' 'Yes, there were.'
8 'Was there a swimming pool?' 'No, there wasn't.'

LESSON 8D

Speaking

1

A 30/11/18
B 10:05

2

a 6 b 2 c 7 d 3 e 8 f 1 g 4 h 5

3

1 I'd like a return ticket to Brisbane.
2 What time does it leave?
3 When does it arrive in London?
4 Would you like a single or return ticket?
5 It's £8.90 for a single ticket.
6 When do you want to return?

4

1 Hello, This is, morning, My name is, calling, Goodbye
2 afternoon, speaking, This is, your call, Bye

REVIEW and PRACTICE 8

Listening

1

a 3 b 5 c 2 d 8 e 6 f 1 g 7 h 4

2

1 b 2 a 3 b 4 b 5 c 6 c 7 b 8 a 9 c 10 a

Reading

1

1 b 2 d 3 a 4 c

2

1 N 2 N 3 N 4 Y 5 DS 6 Y 7 N 8 DS 9 N 10 Y

LESSON 9A

Grammar

1

1 making
2 are
3 am
4 using
5 aren't
6 Are
7 aren't
8 isn't
9 watching
10 are

2

1 A are you doing
B I am/I'm going
2 A Are you staying
B aren't/are not
3 A are you talking
B I'm visiting
4 A Are they swimming
B are
5 A Is, getting
B 's/is making
6 A 's/is she doing
B 's/is having
7 A Are you driving
B 're/are stopping
8 A Is, sitting
B 'm/am leaving

Vocabulary

3

1 shoes, socks/socks, shoes
2 coat, hat
3 dress, boots
4 jumper
5 trousers, belt
6 jeans, T-shirts

4

Across
1 suit
3 coat
5 shoes
6 boots
7 skirt
8 jumper
9 jacket

Down
1 socks
2 dress
4 trousers
5 shirt
8 jeans

LESSON 9B

Listening

1

1 d
2 a, d
3 b, c, e
4 a, b, e
5 f

2

1 b 2 c 3 d 4 a

3

1 er
2 well
3 So
4 um
5 er
6 So

4

1 A angry
B surprised
2 A excited
B worried
3 A hungry
B thirsty
4 A scared
B calm
5 A happy
B tired
6 A sad
B bored

LESSON 9C

Grammar

1

a 5 b 7 c 2 d 4 e 1 f 9 g 10 h 8 i 3 j 6

2

1 A How often does Lupita visit her family?
B She usually goes twice a year.
2 A Does he exercise every week?
B He goes to the gym once a month.
3 A I have a haircut twice a year.
B That's not very often.
4 A How often do they see their parents?
B They visit them three times a month.
5 A Do you check your emails every day?
B I check three or four times a day.
6 A Does she always go out on Saturdays?
B She goes out once or twice a month.

Vocabulary

3

a 1 b 3 c 2 d 4 e 6 f 9 g 8 h 7 i 5

4

1 go shopping, shopping centre
2 market, buy
3 department store, pay by
4 spend, money, online
5 sells, local shops
6 try on
7 with cash

Pronunciation

5

1 He goes swimming twice a week.
2 They watch films two or three times a month.
3 I finish a book about once a week.
4 We have a holiday in Thailand every year.
5 Do you drive every day?
6 She has a shower once or twice a day.

LESSON 9D

Writing

1

(in any order)
1 There are four people in the photo, not three.
2 Izzie is wearing a grey hat, not a black hat.
3 David is wearing a jumper and coat, not a T-shirt.

2

1 There is a shop window on the right of the photo.
2 There are four people in the photo.
3 They are looking in a shop window.
4 David is standing at the top.
5 The man on the left is Alex.
6 The other woman in the middle is Paula.

3

1 That's our mother in the middle.
2 My little sister Sofia is at the top.
3 She's sitting on my Dad.
4 David is in the middle, next to Mum.
5 There's Blackmoor Forest at the top.
6 And that's me on the right.

REVIEW and PRACTICE 9

Listening

1

a 9 b 10 c 8 d 2 e 4 f 5 g 1 h 3 i 7 j 6

2

1 week
2 three
3 year
4 day

3

1 shirt
2 shopping centre
3 hat, shoes
4 credit card
5 jeans
6 online
7 jumper
8 son
9 dress
10 coat

Reading

1

c

2

1 b 2 b 3 a 4 c 5 a 6 c

LESSON 10A

Grammar

1

1 What are you doing this weekend?
2 I am looking after my grandfather.
3 Are you studying tomorrow?
4 Yes I am.
5 Are you going out on Sunday?
6 We are practising for our concert.
7 Patricia is driving there after lunch.
8 We are going swimming in the morning.

2

1 am/'m flying, am not/'m not seeing
2 are/'re visiting, are/'re having
3 Are ... doing, are going
4 is/'s running, is/'s planning
5 are not/aren't sailing, are/'re driving
6 Is ... meeting, is ... taking
7 is ... writing, am/'m enjoying
8 am/'m helping, is/'s cooking

Vocabulary

3

1 video
2 home
3 a film
4 museum
5 art gallery
6 a video

4

1 *watching a film*
2 visiting a museum
3 going to a concert
4 staying at home
5 visiting an art gallery
6 having a barbecue
7 going to a festival

Pronunciation

5

1 A Who is she seeing tonight?
B She's meeting her friends from university.
2 A Are they watching a film?
B No, they aren't. They're watching the football.
3 A I'm visiting a friend in Dublin.
B Are you taking the bus?
4 A Is he staying at home this evening?
B Yes, he is. He's doing the housework.
5 A Which beach are you going to?
B We're talking about that now.
6 A How are we getting there?
B We're taking the train.

LESSON 10B

Reading

1

1 C 2 B 3 - 4 A 5 - 6 D 7 E

2

1 How many bands are playing on Friday?	three
2 Which event is only in the morning?	D
3 How many events are free for students?	1 (E)
4 How old do you need to be to watch the film?	12
5 What type of film is at the cinema this weekend?	Action comedy
6 How much is the art exhibition if you aren't a student?	£3
7 What time does the event at Cambalache start?	10 p.m.
8 Which two places are in the same road?	B and E

3

1 Don't buy
2 come
3 don't wait
4 book
5 have
6 Don't close
7 Don't go
8 Don't tell

4

types of film: *action*, comedy, drama, horror, romance, science fiction
types of music: classical, electronic, hip-hop, jazz, pop, rock

LESSON 10C

Grammar

1

1 How often do you go to the cinema?
2 Who are your favourite actors?
3 Are they making any new films soon?
4 When did Fabien last visit a museum?
5 Did he like the concert?
6 Where was the festival?
7 Can we watch it on DVD?
8 What bands can I see at the moment?

2

a 3 b 6 c 1, 2 d 5 e 8 f 4, 7

3

1 Are … reading
2 did … like
3 is
4 do … fly
5 were
6 Are
7 Can … play
8 are … going
9 Does … listen
10 Did … see

Vocabulary

4

1 c 2 a 3 c 4 a 5 b 6 b
7 c 2 c

5

1 hockey
2 karate
3 rugby
4 swimming
5 basketball
6 Pilates
7 volleyball
8 walking
9 tennis
10 cycling

LESSON 10D

Speaking

1

a 2 b 1 c 3 d 5 e 4

2

1 F 2 T 3 F 4 F 5 T 6 F 7 T

3

1 café
2 Which days
3 open
4 get there
5 special events
6 if it rains

4

2, 3, 5, 6, 8
Graham sounds more interested than Tara.

REVIEW and PRACTICE 10

Listening

1

1 *China*, films
2 UK, *Comedy* and theatre
3 USA, art
4 Argentina, dance
5 India, music

2

1 F 2 NG 3 F 4 F 5 T 6 NG 7 F
8 F 9 F 10 T

Reading

1

a 3 b 2 c 5

2

1 d 2 f 3 b 4 e 5 a 6 c

3

1 karate
2 ballet
3 rugby
4 chess
5 rock climbing
6 skiing
7 gymnastics
8 cycling
9 basketball
10 walking

WRITING PRACTICE

Writing: Completing a form

1

1 Brewer
2 12
3 Padham
4 abrewer
5 1992
6 31

2

1 Ms
2 55 New Street
3 GY2 7HU
4 Patel
5 053877729005

3

1 He's in the USA but he's Japanese.
2 I am from Rouen, in France.
3 My post code is N2 R45.
4 His sister speaks Polish and French.
5 These are Michael's keys.
6 She lives at number 6, Green Street.

4

1 Mrs
2 Michi
3 Fujioka
4 40, Park Road
5 Cromton
6 CR 89EV
7 m_fujioka@starmail.jp
8 01656889846
9 Japanese
10 31/08/2000

Writing: Punctuation

1

1 b 2 c 3 a

2

a At seven in the evening he gets home. (4)
b David's house is in the mountains. It's a clean place far from the cities of the coast. (3)
c Do you like your journey to work? (5)
d Every morning I cycle to the station and get on a busy train into the city. (2)
e I work in London and like many people I spend a lot of my day between home and work. (1)

3

1 but
2 but
3 and
4 and
5 but
6 and

Writing: Describing yourself

1

a - b 3 c 4 d - e 2 f 1

2

1 F 2 T 3 T 4 F 5 F 6 T
7 F 8 T

3

1 Abbie never goes dancing because it's very expensive.
2 I don't need a car because there's a shop/there are shops near our house.
3 Jamie loves weekends because he sleeps late/he can sleep late!
4 Why does she do yoga? Because she wants to make friends.
5 I can't run today because I have a bad knee.
6 Why do I like this cinema? Because it's cheap!

Writing: Writing informal emails

1

1 d **2** e **3** f **4** g **5** a **6** b

2

1 Hello
2 How
3 things
4 well
5 about
6 ask
7 See
8 care

3

1 First, Then, After that
2 First, Then, After that
3 First, Then
4 then, After that

Writing: Describing a photo

1

1 c **2** c **3** a **4** b **5** c

2

1 *is (c)*
2 is (e)
3 are (f)
4 is (b)
5 are (g)
6 were (d)
7 was (a)

3

1 bottom
2 left
3 right
4 top
5 in the middle

Richmond
58 St Aldates
Oxford
OX1 1ST
United Kingdom

Printed in Spain
ISBN: 978-84-668-2507-8
CP: 779799
DL: M-10069-2017

Publishing Director: Deborah Tricker
Publishers: Luke Baxter
Editors: Glenys Davis, Laura Miranda
Proofreaders: Debra Emmett, Shannon Neill
Design Manager: Lorna Heaslip
Cover Design: Richmond
Design & Layout: Lorna Heaslip, Dave Kuzmicki

Illustrators:
Simon Clare; Guillaume Gennet c/o Lemonade; John Goodwin; Sean Longcroft c/o KJA Artists; The Boy Fitzhammond c/o NB Illustration Ltd.

Photos:
J. Escandell.com; J. Jaime; J. Lucas; S. Enríquez; 123RF; ALAMY/ GerryRousseau, Jim Corwin, Moviestore collection Ltd, Simon Reddy, Stephen French, IanDagnall Computing, Joern Sackermann, dpa picture alliance, Serhii Kucher, ZUMA Press, Inc., All Canada Photos, London Entertainment, Everett Collection Inc, imageBROKER, Pongpun Ampawa, Peter Noyce GBR, Ian Allenden, AF archive, Elizabeth Livermore, Lex Rayton, Ted Foxx, Alvey & Towers Picture Library, Elizabeth Wake, Kristoffer Tripplaar, Lucas Vallecillos, Joe Fairs, Dinodia Photos, Peter D Noyce, Brigette Supernova, Pictorial Press Ltd, Collection Christophel, Jonathan Goldberg, Paul Hastie, Tierfotoagentur, REUTERS, Viktor Fischer, Art of Food, Andrey Armyagov, Alex Ramsay, Blend Images, B Christopher, Judith Collins, David Cabrera Navarro, Roman Tiraspolsky, robertharding, Michael Neelon(misc), Fredrick Kippe, Oleksiy Maksymenko Photography, Patti McConville, D. Callcut, Matthew Taylor, Rafael Angel Irusta Machin, Igor Kovalchuk, MallorcaImages, Paul Quayle, Jozef Polc, Mick Sinclair, Michael Willis, Hugh Threlfall, ITAR-TASS Photo Agency, Bailey-Cooper Photography, jeremy sutton-hibbert, creativep, James Jeffrey Taylor, Oleksiy Maksymenko, Paul Smith, David Levenson, United Archives GmbH, Justin Kase zsixz, Simon Dack, Jeremy Pembrey, Barry Diomede, Alex Linch, Tomas Abad, Valentin Luggen, Sergey Soldatov, Iakov Filimonov, Anton Gvozdikov, Alex Segre, MBI, Paul Gibson, Stocksolutions, MEDIUM FORMAT COLLECTION/Balan Madhavan, allesalltag, David Robertson, Dmytro Zinkevych, Simon Dack News, Vaidas Bucys; CATERS NEWS AGENCY; FOCOLTONE; GETTY IMAGES SALES SPAIN/bjdlzx, Yuri_Arcurs, Reenya, Nikada, Paul Almasy, Martin Rose, Maskot, Lars Baron, JamieB, Annie Engel, Fosin2, Darumo, BraunS, artisticco, ajr_images, Bison_, AzmanL, artursfoto, pringletta, Dobino, Berezka_Klo, Indeed, Hero Images, KingWu, Tom Merton, NI QIN, Sam Edwards, Portra, ajaykampani, bgblue, leungchopan, c_kawi, s-c-s, kali9, SensorSpot, LeoPatrizi, Talaj, Pix11, Neyya, Dan Dalton, Chimpinski, DKart, shank_ali, Chris Ryan, londoneye, kickstand, kiankhoon, joto, Fuse, skynesher, asbe, gavran333, Zinkevych, KJA, AFP, ViewStock, John Lund/Sam Diephuis, Hiya Images/Corbis/VCG, Tom Dulat, vm, imaginima, TF-Images, Ben Pipe Photography, Ridofranz, PPcavalry, Edda Dupree / EyeEm, Dave Hogan/MTV 2016, Lightcome, Isovector, VikramRaghuvanshi, FaraFaran, Cimmerian, Bet_Noire, David C Tomlinson, Dave & Les Jacobs, unaemlag, technotr, Zoran Kolundzija, tarras79, stockcam, MacLife Magazine, Jetta Productions, Maya Karkalicheva, DGLimages, innovatedcaptures, FatCamera, Power Sport Images, Jasmina81, Lorraine Boogich, Mirrorpix, Kevin C. Cox - FIFA, Purestock, Caiaimage/Tom Merton, Stockbyte, Jason England / EyeEm, Ted Soqui, scyther5, Steven Swinnen / EyeEm, Weedezign, Westend61, Dave and Les Jacobs/Kolostock, chachamal, Cultura RM Exclusive/ Frank and Helena, Echo, imagotres, julief514, karandaev, kpalimski, demaerre, Danny Martindale, Art-Y, omda_info, colematt, clubfoto, Allan Tannenbaum, DNY59, stevecoleimages, David Lees, DonNichols, JB Lacroix, asiseeit, Tuutikka, Tarzhanova, Thinkstock, Vladimir Godnik, Uwe Krejci, Venturelli, VladTeodor, Synergee, NurPhoto, Samuel de Roman, nycshooter, RuslanDashinsky, sorincolac, AndreyPopov, AngiePhotos, MistikaS, JGalione, Choreograph, Fotoplanner, Leah Puttkammer, Hero images, John Keeble, Liam Norris, JANIFEST, LWA/Dann Tardif, Ron Galella, Rose_Carson, IvanMiladinovic, Shana Novak, Simon Sarin, T3 Magazine, Floortje, Hung_Chung_Chih, artlensfoto, domin_domin, Frank van Delft, macrovector, michaeljung, penguenstok, Flashpop, DenisKot, Wavebreakmedia, Creative, Claudiad, Sheikoevgeniya, Philipp Nemenz, Bettmann, Al Freni, EmirMemedovski, wir0man, pshonka, Anthony Harvey, Anadolu Agency, mrak_hr, mixetto, i love images, mbbirdy, kivoart, SnegiriBureau, Rick Friedman, jsnover, iconeer, Monty Rakusen, gilaxia, Maksim Ozerov, gerenme, MStudioImages, MATJAZ SLANIC, andresr, Jupiterimages, Jon Feingersh, adekvat, Jamie Garbutt, Jack Mitchell, Mark Cuthbert, R-O-M-A, Paras Griffin, Peathegee Inc, Radius Images, Gabriel Rossi, FrozenShutter, blueringmedia, davidcreacion, NuStock, justhavealook, reportman1985, zeljkosantrac, Dougal Waters, David Redfern, Askold Romanov, Digital Vision, Krasyuk, Javier Pierini, Marc Romanelli, Neustockimages, Andersen Ross, Alistair Berg, Steven Puetzer, Todor Tsvetkov, Devonyu, franckreporter, Anthony Charles, Danita Delimont, senkoumelnik, ferrantraite, Chesnot, ersinkisacik, bluejayphoto, NicolasMcComber, Photos.com Plus, Robyn Mackenzie, Astarot, Tony Vaccaro, Santiago Felipe, Tristan Fewings, Tetra Images, dogayusufdokdok, nicoletaionescu, praetorianphoto, vgajic, Sofie Delauw, Birgit R / EyeEm, Christopher Polk, PeopleImages, Henn Photography, KavalenkavaVolha, Kittisak_Taramas, tunart, Mike Coppola, Nicolas McComber, Tatjana Kaufmann, LuisPortugal, christopherarndt, Adrian Weinbrecht, Chris Sattlberger, subjug, JuliarStudio, Juice Images, Jrg Mikus / EyeEm, sturti, Roberto Westbrook, Tanya Constantine, Valery Sharifulin, Jason Hawkes, Image Source, IMAGEMORE Co, Ltd., Jacob Wackerhausen, seb_ra, crossroadscreative, m-imagephotography, DEA PICTURE LIBRARY, Hiroyuki Ito, Erik Isakson, EvgeniyaTiplyashina, Hill Street Studios, lushik, Mondadori Portfolio, Andreas Hein / EyeEm, Axelle/ Bauer-Griffin, Emad Aljumah, Deborah Kolb, monkeybusinessimages, Alexandr Sherstobitov, laflor, Michael Ochs Archives, Science Photo Library, BJI / Blue Jean Images, Dan MacMedan, ChrisHepburn, kzenon, Banar Fil Ardhi / EyeEm, PhotoAlto/Sigrid Olsson, Jade Albert Studio, Inc., New York Daily News Archive, Constantinos Kollias / EyeEm, Chris Walter, Photo by Claude-Olivier Marti, Kelly Cheng Travel Photography, Blend Images - Jose Luis Pelaez Inc, shapecharge, Compassionate Eye Foundation/Steven Errico, gbh007; HIGHRES PRESS STOCK/AbleStock.com; I. PREYSLER; ISTOCKPHOTO/ Getty Images Sales Spain, Devasahayam Chandra Dhas, Andreas Herpens, calvindexter, popovaphoto, Phazemedia, denphumi, SolStock, Pali Rao, JoeLena; J. M.ª BARRES; SHUTTERSTOCK/Glenn Copus/Evening Standard, Olivia Rutherford, MARIUS ALEXANDER, Iakov Filimonov, Sergey Novikov, Blend Images, terekhov igor; Farmer's Daughter; Jono Williams; Andrew Hyde; Aimee Giese; Museum of London; Samsung; SERIDEC PHOTOIMAGENES CD; Telegraph Media Group Limited; ARCHIVO SANTILLANA

We would like to thank the following reviewers for their valuable feedback which has made Personal Best possible. We extend our thanks to the many teachers and students not mentioned here.
Brad Bawtinheimer, Manuel Hidalgo, Paulo Dantas, Diana Bermúdez, Laura Gutiérrez, Hardy Griffin, Angi Conti, Christopher Morabito, Hande Kokce, Jorge Lobato, Leonardo Mercato, Mercilinda Ortiz, Wendy López